THE GOLDEN AGE OF BRAZIL

DOM JOÃO V BY DOMENICO DUPRA
COMMEMORATING THE BATTLE OF CAPE MATAPÁN, 1717

THE GOLDEN AGE
OF BRAZIL · 1695-1750

Growing Pains of a Colonial Society

by C. R. BOXER, *Camoens Professor of Portuguese. King's College, University of London*

Published in coöperation with the Sociedade de Estudos Históricos Dom Pedro Segundo, Rio de Janeiro, by the University of California Press · Berkeley and Los Angeles · 1969

University of California Press
Berkeley and Los Angeles, California

University of California, Ltd.
London, England

© 1962, by The Regents of the University of California
Library of Congress, Catalog Card No. 62-11583

Third Printing, 1969

Published with the assistance of
a grant from the Ford Foundation

Designed by Ward Ritchie

Printed in the United States of America

ACKNOWLEDGMENTS

THIS BOOK owes its existence to the generosity of Senator Assis Chateaubriand, Brazilian Ambassador to the Court of St. James's. With that regal munificence from which so many people of all nationalities have benefited, he arranged for me to visit Brazil in the spring of 1959, under the auspices of the Sociedade de Estudos Históricos Dom Pedro II and the Diarios Associados. This was not the first time I had experienced the lavishness of Brazilian hospitality, or the warm welcome with which the researcher is received in the Brazilian libraries and archives; but the facilities accorded me could not have been bettered for a crowned head or for a film star. It is impossible to name all those who were so generous with their time and assistance, but I must make particular acknowledgments to the following: Dr. Austregésilo de Athayde, President of the Academia Brasileira das Letras; Dr. Iraney, Senhor Eduardo Pires de Campos, Dr. Onofre de Miranda, Dr. Odorico Tavares, all of the Diarios Associados; Dr. Rodrigo Melo Franco de Andrade and the regional representatives of the Patrimonio do Estado which he so ably directs from Rio de Janeiro; Dr. Gil Metódio Maranhão, who placed the files of the transcripts made from various archives for the Instituto do Açucar e Alcool at my disposal and thus saved me many days of donkey work; Dr. António Joaquim de Almeida of the Museu de Ouro at Sabará; Dr. João Gomes Teixeira of the Arquivo Publico Mineiro at Belo Horizonte, who procured for my use a set of the invaluable *Revista* published by that archive, in addition to affording me every facility there. To another scholarly *Mineiro,* Dr. Alexandre Eulálio Pimenta da Cunha, of the Instituto do Livro at Rio de Janeiro, I am likewise deeply indebted for his tireless generosity in ferreting out for me many books on Brazilian history that are difficult to get in South America and virtually impossible elsewhere, and sending them to London. My old friend, Professor José António Gonsalves de Mello of the University of Recife, also gave me the use of his magnificent library and collection of transcripts, and secured for me several out-of-print books on the history of the Northeast. For stimulating conversation on the period covered by this book and for other help of various kinds I am also greatly indebted to Dr. Pedro Calmon, author of several standard works on Brazilian colonial history that are frequently quoted in this book; Dr. José Honório Rodrigues, Director of the Brazilian National Archives, who kindly supplied me with the relevant *Publicacões;* Professors Sérgio Buarque de Holanda, Myriam Ellis, and Alice Canabrava of the University of São Paulo; Augusto de Lima Júnior at Belo Horizonte; Mr. and Mrs. Macartney at Diamantina; Dr. Godfredo Filho, Mr. Erik Loeff, and the unforgettable "Manú" at Bahia. Last but not least to the Magnifico Reitor, Dr. Edgard dos Santos and the University of Bahia, who not only invited me in August, 1959 to the Fourth Luso-Brazilian Colloquium as their guest, but gave me an honorary degree.

July, 1960   C. R. B.

CONTENTS

Contents

District—Intendants and Their Role—Dragoons of Minas Gerais—Garimpeiros and Calhambolas—Methods of Mining—Negro Slaves and Smugglers—Life in the Arraial do Tijuco—Contract System—"In the time of the Caldeiras"—Alvará of August, 1753—Real Extracção—Diamond Production and Exports

ILLUSTRATIONS

Illustrations

CHAPEL OF THE ROSARY OR OF PADRE FARIA, VILLA RICA DE OURO PRETO, MINAS GERAIS

Photograph by Erich Hess from the collection of the Diretoria do Patrimônio Histórico e Artístico Nacional, Rio de Janeiro

CHAPEL OF NOSSA SENHORA D'O, SABARÁ, MINAS GERAIS

Built circa 1720. Photograph by Erich Hess

CHINOISERIE DECORATION IN THE CHAPEL OF NOSSA SENHORA D'O SABARÁ, MINAS GERAIS

Photograph by Erich Hess

FAÇADE OF SÃO FRANCISCO DE ASSIS, SALVADOR, BAHIA

Built in the early eighteenth century. Courtesy of Mr. John Bury

MAPS

I. EMPIRE OF THE SOUTH ATLANTIC

"A HELL FOR BLACKS, a purgatory for Whites, and a paradise for Mulattoes"—such was a popular Portuguese characterization of Brazil in the second half of the seventeenth century.[1] This sarcastic observation was probably made as much in jest as in earnest by the anonymous wit who first propounded it, but it contains a basic element of truth. Negro slave labor produced the sugar and tobacco which then formed the basis of the Brazilian economy. Slavery, whether in house, field, or mine, affected life in colonial Brazil more deeply and widely than did any other single factor. Planters and priests, officers and officials, in short all categories of educated men were alike agreed that without an assured supply of slave labor from Negro Africa, Portuguese America was not viable. Our survey of the Lusitanian empire of the South Atlantic at the time when Dom Pedro II assumed the crown (as distinct from the regency) of Portugal in 1683, can therefore best begin by considering the interdependence of Brazil and the slave markets of West Africa.

As a Portuguese colonist wrote from the Maranhão about 1730: "It is not the style for the white people of these parts, or of any other of our colonies, to do more than command their slaves to work and tell them what to do."[2] Similarly, an Augustinian friar with long experience in the Zambesi mission field observed a few years later that it was "not fitting that the natives should see Portuguese doing manual labor," and it would be very easy to multiply such quotations. One more, however, will suffice. The Archbishop of Bahia informed the Crown in 1702 that there were then some 90,000 souls in his diocese, of whom the majority were Negro slaves, "the whites only serving to tell the slaves what they have to do, whether they are their masters or the overseers of their masters." [3] The idea of the dignity of labor was nowhere widespread at that time and for long afterwards—least of all in the tropical possessions of the European powers. Since the early days of the colonization of Brazil a slave was commonly termed "the hands and feet" of the master (or of the mistress), and all but the most impoverished whites relied on slave labor. "Excepting people of the lowest degree of all," wrote William Dampier after a month's stay at Bahia in 1699, "here are scarce any but what keep slaves in their houses." Those who could not afford imported Negro slaves made shift with the local Amerindians, particularly in the poorer and remoter districts such as São Paulo and the Maranhão. Though the Amerindians were useful as trappers, hunters, fishers, and (above all) as guides in the unknown forests and backlands (*sertões*) of the interior, their original stone-age environment and mentality rendered them unfitted for sedentary and servile employment in the white settlements dotted along the coast. Whether as toilers in the plantations or in the sugar mills, whether as domestic servants in the home, or whether as shipwrights, carpenters, cobblers, masons, and other "mechanics," Negro slave laborers had become indispensable by the end of the sixteenth century.

The Portuguese were not the inventors of the Negro slave trade, and in due time they were surpassed in this traffic by both Dutch and English,[4] but they were the pioneers of plantation slavery, at any rate as practiced on a considerable scale. The bulk of the slaves whom they secured from West Africa were originally bought on the Guinea coast and were mostly of Western Sudanese

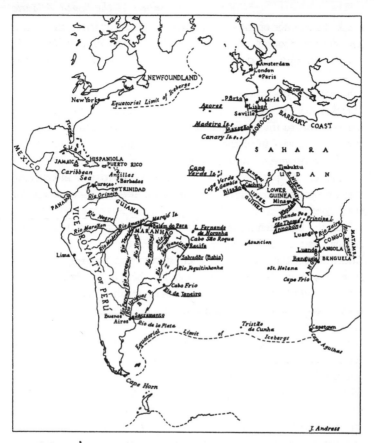

PORTUGAL'S ATLANTIC EMPIRE IN THE EIGHTEENTH CENTURY

stock. The center of the trade then shifted southward to the Bantu kingdom of Congo, and, after the foundation of São Paulo de Luanda in 1575, to the "kingdom" of Angola, which later was extended to include Benguela.[5] An enthusiastic official, writing of what seemed to be the limitless possibilities of this market for "black ivory" in 1591, assured the Crown that the hinterland of Luanda was so thickly populated that it would furnish a copious supply of slaves "until the end of the world." [6] Less than a century later, however, various authorities were deploring the serious decline in the population of Angola, owing to the internecine wars, excessive forced labor and slave raiding, and the ravages of smallpox.[7]

Despite this demographic decline in what had once been Africa's most populous slave mart, the Portuguese of Brazil continued to get the majority of their slaves from this region. Apart from anything else, it was cheaper for them to buy slaves from Angola, where they controlled the coast and had no foreign competitors, than on the Guinea coast where they had been ousted from their original settlements by the Dutch and supplanted in other places by the English. They still maintained a precarious footing at Cacheu and Bissau opposite the Cape Verde Islands, and they could also trade with Lower Guinea from the islands of São Tomé and Principe; but their commerce in the Gulf was much hampered by the powerful and aggressive Dutch West India Company.[8]

Slaveowners in Brazil were not unanimous about whether Sudanese slaves from Guinea or the Bantu from Angola were the best; and fashions in slaves, as in other commodities, were not always the same. Broadly speaking, the slaves of Sudanese origin tended to be more intelligent, more robust, and more hardworking (when they did work), but they were also more rebellious and less disposed to become reconciled to their menial lot. The Bantu, on the other hand, were more cheerful, adaptable, and loquacious, but were not so strong or so resistant to disease. We shall have occasion to discuss this matter again; but for

4

economic and other reasons, Bantu slaves from Angola and Benguela predominated in Brazil at the end of the seventeenth century. The celebrated Jesuit, Padre António Vieira, in a sermon preached at Bahia in 1695 spoke rhetorically but accurately of "the kingdom of Angola on the opposite Ethiopian shore, by whose sad blood, and black but fortunate souls, Brazil is nurtured, animated, sustained, served and preserved." [9]

The slaves obtained from Guinea, whether by the Portuguese or by other White traders, were bought from local rulers or their agents in the European coastal trading bases, some of which were fortified and others not. A different system prevailed in Angola, where, apart from slaves obtained by the Portuguese punitive columns which frequently operated against unsubdued or rebellious tribes in the interior, itinerant mulatto and Negro agents known as *pumbeiros* purchased slaves from the inland chiefs and took them to Luanda in chain gangs. These gangs were called *alimbambas* or *libambos* and held from eight to twelve persons. Since they often had to travel hundreds of miles, and consequently reached Luanda in very poor condition, they were usually placed in barracoons by the seashore and fattened up before embarkation. During this time they were subjected to what can only be termed a farcical form of mass baptism which made them Christians in nothing but name. [10]

On embarkation at Luanda, slaves were classified by a standard measurement known as the *peça de Indias* ("piece of the Indies"), which was defined in 1678 as being "a Negro from fifteen to twenty-five years old; from eight to fifteen, and from twenty-five to thirty-five, three pass for two; beneath eight, and from thirty-five to forty-five, two pass for one; sucking infants follow their mothers without accompt; all above forty-five years, with the diseased, are valued by arbiters." [11] The mortality on the Atlantic crossing was often very heavy, especially in the ships from Guinea that had a longer voyage with the prevailing winds and tides, so that these vessels deserved their nickname of *tumbeiros* or "undertakers." In March, 1684, the Crown endeavored to reduce this mor-

Lisbon

MOROCCO BARBARY STATES EGYPT

Cape Bojador

S A H A R A

R. Nile

Cape Verde

R. Senegal
R. Gambia
R. Grande
Cacheu
Bissão

Timbuktu

W E S T E R N
S U D A N

R. Niger
R. Volta
R. Mono

Sierra Leão

Mandinga

Ashanti DAHOMEY ARDRA
Ivory Gold Coast Slave Cst BENIN
Coast CALABAR
Cabo Palmas Popo
Cabo Tres Pontas Whydah
Mina (Elmina)

Fernando Po

Zaire

Principe I.
São Thomé

Annobón

LOANGO

Rio Congo

A
N
CONGO G
O
ANGOLA L
A

B
A
N
T
MATAMBA U

Luanda
Rio Cuanza
BENGUELA

São Felipe

Cabo Negro

Cape of Good Hope
Cape Agulhas

J. Andress

WEST AFRICAN AREAS WHERE THE PORTUGUESE OBTAINED SLAVES

tality by enacting a law which regulated the number of slaves any vessel could embark in accordance with her tonnage. Shipowners and captains were also ordered to provide adequate rations and drinking-water for this number, an elementary precaution which they had frequently failed to observe. The duration of the voyage from Luanda to Brazilian ports was calculated at thirty-five days for Recife, forty for Bahia, and fifty for Rio de Janeiro. Rules were also given concerning the care of the sick, the provision and the pay of chaplains in slavers, and other matters. This law applied only to ships sailing from Angola and Benguela, since the Crown had no adequate control over those sailing from Guinea. It seems that this law was no more effective than similar legislation against overcrowding and under-supplying slave ships which had been promulgated in 1664 with no lasting results.[12]

On reaching their port of destination the surviving *peças de Indias* were registered and marketed like any other merchandise, "there being no difference between Negroes and goods."[13] The prices they fetched naturally varied in accordance with their age, sex, physical condition, and the use for which they were intended. The lot of those who were employed in domestic service will be familiar enough to most readers from Gilberto Freyre's *The Masters and the Slaves* (*Casa Grande e Senzala*), but a few words may be said here about the daily life of the greater number who were destined for work in the sugar plantations which formed the basis of the Brazilian economy.[14]

At harvest time and when the mills were grinding the cane, work on a plantation was sometimes continued round the clock, and otherwise lasted at least from dawn to dusk. In the winter or rainy season, the hours were not so long, and the more considerate planters did not compel their slaves to work until after the sun was high in the heavens and they had received a breakfast of "broth, or honey when there is some." On Sundays and the principal saints' days the slaves were supposed to be free to tend their own allotments after hearing mass. Some planters evaded this concession whenever they could, but others extended it to include

7

Saturdays as well in the winter season when the mills were idle. Manioc and vegetables formed the slaves' staple diet, meat and fish being luxuries for them. All slaves were supposed to receive the rudiments of religious instruction from the local chaplain, to go to confession once a year, and to have all their newborn children baptized. On some plantations the slaves were allowed, or even encouraged, to indulge in their own African tribal dances and music on high-days and holidays, but such practices were frowned on by the stricter clergy and forbidden from time to time. The plantation factor (or foreman) had to inspect the slave quarters (*senzala*) daily, to ensure that they were kept clean and tidy, to hunt out malingerers, to see that slaves who were genuinely ill got medical treatment, and to send for the confessor if they were dangerously so.

Discipline was maintained with a severity that often degenerated into sadistic cruelty where the infliction of corporal punishment was concerned. Some planters "for trifling offenses threw their slaves alive into furnaces, or killed them in various barbarous and inhuman ways." [15] These sadistic excesses were naturally avoided on the better-run plantations, where the recognized punishment "was not to beat them with a stick, nor to pelt them with stones and tiles, but, when a slave deserves it, to tie him to a cart and flog him. After being well flogged, he should be pricked with a sharp razor or knife, and the wounds rubbed with salt, lemon juice, and urine, after which he should be put in chains for some days." Female slaves were usually flogged indoors for modesty's sake. [16] It is, perhaps, needless to add that mistreatment of slaves was not confined to Portuguese owners. Indeed, the French traveler, Froger, who visited Bahia in 1696 and described the cruelties inflicted on the slaves there, adds: "though all this is bad enough, yet the Spaniards and the English treat them in a still more cruel manner."

The treatment (or mistreatment) of slaves naturally varied widely in accordance with the character of the owner and the amount of supervision which he exercised over his factor—the factors often being mulattoes and brutal disciplinarians. Where the owner was humane and where the slaves were adequately clothed and fed, they raised families and led an existence which was not, perhaps, much worse than that of the working class in many countries of contemporary Europe. The slave children reared on such plantations frequently pined and died, or ran away, if they were sold in adult life to harsher masters. Where the master was sadistically brutal, the slaves deserted if they could, or committed suicide, and the females aborted themselves rather than rear children in such surroundings.

It is arguable whether the majority of slaveowners were humane or the reverse; but cases of wanton cruelty were frequent enough not only to inspire the remonstrances of men like Vieira, Benci, Antonil, and Marques Pereira, but to arouse, somewhat belatedly, the conscience of the Crown. Writing to the governor-general of Bahia in February, 1698, the king ordered him to enquire into the alleged inhuman treatment of slaves in Brazil. If these allegations were justified, the governor-general was to check such atrocities by the most prudent and efficacious means; taking care, however, that these measures "do not arouse resentment among the [white] people, and that the desired end be secured without causing excitement or disturbance among the slaves themselves." The higher ecclesiastical authorities also repeatedly denounced the sadistic maltreatment of slaves; but judging by the frequency with which such admonitions were repeated, they do not seem to have been very widely heeded. Brazil continued to be, by and large, "a hell for Blacks." [17]

So far as Brazil was a "purgatory for Whites," this was true chiefly of cultured courtiers such as Dom Francisco Manuel de Mello, who employed the phrase feelingly after his banishment thither. For most of his countrymen it was on the contrary a land of promise, and, in many cases of fulfillment. The heady "fumes of India" no longer exercised the attractions of an earlier day and generation when "Golden Goa" was in its prime. The majority of Portuguese who went out to the East in the late seventeenth cen-

9

tury went either as conscript soldiers or as banished convicts. Brazil had her share of these categories, too, but in the main her immigrants were voluntary if impoverished expatriates who were in search of a better life and a new home.

As Gaspar Dias Ferreira wrote in 1645: "Portugal has no other region more fertile, nor closer at hand nor more frequented, nor have its vassals a better and safer refuge than Brazil. The Portuguese who is overtaken by any misfortune, emigrates thither." [18] Emigration from Portugal naturally increased still further after the recovery of Pernambuco and the end of the Dutch war; and even though Brazil was affected by the economic depression of the late 1670's, an eyewitness at Bahia reported that every ship arriving from Oporto and the Atlantic islands of Madeira and the Azores brought at least eighty peasants to the New World. Ten years later, an anonymous writer with wide experience of Brazil, averred that every year, "nearly two thousand men from Vianna, Porto, and Lisbon emigrate to Pernambuco, Bahia, and Rio de Janeiro." [19] White women did not emigrate in comparable numbers, but at any rate many more made this short and secure passage with their menfolk than embarked on the long and dangerous six-month voyage to India.

Nor was immigration confined to those who had come down in the world, or who were unemployed at home. Brazil had a European reputation as a country where longevity was common, both among the aboriginal inhabitants as among European settlers. Sir William Temple records in one of his *Essays:* "I remember Dom Francisco de Mello, a Portugal Ambassador in England, told me, it was frequent in his country for men spent with age or other decays, so as they could not hope for a year or two of life, to ship themselves away in a Brazil fleet, and after their arrival there, to go on a great length, sometimes of twenty or thirty years, or more, by the force of that vigour they recovered with that remove." [20] The most illustrious example of such a new lease of life was that afforded by the ailing Padre António Vieira, who returned to Brazil in 1681 to die, but who lived for another sixteen years before he did so. Apart from such valetudinarians, many colonial officials, merchants, and others who had made their pile, settled in Brazil and raised families there, although many others returned to Portugal.

We have no adequate statistics concerning this current of emigration, but sufficient stray references to prove that the majority of emigrants to Brazil came from the provinces of Entre Minho e Douro in northern Portugal, from Lisbon, and from the Atlantic islands of the Azores and Madeira. Minho was the best cultivated province but had insufficient land to support the teeming population bred by its exceptionally fecund women; and several of the Atlantic islands inevitably contained many more people than they could properly support. The Azorean emigrants particularly favored the Rio de Janeiro region, where their predominance was very marked by 1630, but efforts were also made, though without great success, to transplant groups of peasant families from the Atlantic islands to the Maranhão and Northeast Brazil.[21] Lisbon likewise provided a large quota of emigrants and Beira a fair number; but Alemtejo, Tras-os-Montes, and the Algarve seem to have been pretty thinly represented among those who sought to better themselves by emigrating to the New World.

As was inevitable under the circumstances, a class of white peasant-proprietors, owning the land they tilled, could not be formed in colonial Brazil. Even those who had earned their living by wielding the mattock and the hoe in Portugal and the Azores, had no intention of doing so in Brazil if they could possibly avoid it. Some became *lavradores* or sharecroppers on the larger sugar plantations; though they did not do the work themselves but merely supervised a few slaves. Others cultivated tobacco, and since this crop was commonly raised on smaller divisions of land than the sugar estates required, some of these men seem originally to have done their own labor, but by the end of the century the average grower had at least one or two slaves. Others earned a living as carpenters, masons, and so forth, in the towns; but here again, as soon as they earned sufficient money to buy a slave they did so.

"All these tradesmen buy Negroes," wrote William Dampier after his visit to Bahia in 1699, "and train them up to their several employments, which is a great help to them." These "mechanics" as they were contemptuously termed, formed brotherhoods of a guild character in the principal towns, but they never achieved the wealth and importance of their counterparts in Spanish America. Nevertheless, some gifted individuals overcame the deeply ingrained prejudice against anyone who worked with his own hands. The success story of António Fernandes de Matos, who emigrated to Pernambuco as a poor stone mason and rose to be one of the richest and most respected inhabitants of the captaincy was not unique.[22]

Those of the emigrants who were literate became by preference clerks, cashiers, shop assistants, or hawkers working on their own account or on a commission basis. Employed on their arrival, often "poor and in rags," by some relative or acquaintance who had emigrated earlier and already established himself, they usually succeeded in amassing at least a modest competence if they were industrious and thrifty. Those of them who were successful often married their employer's daughter or some local girl; but it was more common for them to employ new arrivals in their turn, than to entrust the conduct of their business to one of their own children. Their America-born descendants were allegedly lazier and more spendthrift than the newly arrived immigrants. The Lancashire proverb of "clogs to clogs in three generations," had its Brazilian equivalent: "father a taverner, son a gentleman, and grandson a beggar."[23] The fact remained that the immigrants usually succeeded in monopolizing many of the openings which the *filhos da terra* or "sons of the soil" might otherwise have filled, however inadequately; and moreover, the former were often favored by the government officials, the great majority of whom were likewise European-born. For these and other reasons, there was usually a good deal of mutual dislike and mistrust between these two categories of the vassals of the Portuguese Crown. We shall see in due course how this ill-feeling on two occasions culminated in civil war.

Various contemporary writers, evidently with a view to encouraging potential emigrants, depicted Brazil as an earthly paradise of perpetual spring, where the climate, scenery, products, and fertility of the soil, were all vastly superior to those of Europe.[24] The majority of the emigrants were probably illiterate, but any who might have read such eulogistic works must have been cruelly deceived soon after their arrival. While extolling the variety of delicious fruits which Brazil afforded, the beauty of the evergreen scenery, and the serenity of the tropical nights under the Southern Cross, these writers discreetly forbore to mention the numerous insect pests which made any kind of agriculture a gamble, and which all the resources of modern science are still far from controlling. A Dutch eyewitness account of 1623 tells us that the harassed settlers christened the ant the "King of Brazil" (Rei do Brasil). Dangerous fevers were endemic in many areas, and the causes and cures of tropical diseases were either only dimly perceived or else (and more usually) completely misunderstood. Droughts ravaged some regions of the country for years on end; and elsewhere the capricious climate was likely to alternate between excessive rain and floods on the one hand and totally insufficient rainfall on the other. Though the soil was rich enough in some places, such as the sugar-growing regions of the *reconcavo* at Bahia and the *várzea* of Pernambuco, it was mostly very poor in organic chemical elements once the tropical jungle and vegetation were cleared to make room for cultivation. The dearth of calcium was (and is) particularly serious, adversely affecting the nutritional value of such food plants as did grow. The hazards of tropical agriculture were pungently expressed by João Peixoto Viegas, who wrote from Bahia in 1687 that "it is just like the act of copulation, in which the participant does not know whether he has achieved something, or whether the result will be a boy or a girl, or sound or deformed, until after the birth is achieved."[25]

13

Nor was it only with capricious Nature that the pioneers had to contend. In some captaincies, such as Ilheus and Espirito Santo, the unsubdued cannibal tribes were still a menace. In other regions the *quilombos,* or communities of runaway African slaves in the forest, formed an irresistible attraction for servile labor on the neighboring plantations. Colonial justice was notoriously corrupt and inefficient, and adventurers who succeeded in making some sort of a living in the interior often found their lands or stock appropriated by a latifundian landowner who knew how to grease the palms of the law. Crushing imposts were levied on sugar, tobacco, and all the principal colonial exports, though widespread smuggling evaded some of this burdensome taxation. Among essential imports, salt was a Crown monopoly since 1631; wine, flour, olive oil, and codfish were all monopolized by the chartered Brazil Company created in 1649. With all these handicaps, and others which will be enumerated later, Brazil was still a land of genuine opportunity, but only for the hardy, the lucky, or the unscrupulous.

Colonization was mainly limited to a number of loosely connected settlements in a coastal belt extending from the Amazon delta to São Vicente, which was seldom more than thirty miles wide. In this, as in several other ways, Portuguese America was a striking contrast to the Spanish viceroyalties of Mexico and Peru. The penetration of the Brazilian interior, which was for long limited to the widely ranging slave raids organized by the (largely halfbreed) inhabitants of São Paulo, had, it is true, taken on a more durable form after the end of the Dutch war, with the opening up of the hinterland of Pernambuco and Bahia. Cattle punchers and other pioneers had pushed more than 900 miles up the valley of the great river São Francisco by 1690, but permanent settlements were very few and far between, being confined to a few primitive ranches and the like. The Jesuit missionaries had pushed a long way up the Amazon and some of its tributaries, but their *aldeias* cannot be considered as settlements of white colonization, as will be shown abundantly below. For practical purposes, white colonization was still restricted to the narrow coastal belt, and mainly to the three relatively populous areas of Pernambuco, Bahia, and Rio de Janeiro.[26] In the thriving ports of Recife, Salvador, and São Sebastião, life may have been something of a purgatory for the penniless newcomers from Portugal but a large proportion of them undoubtedly made good.

Regarding the position of the mulattoes in colonial Brazil, I cannot do better than quote Antonil's summary account of their situation:

Many of them, abusing their owners' favors, are arrogant, vicious, and pride themselves on being bravoes ready to commit any outrage. And withal they, both male and female, are usually luckier than anyone else in Brazil. For thanks to that portion of their white blood which is in their veins and which is perhaps derived from their own masters, they bewitch these latter to such an extent that some of these will put up with anything from them, and forgive them any excess. It would seem as if their owners not only dare not scold them, but will deny them nothing. And it is not easy to decide whether masters or mistresses are more blameworthy in this matter. For among both of them alike can be found persons who let themselves be ruled by mulattoes who are none of the best, thus verifying the proverb which says that Brazil is hell for Negroes, purgatory for whites, and paradise for mulattoes both male and female. Save only when on account of some suspicion, or jealousy, this love changes into hate and becomes armed with every sort of cruelty and rigor. It is a good thing to profit from their abilities when they are prepared to make good use of them, as some indeed are. But they should not be indulged so far that being given an inch they take an ell, and from being slaves become masters. To emancipate troublesome female mulattoes leads straight to perdition; for the gold with which they buy their freedom rarely comes from other mines than their own bodies with reiterated sins; and after they are freed they continue to be the ruin of many.[27]

The sexual attraction which colored women exercised for many Portuguese is too well known to need additional emphasis here, and a couple of examples from the seventeenth century will suffice.

In 1641 the municipal councillors of Bahia deplored the fact that the local slave girls were so gaily dressed "with the finery which their admirers gave them that things have come to such a pass that many married men have left their wives and spent their estates" to enjoy those colored damsels' favors. Similar complaints were voiced by the Governor-General, Dom João de Lencastre, and echoed by the Overseas Council in 1695–1696, when it was alleged that not even priests were immune from these temptations.[28] These complaints, incidentally, recall Thomas Gage's inimitable account of life in contemporary Mexico City, where he noticed that the attire of the mulatto girls was so seductive "and their carriage so enticing, that many Spaniards of the better sort (who are too prone to venery) disdain their wives for them . . . who with their bravery and white mantles over them seem to be, as the Spaniard saith, *mosca en leche,* a fly in milk." Gage adds, in words which anticipate those of Antonil, that "most of these are or have been slaves, though love have them loose at liberty to enslave souls to sin and Satan." [29]

Another eyewitness in Brazil relates how during the Dutch conquest of Pernambuco in 1637, many of the "pot-bellied" sugar-planters fled southward with their pretty mulata mistresses riding pillion behind them while their neglected white wives struggled dishevelled and barefoot through swamp and scrub.[30] It was not, of course, only wealthy planters and respectable citizens who increased the *mestiço* population by consorting with Negresses and mulattoes; in fact, the lower down the social scale the more there was of this miscegenation, for obvious reasons. The soldiers of the garrison towns, sailors from visiting ships, and poor whites of all kinds mingled freely with Negresses, "owing to the lack of white women," as the soldier-chronicler Cadornega noted in Luanda on the other side of the Atlantic.[31] The great majority of the mulatto children born of such (for the most part fleeting) unions, naturally had no proper upbringing or stable family life. Lacking even the protective discipline (such as it was) of the *senzala* or slave quarters, they inevitably became the truculent desperadoes and the brazen prostitutes who gave the colonial authorities continual trouble by their unruly behavior.

Antonil admitted that mulattoes, when properly disciplined, were better fitted for any kind of a skilled job than were Negroes; but colonial legislation discriminated against them much more than it did against the *mamelucos, or caboclos,* as the products of crossbreeding between the whites and Amerindians were termed. Even free mulattoes were often coupled with enslaved Negroes in the laws which either forbade them to carry weapons and to wear costly clothes and so on, or else restricted their use of these and other things which might tend to place them on a level with the whites. They were not allowed to hold official positions in Church or State, though this prohibition was often ignored in practice, as in the case of the famous Padre António Vieira, whose humble mulata grandmother was no bar to his entry into the Society of Jesus. The enduring passion felt by many white men for black or mulata women, best exemplified in the career of Xica da Silva which is discussed in Chapter viii, had its obverse side in the disdain with which the products of such unions were usually regarded. An Italian Capuchin observed of the position of the mulattoes in Angola, which was in some ways similar to that in Brazil: "They hate the Negroes mortally, even their own mothers that bore them, and do all they can to equal themselves with whites; which is not allowed them, they not being permitted to sit in their presence." Mulattoes could and did rise to great heights in the Brazilian colonial world, as exemplified by the career of João Fernandes Vieira, the by-blow of a mulata prostitute. He rose to be a wealthy sugar planter, leader in the "war of divine liberty" against the Dutch in 1645–1654, and finally, governor of Angola and Paraíba. But Fernandes Vieira and others who achieved eminence did so in spite of the official and the social prejudices which existed against them throughout the whole of the colonial period. These prejudices were based, as in other European colonies, upon the conviction that mulattoes almost invariably embodied the vices rather than the virtues of the two races whose blood was intermingled in their own. The lighter their skin, the greater their chances of passing themselves off as white and of ascending the social ladder.[32]

The proverb which characterized the relative positions of the white, black, and coffee-colored inhabitants of Brazil, made no mention of the condition of copper-colored Amerindians and of those who inherited their blood. Their importance was, by this time, vastly less than that of the three other races, but something must be said about them here. In the three cornered clash and fusion of cultures between the seventeenth-century European, African, and Amerindian, the last-named undoubtedly came off the worst. This fact is not surprising since the Amerindians of Brazil were still in the Stone Age when the Portuguese arrived; as, indeed, the great majority of those who have survived by withdrawing into the remotest regions of the forested interior still are. Whereas the Africans, whether Sudanese or Bantu, knew something of slavery in their native habitat and had experience of a sedentary form of civilization and settled agriculture, the primitive Amerindians of Brazil were wandering groups of food-gathering families or tribes, singularly ill-adapted for the routine of agrarian or any other kind of forced labor.

This disadvantage did not prevent the Portuguese colonists from doing their best to enslave them, mainly because white men were loath to do any kind of manual labor in the tropics; but partly, perhaps, because the savages were often fine upstanding physical specimens, when uncontaminated by contact with the Europeans, and hence gave the impression of being strong laborers if only they could be made to work. I have already alluded to the common belief among the colonists that the Amerindian in his native state lived to a great age; and the contemporary Portuguese impression of their physical fitness and appearance is reflected in the following quotation from Padre Simão de Vasconcellos, S.J.:

It is very rare to find among them anyone who is misshapen, blind, crippled, dumb, deaf, hunchback, or who has any other kind of deformity—things which are so common in all other parts of the world. They have black eyes, flat noses, large mouths, sleek black hair; but no beard, or only very occasionally. They are very long-lived, and many of them live more than a hundred or even a hundred and twenty years; nor does their hair whiten until they become decrepit. When children they are very docile, ingenious, clever and affectionate; but when they become adults they gradually lose all those qualities, as if they were no longer the same persons. They treat each other gently when they are not drunk; but as soon as they get intoxicated they scream and dance about all day and all night, quarreling and fighting.[33]

Ungodly by European standards these Amerindians may have been, but there is no doubt that in cleanliness and personal hygiene they were vastly superior to the newcomers. They bathed frequently whenever they had the chance, whereas most good Christians dreaded washing in water almost as much as the proverbial burnt child dreads the fire. The fact is that the European was a filthy animal in comparison with the average Asian, African, or Amerindian; and it is amusing to note the white man's reaction when confronted with the idea of a regular wash and a frequent bath. The Jesuit Padre Alexandro Valignano in Japan, the Portuguese Captain João Ribeiro in Ceylon, and indeed every observant traveler bore testimony, whether wittingly or otherwise, to the superiority of the so-called "barbarians" in this respect. Even the despised African Negro, commonly regarded as a revoltingly dirty individual, was admitted by intelligent observers to be more hygienic than a white man, if he was not forced to live in squalor. A much traveled Spanish Dominican friar even claimed that the lice which commonly infested Europeans in their own unwashed continent disappeared when their hosts went to Asia or America; only to become inseparable companions again when the returning wanderer set foot on his native shore.[34]

The Portuguese pioneers mated freely with the Amerindian women whenever they had the chance, and they adopted certain traits of the native culture, such as a fondness for bathing, the substitution of manioc flour for bread, and the use of the hammock, which are basic factors in Brazilian life today. This did not prevent the great majority of them and their descendants down to the time of Pombal from regarding the Amerindian male with the utmost contempt and aversion, and from enslaving him whenever they could. Although the idea of the "noble savage" has been traced to early French literary conceptions of the Brazilian Indian,[35] this notion was most emphatically not entertained by the Portuguese who came into contact with him, and who were resolved either to domesticate, or to enslave, or to kill him. The idealization of the Amerindian did not take hold in Brazil itself until that country broke loose from Portuguese domination in the early nineteenth century. In a purely artificial and romantic revulsion against their Lusitanian origins, many Brazilians without a drop of Amerindian blood in their veins then changed their Portuguese patronymics of Sousa, Costa, and the like, for mellifluous Tupí-sounding names like Paraguassú. Moreover, even in colonial days, Amerindian ancestry and blood were always regarded as being more honorable—or, at least, less dishonorable—than those of the African Negro, with their inevitable connotation of slavery. Hence many people with African blood sought to pass themselves off as being descended from Amerindians; for Church and State alike condemned the enslavement of the Amerindian while condoning, and at times even promoting, the enslavement of the African.

The Jesuit missionaries, in particular, strove to prevent the enslavement of the Amerindians, whom they endeavored to domesticate and Christianize by gathering them together in village mission-settlements (*aldeias*). In so doing, they preserved the Red man from total extinction or from complete absorption by the White; but their own rigid system of supervision, and the enforcement of Christian *mores,* was in many ways unsuited for the further development of the Amerindians. The *aldeias* resembled orphanages or boarding schools run by prudish if devout priests; and by enforcing such European ideas as clothing the inmates, the missionaries unwittingly did their charges more harm than good.[36]

The Jesuits, unlike the colonists, believed that the Amerindians had certain natural virtues, which they endeavored to foster. But they took the line, after a few preliminary and disastrous experiences in the contrary sense, that the Amerindians should be treated as adult children and could not, in the foreseeable future, progress to a point where they could be safely ordained as priests. Through force of circumstances which will be explained later, they were reluctantly compelled to allow the Amerindians of the *aldeias* to perform manual labor for the colonists under certain conditions and safeguards. But they strove to limit this concession as far as possible, and to shield their neophytes from demoralizing contacts with the whites and half-castes.

The colonists looked at the Amerindians with completely different eyes, being resolved to use the men for servile labor and the women as wives, concubines, or handmaidens. Even after experience had shown that the Negro was vastly superior both as a house servant and as a field hand, enslavement of the Amerindians continued in regions where the colonists could not afford to import Negro slaves, or where their way of life was more suitable for the Red man. As indicated above, this was particularly so in the southern region of São Paulo de Piratininga, and in the northern state of Maranhão-Pará.[37] On the plateau of Piratininga, the colonists mated with Amerindian women to a greater extent than elsewhere, and they adopted much of the savages' jungle craft and forest lore. The Paulista, or *Bandeirante* as he was later called, was the South American equivalent of the French Canadian *métis* or *coureur-des-bois*. More at home in the forest paths and bush trails of the remote backlands than in their own houses, the Paulistas penetrated hundreds of miles inland in the course of their frequent expeditions in search of slaves, precious metals, and emeralds, as will be explained in the next chapter.

In the Maranhão-Pará region, life was dominated by the network of great rivers and their numerous affluents, which formed the sole means of communication between the few and sparsely populated settlements, and which, in the river Amazon, afforded a magnificent highway into the interior. The complete dependence of the colonists on Amerindian labor, and the scant regard they showed for those who toiled on their behalf, were described as follows by Padre António Vieira, S.J., during a voyage up the river Tocantins in 1654.

> Here it will be well to note that the Indians are those who make the canoes and their awnings, who caulk them, sail them, row them; and many times, as we shall see, they are those who carry them on their backs over the portages. They are also those who, after rowing for days and nights on end, go out to seek food for themselves and the Portuguese (who always get the most and the best). They are those who build huts for us, and, if we have to march along the banks, they are those who carry the loads and even the weapons. All this the poor Indians do for no other payment than being called "dogs" and other names which are much more insulting. The best reward that these poor wretches can hope for on such expeditions, is to find a commander who does not treat them so badly, but this very rarely happens. There have been expeditions on which more than half the Indians who set out did not return, because they died from sheer overwork and harsh treatment.[38]

The Amerindians' religious beliefs, and to a lesser extent those of the African Bantu, were essentially based on fear. Both races were compassed about by a network of taboos, partly inspired by the terrors of the jungle, and the spirit world was very real for them. Witchcraft and sorcery thus played a great part in their lives; and I need hardly add that belief in the "black arts" was by no means extinct in Europeans. Jesuit missionary writers in South America and elsewhere often relate startling tales of how the devil or his agents directly intervened in the concerns of everyday life. Both Bantu slaves and Amerindian converts thus made little difficulty in conforming to the outward signs and symbols of Roman Catholic Christianity, such as the wearing of crosses and rosaries and the veneration of saints' images. Alexander Hamilton wrote of the Negro slaves from Mozambique: "after baptism, they have a little crucifix, or a saint of brass or ivory, hung about their necks, which they are as fond of, as a monkey is of a young kitten to play with." [39] This unflattering comparison does not, of course, hold true of all colored converts. The lay brotherhoods of Our Lady of the Rosary, the favorite saint of Negro slaves in Brazil, may have contained members who professed their faith in its purest form. But for obvious reasons, the bulk of the servile population had only the dimmest notion of Christianity. Their ancestral and spiritualist beliefs strongly influenced their peculiar form of Roman Catholicism and for that matter deeply affected their descendants to the present day.[40]

Concluding this rapid and inevitably somewhat superficial survey of the Brazilian social scene in the last quarter of the seventeenth century, we may note that the majority of the population already consisted of mixed bloods, although the mixture varied widely in different regions. Going from north to south, the State of Maranhão-Pará contained mainly Amerindians, the *mamelucos* or *caboclos* in the second place, whites and mulattoes in the third, and Negroes a poor last. In the populous ports of Recife, Salvador, Rio de Janeiro, and their immediate hinterlands, Negroes and mulattoes predominated, with pure whites in the second place, and Amerindians and *caboclos* in the third. In the São Paulo region, *mamelucos* were the most numerous, and persons with an admixture of Negro blood were (like pure whites) comparatively rare. In the recently occupied cattle-raising areas of the backlands, such as the valley of the river São Francisco, the three races were mixed to such a degree that any assertion is a pure guess; but perhaps the Amerindian and Negro strains predominated in the *vaquerios* or cowboys. In any event, there were strong currents of immigration from Portugal and the Atlantic islands on the one hand, and from West Africa on the other; whereas the Amerindians were being decimated by disease, hard labor, the rigid Jesuit *aldeias,* and other factors, and thus formed a rapidly diminishing contribution.[41]

Despite the hazards of tropical agriculture in Brazil and the vicissitudes of the slave trade in Angola, Portugal's existence as an independent nation was now largely based on the resources which she derived from her control of those two regions in the South Atlantic. A visiting English seaman noted of Brazil in 1664: "the country is much abounding with sugars, which is the best sugar for the most part that is made." He added that Rio de Janeiro, Salvador, and Recife, "all yearly lade many ships with sugar and tobacco and brazilwood for the merchants of Portugal, it being a great enriching to the Crown of Portugal, without which it would be but a poor kingdom." Not only in jest did the first Braganza king characterize Brazil as his milch cow (*vacca de leite*), and the economy of Brazil depended in its turn upon the continual arrival of slaves from Angola. The competition of sugar exported from Barbados and other Caribbean islands was becoming increasingly felt in the last quarter of the seventeenth century; but old Consul Maynard at Lisbon, "a very stirring man on his nation's behalf," could still write in 1683 that the English were exporting from Brazil via Portugal, "wonderful quantities of sugars." Sixteen years later William Dampier bore convincing testimony to the superiority of Brazilian over West Indian sugar, on observing how the former was cultivated and refined at Bahia.[42]

The English had an important share in the carrying trade between Lisbon and Brazilian ports, since Portugal did not have sufficient shipping of her own to maintain the annual Brazil fleets, but was forced to rely to a considerable extent on freighting foreign bottoms. Maynard observed in 1670 that "the employment of English shipping from Portugal to Brazil is very advantageous to this kingdom [England], ten to twelve great ships going yearly thither, being ships of force, well manned, which advanceth our navigation and encourageth the building of ships fit for war." The English were not satisfied with this, but continually pestered the Portuguese government for permission to trade with Brazil on their own account, quoting the treaties of 1654 and 1661 in support of their claim. The Portuguese, however, remained adamant on this point, for the reason stated by Charles Fanshawe, the English envoy at Lisbon in 1682. The Brazil trade, he wrote, "is as the apple of their eye, it being the only navigation left them, which they think strangers would wholly carry from them," if admitted on equal terms.[43]

The pattern of trade on which the English were so anxious to "horn in," was a triangular one between Portugal, Angola, and Brazil. The ships which left Lisbon and Oporto for Luanda, or for Brazilian ports, carried European manufactured goods of every description, and also a certain amount of Chinese and Indian wares, which had been imported into Lisbon from Goa. Since Portugal's own production was insufficient to supply the demands of her South Atlantic empire, a large proportion of the outward-bound cargoes consisted of goods purchased from other European countries, of which England provided the lion's share. More than eighty ships "great and small," were engaged in the annual export of woollen manufactures from London, Bristol, and West Country ports to Portugal. This figure was exclusive of sixty ships engaged in the Newfoundland codfishing trade with Portugal and an unspecified number of other ships which exported fish direct from England.[44]

Angola exported practically nothing besides Bantu slaves and elephants' tusks—"black" and "white" ivory in other words. Business in these two commodities was pretty brisk despite the economic crisis which the Portuguese empire was then experiencing, owing to the fall in price of Brazilian sugar and tobacco and the rise in price of corn, cloth, and other essential imports from Northern Europe. The price of slaves had also doubled between 1640 and 1680. Writing in 1681, Cadornega tells us that between eight and ten thousand head of adult slaves were exported annually to Brazilian ports from Luanda, where there were always to be found about twenty merchant ships in the harbor, some of them large and well gunned. The slaves were purchased with European or Brazilian products, such as textiles, rum and sugarcane brandy (*cachaça; giribita*), and tobacco. The duties levied on the export of slaves furnished most of the money (or payment in

kind) for the upkeep of the garrison, salaries of the Crown officials
and the clergy, to say nothing of substantial contributions to the
instalment payments made in Lisbon for the price of peace with
the United Provinces and the dowry of our Queen Catherine. The
right to buy slaves was vested in successive contractors, who paid
the Crown an agreed sum for exercising this privilege over a
varying number of years. They could then either buy slaves on
their own account, or, as was more usual, sublet their rights to
anyone who paid them a licensing fee.[45]

On reaching Brazil, the slaves were usually sold for sugar or
tobacco, which was then remitted in the annual fleet to Portugal.
With the decline in sugar prices in the last quarter of the seventeenth century, many Lisbon merchants insisted on being paid in
cash rather than in kind, and the resultant export of coin produced a serious financial crisis in Brazil. The sugar fleets sailed
in convoy, a precaution originally instituted against Dutch
privateers in 1649, but which was continued after the definitive
conclusion of peace with the United Provinces (1669), owing to
the menace of the Barbary corsairs cruising off the coast of
Portugal and the Azores. The convoy system was very unpopular
in Brazil, for the times of arrival and departure were very uncertain and seldom coincided with the harvest. In 1690 an effort
was made to reform this state of affairs by fixing the time of departure of the Brazil fleets from Portuguese ports between December 15 and January 20, and their return sailings from Brazil
between the end of May and July 20, but deviations from these
norms were frequent. Stocks piled up in the warehouses, and
sugars were sometimes awaiting shipment for two years. These
delays adversely affected the quality of the sugar, and this was one
of the reasons for the growth of exports from the Antilles at the
expense of those from Brazil, despite the superior quality of the
latter at the port of embarkation.[46] Nevertheless, Bahia still drove
a relatively thriving trade, as William Dampier testified after his
stay there in 1699, and it was the most important city in the
Portuguese empire after Lisbon.

With the proceeds of the sale of his sugar or tobacco at Lisbon, the seller could then buy European or Asian goods for re-export to Angola or to Brazil. These exports included wigs, ribands, silk stockings, and other luxuries for wealthy planters, traders, or officials, as well as necessities like wine, olive oil, codfish, wheaten flour, and textiles. This triangular trade might, of course, be carried on in any direction between the three countries concerned. A Lisbon merchant could, for example, send goods for sale in Brazil and then invest the proceeds in the purchase of slaves from (or at) Angola. Similarly, a planter or trader in Brazil could send sugar, tobacco, or dyewood to Lisbon and receive the return in European goods; or he could send tobacco, brandy, or rum to Angola and receive the return in black or white ivory or in both.[47]

At all the principal ports on both sides of the Atlantic, the Crown levied heavy and sometimes crippling duties either on imports, or on exports, or on re-exports, or on all three. One of the leading landowners at Bahia complained in 1680 that out of a hundred rolls of tobacco which he sent to Lisbon, more than seventy-five were needed to pay the Customs dues and freight charges. "And as regards the remaining twenty-five," he wrote bitterly, "I am not allowed to sell them, nor consume them, nor even throw them into the sea, but am held responsible for them." [48] These excessive fiscal burdens in turn gave rise to a flourishing contraband trade, which frequently attained alarming proportions from the Crown's point of view. This was particularly true with Brazilian tobacco, despite the stringent rules and regulations framed to prevent unlicensed exports. The officers and crews of homeward-bound East Indiamen, which now regularly called at Bahia, were notorious for the skill they displayed in smuggling tobacco aboard.

Some of the wealthier traders acted as merchant-bankers, issuing and cashing money and drafts, or advancing money to Crown officials whose salaries were in arrears. These officials were for the most part ill paid, and virtually all of them engaged in commerce whenever they had the chance. The governors of Angola, for in-

stance, actively participated in the slave trade; it being nothing un-
usual for about twenty-five per cent of the Negroes exported annually from Luanda to be shipped on the governor's account.[49]

The economic revival of Portugal which had been expected to
follow the definitive conclusion of peace with Spain and the
United Provinces in 1668–1669, had largely failed to materialize.
On the contrary, and as indicated above, Portugal was confronted
with a decline in the prices which her colonial primary products,
such as sugar and tobacco, fetched on the Lisbon market, and with
a rise in the prices of her most essential imports from Northern
Europe. The position was aggravated by a simultaneous decline in
the annual importation of silver bullion to Lisbon from Spanish
America via Seville and Cadiz, and by a similar monetary crisis in
Brazil and Angola, both of which suffered from an acute shortage
of coin. The Governor-General of Brazil complained that in the
year 1690 more than 80,000 cruzados had been exported from
Bahia to Oporto alone, and that if Brazil's unfavorable balance of
trade continued at this rate, her economy would soon collapse.
Finally, the deteriorating economic situation of Portugal's Atlantic
empire was worsened by the ravages of smallpox throughout
Angola during the 1680's, and by the simultaneous introduction of
yellow fever into Brazil, where Bahia and Pernambuco were both
seriously affected. Writing from Bahia to a friend at Lisbon in
July, 1689, Padre António Vieira, S.J., observed gloomily: "we
shall shortly relapse into the savage state of the Indians, and become Brazilians instead of Portuguese." [50]

The home government did not watch this prolonged economic
crisis with folded arms, but strove to avert disaster by a combination of stop-gap and more far-reaching measures. Persistent efforts
were made to foster the growth of the cloth industry in Portugal
by protectionist legislation on Colbertian lines and by contracting
foreign technicians. Sumptuary laws were enacted against the
importation of luxury goods, particularly those from France.
In 1688 the nominal value of the coinage was increased by twenty
per cent, while leaving its intrinsic value unchanged, and another

increase of ten per cent was made six years later. In 1694 a colonial mint was established at Bahia, partly as the result of repeated representations by Padre António Vieira. In 1680 a Portuguese colony was founded at Sacramento on the northern branch of the Rio de la Plata opposite Buenos Aires, largely in the hope of diverting the stream of silver from Potosí through this backdoor of High Peru, as had happened in the years before 1640. Last not least, the search for gold, silver, and emerald mines in Brazil, which had been carried on intermittently ever since the mid-sixteenth century, was more actively stimulated by the Crown.[51]

Not all these measures were equally successful. The industrialization program collapsed with the suicide of its protagonist, the Count of Ericeira, in 1690, and his successors were more interested in developing the wine trade. A succession of bad sugar harvests, unseasonable rains, and the continued ravages of yellow fever, with heavy mortality among slaves, oxen, and horses brought the Brazilian sugar industry to the verge of collapse in 1691. The monetary revaluations were only temporarily successful;[52] and the colony of Sacramento, though it quickly became a center of contraband trade with the viceroyalty of Peru, proved very expensive to maintain in the face of Spanish hostility. The search for mines was concentrated partly on the legendary silver-bearing region of Sabarábussú, the "shining mountain," which was supposed to conceal a second Potosí. No silver was forthcoming, but just when the Crown had almost abandoned hope of finding rich deposits of silver in this remote and melancholy region, some Paulista adventurers encountered alluvial gold on a hitherto unprecedented scale, and the first of the great gold rushes began.

II. THE GOLD RUSH
IN MINAS GERAIS

T HE BELIEF that Brazil must contain mines of precious metals and of precious stones was almost two centuries old when hope long deferred was at last translated into reality on a dazzling scale. There is no need to recapitulate here the various forms which the search for gold, silver, and emeralds took at different times and places, whether inspired by the Spanish tales of *El Dorado* ("The Golden Man"), which likewise haunted Sir Walter Raleigh, or by misunderstood Amerindian legends, or simply by the (misconceived) geographical propinquity of silver-bearing Potosí. The width of the South American continent was underestimated, and the conviction that the Cerro de Potosí was not so very far distant from the vaguely conceived Brazilian frontier encouraged people to continue the search westward in spite of repeated disappointments. This belief was reflected in a report of Consul Maynard, compiled at Lisbon in 1670, concerning Paulista activity (or, in Maynard's view, inactivity) in the hinterland of Piratininga. He referred optimistically to "the probability of the discovery of gold and silver and other riches, which the situation promises, as much as any place in the world, it lying in the same latitude and same continent with Peru, only separated by the River of Plate and the Amazons."[1] Since, in fact, it was the Paulistas who discovered alluvial gold in this region, we may consider this peculiar breed in more detail than was necessary in the previous chapter.

The most distinguishing feature of the Paulistas was their strong admixture of Amerindian blood, and in this they resembled the Spaniards settled in Paraguay, who mated with the Guaraní women on a similar scale. The majority of the Paulistas spoke Tupí-Guaraní (the *lingua geral* or lingua franca) in preference to Portuguese, at any rate when at home with their womenfolk or when absent on their far-ranging expeditions into the interior (*sertão*). This preference for the maternal tongue did not, perhaps, apply to those of them who had been educated at the Jesuit Colleges of Santos and São Paulo, but even these men were bilingual. Presumably because of their Amerindian blood, the Paulistas were infected with a wanderlust which was absent in the other settlers of coastal Brazil, who for more than a century made relatively few, feeble, and sporadic efforts to penetrate deeply into the hinterland. The Paulistas, on the contrary, were continually sending roving bands ever further into the *sertão;* and by 1651 they had blazed trails to High Peru and through the dense forests of central Brazil to the Amazon delta.[2] The highland region of São Paulo de Piratininga was a poor and isolated—though a healthy —one, and these expeditions were principally in search of Amerindians whom the Paulistas then enslaved (or domesticated) for use in their cultivated fields (*lavouras*). More or less as a sideline, they also searched for gold, silver, and emeralds; and they had discovered the alluvial gold-producing streams of Paranaguá by about 1572.

These roving bands were known as *bandeiras,* a term originally applied to Portuguese militia companies, and they were organized on a para-military basis.[3] They varied in strength from a mere fifteen or twenty men to several hundred individuals provided with one or two friars as chaplains. The majority of any *bandeira* usually consisted of Amerindian auxiliaries, whether bond or free, for use as scouts, food gatherers, guides, porters, and so forth, with the white and half-breed Paulistas forming the kernel. In course of time, the Paulistas became as proficient in jungle and bush craft as the Amerindians already were, or even, according to some contemporaries, "as the very beasts themselves." These *bandeiras* frequently roamed the interior for months and occasionally for years on end. Sometimes they planted manioc in forest clearings, and camped in the neighborhood until they could harvest the crop; but they chiefly depended on the products of the chase, on fish from the rivers, on fruits, herbs, roots, and wild honey. They made as much use of bows and arrows as they did of muskets and other firearms, and except for their weapons they traveled remarkably light.[4]

Most modern representations of seventeenth-century Paulistas, whether in painting or in sculpture, depict them in a sort of "Pilgrim Father" attire with high jack boots; but in point of fact they seem to have worn little else but a broad-brimmed hat, beard, shirt, and drawers. They generally marched barefooted and in single file along jungle trails and bush paths, though they often carried a variety of weapons. Their gear likewise included thick wadded cotton jerkins, which were so effective against Amerindian arrows that in 1683 it was suggested they should be used in warfare against the bellicose Negroes of Angola on the other side of the Atlantic.[5] The feminine element was not lacking in the larger *bandeiras,* for though the Paulistas did not take their lawful wives with them on their expeditions, they were often accompanied by Amerindian women as cooks and concubines.

Although the highland plateau of São Paulo de Piratininga is only about thirty miles from the sea as the crow flies, the region was isolated from the rest of the colony by the singularly rugged Serra do Mar. Communication with the port of Santos was by a mountain trail so winding and precipitous that in many places the traveler was obliged to use his hands as well as his feet in ascending it. There was a certain amount of livestock in the captaincy, but the shoulders and heads of the Amerindian porters formed the principal means of carriage. It was also the enslaved and domesticated Amerindians who cultivated the manioc and other food plants that were grown. As the town council of São Paulo wrote ingenuously to their lord-proprietor in 1606, "Your worship well knows that the Portuguese are not hard workers, especially when they are out of their own country." [6]

The geographical isolation in which the Paulistas lived naturally made this region a refuge for malcontents, deserters, and fugitives from justice, as likewise for foreigners who were regarded with suspicion by the colonial authorities. Spaniards, French, English, Dutch, and Italians were all represented among the founding fathers of São Paulo; but the assertion of some Spanish Jesuits that the Paulistas mainly consisted of "Jewish banditti" need not be taken seriously. Given these very mixed origins and the nature of their physical surroundings, it is not surprising that the Paulistas showed themselves suspicious and resentful of the representatives of royal authority, although they always professed a whole-hearted respect for the person of the reigning monarch. The colonial authorities, on their side, did not as a rule concern themselves overmuch with São Paulo; partly because it was not part of a Crown captaincy but of one belonging to a *donatório* or lord-proprietor, in the person of the Count of Monsanto, and partly because the region was sparsely populated and economically backward compared with the rich sugar-producing regions of Rio de Janeiro, Bahia, and Pernambuco.

When the officials at Bahia and Rio did have occasion to try and enforce their authority or their orders in São Paulo, they usually failed to do so, except so far as the Paulistas were prepared to obey these instructions for the sake of their own convenience. On occasion, the Paulistas expelled the Jesuits from both Santos and São Paulo, and the padres only gained readmittance to the latter town by compromising over the problem of the freedom of the Amerindians. Nor did the Paulistas send many men to fight against the Dutch during the campaigns of 1630–1654, though they were repeatedly urged by the colonial governors to do so. Similarly, the Paulistas only paid the quint, or tax of the royal fifths on all gold mined or washed, to the extent that it suited them. They were more than once accused of obstructing the efforts of the technicians who were brought in to improve mining methods, and of reluctance to allow outsiders to search for new mines. This obstruction was motivated by the fear that if gold or silver was found in abundance, the colonial authorities would have every inducement to bring São Paulo under their direct and effective control.[7]

A disgruntled colonial governor wrote in 1662 that São Paulo was a veritable La Rochelle, since deserters and criminals who took refuge there could never be arrested nor apprehended by the authorities. Thirty years later another exasperated governor-general wrote that the monetary reform of 1691 was enforced without difficulty or opposition in the whole colony, "save only in São Paulo, where they know neither God, nor Law, nor Justice, nor do they obey any order whatsoever." Dom João de Lencastre described the Paulistas in 1700 as being "people of an independent and inconstant character, most of whom are criminals; and above all they are deeply devoted to the freedom in which they have always lived since the creation of their town." Such unflattering observations abound in the official correspondence between Rio, Bahia, and Lisbon. Admittedly there were a few Crown officials and others who defended the loyalty and praised the pioneering spirit of the Paulistas, but the consensus of opinion was strongly hostile to them. It is no wonder that Dampier, Froger, and other foreigners who visited the Brazilian coast in the last decade of the seventeenth century were told that the inhabitants of São Paulo were "a sort of Banditti, or loose people that live under no government."[8]

Despite their truculent independence and their feeling that they were different from and not beholden to the inhabitants of the rest of Brazil, the Paulistas were surprisingly amenable to direct requests or orders from the Crown as distinct from those of its representatives. The desire of their leading men for titular honors and distinctions was remarkable even in an age when this was common form in all European countries. The Crown exploited this vanity to the full when soliciting the help of the Paulistas during the prolonged search for gold and silver mines in 1674–1682. These particular attempts failed; but a decade later the Crown explicitly authorized the governor of Rio de Janeiro to tempt the principal Paulistas to join in prospecting for mines by the promise of making them gentlemen of the royal household and knights in the three military orders of Christ, Aviz, and Santiago.[9] These last orders reached Rio de Janeiro just about the same time as the Paulistas, who were already searching for silver and emeralds in the interior, struck alluvial gold in paying quantities.

The exact date and place of the first really rich strike will probably never be known. The traditional accounts vary, and the official correspondence of the governors of Rio and Bahia only tardily and inadequately reflect the finds of the first ten years. Collating such fragmentary and contradictory accounts as have come down to us, it would seem that gold was found almost simultaneously in different regions of what is now Minas Gerais by different individuals or parties of Paulistas in the years 1693–1695. *Bandeiras* from São Paulo had briefly traversed much of this region in the previous century, and with more thoroughness during the long search for emeralds by Fernão Paes and for silver by Dom Rodrigo de Castel-Blanco in 1674–1682.[10] As mentioned above, these attempts failed; but a leading Paulista, Manuel de Borba Gato, who was implicated in the assassination of Don Rodrigo in the Sumidouro area (August 28, 1682), subsequently took refuge with his followers in the region of the Rio das Velhas, where he discovered alluvial gold in paying quantities. He is alleged to have kept this discovery to himself until the end of the century; but since he was not completely cut off from all contact with São Paulo and the outer world, it is probable that news thereof, in a somewhat garbled form, had filtered through to Rio de Janeiro by 1695. Moreover, the *bandeiras* which traversed the region between the Serra de Mantiqueira and the headwaters of the Rio São Francisco had noticed that the beds and banks of

35

many of the rivers and streams which they crossed were similar to those at Paranaguá and elsewhere which produced alluvial gold, although in such small quantities as did not tempt them to try their luck for long in this region where Amerindians formed an easy quarry.

It has been argued that the first gold strikes in the region of the Rio das Velhas were not made by Paulistas but by adventurers from Bahia who had penetrated as far as Sabarábussú by way of the rivers São Francisco, and Rio das Velhas. This is admittedly a possibility, but the weight of evidence seems to me to confirm the traditional priority of the Paulistas, though only by a short head. Both contemporary and contemporaneous accounts usually ascribe the discovery to the Paulistas, even when written by persons who were hostile or unfriendly toward them. One of these Portuguese pioneers recorded in his old age, "there is no doubt that the Paulistas were the first discoverers of this continent of the Mines, and after they had found gold in them, both Europeans and Brazilians joined in the rush." Another pioneer of European origin, who had served in one of the Paulista *bandeiras* in Minas Gerais at the end of the seventeenth century, recalled that some Paulistas, roaming the region of the Rio das Mortes in search of the Cataguazes Indians who wore gold ornaments in their lips and ears, were shown by a local chief the site of the first gold finds in this region.[11] However this may have been, the discovery of alluvial gold in the valleys of the Rio das Velhas, Rio das Mortes, and Rio Doce, respectively, occurred at very short intervals in the years 1693–1695.

The scenery of the gold-bearing region of Minas Gerais is now very different from what it was 260 years ago, but the basic geological features are, of course, still the same. The region forms part of a vast plateau, whose most prominent feature is the Serra do Espinhaço, the oldest geological formation in Brazil. This range runs roughly north and south along a line drawn through Ouro Preto and Diamantina, separating the basin of the Rio Doce to the east from that of the Rio São Francisco to the west. It was on the flanks of the Serra do Espinhaço and its offshoots that the gold-bearing streams and valleys were chiefly found. These were sometimes in the *chapadas,* a name applied to small elevated plateaus, usually consisting of horizontal deposits and separated by deeply eroded valleys. To gain access to the gold-bearing region, the Paulistas had first to scale the formidable barrier of the Serra da Mantiqueira, in which lies the Pico do Itatiaiossu (8,900 feet), the highest point in Brazil, and then to cross the Campos Gerais which lay between the Mantiqueira and the Espinhaço, and was originally infested by the hostile Cataguazes Indians.

Ever since the first settlement of Minas Gerais, successive generations have burnt the trees and vegetation in order to clear the ground for mining or for agricultural pursuits, which accounts for the desolate appearance of most of the countryside today. The summits of the higher peaks, such as the Itacolomí and Itambé, were presumably as bare then as they are now, but the lower slopes of the hills were probably thickly wooded. This certainly applied to the deeply eroded river valleys, with a soil enriched by millennial deposits of humus, derived from the heavy annual rainfalls between September and April, often accompanied by violent lightning and thunder storms. In many districts the undergrowth that faced the first pioneers was evidently very tangled and thick. One of these men recalled in his old age that it had originally taken four days to go from the mining camp at Villa Rica de Ouro Preto to neighboring Ribeirão do Carmo (later Mariana): "for it took so long in that time because of the huge woods which barred the certainty and brevity of the way; whereas being subsequently frequented by travelers, it has become so short and easy that nowadays they take less than two hours to cover the two brief leagues which separate Villa Rica from the city of Mariana." [12]

The pioneer Paulista prospectors in Minas Gerais first found alluvial gold in the beds of rivers and streams. Deposits of this gold were called *faisqueiras,* because the larger particles gleamed or glittered in the sun; whence the word *faisqueiro* for an

37

itinerant prospector or miner of placer gold. When the rivers were in flood and too deep to work, the *faisqueiros* turned their attention to the banks and their immediate vicinity (*taboleiros*) where they often found gold as well. When these deposits were exhausted, or when newcomers found them already being worked by their predecessors, the prospectors went farther afield, and searched for gold in the rifts and clefts of the neighboring hillsides (*grupiaras* or *guapiaras*). All the early gold workings were of the placer variety; and only when the alluvial gold was becoming scarce, did the miners drive tunnels and shafts into the hillsides, as we shall see in Chapter vii.

The original process of washing and panning for gold was of the simplest. The sole instrument required was the *bateia,* a large, shallow, cone-shaped basin, made of wood or metal, which the miner held with both hands. The gravelly subsoil mixed with quartz (*cascalho*) which contained the gold particles was placed in the *bateia* with a quantity of water just sufficient to cover it. The miner then gently rotated the *bateia* in a circular or elliptical motion, tipping out some of the water and *cascalho* at intervals, and allowing the gold to sink to the bottom until it was clearly visible. The *cascalho* was not usually on the surface of the soil, but at varying depths below a layer of sand, earth, or clay. The pits or diggings made in the course of extracting the *cascalho* were called *catas* and many parts of Minas Gerais were soon honeycombed with them.

As the gold deposits became fewer and deeper, the methods of extraction became more complicated in the first quarter of the eighteenth century. Troughs and hydraulic machines were employed, and in some cases the bed of the river or stream was exposed by damming the water and artificially diverting the flow into another channel. Contrary to what is often stated, subterranean mining was sometimes carried out in colonial Minas Gerais, but this process was admittedly not a common one. This was partly owing to the friable nature of much of the rocky terrain, but mainly for want of expert knowledge. The Portuguese were far behind the Spaniards in mining techniques, and the most extensive underground works in Minas Gerais could not compare with those of Mexico and High Peru. The gold secured by these various methods ranged in color from bright yellow to a rusty gray or black. This latter variety was known as *ouro preto,* and another type of dulled and dirty appearance was called *ouro podre.* The touch of the gold found in Minas Gerais oscillated between 21½ and 22½ carats.[13]

When the news of the rich gold strikes finally percolated through to the settled districts of coastal Brazil in the years 1695–1696 there were only two practicable trails by which those who sought the gold diggings of Minas Gerais could reach them. The oldest was the one by which the *bandeiras* had traveled from São Paulo to the upper reaches of the Rio São Francisco, and it was known as the "highway of the Backlands" (*Caminho Geral do Sertão*). It ran by way of the river Paraíba, across the Serra da Mantiqueira to the north side of the Rio Grande, whence it bifurcated to the Rio das Velhas and the Rio Doce. Within a few years, by 1700 at the latest, a feeder route to this trail had been developed from the little port of Paratí, a few days sail below Rio de Janeiro. This trail, the "Caminho Velho" or "old highway" as it was soon called to distinguish it from the more direct "Caminho Novo" which was opened a few years later, ran inland for the distance of a five-day march over difficult country until it joined the original Paulista trail at Pindamonhangaba. These two trails then became a single one which took the traveler about twenty days to cover before he reached the first gold mining camps in the region of the Rio das Mortes. The Paulistas, incidentally, did not usually travel from sunrise to sunset, but only from sunrise to noon, or until two or three o'clock in the afternoon at the latest. The rest of the day was given over to pitching camp, and to hunting in the bush and fishing in the river (if there was one nearby). In this way they usually took a couple of months to travel from the town of São Paulo to the gold diggings, whereas the adventurers who made forced marches over the Paratí route averaged three or four weeks.

The other main route, which soon became the most important, ran along the right bank of the Rio São Francisco, which at that time formed the boundary between the captaincies of Bahia and Pernambuco. This river was usually approached from the coast by way of the little port of Cachoeira, center of the tobacco-growing district in the *Reconcavo* of the city of Salvador. The Rio São Francisco could also be reached overland from Pernambuco, and even from the interior of the Maranhão by way of the recently opened region of Piauí. Trails from all over the hinterland of the captaincy of Bahia converged on the Rio São Francisco at a ranch called the camp of Matthias Cardozo (*arraial de Matthias Cardozo*), whence the way to the gold diggings ran along the bank of the river for about 160 miles as far as the junction with the Rio das Velhas. The mining camps strung along the Rio das Velhas were soon connected by a network of paths and trails with other similar camps, including the remote outposts established in the forbidding Serro do Frio and part of the valley of the Rio Jequitinhonha.

Although the Cachoeira–Rio São Francisco–Rio das Velhas route was longer than those from Paratí and São Paulo, it afforded on the whole easier going. Cattle ranches were established along much of the length of the Rio São Francisco, often separated from each other by only half a dozen miles. The terrain was far less rugged, and water was more easily available. Cattle and horses could traverse this route with relative ease, whereas the mountain trails from Paratí and São Paulo were in places only practicable for pedestrians, or for exceptionally sure-footed horses and mules.[14]

By the middle of 1697, even those who were inclined to be skeptical of the news of the first discoveries had come to realize that there was indeed "gold in them thar hills" on an unprecedented scale. Writing to the Crown in June of that year, Artur de Sá, the governor of Rio de Janeiro, reported that the Caeté mines alone "extend in such a fashion along the foot of a mountain range that the miners are led to believe that the gold in that region will last for a great length of time." New and rich workings were discovered almost daily over a wide area, where every river, stream, and brook seemed to contain gold. Inevitably, the Paulista discoverers and pioneers were not left in unchallenged possession of the diggings, and a swarm of adventurers and unemployed from all over the colony converged on the region by way of the routes described above. "Vagabond and base people, for the most part low-class and immoral" as the Governor-General Dom João de Lencastre unflatteringly described them at Bahia.[15]

The Jesuit Antonil, in his classic account of those bonanza days in Minas Gerais, described the current of immigration in less jaundiced terms. "Each year a crowd of Portuguese and of foreigners come out in the fleets in order to go to the Mines. From the cities, towns, plantations, and backlands of Brazil, come Whites, Colored, and Blacks, together with many Amerindians employed by the Paulistas. The mixture is of all sorts and conditions of persons: men and women; young and old; poor and rich; nobles and commoners; laymen, clergy, and religious of different orders, many of which have neither house nor convent in Brazil." The same authority adds that no proper control was exercised over these people when they reached the mining area. They lived in anarchic conditions, and obeyed only the local rules that had been evolved to settle the conflicting claims to ground in the gold diggings and river beds. Crimes went unpunished, save by private vengance, and murders and thefts abounded. Ecclesiastical jurisdiction was likewise at a discount, since the bishops of Bahia, Rio de Janeiro, and Pernambuco disagreed as to their respective spheres of jurisdiction in this unmapped and undemarcated region. Moreover, many of the miners were itinerant, being frequently on the move in search of new and richer strikes.[16]

The senior colonial authorities regarded this gold rush with mixed feelings, and their ambivalent attitude was reflected in the reactions of the Crown and the Overseas Council at Lisbon. In his above-quoted dispatch of January, 1701, Dom João de Lencastre rejoiced that the latest news from the mines formed a singularly auspicious opening to the new century and gave promise of great wealth and prosperity to the mother country. Nevertheless, he added, there was a grave risk that Brazilian gold would ultimately be of no more use to Portugal than American silver had been to Spain. Gold, on entering the Tagus, might leave the same river soon afterwards to pay for imports from France, England, Holland, and Italy, "so that these countries will have all the profit and we will have all the work." Doubtless, he wrote, the king's advisers were seriously considering this matter, but meanwhile the repercussions in the colony itself were causing grave concern.

The chief danger, he explained, was that the hordes of adventurers who were now swarming into the mining region, "leading a licentious and unchristian life," would speedily transform that district into a "sanctuary for criminals, vagabonds, and malefactors," who could easily imperil the whole of Brazil if they developed the same freedom-loving propensities as the Paulistas. Another and more imminent danger was the fatal attraction exercised by the gold fields on people who otherwise would have contented themselves with cultivating the staple Brazilian crops of sugar and tobacco. Apart from the large white immigration into the mining area, many more Negro servants and slaves accompanied their masters. A shortage of field hands was already being felt in Bahia, Pernambuco, and Rio de Janeiro, "and will soon be felt in Portugal itself if something is not done in time to stop it." Last not least, was the difficulty in collecting the payment of the *quintos,* or royal fifths, from the unruly and uncontrolled miners in such remote and undeveloped a part of the country.[17]

Dom João de Lencastre proved a true prophet. Much of the gold that was so laboriously mined in Minas Gerais, quickly found its way to foreign countries, as Antonil and the Overseas Council bewailed in very similar terms ten years later.[18] The adventurers who swarmed into the mining region likewise remained for more than a decade outside the effective control of the colonial authorities, despite two extended visits paid to the gold diggings by the governor of Rio de Janeiro in 1700–1702. Had the miners remained united, they might easily have defied effective Crown control for longer; but the outbreak of civil war between the Paulista pioneers and the newcomers of chiefly European origin in 1709, enabled the representatives of the Crown to assert their authority in the following year. Even so, another decade elapsed before the consolidation of Crown control was effected by the suppression of the revolt at Villa Rica. The shortage of Negro field hands continued to plague tobacco and sugar planters for the first half of the eighteenth century, being only eased by the subsequent steep decline in the gold and diamond mining industries. Finally, the problem of the royal fifths was never satisfactorily solved for as long as this hated tax continued to be imposed.

Since the government was unable to exercise any firm control in Minas Gerais itself for more than a decade, the authorities of Bahia and Rio de Janeiro tried to atone for this by limiting the traffic and policing the trails leading to that region, but likewise with little success. The construction of a new and (it was hoped) shorter route to the mining fields from the captaincy of Espirito Santo was begun in 1700; but work was stopped two years later by order of the Crown, whose advisers considered that the fewer the routes leading to the mines, the easier it would be to supervise them.[19] In pursuance of this policy, the closure of the River São Francisco route was decreed by the Crown in February, 1701, despite the fact that most of the essential supplies for the mining camps came in by this way.[20] Another restrictive measure proposed by Dom João de Lencastre in 1701, was that nobody should be allowed to go to the mines without a passport signed by the governor-general at Bahia, or by the governors of Rio de Janeiro and Pernambuco, and that these passports should only be granted to persons of credit and substance. This measure was in fact adopted by the Crown but its enforcement proved to be impracticable.[21]

The folly of these restrictions was pointed out to the Crown more than once. As regards the *caminho velho,* this ran through such rugged and thickly wooded country that the nature-wise Paulistas could evade any guards that were placed there, "even if these were as numerous as the trees of the same woods." The attempt to close the Rio São Francisco route was even more fatuous, for the miners could not live without the meat that they secured by this route. The Paulista officials who were entrusted with confiscating droves of cattle that entered Minas Gerais from the north, coöperated with the ranchers and cowboys in bringing them in, even to the extent of forcing reluctant owners to send supplies. Moreover, slaves, salt, flour, iron tools, and other necessities of life were cheaper to import from Bahia than from São Paulo and Rio de Janeiro; not only because the river route was easier going, but because the southern captaincies barely produced enough for their own consumption. The Bahia ranchers and merchants were equally keen on ignoring this prohibition, since the prices they got for their cattle in Minas Gerais were greatly in excess of anything that they could expect to get in the coastal towns. Oxen which fetched from three to five *oitavas* (drams) of gold a head in these last places, fetched from fifteen to thirty in Minas Gerais. Finally, cattle driven from the remoter backlands to the coast were sometimes more than a year on the road; whereas droves from the middle reaches of the São Francisco could reach Minas Gerais in about a month or six weeks.

Apart from the economic facts of life, the human element involved made nonsense of these paper prohibitions. Both the Paulistas and the *vaqueiros* (cowboys) were such adepts in bushcraft and use of ground, that any one of them who "sought refuge with his musket in the woods could not be prevented by all the armies of Europe from coming and going as he wished." The powerful Paulista leaders and the richer ranchers, with their scores of hired bravoes, armed slaves and hangers-on, behaved like independent princelings, "insulting persons of the highest rank, without any regard for human or divine laws." The majority of the newly arrived immigrants from Portugal were also people who would stop at nothing, and most of the ill-paid colonial officials were easily bribed or intimidated. The mining code promulgated in 1702, to which reference is made on p. 52 below, allowed droves of cattle to be driven into the mining region by this route, but rigorously maintained the prohibition on all other forms of transit, trade, and traffic. Under these conditions the closure of this route was never more than a farce, and the authorities at Bahia admitted as much in their correspondence with the Crown.[22]

Efforts to limit the number of Negro slaves entering Minas Gerais were equally futile. In January, 1701, the Crown decreed that only two hundred Negro slaves could be imported annually from West Africa via Rio de Janeiro to the mines, and the other slave markets in Brazil were expressly forbidden to sell slaves to the miners. This restriction was relaxed by another decree of March, 1709, but owing to the outcry from the planters, the Crown went into reverse again two years later. The decree of February, 1711 ordained that Negro slaves who were engaged in agricultural labor could not be sold for service in the mines, with the sole exception of those "who by the perversity of their character are congenitally unfitted for work in the sugar mills and fields." The obvious loophole which this concession provided was exploited to the full by the slaveowners, despite the threat of severe punishment for transgressors of the letter and spirit of this law. In 1703 the Crown had instituted an annual import quota of 1,200 African slaves for Rio de Janeiro, 1,300 for Pernambuco, and the balance for Bahia, while maintaining the existing limit of 200 on re-export for Minas Gerais. This law likewise remained largely a dead letter and the quota system was finally abolished in 1715.[23]

The high prices given for slaves by the gold miners, settlers, and merchants in Minas Gerais were reflected in the expansion of the slave trade with Guinea. The governor of Rio de Janeiro complained in 1703 that the inhabitants of the southern captaincies, being unable to get sufficient slaves from Angola, had for some years past been sending ships from Rio and Santos to trade for slaves on the Guinea coast. These slaves were bought with tobacco, rum, and chiefly gold dust and gold bars, most of which had not paid the royal fifths. He admitted that the only way to stop this flourishing contraband trade was to forbid all navigation between Guinea and the southern Brazilian ports. All efforts to stop the large-scale smuggling of tobacco had failed, although this was a bulky commodity which was very difficult to conceal. Gold, on the other hand, was much more easily hidden, "and despite the most rigorous searches, it will not be possible to prevent people from smuggling as much gold as they wish, owing to the small space occupied by even a considerable quantity thereof." [24] Needless to say, the Crown did not endorse this defeatist attitude of Dom Rodrigo da Costa, but the subsequent history of the trade shows that he was not unduly pessimistic.

Much of this contraband commerce in gold and slaves was done with the English and Dutch on the Guinea coast, although the Hollanders often attacked and robbed the Brazilian slavers at sea. On other occasions the masters of slave ships pleaded that they had been forced by pirates to sell slaves against their will, but in many cases collusion was clearly involved. Dutch aggression was sufficiently disturbing for serious consideration to be given to a proposal by the King of Ardra that the Portuguese should build a fortified factory in his territory at Whydah. The Crown at first seemed inclined to accept the suggestion, and some merchants at Bahia offered to build and maintain the fort at their own expense if they were allowed to form a monopolistic slaving company for trade with Guinea. On second thoughts, the Crown rejected this proposal and preferred to seek redress from the Dutch through diplomatic channels. [25]

In 1711, the Crown, always on the lookout for a pretext to replenish the exchequer, slapped an additional duty on African

slaves who were allotted for re-export to the mines, those coming
from Angola being taxed at a higher rate than those from Guinea.
Commenting on this ruling three years later, the governor-general
at Bahia pointed out that this valuation was made on a false
premise. Experience had shown conclusively that the Sudanese
slaves from Guinea were stronger and better workers than the
Bantu from Angola, and the former accordingly fetched much
higher prices, particularly in Minas Gerais. He therefore decided
to amend the law of 1711, by imposing a flat rate of four and a
half *milreis* per head on all imported Negro slaves irrespective of
their origin, "so as to avoid the deals and deceits which usually
occur in such valuations," and the home government accepted
this modification.[26]

This legislation and other similar enactments that I have no
space to mention, failed to prevent the influx of all and sundry
into Minas Gerais, including thousands of Negro slaves who
were badly needed on the coastal plantations. Nothing like it had
been seen before and nothing like it was seen again until the
California gold rush of 1849. The only effective check on the
number which came pouring in was the sterile nature of the soil
and the impossibility of providing food for all those who wished
to come. One of these pioneers recalled in his old age how some
of the early optimists had started out on the month or six-week
journey to the mines without carrying any provisions at all.[27]
Many died of malnutrition or starvation before reaching their
destination, and it was not unknown for a starving man to murder
his comrade for the sake of a handful of maize. Antonil painted
a similar picture when he wrote: "Since the land which yields
gold is exceedingly barren of all that is necessary for human life,
and the trails to the mines are for the most part equally sterile,
it is incredible what the miners suffered in the beginning from
want of food supplies, not a few being found dead with a spike of
maize in their hand, having no other sustenance."[28]

In their frantic haste to exploit the existing diggings, or to
find new ones, the early pioneers neglected to plant sufficient

manioc and maize, with the result that they suffered acutely from famine in 1697–1698 and again in 1700–1701. The governor of Rio informed the Crown in May, 1698, that the shortage of foodstuffs was so critical that most of the miners had been forced to abandon their diggings, and were wandering with their slaves in the woods, looking for game, fish, or fruits to eat. On his subsequent visit to the mines, he reported from the Rio das Velhas at the end of November, 1700, that famine had visited the region again, though he hoped for relief in March of the following year with the harvesting of crops that had been planted and the arrival of more cattle from the Rio São Francisco.[29] Fantastic prices were paid for food during this struggle for survival. A cat or a little dog sold for 32 drams of gold, an *alqueire* of maize for 30 or 40, and a scrawny chicken for 12. However, it was also admitted that about this time a Negro slave often produced 16 drams of gold as a result of his day's work.[30]

Conditions improved considerably once the crisis at the turn of the century had been surmounted, although the food supplies of Minas Gerais were never superabundant throughout the first half of the eighteenth century. Small farms and ranches were quickly established along the principal trails, and more attention was paid to planting vegetables, maize, and to raising livestock in the neighborhood of the principal mining camps which were slowly turning into townships. Indeed, many people soon found it more profitable to grow food for sale to the miners than to do any mining themselves, since prices remained very high owing to the demand being greater than the available supplies. The early settlers planted mainly maize, pumpkins, beans, and occasionally potatoes. By 1703 they were raising a fair amount of pigs and chickens, "which they sell for a high price to travelers, raising it higher according to the necessity of those who pass by. And this gives rise to the saying that all those who pass the Serra de Mantiqueira leave their conscience either hanging or buried there." [31]

After the tide of immigration was resumed at full flood in

the opening years of the eighteenth century, it was calculated with a fair degree of probability in 1709 that there were then some thirty thousand people engaged in mining, agricultural, and commercial pursuits in Minas Gerais. Other contemporary estimates range from six to sixty thousand, but Antonil, who gives the figure of thirty thousand, took particular care to get his information from reliable persons who had visited the whole mining region. On the strength of a hyperbolic remark in the *Triunfo Eucharistico* of 1734, where the writer states that "half Portugal" was emigrating to the mines, it has been claimed by several modern authorities that no fewer than 800,000 persons reached Minas Gerais from the mother country between 1705 and 1750.[32] This is palpably absurd. Considering the volume of shipping involved in the Brazil trade, and the limited carrying capacity of many of the ships, it is doubtful if more than five or six thousand people ever emigrated from Portugal in a single year—and not all those went to the mines. Probably three or four thousand would be nearer the annual mark in the "rush" years; but even this number was a considerable drain for a small country like Portugal, particularly since the majority were able-bodied men. At any rate, the drain of people emigrating from Minho province was sufficiently alarming to induce the Crown to promulgate a decree in March, 1720, drastically limiting the emigration to Brazil, which thenceforth was only permissible with a government passport. Of course this decree was not always strictly observed; but it may be doubted whether the annual number of emigrants ever exceeded two thousand thereafter.

The earliest mining camps were naturally of the most makeshift description, and even when they began to take on a more permanent form and become embryo townships, the housing elements were very simple. Walls were of crossed sticks and mud, or of poles on end (*pau a pique*), with roofs of palm thatch, leaves, or straw. The next development was dwellings of the wattle-and-daub type with a cover of thatch, but the floor in all cases was of bare earth. As the settlements grew in prosperity and stability, the walls became plastered, inside and out, wooden or stone floors were provided, and thatched roofs were replaced by tiled. Verandas and balconies were later refinements, and finally came the best type of colonial house with cedar corner posts and sleepers, tile roofs, and plastered-over bricks. This last type evolved slowly, and even in 1711 there was only a single tiled house in Ouro Preto, which was one of the oldest and most prosperous settlements.[33]

Agricultural methods were equally simple, and can be defined as of the fire cum hoe variety. Ploughs were unknown, spades and shovels are rarely mentioned, and the axe, billhook, knife, and hoe were the chief tools employed. The first step was to cut down the trees and brushwood to the extent that the owner of a particular tract of land and his slaves could manage. The vegetation thus felled was left for a few weeks to dry out and then fired. The yield of the subsequent harvest depended largely on the success of this burning. If the whole was reduced to ashes, a good crop was forecast; if, through wet weather, the felled trees were only half burned, a bad one. When the ground had thus been cleared the Nego slaves dibbled it with their hoes and sowed the maize, bean, and other subsistence crops. After some years, when the soil became exhausted, a new felling and burning was made in another place. In other words, the cycle was felling, burning, clearing, planting, and harvesting. A rickety vegetation, the second growth, gradually took the place of the primeval forests and thick woods that originally covered a great part of Minas Gerais.[34]

The early settlers' domestic animals were largely limited to pigs and chickens, which also fulfilled the functions of scavengers in the absence of any sanitary facilities other than chamberpots. As time went on, ranches of cattle were formed, but for many years the inhabitants of Minas Gerais depended mainly on the importation of meat on the hoof from Bahia and to a lesser extent from São Paulo. Horses were only owned by the wealthiest settlers and officials; and owing to the vile nature of the trails it was a considerable time before the use of mules, donkeys, and asses as pack animals became common. In the first decade of the eighteenth century, virtually all goods were transported on the shoulders and heads of Negroes and Amerindians.

The mining region was prospected, occupied, and to a lesser extent, settled with astonishing rapidity. The chief camps at Ribeirão do Carmo, Ouro Preto, and Sabará had become thriving settlements by the end of the century. Catas Altas, Villa do Principe, and others too numerous to mention, had followed suit a couple of years later. One of the first indications of permanent settlement was the erection of one or more chapels. These were naturally of the *pau a pique* or wattle-and-daub variety, though they were usually among the first buildings to be graced with a tiled roof. *Vendas,* or small trading shacks, sprang up about the same time; whether these or the chapels came first is a problem similar to that of the chicken and the egg. In any event, conglomerations of neighboring mining camps (*arraiais*) united to form the present towns, which still straggle up hill and down dale, with long winding streets and steep stairways connecting the original nuclei. This loose pattern of town settlement can clearly be seen today in cities such as Ouro Preto, Sabará, and São João d'El Rei, where some of the wards (*bairros*) retain the names of the original settlers, as, for instance, that of António Dias in Ouro Preto.[35]

The distribution of *datas* or mining allotments was carried out anything but smoothly in the first turbulent years. Rich and powerful miners who had numerous armed slaves were likely to usurp the *datas* of those who had none. As for these luckless wights: "when they were working the *datas* that had been allotted to them, if fortune should happen to give them more gold than it did to their more powerful neighbors, so overweening was ambition that these men, forgetful of their bounden duties, and especially that of Catholics, without fear of God and the justices forcibly expelled the former from their rightful property; or else they went and mined therein against their express wishes." To prevent this abuse and to settle other disputes which inevitably arose among the rough crowd of pioneer prospectors, the governor of Rio de Janeiro promulgated a mining code for Minas Gerais in March, 1700. With minor modifications and additions this code was accepted and enacted by the Crown a couple of years later and it remained in force for the rest of the colonial period.[36]

Under the provisions of this code, the first man who discovered gold in any place had the right to choose the site of the first two *datas*. The third was allotted to the Crown, and the fourth to the Crown's representative or *Guarda-Mór*. These were called *datas inteiras* (complete allotments) and they each measured thirty square *braças*.[37] All the other *datas* were distributed by drawing lots, and they were demarcated in proportion to the number of working slaves that each miner employed, on the basis of two square *braças* for each slave. The Crown's *data* was immediately sold to the highest bidder to mine on his own account, the price being credited to the royal exchequer. Once the distribution of *datas* was made, miners could buy, sell, exchange, or amalgamate their holdings by mutual arrangement. Antonil notes that this system led to many strange twists of fortune: "one miner extracting a great deal of gold from a few *braças,* and others a very little gold from many *braças*. And there was a man who for just over 125 ounces sold his *data,* from which the buyer subsequently extracted 224 pounds of gold." The distribution of the *datas* was the responsibility of the superintendent, *Guarda-Mór,* and other Crown officials appointed for the purpose, all of whom received a handsome rake-off for their pains. There were a few districts where *datas* were not officially distributed, and where ownership of a gold digging (or washing) was established simply by prior possession. These were the so-called General Mines of the Ouro Preto district which soon gave their name to the whole region of the Serra do Espinhaço and beyond.[38] The district boundaries were, for the most part, vaguely or wholly undelimited, even on paper and such few maps as existed. Nobody had any clear idea of how far the region came under the authority of the governor-general at Bahia and how far under the governor of Rio and the southern captaincies.

During his visit to the mining district, Artur de Sá appointed various officials to look after the interests of the Crown in such matters as collecting the royal fifths, auctioning the Crown *datas,* and confiscating contraband goods brought in by the river São Francisco route. Among these officials was the old Paulista pioneer, Manuel de Borba Gato, who earned the hatred of the smugglers, "since he confiscated many of the convoys of goods coming from Bahia, remitting the proceeds in gold to the royal treasury at Rio de Janeiro, as also the proceeds from the sale of Crown mining allotments. The total yield from these sources amounted to more than eight *arrobas* in the time of Borba, who sent them through a certain João Martins, and this was the first gold that the King received from these mines." [39]

Many fortunes were made—and lost—in those golden days. Generally speaking, the individuals who did best for themselves, derived their wealth not from mining alone, but from a judicious combination of mining, farming, slave trading, and merchandising. This was true of Francisco do Amaral, whom Antonil cites as the richest man in Minas in his day (1709), with a fortune of more than fifty *arrobas* in gold. As with the later California, Australia, South Africa, and Klondyke gold rushes, successful miners would pay any prices that were asked, and they made a point of spending their money extravagantly and ostentatiously. Wrote Antonil: "those who had amassed great wealth from their diggings were led thereby to behave with pride and arrogance. They went about accompanied by troops of matchlock men, ready to execute any violence and to take the greatest and most frightful revenge, without any fear of the law. The gold incited them to gamble lavishly, and heedlessly to squander vast sums on vain luxuries. For instance, they would give one thousand *cruzados* for a Negro trumpeter; and double that price for a mulata prostitute, in order to indulge with her in continual and scandalous sins." [40]

Nor was it only the laymen who were perverted by the traditional *auri sacra fames*. The correspondence of the governors of Bahia and Rio de Janeiro with the Crown contains a litany of complaints concerning the renegade friars and "bad clergymen" (*clerigos maus*) who infested the mining region. They were stigmatized as being among the worst offenders in leading irregular lives, in defrauding the royal fifths, and indulging in contraband trade on a lavish scale. They early spread "the pestiferous doctrine that the defrauding of the royal fifths does not demand the restitution of the amount thus stolen, because of the application of civil punishment when the crime is discovered." Clerical immunity enabled many of these men to escape search at the control points along the trails; one of their favorite devices being to conceal contraband gold dust in hollow wooden saints' images (*santinhos de pau occo*). Ten years after the gold rush had begun, it was alleged in 1705 that not a single priest in Minas Gerais took an active interest in the religious needs of the people. So bad did the situation become, that six years later the Crown took the unprecedented step of banning not only unauthorized friars but the establishment of the religious orders in Minas Gerais. Another set of men who gave the authorities great concern were deserters from the garrisons of Bahia, Rio de Janeiro, and Sacramento. These men left their units and flocked to the mines in such numbers that the security of the seaports was seriously affected.[41]

The gold rush to Minas Gerais further unbalanced the already rickety price structure of Portugal's Atlantic empire. The excessively high prices given for both necessities and luxuries in the teeming mining camps and townships meant that merchandise, slaves, and foodstuffs tended to gravitate thither, irrespective of whither they were originally consigned. This resulted in a shortage of these commodities in their normal markets, with a consequent rise in prices, which all efforts at legislation failed effectively to control. Craftsmen and artisans flocked to the mines for more remunerative employment, and this in turn led to an increase in the cost of essential services in the rest of Brazil. In

January, 1703, for example, the municipal council of São Paulo was informed that "there was a general complaint in the town that tailors and cobblers were charging outrageous prices for their work." Cattle owners in the district refused to supply the local market with meat, preferring to send their beasts for sale in Minas Gerais, where they fetched vastly higher prices despite the poor condition in which they arrived. In September, 1702, the governor at Rio complained that the city was without the requisite stocks of meat and flour, since the people who ordinarily supplied those products had left for Minas Gerais.

Everywhere it was the same or a similar story. In Bahia the immigrants from Portugal who normally filled the posts of overseeers, bookkeepers, and cattle rangers were leaving en masse for the mines. New arrivals who were hired scarcely worked longer than the time necessary to earn the purchase price of a horse or some other means which would enable them to leave for the gold fields. The slave exporters of Angola preferred to ship their slaves to Rio de Janeiro, where they would fetch higher prices for re-export to the mines, thus aggravating the acute labor shortage in Bahia and Pernambuco. Worst of all, as Antonil wrote in unconscious fulfillment of Dom João de Lencastre's forecast of 1701: "the greatest part of the gold which is extracted from the mines is carried in gold dust and in coins to foreign kingdoms. The lesser part is that which remains in Portugal and in the cities of Brazil—save what is spent in braids, ornaments, and other fripperies with which the women of ill-fame and the Negresses are plentifully adorned nowadays, much more so than their lady owners." [42]

Some years elapsed before the Crown and its advisers realized the full import of the gold rush in Minas Gerais, and then they were at first chiefly concerned with trying to check the movement of people to that region and with preventing the decline of the sugar and tobacco plantations. In March, 1701, the Crown still had only the haziest notion of what was going on in the mining districts, and Dom João de Lencastre was asked for a report on the conditions prevailing there, so that the Crown could decide on its future policy in the light of the information thus received. The official correspondence at this period reflects greater concern with the working of the tobacco monopoly than with the production of gold in Minas Gerais.[43] This concern was also mirrored in Antonil's *Cultura e opulencia* of 1711, which purported to show that the value of the Brazilian gold received in Portugal was far less than that of either sugar or tobacco and was equaled by that of hides. Presumably this estimate took no account of contraband gold; and another chapter of Antonil's book shows that the Crown was becoming seriously worried with the problem of collecting the royal fifths.

When the gold rush started in the late 1690's, the collection of the fifths was confined to four smelting-houses in the São Paulo region, of which only one, that of Taubaté (established in 1695) was anywhere near the newly discovered mines. The miners were supposed to bring their gold dust or nuggets to one of these establishments, where the ore would be cast into bars after deducting a fifth of the value for the Crown. Since compliance with the law was left to the honesty of the individual, and the nearest smelting-house was only reached after a toilsome journey, most of the miners naturally disposed of their gold clandestinely, or else used it to pay for the necessities and the luxuries which they required. Gold dust was used instead of coin for daily purchases, and the man who was finally left with it was theoretically responsible for paying the fifths at a smelting-house or a mint. Goldsmiths, who soon entered the region in considerable numbers, frequently melted gold for interested parties in return for a consideration and in defiance of reiterated laws against this practice. The smelting-houses were not mints, and they were not authorized to buy the melted proceeds. This could only be done by the mint at Lisbon, to which owners were freely permitted to send their smelted gold, and where it was paid for in coin.[44]

As mentioned on page 29 above, a mint had been opened at Bahia in 1694 for the purpose of striking a provincial coinage of such reduced value as to discourage its being taken out of Brazil. At the suggestion of the governor of Rio de Janeiro this mint was moved thither in 1699, where it carried out a similar operation before being transferred to Pernambuco for the same purpose a year later. Both the governor of Rio and the city council repeatedly urged the Crown to establish a permanent mint at Rio which would, so they argued, secure a handsome return from collecting the fifths and from seigniorage and brassage. This step was taken in 1702–1703, a smelting-house being established at the same time for the convenience of those who might prefer gold bars to coin. The result did not come up to expectation so far as collecting the fifths was concerned, but the Crown made a handsome profit from the other two sources, as Antonil admitted in 1709.

During his visit to Minas Gerais in 1701–1702, Artur de Sá appointed agents to assess the fifths in various districts and he established inspection stations on the principal trails leading out of the mining region. All persons were prohibited from leaving this area without an official receipt (*guia*) showing the amount of gold that they were carrying, and the smelting-house for which they were bound and where the fifths would be paid. The mining code of 1702 reinforced these provisions, and arrangements were also made for collecting locally the fifths on the gold dust with which purchasers paid for the cattle imported from Bahia and elsewhere. As will be seen from the figures given in Appendix II, these measures met with relatively little success, the yield from the fifths being particularly disappointing. From another source we learn that there were only thirty-six persons who paid the fifths in Minas Gerais in 1701, these contributors including a woman, a priest, and a friar. Only one such payment is recorded in 1702, and though there were eleven next year (including one of 504 drams), not until 1710 did the number of contributors to the fifths reach more than three figures.[45] The proceeds from the confiscated cattle and the sale of the Crown mining allotments were far more substantial; but, even so, the total income of the

Crown from all these and other sources was relatively small during the first decade of the eighteenth century, considering that more than thirty thousand people were then living in Minas Gerais. These figures do not, of course, tell the whole story, since we have only a few stray references to the payments made at Rio de Janeiro, and none to those made at São Paulo and Taubaté. In 1704 the closure of the smelting-houses at these places was ordered, their operations being transferred to the little ports of Santos and Paratí. It was hoped that the fifths would be easier to collect at these terminal points, but this expectation was not fulfilled.

An interesting sidelight on the amount of gold leaving Minas Gerais is supplied by some revealing entries in an account book kept by the Reverend Guilherme Pompeu, a Paulista secular priest and a wealthy landowner, who also acted as a moneylender and merchant banker. In January, 1699, for example, he received 7,360 drams (nearly twenty-six kilograms) of gold, to send for payment of the fifths on his own behalf and that of others. This was admittedly an exceptionally large amount; but he was not the only person who was acting in this capacity in his home town of Parnahyba, although he was undoubtedly the most important. From the same source we learn that the usual rate of interest which he charged on personal loans was eight per cent, by no means an excessive rate for his day and generation. Defaulting debtors were rare exceptions, and strict honesty on the part of his clients was the general rule. This is a point particularly worth noticing, since so much of the official correspondence of the period gives the impression that all the inhabitants of Minas Gerais were unscrupulous rascals who would defraud not only the Crown's fiscal agents but their next of kin. The priestly banker had business correspondents in Santos, Rio de Janeiro, Bahia, Lisbon, Oporto, and Rome; and he prudently maintained deposit accounts in those places though he himself never left Brazil.[46]

The amount of gold which left Minas Gerais through São Paulo and Rio de Janeiro, whether legally or illegally, large as it evidently was, still remained far less than that which flowed out by the river São Francisco route to Bahia. As noted on page 45 above, all legislation which attempted either to restrict the use of this road or to close it entirely, failed to achieve any results whatsoever. Apart from the convoys of cattle, slaves, and goods which poured into the mines by the trail which led along the banks of the São Francisco, many miners came down this river from the Rio das Velhas in canoes, either to buy supplies or to leave with their winnings for the city of Salvador and beyond. As early as 1699, an Italian visitor to Salvador reported that "they sent a great number of gold bars to the city, the royal fifths yielding that year as much as twenty million [*cruzados*] to the Crown." The last part of this statement was entirely erroneous, since there was then neither mint nor smelting-house in Bahia, and the gold involved was virtually all contraband. "Your Majesty is losing millions," an anonymous observer informed the Crown six years later, "so much gold is sent to the said city of Bahia that the amount cannot be counted in pounds but in hundredweights." [47] The local authorities suggested that the best way of stopping this drain was to reëstablish the mint in the colonial capital, but this was not done until 1714.

If we cannot estimate even approximately the amount of gold which left Minas Gerais, Rio de Janeiro, and Bahia respectively, such figures as we possess for the amounts received annually at Lisbon are an equally unsafe guide. The latest writer on the subject shows that a steady increase in this gold was recorded during the first decade of the eighteenth century. From 725 kilograms in 1699, it rose to 1,785 kilograms two years later, and to 4,350 kilograms in 1703. This rise continued until the impressive total of 14,500 kilograms was reached in 1712. [48] In addition there was a parallel stream of contraband gold imported, and this is naturally where the official figures fail us, except for registering occasional seizures and intelligent guesses. Antonil estimated that less than one third of the gold actually mined was declared, and another contemporary authority alleged that less than a tenth of such gold eventually found its way to the smelting-houses and the mints.[49] This last estimate may well be an exaggeration, but it is undeniable that a vast amount of Brazilian gold was soon in circulation, whether lawfully or otherwise, on both sides of the Atlantic. Magalhães Godinho states that by 1703 at the latest the amount of gold secured from Minas Gerais greatly exceeded all the gold that Portugal had hitherto received from Guinea since the foundation of Mina in 1482, or all that Spain had ever received from her American possessions during the whole of the sixteenth century.

In November, 1695, and thus on the eve of the startling discoveries of the next two years, the authorities at Lisbon had viewed the prospect of extensive gold smuggling with enlightened complacency. The Overseas Councillors then observed that even though contraband gold which reached the Tagus did not enrich the royal treasury it did enrich the king's subjects, "who as much and even more than the treasury itself, made kings rich." [50] When the Crown and its advisers belatedly realized the extent and permanence of the new gold fields, they resolved to change their declared policy of subordinating the interests of the mining industry to those of the sugar and tobacco plantations. The first efforts to channel the flow of gold through the authorized smelteries and the mint at Rio de Janeiro having conspicuously failed by the end of the first decade of the eighteenth century, they determined to tighten up the collection of the fifths in Minas Gerais itself. Luckily for them, the unexpected outbreak in 1708 of civil strife between the Paulistas and the later arrivals in that region afforded the Crown both a pretext and an opportunity for effective intervention.

III. PAULISTAS AND EMBOABAS

A GREAT DEAL of ink has been expended by Brazilian writers in discussing the so-called *Guerra dos Emboabas* (War of the Emboabas) which plunged Minas Gerais into civil strife at the end of 1708, but the actual course of events is still far from clear. Such contemporary—or contemporaneous—accounts as have found their way into print, virtually all stem, directly or indirectly, from the opponents of the Paulistas. The sole important exception is the dispatches of the governor of Rio de Janeiro, Dom Fernando Martins Mascarenhas de Lencastre, who favored the Paulistas, but he made only a tardy and fleeting appearance on the scene of action. The historian is faced, therefore, with a dearth of evidence on one side of the contending parties, but the basic reasons for the outbreak are fairly clear.

From the beginning of the gold rush there was little love lost between the pioneer Paulista discoverers and the *forasteiros* ("strangers" or "outsiders") who came in their wake. This was natural enough, for the Paulistas not only felt that they had prior claims as the original discoverers, but their way of life was in some respects more Amerindian than European. Inured to a nomadic existence, speaking Tupí among themselves, and thoroughly at home in the wilds of the *sertão,* they had little enough in common with the newcomers from the coastal ports, whether townsmen born and bred or whether peasants who had just left the tail of a plough in Portugal. The fact that many of the claims originally staked by the Paulistas had been jumped by later arrivals from the coast when the first owners had evacuated their diggings in the famines of 1698 and 1700, did not make for harmony between the two parties. The Paulistas tended to look upon the mining region as their special preserve, as evidenced by the town council of São Paulo petitioning the Crown in 1700 to limit the awarding of land grants in Minas Gerais to them alone.[1]

Mutual resentment between the two groups was further inflamed by the opprobrious terms which they used to describe each other. We saw in the previous chapter that the Paulistas were often characterized as lawless banditti; and they in turn voiced their contemptuous dislike of the newcomers from Portugal and the Atlantic islands by dubbing them *Emboabas*. This was an Amerindian word of obscure etymology, but one which was obviously used in a derogatory sense.[2] It is true that one of the very few sources which takes the side of the Paulistas claims that most of them magnanimously befriended the pioneer Emboabas, freely sharing their diggings with these poor and needy "sons of Portugal"—only to be rewarded with the blackest treachery and ingratitude in the long run.[3] Doubtless this did happen in certain individual instances; but the attitude of most of the Paulistas was certainly reflected in their town council's above quoted petition of April, 1700.

A minor source of discord was formed by the slaves. Those of the Paulistas were mostly Amerindians, lumped together under the generic but inaccurate term of Carijós and Tapuyas. Those of the Emboabas (when these latter could afford them) were almost invariably Negroes. There was apparently as little love lost between these two groups of the servile population as there was between their respective masters.

One other factor which deserves mention here is that, contrary to what might have been expected, those adventurers who came to the mines from the hinterland of Bahia, Pernambuco, and other regions of Brazil, sided with the European-born Emboabas rather than with the American-born Paulistas. The great majority of these Brazilian-born adventurers from the northern captaincies were Bahianos; but most accounts of the ensuing civil strife make no distinction between them and the Emboabas, and neither will I. The fact that most of the Paulistas had Amerindian blood in their veins and went about barefooted, did not prevent them from being exceedingly proud of their allegedly aristocratic ancestors. They were correspondingly contemptuous of the Emboabas whether these were European or Brazilian-born. It was, in a way, a case of the Paulistas versus the rest, rather reminiscent of the civil strife between the Basques and the rest in Potosí seventy-five years earlier.[4]

Tempers on both sides had been steadily rising for several years when the first noteworthy incident occurred in the Arraial Novo or New Camp, which later became the township of São João d'El Rei. This was provoked by the provocative arrogance of the local Paulistas, who used to say whenever they heard a shot fired in the distance: "there dies a dog—or an Emboaba!" These Paulistas lived mostly outside the camp in the bush, "so as to be near the wild beasts whose hearts they inherited"; but from time to time, groups of them would swagger through the Emboaba mining camps in a singularly bellicose manner. On such occasions, "their leader would go in front, barefooted, in cotton drawers tied in just below the knee, sword in hand, bandoleer girded on, a brace of pistols at the waist, a knife slung on the chest, a carbine under the arm, and with either a hooded cap or a floppy-brimmed hat on his head, shouting to the sound of drums and trumpets, 'kill the Emboabas'." This walking armory was usually followed by a throng of Amerindian slaves and halfcastes, likewise armed to the teeth.[5]

The Emboabas, by their own account, were for long overawed by these displays of truculent bellicosity, but eventually their pent-up tempers exploded in savage wrath. On June 27, 1707, two of the leading and most provocative Paulistas were lynched by an infuriated mob of Emboabas in the Arraial Novo, after the smithy in which they had taken refuge had been burnt by the mob about their ears. When this first impulse of blind rage was over, the majority of the Emboabas hurriedly evacuated the camp and took refuge in the bush, fearing a condign revenge on the part of the Paulistas. A number of bolder spirits, however, barricaded themselves in an outlying house and prepared to resist the expected counterattack. The Paulistas did indeed appear on the scene like enraged lions; but finding that this little group was prepared to fight to the last, they contented themselves with burying their slaughtered compatriots, and then withdrew like gentle lambs. Greatly encouraged by this anticlimax, the refugee Emboabas returned to the camp and resolved to stand no more nonsense from their opponents. The latter made several ineffective overtures for a peaceful understanding, but these were resisted by the Emboabas, who, rightly or wrongly, were convinced of the Paulistas' duplicity. An uneasy state of truce now supervened for more than a year, with both sides watching each other suspiciously while arming themselves and their slaves for the showdown they considered inevitable.

The three most densely settled regions in Minas Gerais were the valleys of the Rio das Velhas and the Rio das Mortes and the district surrounding the *Morro,* or high hill, overlooking the mining camp that later became the town of Villa Rica de Ouro Preto. Paulistas and Emboabas were scattered, and to some extent intermixed, throughout these regions, but the Emboabas had an over-all numerical superiority. Both sides were strongly represented in the Rio das Velhas area, where the old Paulista Superintendent of the Mines, Manuel de Borba Gato, was the senior Crown representative in the whole mining region. As a Paulista, he could hardly avoid favoring his kinsmen, though on the whole he seems to have held the scales fairly even.[6] It was obviously essential for the Emboabas to find a leader who could make an effective counterweight in real power and influence, if not in lawfully constituted authority. This man they found in the person of Manuel Nunes Viana.

As his surname implies, Manuel Nunes Viana was born in the little seaside town of Viana do Castello in northern Portugal. Of humble birth, he emigrated to Brazil at an unrecorded date when still a lad, like so many other peasants and workers from the Minho. He first came to notice as the result of a street brawl in the viceregal city of Salvador (Bahia), when he was set upon one day by two or three armed men. His own sword broke off at the hilt in the ensuing scuffle; but nothing daunted, he defended himself with his hat and contrived to disarm one of his opponents. He killed his man with the sword thus secured, whereupon the other(s) fled, and he himself subsequently went into hiding. When the governor heard of this feat, he gave him what amounted to a conditional pardon, by banishing him to the far interior, but providing him with letters of recommendation to some of the cattle barons of the Rio São Francisco.[7] In this remote region he speedily made his name and fortune by large-scale contraband trade with Minas Gerais. He amassed great wealth and large herds of cattle on his own account, besides what he secured by acting as administrator of the vast estates of Dona Isabel Maria, daughter and heiress of António Guedes de Brito, who was in her own right one of the principal latifundian landowners of Brazil. By 1707 he was the owner of several lucrative gold diggings at Caeté and elsewhere in Minas Gerais.

Early in October, 1708, the acute tension between Paulistas and Emboabas which had subsisted ever since the lynching at the Arraial Novo in June of the previous year, was further aggravated by another incident, this time at Caeté. A quarrel arose there between an Emboaba and a Paulista over the possession of a firearm, the former appealing to Manuel Nunes Viana for support, while the latter sought the protection of a prominent Paulista, Jeronimo Pedroso. When the latter insisted on satisfaction for his protégé, Manuel Nunes Viana challenged him to a duel—

something very rare in the Portuguese-speaking world.[8] Jeronimo Pedroso first accepted the challenge, but subsequently evaded meeting his opponent in the field alleging "safer rather than honorable pretexts."[9] Smarting under this discomfiture, the Paulistas began to scheme for revenge (or so it was alleged) under the leadership of Jeronimo's brother, Valentim Pedroso, who was said to have vowed to "kill all the sons of Portugal." A large party of Paulistas was reported to have agreed "that on a given Monday they should all meet in Caeté" to exact revenge. True or not, these allegations lost nothing in the telling. Each side suspected the other of plotting a massacre of its opponents on the lines of the Sicilian Vespers, and the tension reached breaking point.

At this juncture Manuel de Borba Gato intervened, ostensibly as an impartial mediator desirous of averting bloodshed, but in effect on the side of his Paulista kinsmen—the Pedroso brothers being his distant relatives. On October 12, 1708, he posted a public notice on the church door at Caeté, banishing Manuel Nunes Viana from the Rio das Velhas district within twenty-four hours, as a disturber of the public peace and a defrauder of the Crown's dues. Viana replied next day with a formal letter of disavowal, indignantly denying the allegations against him and disputing Borba Gato's authority to banish him. He claimed that far from being a fomenter of discord and usurper of authority, he had always acted as a pacifier and conciliator in the Rio de São Francisco region and elsewhere. He accused Borba Gato of siding with the unruly Paulistas who were the cause of all the trouble, and who were continually provoking conflicts everywhere, although the superintendent had never tried to banish any of them. His own quarrel with Jeronimo Pedroso was a purely private affair and no concern of Borba Gato. If the latter persisted in his unreasonable attitude, he would be solely responsible for any unfortunate consequences which might ensue.

Borba Gato riposted by posting a second public notice, repeating his order for Manuel Nunes Viana to leave the district within twenty-four hours. "I warn you" this edict concluded, "that if you make any resistance to this order, I will not only confiscate your goods, which I see have come by the forbidden trail from Bahia, but all your property wherever found, as belonging to a mutineer and rebel leader against the orders of His Majesty whom God preserve." This fulmination was reinforced by another edict forbidding anyone from giving aid and comfort to the outlawed Viana, on pain of arrest and confiscation of their belongings.

Despite his brave words, Borba Gato was evidently intimidated by the resolute stand of Viana and his followers, who all rallied round the Emboaba leader in this crisis. At any rate, the superintendent made no serious attempt to enforce his threats, but, on the contrary, arranged a meeting at Caeté between the two protagonists when an outward reconciliation was effected in his presence. The hollowness of this formal agreement was quickly made manifest.

No sooner had Borba Gato returned to his headquarters in the Rio das Velhas district at the end of November, then trouble broke out again in Caeté. A Paulista named José Pardo was lynched by an Emboaba mob after his two sons had killed a Portuguese in the street in broad daylight. In the belief, real or assumed, that the Paulistas were plotting a general massacre of their rivals, the Emboabas then proceeded to disarm the former wherever they could find them and were strong enough to do so. Since they had an overwhelming advantage in numbers, this was effected with little or no loss of life, first of all in the Rio das Velhas district and then in the region of Ouro Preto. Only a very few individual Paulistas offered any armed resistance. The majority fled from these two districts either before or after they were disarmed. The remainder either sullenly surrendered or else declared their allegiance to the winning side.

Oddly enough, none of the contemporary accounts make any allusion whatsoever to the action of Borba Gato at this critical time.[10] Since he appears on the scene just over a year later, either the Emboabas must have left him severely alone or else he temporarily withdrew to São Paulo. The makeshift mining camps at Ouro Preto and Ribeirão do Carmo were burnt in the course of this operation, the former by retreating Paulistas and the latter by the victorious Emboabas. No lives seem to have been lost on either of these occasions, and it was an easy matter to rebuild the mud huts and ramshackle wooden structures which formed the dwellings. By the end of 1708, therefore, the Emboabas were in full control of two out of three principal mining areas, and the demoralized Paulistas had fallen back on the district of the Rio das Mortes. They had not suffered many fatal casualties, but they had lost a great deal of "face," and were breathing dire if rather futile threats of revenge.

In the last week of December, 1708, the leading Emboabas and Bahianos met at Cachoeira do Campo, where they formally proclaimed Manuel Nunes Viana acting governor of the whole mining region until such time as the home government might send regularly constituted officials. Viana accepted the post with a show of reluctance,[11] but proceeded to act as if he was the lawful representative of the Crown. He organized his adherents into three militia regiments and made a series of civil and military appointments to gratify his principal supporters. These included some men who had what can only be termed criminal records, remarkable for even that rough and turbulent milieu. Three of them deserve further mention here because of the important parts which they played then and subsequently.

Francisco do Amaral Gurgel had organized the brutal and treacherous murder of a senior colonial official, Pedro de Sousa Pereira, near Rio de Janeiro on September 20, 1687. He had subsequently fled to the remote hinterland of São Paulo and had thus been able to participate in the first years of the gold rush to Minas Gerais. Here he not only made a fortune but became the richest man of them all according to Antonil's calculation.[12] Bento do Amaral Coutinho, who is sometimes described as Francisco's brother and sometimes as his nephew, but was probably neither, had likewise taken refuge in the mining region after perpetrating the singularly vicious murder of a Rio sugar planter in 1706.[13] Both these Amarals were Brazilian-born, being natives of Rio de Janeiro or its vicinity, but the third of our rascally trio, Fr. Francisco de Menezes, was a renegade Trinitarian friar and a scion of the noble Portuguese family who were lords of the manor of Aguas Belas.[14] He made his appearance at Sabará in 1704 or 1705, and speedily blossomed out as a monopolistic contractor, sometimes in conjunction with Francisco do Amaral and sometimes on his own. His efforts to corner the meat market made him highly unpopular with the Paulistas, who succeeded in preventing the extension of his contract for the exclusive supply of butcher's meat by appealing to the governor at Rio. This so infuriated the friar that he swore eternal enmity to the Paulistas, and was very active in disarming them during the disturbances of 1708.

Having consolidated their hold on most of Minas Gerais, the Emboabas took the offensive against the last Paulista (potential) pockets of resistance along the Rio das Mortes. Bento do Amaral Coutinho was in charge of this operation and he encountered no resistance worth the writing, most of the Paulista bands withdrawing to Paratí or to São Paulo without putting up a fight. Those in the principal mining camp (that later became the town of São João d'El Rei) remained there for the nonce, and were left severely alone. One *manga* or detachment of about fifty men, most if not all of whom were probably Amerindians and half-breeds, was surrounded in a *capão* or copse, after firing some shots which wounded a few Emboabas. Bento do Amaral allegedly promised these men quarter if they would lay down their arms. After some hesitation they did so, only to be pitilessly massacred to a man by his orders. This atrocity of the *Capão da Traição* ("Copse of Treason"), as it was subsequently called, was greatly exaggerated by later writers, beginning with Rocha Pitta in 1730 and culminating in Diogo de Vasconcellos' highly colored but completely fictitious version in his *História Antiga* of 1904. These writers state or imply that many hundreds of white Paulistas were killed in this shambles; but a close examination of such contemporary (as distinct from contemporaneous) accounts as have survived, shows conclusively that only a very small force was involved.[15]

Even before news of this last incident reached Rio de Janeiro, the worsening of the situation in Minas Gerais had been watched in that city with increasing alarm and concern. This is reflected in several private letters written by officials and merchants in Rio to influential friends at Lisbon and which have fortunately been preserved for posterity. I quote some extracts *verbatim,* since unofficial correspondence of this kind is excessively rare in the Portuguese archives, and they give a better idea of the situation than do official dispatches.

What I will tell you as the latest news [wrote an official at Rio to a friend at Lisbon toward the end of January, 1709], is that the Emboabas have risen against the Paulistas in the Mines. They have elected their own captain-major and colonel of foot and other military officers, so as not to obey any others, and there have already been some deaths. The Paulistas have sent to block the new trail, so that no loads of merchandise can go to the Mines. [They have seized] gunpowder, lead, and weapons to distribute among their troops. It is rumored that the Emboabas will come down to burn the Paulistas, and I believe there will be great slaughter on both sides. Although you people have your battles there, we are also beginning to have ours here, though not against the French or the Spaniards . . . P.S. Just now a council meeting has been held about the rising in the Mines, and it was decided that our governor should go there to appease the quarrels. Half Rio is preparing to leave and go with him, for many people are going in the hope of doing some business and collecting their debts, so that it is said for certain that he is going and many people will go with him.[16]

A fortnight later another official wrote as follows:

Business in the Mines has been at a standstill these many days, for the settlers there are divided into two armed camps. The leader of one of them, comprising all those who are not Paulistas, is a certain Manuel

Nunes Viana, a native of the town of that name and a settler in the hinterland of Bahia. He has taken the field with more than three thousand armed men; and he is a man who commands a large following, since he is very rich, unscrupulous, and bold. For these reasons he is the chief person who brings many herds of livestock into the Mines from Bahia, whither goes the greatest part of the gold which they fetch, against the orders of His Majesty, whom God preserve, and to the great detriment of his royal treasury, since they pay no fifths, and in the local treasury there is only a little more than two *arrobas* of gold. The governor of this town has resolved to go to the backlands of the Mines, to see if he can appease those settlers in person. God grant that he may do so, since this matter is a vital one for our lord the king. . . .[17]

These two correspondents were fairly impartial in their reporting, but a third was an outspoken supporter of the Emboabas, whom he represented as being driven to act as they did by the outrageous provocations of the Paulistas. He was very contemptuous of the fighting ability of these latter, observing scornfully that "in truth they only know how to kill when hiding behind trees." [18] He reported their discomfiture in the Rio das Mortes with unconcealed satisfaction, and was distinctly skeptical of the efficacy of the governor's intended intervention. "The governor is leaving for the Mines," he wrote on February 10, 1709, "They say that he is going to settle this dispute, but God grant that he does not make things worse, for now the Portuguese will not yield. Our people there muster some thirty thousand men, admittedly including slaves." The king would also suffer, he added, "for he will receive neither the fifths nor coin, and none will arrive, because in fact there are none. To tell you the whole truth, brother, everyone here is completely ruined, and I especially, for God so willed it that on this occasion I should have my money in the Mines . . . and although the debtors are men of substance they cannot pay now. And I will tell you frankly that even after these difficulties are settled, it will take more than two years for the Mines to get back to normal. In the meantime, may God have pity on the many people who have their wherewithal in those parts!" [19]

The governor's decision to intervene personally as a mediator in Minas Gerais had been taken at a council meeting attended by the principal ecclesiastical, civil, and military authorities on January 10, 1709.[20] His standing orders forbade him to leave the city, save in case of grave emergency; but all those at the meeting unanimously endorsed his opinion that just such an emergency had now arisen. Although one of the above quoted correspondents stated that "half Rio" was going with the governor, in the upshot he left in March with only two companies of infantry from the local garrison and a small personal suite. Portugal was involved in the War of the Spanish Succession, and the risk of a French attack made the employment of any large force out of the question. Dom Fernando Martins Mascarenhas de Lencastre hoped that his personal authority would suffice to restore order; but if it came to a showdown he was prepared to rely on help from the Paulistas, since he regarded them as the wronged party and he was resolved to reinstate them in the Mines. He considered that they had prior claims as the original discoverers, "and they alone are capable of developing and increasing them, since the outsiders have not got the ability to open up the Backlands, without which the Mines will collapse."[21]

Dom Fernando was not impressed by the arguments of Bento do Amaral in his letter of January 16, that the Emboabas had been reacting only in self-defense against the intolerable provocations of the Paulistas. The governor knew the criminal backgrounds of most of the Emboaba leaders and he found Manuel de Borba Gato's version much more convincing. Matheus de Moura, whom Viana had appointed superintendent of the mines in the place of Borba Gato, was the assassin of his own sister, "and these are the sort of people who comprise this gang," Dom Fernando wrote disgustedly on February 16, 1709. Manuel Nunes Viana had not attempted to justify his treasonable actions, and this led the governor to fear that the Emboaba leader might oppose his entry into the mining region when he saw that he was accompanied by such a small force. In that event, wrote Dom Fernando, "I will avail myself of the Paulistas"; but he urged that the only way of establishing effective Crown control in Minas Gerais was to install a governor and a garrison there, together with the full apparatus of the law.[22]

Having left Rio de Janeiro some time in March, the governor reached the Rio das Mortes on an unascertained date in April, 1709. He was received in the principal mining camp by both Paulistas and Emboabas with due honors, "including three successive nights of illuminations." Here he remained ostensibly inactive for three days, presumably making confidential soundings on both sides. Early on the afternoon of the fourth day, he ordered a mass turnout of the rival parties, and made them a spirited harangue on their duty to live together in peace and amity as vassals of the same king. He told each side to nominate two representatives and then instructed these four men to hammer out a compromise settlement of their differences. This they eventually did, but their mutual mistrust was still too deep for the apparent reconciliation to be more sincere and lasting than the earlier one achieved by Borba Gato's intervention at Caeté in the previous November. The governor, however, professed himself satisfied, distributed a number of militia commissions and other honors to the principal participants, and then continued his march northwards toward the heart of the mining district. Many people, both Paulistas and Emboabas, offered to accompany him, but he courteously declined their overtures.[23]

Encouraged by his apparent success at the Rio das Mortes, Dom Fernando was chagrined to find his passage barred some days later at Congonhas do Campo by a strong Emboaba force drawn up in battle array under Manuel Nunes Viana himself. The exact details of what followed are obscure, as no two contemporary accounts agree on this point, and later narratives are even more widely divergent.[24] It is clear, however, that the Emboabas flatly declined to let Dom Fernando proceed any further, though it is uncertain whether they did this rudely or courteously. It is also clear that Manuel Nunes Viana either advised or compelled the governor to give up his plan of reinstating the Paulistas and expelling the Emboabas who had come by the forbidden Bahia trail. In any event, the expedition which had begun so promisingly at the Rio das Mortes ended in a humiliating fiasco at Congonhas do Campo, whence the angry and frustrated governor returned to Rio faster than he had come. No sooner had he gone, than the Paulistas still remaining in the Rio das Mortes region withdrew to their home town, vowing vengeance for the shameful disaster at the Capão da Traição.

The citizens of São Paulo, incidentally, were badly shaken by the speed and thoroughness with which the Emboabas had effected the expulsion of their kinsmen from the Mines. A town meeting held in mid-February, 1709, resolved that something should be done about "the rising of the outsiders in the Mines, which conquest belongs to us"; but it was decided to organize an expeditionary force to uphold Paulista rights only in the following April. Four more months elapsed, however, before anything concrete was done, and by that time the Crown had established effective authority in Mīnas Gerais.[25]

The first reliable news of the critical situation in Minas Gerais had reached Lisbon in July, 1709, having come via the Azores.[26] Naturally enough, it caused a good deal of alarm, particularly since the home government had more than enough on its hands as a result of Portugal's unhappy involvement in the War of the Spanish Succession. The reports of fighting between Paulistas and Emboabas were disquieting enough; but what caused even greater concern was the fact that Manuel Nunes Viana had usurped the function and authority of the Crown in making numerous military and civil appointments on his own initiative. On the other hand, private advices from Rio de Janeiro, of which typical extracts have been given above, convinced the Overseas Councillors that the Emboabas were not solely to blame for the outbreak, as the dispatches of Dom Fernando Martins Mascarenhas had claimed. It was obviously necessary for the Crown to intervene at once, despite the lack of royal authority in that region, lest the trouble spread and threaten the defense of the southern captaincies, on which both French enemies and English allies were believed to be casting covetous glances.[27]

After a flurry of consultations between the king and his principal advisers, it was decided that, since Dom Fernando's triennial term of office had already expired and his successor must have arrived in Rio, the new governor should be ordered to go to Minas Gerais and proclaim a general amnesty. Manuel Nunes Viana and Bento do Amaral Coutinho were to be specifically exempted from this amnesty, since their crimes had been outrageous and they had deliberately usurped the royal authority. The governor was empowered to take an escort of some soldiers from the garrison of Rio de Janeiro, and to call upon the governor-general at Bahia for further reinforcements if necessary. These orders were dispatched in a royal letter dated August 22, 1709, but the new governor of Rio, António de Albuquerque Coelho de Carvalho, had already taken similar action on his own initiative before these instructions reached him exactly three months later.[28]

António de Albuquerque, as I shall henceforth call him for short, was no stranger to Brazil, though he was not American-born as most of his biographers wrongly claim. He came from a Beira family of the minor aristocracy, which had long been connected with Brazil and the Maranhão; but he himself was born at Lisbon, according to his baptismal registry in the church of Santa Engracia, dated September 14, 1655.[29] Twelve years later he accompanied his father and namesake to the Maranhão, where he stayed for the four-year term of the latter's governorship. Returning to Portugal in 1671, he went back to the Maranhão with another governor seven years later, partly to look after the family estates at Santa Cruz de Camutá. His second stay in South America was prolonged for many years, and he became successively governor of Grão-Pará (1685–1690) and of the Maranhão (1690–1701), filling this last post with unusual-distinction according to the testimony of the grateful colonists. During his tenure of office he repelled an attempt by the French from Cayenne to occupy a post in the Amazon estuary, and in 1697 he made an extensive visit of inspection up the Amazon and the Rio Negro.[30] His health being undermined by long service in that fever-stricken region, he repeatedly begged to be relieved of his office, which the Crown somewhat reluctantly granted in 1701. He returned to Portugal to recuperate, but his convalescence was interrupted by the outbreak of the War of the Spanish Succession, in which he took a minor but honorable part as commander-in-chief in Lower Beira (1706–1708) and governor of Olivença (1708–1709). His appointment to the governorship of Rio de Janeiro was already rumored in February, 1708, but it only materialized when his transfer to that post was signed by the king in March, 1709.[31]

Albuquerque reached Rio the following June, and despite some local opposition from people who feared that he might repeat his predecessor's fiasco, soon made up his mind to leave for Minas Gerais. According to some accounts, the victorious Emboabas had already fallen out among themselves, and Manuel Nunes Viana was at cross-purposes with the principal Bahiano leader, Sebastião Pereira de Aguilar, who likewise had vast cattle ranches along the Rio São Francisco and extensive gold diggings in Minas Gerais. Viana had also made himself unpopular with the settlers of Sabará by trying to secure the local meat monopoly after the renegade Trinitarian friar, Francisco de Menezes, had left for Rio and Portugal to plead the Emboabas' cause before the Overseas Council at Lisbon. It is more than likely that Albuquerque had some intimation of these dissensions in the insurgent camp when he left Rio in July, 1709, accompanied by only about a dozen men. The instructions, which he brought with him from Lisbon, authorized him either to use force or else to grant a general amnesty (Viana and Amaral Coutinho alone excepted) in accordance with the situation that he might find in Minas Gerais. The fact that he left with so small an escort shows that he was resolved to rely solely on conciliation.

Traveling by forced marches the little party reached Caeté unheralded, and Albuquerque, "with his beard grown" [32] took up his quarters in the biggest house in the mining camp, most of whose inhabitants were away in the neighboring diggings. From here he sent a message to Manuel Nunes Viana, ordering him in the king's name to leave Minas Gerais within three days and to return to his ranches along the Rio São Francisco. Whether out of loyalty to the Crown and its representative, as he later protested, or whether because he could no longer count on the support of Pereira de Aguilar and the Bahianos, Manuel Nunes Viana offered no resistance to this order; but he asked for an extension of six days, so that he could get a train of pack horses and his baggage together. Albuquerque readily granted this request, and the Emboaba leader left for his estates on the Rio São Francisco without further ado.

After spending a few days at Caeté, Albuquerque proceeded to Sabará, and then visited successively the other main mining camps in the region of the Rio das Velhas and Ouro Preto. He was unhesitatingly acknowledged as the lawful governor in all of them; and for the first time the authority of the Crown was now accepted with more than token respect in Minas Gerais. Albuquerque confirmed many of the appointments made by Nunes Viana, but he rescinded some of them, and reinstated Borba Gato as superintendent in the Rio das Velhas region. He also created a number of administrative and militia posts, where he considered these to be either necessary or desirable for placating influential people who might otherwise feel disgruntled. His success was partly due to his own tact and personality, but mainly to the fact that the Emboabas, having won the war and expelled the Paulistas, were naturally anxious to get back to their gold diggings and to reopen the trade with Rio de Janeiro.[33]

Equally naturally, this feeling was not shared by the Paulistas. They were still smarting under the humiliation of having been expelled so opprobriously from what they all regarded as "our conquest" by right of prior discovery and occupation.[34] As noted above (p. 74), it took them several months to organize an expeditionary force, whose total Albuquerque later estimated at just over two thousand men. One of the richest Paulistas, Amador Bueno da Veiga, was elected to command this "expedition to the Mines for the good of the fatherland," as this punitive column was euphemistically termed. The instructions given by the Town Council of São Paulo to Amador Bueno on August 21–24, 1709, stressed that he should concentrate on the peaceful reinstatement of the Paulistas in their gold diggings, only using force as a last and unavoidable resort. Albuquerque's arrival in the Mines had been reported to the Town Councillors, and they instructed Amador Bueno strictly to obey the orders of the newly arrived governor as the lawful representative of the Crown.[35]

Rumors that the Paulistas were about to launch a large-scale invasion of the Mines were seriously worrying the Emboabas in the district of the Rio das Mortes when Albuquerque arrived there early in October on his way back to Rio de Janeiro. He thought that these rumors were exaggerated; but finding that the settlers would not be reassured, he decided to go and meet the Paulistas, with the object of dissuading them from their undertaking if they had already started. He met their main body at Guaratinguetá, and found that their force was almost entirely composed of Amerindians and half-breeds, "with very few whites." [36] Their leaders, incidentally, included the Pedroso brothers whose arrogance had been one of the principal causes of the outbreak of the war.

Though suffering from a severe bout of malaria, Albuquerque argued for some days with Amador Bueno and his staff, promising that he would see justice done for such Paulistas as had been unfairly deprived of their diggings, and warning them that they would be guilty of lese majesty if they tried to dispossess the Emboabas by force. The Paulistas retorted that "they could not fail to exact satisfaction themselves for the affront they had suffered, since they were the lords of those mines by the virtue of their discovery of them, and under no circumstances was it convenient that outsiders should live there; for which reason they wished to go and drive out the latter and take possession of the former." They added that the king could raise no objection to their having done so when he heard their explanations. When Albuquerque again tried to persuade them to retire, for their arrival in the Mines would inevitably be followed by a renewal of the struggle, the Paulistas replied that he could accompany them thither and expel the Emboabas on his own authority and with their backing. "To which I answered," he reported to the Crown, "that even if my fever had allowed me to go with them, I would never do as they suggested, since without Your Majesty's order, I could neither tell the outsiders to leave the Mines, nor could they expel them." [37]

Finding threats and persuasions alike wasted, and according to some accounts being threatened with death by the Paulistas, Albuquerque finally abandoned his efforts and left for Paratí and Rio de Janeiro. He sent ahead an emissary named Estevão Rodrigues, who had accompanied him from the Rio das Mortes, to warn his compatriots that the vengeful Paulistas would soon be upon them. Traveling night and day with relays of post horses provided by Albuquerque's orders along the Caminho Novo, Rodrigues reached the Rio das Mortes before the slow-moving Paulistas had finished their concentration and resumed their advance.

The alarm having been given, some 260 whites and 500 Negroes concentrated in a makeshift fort which had been built during the troubles of the previous year, where they awaited the Paulista column which made its appearance on November 14, 1709. Four or five days of inconclusive skirmishes followed, but just when the Emboabas were beginning to run short of ammunition and food, the attackers withdrew under cover of darkness one night. They had inflicted some eighty casualties by long-range musket fire; and although their own losses are not stated, they were probably rather fewer, since they were admittedly the better marksmen. The reasons for their precipitate withdrawal are likewise conjectural, but were probably due partly to reports of the rapid advance of a powerful Emboaba relieving column from Ouro Preto, and partly to dissensions between the Paulista commanders.

It seems that Amador Bueno was inclined to interpret somewhat strictly the São Paulo Town Council's injunctions to avoid the use of force, whereas the Pedroso brothers and a few others were for exacting a condign revenge for the atrocity of the Capão da Traição.[38] Three days after their departure, the relieving column arrived from Ouro Preto and set off in pursuit of the retreating Paulistas. The latter had got a good start, which they had further improved by destroying the boats and bridges at the river crossings. The Emboabas, therefore, soon broke off the pursuit and dispersed quietly to their own home districts during the month of December, 1709.

As things turned out, this marked the final stage of the "War of the Emboabas," which had thus lasted, with intervals, for almost exactly a year. Fortunately, the loss of life had not been heavy, and it is doubtful if more than a hundred fatal casualties had been suffered by either side. One eyewitness later claimed that the disturbances had not amounted to an actual civil war;[39] but even if there had been more sound and fury than death and destruction during that eventful twelvemonth, the upshot was a decisive victory for the Emboabas. We may note that, contrary to the fears expressed by merchants and officials at Rio de Janeiro early in 1709, the fighting in the Mines did not prevent Manuel Nunes Viana from sending the royal fifths to Rio later in the year.

When Albuquerque got back to Rio de Janeiro at the end of October or beginning of November, 1709, he was still deeply resentful at the way he had been snubbed by the Paulistas at Guaratinguetá. Indeed, he seems to have contemplated the conquest of São Paulo itself with the aid of the victorious Emboabas.[40] However this may have been, on November 22 he received the royal orders of the previous August which enjoined him to grant a general amnesty to both sides and to seek a peaceful solution of the conflict at any price. Three months later (February 26, 1710), he received another royal dispatch, which ordered him to relinquish the governorship of Rio de Janeiro and assume that of a newly created and much larger region which was to be entitled the "Captaincy of São Paulo and the Mines of Gold," with head-quarters at the town of São Paulo. The creation of this new captaincy had been mooted at Lisbon for some time, but the final decision had been reached largely as a result of the representations of the Emboabas' emissary, Fr. Francisco de Menezes. This rene-gade friar had convinced the authorities at Lisbon that the Emboabas were not to be trifled with, and that it would be dangerous as well as futile to try to upset the *fait accompli*. Indeed, so impressed were the Overseas Councillors with the strength of the Emboabas, that they allowed the friar to return to Brazil, while secretly authorizing Albuquerque to expel him from the Mines if he found an opportunity of doing so.[41]

Dissembling his smoldering resentment against the Paulistas in view of his new instructions, Albuquerque first proceeded to Santos and then to São Paulo, where he arrived in June, 1710. The Paulistas were by now anxious to atone for their cavalier treatment of him eight months earlier, since they realized that they had no chance of reconquering the Mines by force, and that their only hope of readmission lay in Albuquerque's exerting his authority on their behalf. The new governor was therefore inducted into office with great pomp and rejoicing, including three successive nights of illuminations. During the four months (June–October) that he stayed in São Paulo, Albuquerque on his side became convinced that the Paulistas had a good case for reinstatement in the Mines, and in other respects as well. He therefore wrote to the Crown in support of various requests that they made, includ-ing the proposal that their town should be elevated to a city and the seat of a bishopric.[42] The Crown made no difficulty about granting the first part of this suggestion, but postponed the erec-tion of the bishopric until 1745, mainly for reasons of economy. Albuquerque, with the knowledge and approval of the Crown, had tried to induce the Bishop of Rio de Janeiro to accompany him to São Paulo. Dom Frei Francisco de São Jeronimo, though at first professing willingness to make a pastoral visit to his far-flung flock subsequently evaded doing so. Perhaps he preferred

São
Paulo

the pleasures of Jew-baiting at Rio de Janeiro to the hardships of travel in Minas Gerais.[43]

Among the principal matters decided by Albuquerque in consultation with the leading Paulistas were that he would try to reinstate their expelled compatriots in their former gold diggings; that the royal fifths should be collected on the basis of *bateias;* that a "reasonable tax" should be levied on all merchandise, slaves, and cattle imported into the mining region; that some companies of foot soldiers should be raised for internal security; and that a law should be passed severely restricting the use of arms by slaves, mulattoes, Amerindians and mixed bloods.[44]

Having settled matters in São Paulo to his own and the general satisfaction, Albuquerque departed for Minas Gerais, where he had been authorized by the Crown to raise any three of the most populous mining settlements to the dignity of towns. Meetings held with the leading Emboabas at Ribeirão do Carmo (November 10, 1710), and at Ouro Preto (December 1, 1710), which were also attended by Borba Gato and other prominent Paulistas, ratified the decisions taken at São Paulo in the previous July, and decided that the tax levied on each *bateia* used in the gold diggings was to vary between eight and ten *oitavas* annually. In this connection, it is worth recalling that just before Albuquerque left Rio for São Paulo and the Mines in April of the previous year, he had written to the Crown: "There is no doubt that the three parts of the fifths will be embezzled, whatever precautions are taken to prevent this." [45]

After further consultations and mature reflection, Albuquerque decided that the three mining camps to be erected into townships should be Ribeirão do Carmo, Ouro Preto, and Sabará. They were successively inaugurated by him personally under the respective styles and titles of Ribeirão do Carmo (April 8, 1711), Villa Rica d'Albuquerque (July 8, 1711) and Nossa Senhora da Conceição do Sabará (July 17, 1711).[46] He formally established an elected senate or municipal council at each one of these new townships amid scenes of great enthusiasm and rejoicing. In coöperation with these brand-new municipalities, Albuquerque initiated a number of other measures to improve local administration, to facilitate the collection of the fifths, and to make a fair distribution of mining allotments (*datas*) and land grants (*sesmarias*) as between Emboabas and Paulistas. He also tried to ensure that these two rival factions were evenly or at any rate fairly represented on the newly created town councils.[47]

One of the problems that caused Albuquerque great concern was the continued presence of renegade friars and unbeneficed clergy in the Mines. Those coming from the hinterland of Bahia and Pernambuco were particularly reprehensible and troublesome,[48] but he was able to prevent Fr. Francisco de Menezes returning to the Mines from Rio de Janeiro. It is clear from his correspondence with the Crown at this period that Albuquerque had forgiven if not forgotten his mortifying encounter with the Paulistas at Guarantinguetá, which had so upset him at the time and for some months afterwards. It is also clear that between June, 1710 and September, 1711 he was really acting as an impartial judge and mediator between Paulistas and Emboabas, and he was obviously respected as such by both sides. On the other hand, he did not neglect his own interests, and Fr. Francisco de Menezes was probably correct in asserting that Albuquerque engaged extensively in private trade.

In the midst of these manifold preoccupations attendant on the pacification and organization of his vast captaincy,[49] Albuquerque suddenly received the alarming news that a powerful French expedition had disembarked at Rio de Janeiro. The fate of the city of São Sebastião was hanging in the balance. Obviously there was not a moment to lose if a relieving force from the Mines was to be raised, equipped, and marched to the coast in time to help the hard-pressed (and ill-led) defenders.

IV. THE FRENCH
IN RIO DE JANEIRO

PORTUGAL'S INVOLVEMENT in the War of the Spanish Succession needs only the briefest recollection here. Her choice of sides in the opening years of the eighteenth century was not an easy one. If she supported the Habsburg candidate, she laid herself open to invasion overland by the vastly superior armies of France and Spain. If she supported the Bourbon candidate, her home ports, and still more, her far-flung and weakly defended empire, would be at the mercy of the vastly superior fleets of the maritime powers. In the light of hindsight, neutrality would have been the best solution; but this was very difficult to achieve at the time owing to the conflicting pressures exercised on her by the stronger governments that were already involved.

Pedro II's first choice, after a good deal of hesitation, was to accept the French Alliance which was proffered him with great insistence by Louis XIV. Yet only a few months after the signature of the Franco-Portuguese Treaty of June, 1701, Dom Pedro began to repent of his decision. Various circumstances, which need not be detailed here, enabled him to get out of his commitments to the Sun King in September of the following year, but he was not allowed to remain neutral. Intense diplomatic pressure was later exerted on him to join the Grand Alliance of England, the Netherlands, the Empire, and Savoy. After seven months of this strenuous diplomacy at Lisbon, the English envoys, John and Paul Methuen, finally induced Dom Pedro to commit himself irrevocably to the Grand Alliance in May, 1703.

Since the allies were anxious to get Portugal into the war so that the English and Dutch fleets could have the unrestricted use of Lisbon as a base for their operations in the Mediterranean, Dom Pedro was able to exact a stiff price for his adherence. The allies pledged themselves to expel the Bourbon King, Philip of Anjou, from Spain, and to install the Habsburg candidate, the Archduke Charles in his place. Great Britain and the Netherlands also promised to provide substantial assistance in men and money for the Portuguese army. The Archduke Charles reluctantly agreed to the cession of Badajos and other frontier towns in Europe, and to yield the region around the settlement of Sacramento on the north bank of the Rio de la Plata in South America. The two political treaties of May, 1703 were rounded off in the following December by the famous Anglo-Portuguese commercial agreement known as the "Methuen Treaty," from its English negotiator, John Methuen. Two of its only three clauses provided that England would admit Portuguese wines at a third less duty than that imposed on French wines, and Portugal removed the existing legal restrictions on the importation of English woolens.[1]

Both Portugal and her overseas empire were completely unready for the war in which they were now involved. An apprehensive diarist wrote despondently of the prevailing inefficiency and confusion, largely resulting from "the thirty-five years of peace in which the possibility of war was never envisaged."[2] The war was not popular with the common people, who had not yet recovered from the sacrifices imposed by the long struggles with Spain (1640–1668) and Holland (1600–1663). The Crown of Portugal was a notoriously bad paymaster, and its troops, when paid at all, had never received more than half pay during those two wars. The prospect of military service was dreaded by the lower classes, who went to great lengths to avoid it. Many men mutilated themselves; others claimed ecclesiastical or statutory immunities; others pretended they were the only sons of penniless widows, or else were under age; others feigned madness, or contagious disease; and one shameless (but humorous) individual even claimed that he was of pure Jewish descent on both sides, in order to escape the attentions of the recruiting sergeant.[3]

Admittedly, the quality of the hardy Portuguese infantrymen was still the same as that praised by Schomberg thirty-five years earlier, when he observed that "although they are generally brought by force into the field, yet do they fight admirably well when once they are got there." [4] This remark presupposed that they would be well led, and unfortunately there were few outstanding or experienced leaders in the senior ranks of the Portuguese army after the long period of peace. The navy was in an even more neglected state, having for years been starved of money and short of trained officers and seamen. So few were Portugal's deep-sea mariners at this period, that great difficulty was experienced in manning the two or three Indiamen that annually left Lisbon for Goa, and even the more popular Brazil fleets were often seriously undermanned.

It is true that the Portuguese army and allied contingents managed to enter Madrid on two occasions, but in each case the triumph was short-lived. After their decisive defeat at Almanza in 1707, the ill-assorted allies never had a chance of conquering Castile for Charles, although Catalonia remained loyal to the Austrian Archduke until the end. The Franco-Spanish forces repeatedly ravaged large sections of Portuguese territory; and the wretched peasantry were often mistreated by their own unpaid and ill-disciplined soldiery as well as by the "heretical and drunken" English and Dutch troops who were quartered on them.[5]

Nor did Portugal find overseas any compensation for the losses in men and material which she suffered as the tide of war swung back and forth across the Iberian Peninsula. The exposed outpost of Colonia do Sacramento had to be abandoned to the Spaniards of Buenos Aires, though the garrison and settlers managed to fight their way out to the ships sent to evacuate them in 1705. French corsairs harried Portuguese shipping in the eastern seas from Mozambique to Macao. French raiders sacked the islands of Principe (1706) and São Tomé (1709) in the Gulf of Guinea, burnt the little town of Benguela in West Africa (1705), and plundered Santiago de Cabo Verde in 1712. The principal French attacks, however, were launched against Brazil, where the city of Rio de Janeiro was regarded as a most desirable prize in view of the great wealth that was channeled through that port from the gold mines of Minas Gerais.

The first attack on Rio was mounted in 1710, and although the French naval historian, Charles De La Roncière, stigmatizes this expedition as "une folle équipée," it came within measurable distance of success. A squadron of six sail carrying about 1,500 men was fitted out at Brest by a privateering company and placed under the command of Jean-François Du Clerc. This officer was a Creole from Guadeloupe, and of so dark a hue that he was mistaken for an "Indian Prince" when he first landed in Brazil. He was described by one who knew him as being "un jeune homme, plein de coeur, entreprennant, et intrepide," but he had not seen much active service hitherto. When selected to command the expedition he was only captain of a fireship, being promoted to *capitaine de frégate* at the end of January, 1710.[6]

It seems extraordinary that such a small force and a relatively inexperienced commander should have been deemed sufficient to take the well-fortified and strongly-garrisoned town of Rio de Janeiro. A contemporary Portuguese pamphleteer suggested that Du Clerc was inspired by the feat of De Pointis, who had taken the even more formidable stronghold of Cartagena de Indias from the Spaniards in 1697, with a heterogeneous force of French regulars and buccaneers. It is more likely, perhaps, that he was encouraged by the observations of his countrymen who had visited Rio and Bahia with de Gennes' squadron in 1695, for they did not think much of the fortifications or of the Portuguese. Froger, the chronicler of that expedition, wrote in his widely read *Relation d'un voyage,* "It is well known, they are no otherwise brave than upon their own dunghill; and that they had rather, upon occasion, have recourse to their beads than to their courage." [7]

Du Clerc appeared off the harbor of Rio de Janeiro on the morning of August 17, 1710 with his six sail, but the alarm had been given on the previous day when his squadron had been sighted by a fisherman. The French vessels, flying English colors, made as if to enter the harbor, but when the forts at the entrance fired some challenging shots they hauled away out of range, and set a course southwards for the Ilha Grande next day. Du Clerc wasted the next three weeks in inconclusive skirmishing with the militia defenders of the island, and in sending small landing parties ashore at various places to reconnoiter the defenders' dispositions and to secure fresh water and provisions. Finally, on the advice of four Negro slaves who had fled from Bento do Amaral Coutinho's *engenho* at the Ilha Grande, he disembarked with some 1,200 men at the undefended beach of Guaratiba, forty miles south of the city, on September 11.[8]

Guided by Amaral's runaway Negroes, the French took a circuitous route through the difficult and thickly-wooded country skirting the base of the Orgãos mountains. This march lasted exactly a week, and on the evening of September 18 they reached the Jesuits' *engenho* on the outskirts of the city, where they camped for the night. During all this time, the governor, Francisco de Castro Morais, contented himself with taking purely defensive measures, though it would have been easy to intercept the French advance at any of the numerous defiles through which it had to pass. He did indeed send out one detachment to harass the rearguard, but this force missed its way and did not make contact with the enemy. As Fr. Francisco de Menezes pointed out in his report to the Crown, the jungle was neutral: "if it was a help for us, it was likewise favorable for them." Only on September 17 did the governor realize what route the French had taken, although the regulars, militia, and Negro auxiliaries at his disposal totaled more than 15,000 men—sufficient to provide him with ample patrols and reconnaissance parties if he had the initiative to use them.[9]

Du Clerc launched his long-awaited attack on the city on the morning of September 19. Despite his overwhelming numerical superiority, the governor with the two regiments of regular soldiers remained completely inactive for most of the day behind some hastily dug earthworks in a locality which the French did not attack. One of the regimental commanders was so old, ill, and fat that he could only mount his charger when hoisted into the saddle from a bench by some of his officers. The dubious quality of his subordinate commanders may explain in part the governor's otherwise inexplicable inaction. Meanwhile, Du Clerc, leading his men in person, battled his way through the streets against stiff opposition to the heart of the city near the waterfront, where he was fought to a standstill by the local militia and armed Negro slaves. Prominent among the defenders were the two rapscallion Emboabas, Bento do Amaral Coutinho and Fr. Francisco de Menezes, whose inspiring leadership more than atoned for the supine behavior of the governor. The external students of the Jesuit College [10] also distinguished themselves by their gallant defense of the governor's palace which marked the turning point in the struggle. Their Jesuit teachers likewise played a vital part by encouraging the defenders and by ringing their church bells at this critical moment. Their conduct was later contrasted by a satirical poet with that of the other religious, "all of whom fled with the Bishop." [11]

Only after the French had been fought to a standstill by the militia, the students, and the Negroes, did a portion of the regular troops tardily (but effectively) intervene to take the invaders in the flank and rear. With nearly half his force wiped out, Du Clerc stormed his way into a strongly built *trapiche,* or warehouse for sugar chests, on the waterfront, which was provided with six cannon, and where he hoped to hold out until his ships could come to his rescue. The Portuguese at first hesitated to press their attack on this improvised stronghold, since sixty of their own women and children had taken refuge there before the French seized it. With the approach of night, however, the governor, who made a tardy appearance on the scene of action, decided that he could not afford to let the invaders strengthen themselves there. Artillery fire having proved ineffective against its thick walls, ostentatious preparations were made to blow up the building with barrels of gunpowder. Seeing the hopelessness of further resistance, Du Clerc at length asked for terms. The governor replied that he would only spare the lives of the French if they yielded forthwith. This they did, "surrendering with their arms and flags just before the hour of the Ave Maria, this victory being celebrated by the renewed ringing of the church bells." [12]

The defenders of the city had given no quarter during the bitter street fighting, and of the 600 Frenchmen who were still alive in the *trapiche,* more than half were wounded, many of them severely. The sole survivor who escaped to tell the tale of the disaster to the ships waiting at Guaratiba was one of Bento do Amaral's runaway slaves. The other three were caught, tortured, and executed by the victors. Estimates of the latters' casualties vary widely, but the most reliable source puts them at 270 killed and wounded. [13] The dead included Colonel Gregorio Castro de Morais, the governor's brother and one of the few regular officers who showed outstanding courage and initiative. Though lying mortally wounded, he urged his men forward, exclaiming as he died, "one man is no loss." Du Clerc and some of his officers were imprisoned in the Jesuit College, others in the Franciscan convent, and the French soldiers were distributed between the warehouses of the mint and the city jail.

Next day three of the French ships appeared off the harbor and exchanged shots with the fort of Santa Cruz two days later. Du Clerc then obtained leave from the governor to send a note under a flag of truce to the French commander, telling him of the disaster, and asking him to send clothing and surgeons ashore for himself and his men. This was done in due course, after the ships had joined forces with those waiting at Guaratiba and the Ilha Grande. After handing over their two smallest vessels to the Portuguese, with the request that they be sold and the money given to the upkeep of the French prisoners, the commander left on October 15 with the other ships for Martinique and home.

During the time that the ships lay off the bar in October, Du Clerc had shown that this bloody reverse had abated nothing of his courageous spirit. He repeatedly tried to escape, by attempting to bribe the sentries and by forcing his way out. After the ships had gone, he frequently petitioned the governor to remove him from the Jesuit College to another residence, "as he was not born to be a friar." Castro de Morais eventually and reluctantly yielded to his importunities, and he was accordingly moved to one of the best houses in Rio. A few weeks later (March 18, 1711), Du Clerc was murdered in his bedroom by a group of masked men who had penetrated unchallenged into the house, and made their exit after the assassination, despite an armed guard at the door. The identity of the murderers was never discovered, although the Overseas Councillors at Lisbon, genuinely horrified when they received the news, persuaded Dom João V to order the most rigorous judicial investigation. Judging by the wording of the petition of the victim's widow to Louis XIV, local gossip credited the governor himself with organizing the crime, two of his illegitimate sons being among the murderers. Another and possibly more reliable allegation was that it was the work of jealous husbands who resented Du Clerc soliciting their wives with love letters.[14]

When the French first appeared off Rio de Janeiro, a message was sent posthaste to António de Albuquerque in Minas Gerais, asking him to be prepared to send reinforcements if these should prove to be necessary. Albuquerque, who had just left the Rio das Mortes, promptly dispatched orders for all the militia commanders and their men to hold themselves in readiness, and he himself returned to São Paulo to supervise the dispatch of reinforcements to Santos and Paratí. The Paulistas responded with an alacrity which was praised even by their old antagonist, Friar Francisco de

Menezes, "for everyone who was capable of bearing arms set out, and showed that they did not want a French king." The "valorous Mineiros" urged their commanders to lead them at once to Rio de Janeiro without waiting for a second order, but their leaders preferred to wait until Albuquerque told them to march. This was just as well, since when he did receive a second message from Rio a few weeks later, it was to notify him "of the great victory which the citizens of Rio de Janeiro had gained over the enemy, killing, wounding, and capturing them all, without one escaping." [15] The goodwill and promptitude shown by both Paulistas and Emboabas on this occasion augured well for their reaction to the much graver crisis of the following year.

The victory of Rio de Janeiro was celebrated with "grandiosas festas" both locally and at Lisbon, where the news formed a welcome change from the depressing tidings of the war in Spain. In France, on the other hand, the natural chagrin was sharpened by reports which alleged that the Portuguese, "insolent victors, were treating their prisoners very cruelly; that they were making them die of hunger and misery in the jails, and even that Monsieur Du Clerc had been murdered, although he had surrendered on terms." [16] The alleged ill-treatment of the prisoners was greatly exaggerated and the governor refused to accept Fr. Francisco de Menezes' advice to ship them off to Benguela, Mozambique, and Cape Verde, "lands where life is short," as the friar cynically observed. But Portuguese jails were no more comfortable than any others, and the wounded prisoners undoubtedly suffered severely.

These reports, coupled with the nicely balanced prospects of gaining great honor and glory on the one hand and a rich booty on the other, inspired the celebrated Breton corsair, René Duguay-Trouin, to organize an expedition to revenge Du Clerc's disaster. Born to a family of merchant seamen at Saint-Malo in 1673, Duguay-Trouin was educated for the Church, but the attractions of Mars and Venus soon made a greater appeal to the adolescent cleric than did the call to a devout and holy life. He insisted on embarking in one of the family privateers at the age of sixteen and promptly distinguished himself in a hard-fought boarding action that same year (1689). From then onwards, save for the short interval of peace in 1698–1701, he saw a great deal of active service in all weathers on the seas between Spitzbergen and Gibraltar. The hero of numerous sea fights in which he was almost invariably successful, his dauntless intrepidity aroused the admiration of his Dutch and English opponents. This respect was increased by the fact that he always showed himself a chivalrous victor (and a perfect host) to any captured commander who was worthy of his steel. By 1710, his exploits had made him renowned as one of the finest fighting seamen of any age or nation, and this reputation holds good today. He was also a singularly handsome man, a skilled duelist, an ardent amorist, but "no friend to the bottle or the table." In short, in the opinion of friend and foe he well deserved his sobriquet of "le parfait gentilhomme." [17]

Duguay-Trouin did not make Du Clerc's mistake of underestimating his opponents, perhaps because he had done so once before. One of his few failures had been his repulse by the escort of the homeward bound Brazil fleet off the mouth of the Tagus in May, 1706, though this failure was chiefly due to the misconduct of some of his subordinates.[18] He was resolved not to be let down this time and he selected his commanders with particular care. The preparations for the expedition were made with great speed, secrecy and thoroughness, for they took only two months from the time that Duguay-Trouin obtained the formal sanction of Louis XIV. In accordance with the usual Saint-Malo practice, the expedition was financed mainly by a group of his wealthy fellow townsmen, who promoted a company for the purpose, while the ships and troops were provided by the Crown. This undertaking being an exceptionally ambitious one, outside subscribers were also secured, and the Count of Toulouse, titular Admiral of France, was a leading investor. Most of the ships were fitted out at Brest, but others were equipped at Rochefort, Dunkirk, Saint-Malo, and elsewhere, so as to give the English the impression that only a number of unconnected privateering cruises were in preparation.

Brest was the original rendezvous for the squadron, but hearing that the English were fitting out a force to blockade that harbor, Duguay-Trouin changed the meeting place to La Rochelle, and slipped out of Brest on June 3, 1711. He was only just in time. Two days later Admiral Sir John Leake appeared off the harbor with twenty sail dispatched expressly to prevent his departure. Being soon joined at La Rochelle by all save one of the frigates from the other ports, Duguay-Trouin finally sailed on June 9, with seven ships of the line, five frigates, one galliot, and three bomb-ketches, bound for "the conquest of the golden fleece under the leadership of a new Jason." He picked up a small English prize off Lisbon and was joined by the tardy frigate at the Cape Verde Islands, so that he crossed the Line on August 11 with eighteen sail.[19]

The speed and secrecy with which the expedition had been prepared did not, in the upshot, deceive the English as to its real destination. When Leake reported that his adversary had given him the slip, a packet boat was promptly sent to Lisbon with the news that Duguay-Trouin had left and that Rio de Janeiro was his objective. There being no Portuguese vessel available in the Tagus to sail to Brazil at a moment's notice, the English packet boat was sent straight on to Rio where she arrived at the end of August, before any sign had been seen of the French squadron.

Luckily for the Portuguese—or so it seemed at the time—an exceptionally strong escort for the homeward-bound Brazil fleet was still in the harbor. This squadron comprised four ships of the line (mounting from 56 to 74 guns) under the command of Gaspar da Costa da Ataide, who was generally regarded as Portugal's best and most experienced seaman. He certainly had many years of service in the Atlantic and Indian Oceans behind him, including a share in Leake's victory over De Pointis off Algeciras in March, 1705.[20]

Under these circumstances it would seem that Duguay-Trouin could not have taken the defenders by surprise, yet this is exactly what he did do. When the English packet boat brought the news of his approach, the governor ordered the garrison to be mustered, the forts to be manned and the militia to stand by. These pre-cautions were intensified some days later, when word was received from the lookout posted at Cape Frio that sixteen sail steering southwards had been sighted far out to sea. The Portuguese war-ships moved their berth to guard the harbor entrance and everyone prepared for action, resolved to repeat the triumph of the previous year. When another three days had passed without any sign of the French fleet, the governor concluded that the report was a false alarm. He accordingly ordered the troops to stand down and the warships to return to their former berth in the Bay of Guanabara. He assured Gaspar da Costa that the lookouts on the surrounding hills could see fifteen miles out to sea. When the French ships were sighted in the offing, he added, there would be ample time to man the ships, forts, and batteries properly. He could not have made a worse miscalculation.

Duguay-Trouin had taken soundings near the Brazilian coast on September 11, which was the same day that the governor had ordered the troops to stand down. Calculating his position to a nicety by a remarkable combination of good luck and good judg-ment, he found himself at daybreak next morning standing straight for the entrance of Rio de Janeiro Bay in misty weather. He at once ordered the Chevalier de Coursérac, who had been there before, to take the lead in the *Magnanime* (74) the rest of the squadron following in line ahead. This order was promptly and skilfully executed.[21] Before the morning mist had fully cleared and the Portuguese had recovered from their astonish-ment, the French ships had begun to sail into the harbor, braving the cross fire of the forts of Santa Cruz and São João which guarded the entrance.

Both of the Portuguese commanders lost their heads at this crisis. Order, counterorder, and disorder followed one another in quick succession, but the governor failed to send reinforcements to the most urgently threatened points. Gaspar da Costa made an in-effective attempt to get his warships to weigh anchor, but they cut their cables and grounded near the city, where three of them were fired then or later to prevent the French taking them. The seventh, the *Nossa Senhora da Barroquinha,* was captured by the French, who afterwards removed her bronze cannon before burning her themselves. The forts were mostly undermanned, that of Santa Cruz having only thirty gunners and soldiers, and that of Boa Viagem only five. The defenders' confusion was increased by the accidental explosion of some barrels of gunpowder on the island of Villegagnon, killing or wounding about fifty people. Nevertheless, despite the complete surprise achieved by Duguay-Trouin, and the resultant demoralization of the defenders, the forts guarding the bar contrived to inflict about 300 casualties on board the French ships before they passed out of range and anchored off the fortified Ilha das Cobras near the city waterfront. This islet, which was the key of the defense, but which had only a skeleton garrison, was seized by the French after the defenders had fled on their approach at dawn next day.

Despite the spectacular success achieved by Duguay-Trouin within twenty-four hours of his unexpected arrival, the position of the defenders was still very far from hopeless. Estimates of the force at the governor's disposal vary greatly, but a reliable English eyewitness alleged that "the Portuguese had 1,000 regular troops, 2,000 marines, 4,000 citizens in arms and 7 or 8,000 Blacks." [22] This estimate is probably near the truth, since there were then five infantry regiments in the Rio garrison, including the *terço* of veterans who had fought their way out of Sacramento. Admittedly, a percentage of these troops seems to have been absent with or without leave in Minas Gerais; but when due allowance is made for this, the number of armed men available for the defense must have considerably exceeded that of the attackers. [23] The subsequent course of events proves the truth of Napoleon's dictum: "There are no bad soldiers, only bad officers."

Francisco de Castro Morais and Gaspar da Costa Ataide blamed each other for acting with cowardly indecision during the next critical days. All the evidence, including their own apologetic accounts, goes to show that they were both right. The rot started at the top and spread downwards, as it so often does in war. Even so, the irresolution and inaction of these two commanders was to some extent offset by the courage and initiative displayed by three of their subordinates, who kept clamoring for offensive action. These were Gil de Bocage, a Norman by birth, who had joined the Portuguese naval service some years previously,[24] and those two redoubtable Emboabas, Fr. Francisco de Menezes and Bento Amaral Coutinho. The friar exposed himself with such reckless courage in his habit that the French sailors christened him "Frère Jacques."

On September 14, Duguay-Trouin landed some 3,300 fit men without opposition on a beach half a mile to the northwest of the city. Nearly 500 men who were suffering from scurvy were disembarked at the same time, and within four or five days they had recovered sufficiently to serve alongside their comrades. The French next occupied some heights overlooking the city, while Duguay-Trouin took up his headquarters in the bishop's country house. Mounting batteries on these eminences and on the Ilha das Cobras, the French began a bombardment of the city which did a good deal of material damage to the buildings but inflicted little or no loss of life.

Acting on his own initiative, Bocage mounted some guns in the dormitory of the Benedictine monastery, whose fire severely galled the besiegers by their own admission. He also disguised himself as a captured French sailor, and in this way was enabled to "pump" some French scouts who had been captured and who unwittingly revealed to him all the attackers' dispositions. On the basis of this information, he persuaded the governor to allow a counterattack to be made on one of the French batteries, something which Francisco de Morais had hitherto refused to do, despite the reiterated requests of Bocage, Fr. Menezes, and Amaral Coutinho.[25] Though taken by surprise, the French repulsed their assailants after a sharp skirmish and several casualties on both sides. The governor then relapsed into his former passivity and categorically forbade any further counterattacks. Meanwhile,

97

Gaspar da Costa, considering that all was lost, was only restrained from fleeing to Bahia by the urgent remonstances of the Jesuits. All this irresolution in high places adversely affected the morale of the defenders, many of whom began to feel they had little hope of final victory with two such palpable poltroons as their senior commanders.[26]

On September 19, everything being nearly ready for a final bombardment and assualt, Duguay-Trouin summoned the governor to surrender. He demanded a large indemnity for the murder of Du Clerc and the mistreatment of his men, the punishment of those responsible, and the immediate release of the surviving French prisoners. Failing prompt compliance, he threatened to reduce the city and the surrounding countryside to ashes. Francisco de Castro Morais rejected this summons in polite but resolute terms. He denied complicity in the murder of Du Clerc and declared that those guilty of this atrocity would be severely punished if they were found. He alleged that the French prisoners had not been ill-treated and that he had saved their lives from the Negroes who would have killed them all. He finished by declaring his intention of defending the city to the last and his conviction that God would support his just cause.[27]

On receiving this resolute reply, Duguay-Trouin renewed his bombardment with greater fury than before, the battery in the Benedictine monastery being his principal target. Some of the defenders began to desert, but the majority stood firm, hoping that António de Albuquerque would soon come to their relief with the militia from Minas Gerais which had been urgently summoned when the French arrived. The besiegers would then be caught between two fires and might well share the fate of Du Clerc's men in the previous year; particularly as the weak offshore breezes would make it much harder for their ships to run the gantlet of the forts when outward bound. But the rot in the senior ranks was spreading.

On Sunday September 21, the governor assembled a council of war at which the majority of those present voted for evacuating the city. The commander of the regiment from Sacramento vehemently denounced this proposal, pointing out that very little loss of life had hitherto resulted from the French bombardment, and that the governor should defend the city to the last as he had promised to do. At six o'clock that same evening the governor made public proclamation that nobody should retire ten paces from his post on pain of death. Soon after nightfall, however, one of the militia regiments began to withdraw, and wild rumors immediately spread that all was lost. When this was reported to the governor, he hesitated no longer but ordered a general *sauve-qui-peut*. Some unit commanders who queried this order were sharply reprimanded and told to retire without delay, the governor setting the example himself about 10:00 P.M.

The retreat now became general and the city was evacuated in the pitch darkness of a torrentially rainy night and amid scenes of indescribable panic and confusion.[28] The oldest inhabitants could not recall such a wild and stormy night and this naturally made confusion worse confounded. Trails leading out of the city became quagmires or torrents, and the women and children suffered particularly severely. So sudden was the evacuation that very few people had time to take anything of value from their homes, although much of the gold and ready money had been sent out of the city some days previously. Luckily for the fugitives, the French had no idea of what was happening and were busy making preparations to storm the city the next day. The first intimation they had was the appearance of Du Clerc's aide-de-camp at daylight, with the news that the city was empty of its defenders.

Duguay-Trouin at first could hardly believe this information, but on entering the city with due precautions, he found that virtually the only occupants were the survivors of Du Clerc's expedition.[29] These had broken out of their prison and were busy plundering the houses; a congenial occupation in which they were soon joined by some of Duguay-Trouin's men despite the stringent orders and drastic punishments which the French commander meted out to stop unauthorized pillage. Vasconcellos Velho stated that Duguay-Trouin shot eighteen of his own men who had robbed treasures from the churches. The loss of the city completely demoralized the defenders of the surrounding forts when they heard of it, and these strongholds were either abandoned or else surrendered at the first summons of the French. The latter were therefore soon in possession of the entire Bay of Rio de Janeiro, together with the shipping in the harbor. In the Jesuits' church on a hilltop, "whence can be seen the most delightful view in the world," the victors thankfully sang their *Te Deum* to the accompaniment of oboes and trumpets.

Considerable as was the booty found in the abandoned city, and in the country houses in its immediate vicinity, it was not sufficient to cover the cost of the expedition and to repay Duguay-Trouin's backers. To achieve this, he had somehow to secure the gold which the Portuguese had evacuated in the early stages of the campaign. Moreover, he had to act quickly, since runaway Negro slaves informed him that António de Albuquerque was rapidly approaching with a strong force from Minas Gerais. Once this "général d'un grand renom chez les portugais" had made his junction with the defeated Rio garrison, Duguay-Trouin would no longer have the cowardly and pliable Castro de Morais to contend with. The French commander therefore sent the latter an ultimatum demanding the immediate payment of a large ransom for the city and forts, failing which he would level them to the ground.

The governor hesitated for a few days, but the death of the enterprising Bento do Amaral Coutinho in a skirmish against the French [30] put the finishing touch to his demoralization. Without waiting any longer for Albuquerque and his daily expected reinforcements, he entered into negotiations with the French when the latter menacingly moved their main body nearer to his makeshift camp at the Engenho Novo. With the Jesuit Padre António Cordeiro acting as chief intermediary, Duguay-Trouin was persuaded to accept the sum of 610,000 cruzados in gold, 100 chests of sugar, and 200 head of cattle as ransom for the city and forts.

Most of the money was raised by handing over the royal fifths received from Minas Gerais and the bullion evacuated from the Mint, but the wealthiest citizens who had saved their gold were also forced to make substantial contributions. It is only just to add that the governor himself made one of the largest individual payments.[31] It was also stipulated that the merchants and citizens who had sought refuge in the vicinity could freely trade with the French and buy back such of their own ships and property as they could afford to pay for. This capitulation was signed on October 10, 1711, and three or four of the leading civilian and military authorities were handed over to the French as hostages for the execution of these onerous terms. A fortnight later António de Albuquerque arrived with the vanguard from Minas Gerais.

Although he arrived too late, the fault was certainly not that of the men he led. On September 21 he had received a verbal message that Duguay-Trouin had forced the harbor entrance with eighteen sail; and without waiting for further information, or a written request from Castro Morais, Albuquerque at once resolved to go to the help of the threatened city. The militia of Minas Gerais was mobilized with a speed and the men joined the colors with an alacrity that formed a striking contrast to mobilization in Portugal, where men were mustered with difficulty and took the field with reluctance. Albuquerque's call to arms was sent out over a roadless country, and to a turbulent mining population which eighteen months previously had been at each others' throats; yet exactly a week later he left Ribeirão do Carmo at the head of "nearly six thousand men of the best and finest people in the Mines, both Outsiders and Paulistas." His force was composed of one regular line regiment, raised on this occasion, three territorial (*auxiliaries*) and six militia (*ordenança*) regiments, together with a cavalry regiment of 320 horse. Several of the senior officers had seen active service in foreign wars, and most of the men provided for themselves and their slaves, others being supported by the wealthier officers. The Emboabas were by far the more numerous but the Paulistas furnished two detachments (*troços*) under their own officers. On leaving at the head of this relief column, Albuquerque left district commanders behind him who were entrusted with the task of mobilizing more men and forwarding more supplies.[32]

Heavy rains made the mountain trails almost impassable and the rivers were in flood, but Albuquerque pressed on by forced marches. Since he had no wheeled transport and relatively few pack animals, his men could not carry much powder and shot. Albuquerque therefore sent reiterated messages to Castro Morais, telling him to have a good supply of these essential munitions in readiness. On October 15, before scaling the Serra do Mar, Albuquerque received a message from the governor of Rio telling him that the city had fallen and asking him to come and retake it. On crossing the mountains a few days later, he got another message from Castro Morais, stating that he was negotiating with the enemy. Immediately afterwards he received a third message, announcing that the capitulation had been concluded and the hostages given for its performance. Still hoping that he was not too late after all, Albuquerque advanced to where Castro Morais was encamped, only to find that, although there was sufficient powder, only four small kegs of shot were available. He also found that the Portuguese had no artillery whatsoever; that the French were strongly posted in all the forts, batteries, and entrenchments; that most of the ransom had been paid; and that Castro Morais had neglected to secure any French hostages in return for his own. In view of these circumstances, Albuquerque reluctantly realized that there was nothing he could do save accept the accomplished fact.[33]

The rest of the story is soon told. Albuquerque's arrival with his whites, mixed-bloods, and Negro slaves "aussi aguerris que des soldats," at least had the effect of inducing Duguay-Trouin to speed up the preparations for his departure. Having received the balance of the payments due, he handed over the city and forts to the Portuguese, and set sail on November 13. His chivalrous treatment of such women and wounded as fell into his hands was gratefully acknowledged by the citizens who returned to their plundered homes, and who made no difficulty about trading freely and amicably with the French. Duguay-Trouin also returned to the Jesuits much of the church ornaments and furniture that he had saved from plunder. Last not least, the "parfait gentilhomme" gave refuge in his ships to some wretched crypto-Jews whom he had found awaiting deportation to Portugal for trial by the Inquisition.[34]

By allowing the citizens and merchants to repurchase their own property and merchandise with gold dust or coin, Duguay-Trouin had collected a substantial sum for his Saint-Malo *armateurs,* in addition to the bullion received for the city's ransom. Since the sugar and most of the other goods seized in the warehouses would not fetch high prices in France, he loaded them on two of the largest Portuguese prizes which he sent round Cape Horn to trade with the Spaniards of Peru. The remaining ships and goods were sold to the Portuguese for what they would fetch. Even Albuquerque, who opposed this brisk trade wtih the French, ended by buying 2,080 barrels of gunpowder from them. Joseph Collett was allowed to ransom the East Indiaman *Jane* with her lading for £3,500 in bills of exchange drawn on London. He likewise acknowledged that Duguay-Trouin had treated him and his compatriots "with a great deal of civility." [35]

Persistent contrary winds forced the French commander to give up his original plan of sacking Bahia on the homeward voyage; just as he had dropped this project on the outward voyage after being delayed by calms in the Gulf of Guinea. When the fleet reached the latitude of the Azores, it ran into a fearful storm (January 29, 1712), in which two ships foundered with all hands. One of them was the *Magnanime* (74) which went down with the brave de Coursérac and the bulk of the Rio ransom aboard. This tragedy recalls a similar fate which befell the homeward-bound armadas of Don Francisco de Toledo and Don Antonio de Oquendo in the same vicinity in 1625 and 1631 respectively. Despite the loss of so much treasure, the expedition showed a handsome material profit when the two ships dispatched to the Pacific finally returned to France after disposing very advantageously of their plundered cargoes. Duguay-Trouin received a well-deserved hero's welcome from the French court, and the renown of his exploits bolstered French morale at a critical period.[36]

Conversely, when the news was received at Lisbon it naturally depressed the Portuguese, particularly since the government had given timely warning. It did not, however, come as a complete surprise. From the pessimistic tone of the correspondence exchanged between the principal advisers of the Crown in October, 1711, it is clear that the Portuguese ministers were prepared for the worst. The Duke of Cadaval, for instance, opined that if the French had captured Rio de Janeiro and had decided to stay there, then it would be impossible to eject them with Portugal's own army and navy. True, the English and Dutch might supply ships for an expeditionary force to recover the city; but the soldiers would have to be Portuguese, "for to accept English troops would be to hand Brazil over to the English." Yet the war was going so badly in Spain that the Duke saw no hope of sparing any considerable body of troops from the defense of Portugal.[37] In the event, Duguay-Trouin had no intention of achieving more than he did, and the peace talks which opened at Utrecht in January, 1712, implied that the end of the war was near. Actually, these negotiations dragged on for another three frustrating years. Portugal, who received little diplomatic support from the English ally who had dragged her into the war, had to be content at the final conclusion of peace with the recognition of her rights in Amazonia and the restoration of the colony of Sacramento.

Albuquerque, though arriving too late through no fault of his own, had been greeted with great relief by the fugitive citizens and soldiery of Rio. They refused to recognize the authority of the cowardly Castro de Morais any longer, and insisted that the former should assume and retain the governorship. This he did, entering the plundered city on November 16, three days after the

French had left the Bay. "On his heels came the numerous refugees who had sought sanctuary in the neighboring woods. And their clamor and cries were such that the said general looking behind him and seeing the extent of their grief, reflected his broken heart in his eyes." [38] He refused to arrest Castro Morais, as the inhabitants demanded, but in due course the ex-governor and most of the principal culprits were sent to Portugal for trial. Castro Morais was then sentenced to be cashiered and to perpetual exile in an Indo-Portuguese fortress, but the sentence was quashed thirty years later. Gaspar da Costa was thrown into prison at Lisbon on the arrival of the homeward-bound fleet, which he took back to Portugal in spite of his misconduct at Rio, but I do not know what sentence (if any) he received. [39]

Albuquerque spent more than a year supervising the rehabilitation of Rio, which, thanks to the gold mines of Minas Gerais, rapidly recovered from the disaster of 1711. He did not forget to remind the Crown of the exemplary zeal which the Emboabas and Paulistas had shown in September of that year, and he asked that their loyalty should be suitably acknowledged. The reconstruction of Rio was not the last service which Albuquerque rendered to Brazil. [40] On his homeward voyage in 1714, he played a part in pacifying the troubles of Pernambuco, where tension between the "sons of the soil" and the immigrants from Portugal had produced an explosion which recalls in some ways the civil war in Minas Gerais.

V. PLANTERS AND PEDDLERS

ALTHOUGH THE PARALLEL between the civil war in Minas Gerais and that in Pernambuco must not be pushed too far, there is no denying one basic similarity: the mutual dislike between the "sons of the soil" and the upstart immigrants from Portugal. Just as the Paulistas, rightly or wrongly, prided themselves on their allegedly noble forebears and looked down on the miners and traders of European origin, so the artistocratic sugar planters of Pernambuco despised the hard-working but humble immigrants who often amassed sufficient wealth to become their economic superiors. The Pernambucan self-styled nobility was not of very illustrious or ancient lineage for the most part. In the mid-seventeenth century a Portuguese governor who knew Brazil well, described their origins as being "none of the best." [1] But they had now been settled on the land for generations; they claimed the major share in the expulsion of the Dutch in 1645–1654; and their way of life as sugar planters and slaveowners inevitably led them to regard themselves as aristocrats and as more than a cut above mere merchants and traders, who, however successful, remained their social inferiors.

The social standing of merchants in Portugal and her overseas empire was a somewhat peculiar one. Theoretically, they ranked lower, in some respects at any rate, than the practitioners of the seven "mechanical arts" of medieval origin: peasant, hunter, soldier, sailor, surgeon, weaver, blacksmith. In Catholic Portugal as in Confucian China—or in Marxist Russia—the merchant was likely to be regarded as a parasitic and profiteering middleman, determined to enrich himself at the expense of his fellow men.[2]

Theoretical disdain for the merchant's calling was sharpened by the fact that in the Portuguese-speaking world a high percentage of the successful merchants were of crypto-Jewish or "New-Christian" origin, largely because all other avenues of advancement were officially closed to them. Anti-Semitism was nowhere stronger than in Portugal, despite (or, perhaps, because of) the fact that there was a strong admixture of Jewish blood in many Portuguese families. Foreign residents and travelers were particularly caustic on this point, as exemplified by Froger's account of his visit to Rio de Janeiro at the end of the seventeenth century. "The governor having prohibited the inhabitants to trade with us, and taking upon him to be the sole seller and buyer, we were obliged to afford our commodities at a cheaper rate than they bear in Europe; which sufficiently shows the sinister practices of that nation, of whom three-quarters are originally Jews."[3]

Froger's observation, however exaggerated, serves to remind us of another important feature of Portuguese colonial life, already briefly mentioned in Chapter i. Trade and commerce, despised in theory, were driven in practice by all who could afford to do so, from the viceroy or governor-general downwards. Crown salaries were avowedly inadequate in most cases, and occupants of government posts were expected to recoup themselves by trading, providing this was done discreetly.[4] The Portuguese empire was essentially a commercial and maritime one, though cast in a military and clerical mold. Recognition of this fact was implicit in the grandiloquent title chosen by King Manuel I—"The Fortunate" to his countrymen and "Le Roi-Epicier" to François I— a title proudly maintained by his successors long after it had ceased to have any practical application: "Lord of the Conquest, Navigation, and Commerce of India, Ethiopia, Arabia, and Persia."

It is difficult to visualize any other European monarchs making mention of commerce in their regal styles and titles. Although it would be wrong to assert that Portugal had a commercial class comparable to those which flourished in the United Netherlands, England, France, or Italy, yet Portuguese trading communities at certain times and places achieved a considerable degree of importance, despite the handicaps imposed by vexatious Crown monopolies and competition from greedy governors. The opulent merchants of Macao in the heyday of the old Japan Trade (1557–1640) afford one example, and the *Mascates* of early eighteenth-century Recife another. As a member of the latter community wrote: "In short, it is a land of trade, in which profit is the only motive."

The etymology of the word *Mascate,* like that of *Emboaba,* is disputed by scholars and philologists; but I have no hesitation in rejecting the theory which derives it from the seaport of Muscat (Port., *Mascate*) in Arabia. This place belonged to the Portuguese for nearly a century and a half before it was taken from them by the Arabs of Oman in 1650, but it was never a great commercial center like the more northerly Ormuz, world-famous emporium of the Persian Gulf.[5] In any event, the word *Mascate,* as used in Portugal and Brazil, though not (as far as I am aware) in Portuguese Asia, denoted a peddler or itinerant trader, hawking cheap goods and trinkets from place to place and from door to door. They were usually regarded with contemptuous aversion, but they fulfilled an important function in a country with primitive communications. Koster, in his classic description of early nineteenth-century Pernambuco, terms them "a useful, industrious, and generally honest set of men," [6] and this was equally true a century earlier. At that time, the word *Mascate* also included shopkeepers, cashiers and clerks, most of whom, as mentioned in Chapter i, were immigrants from Portugal. Just as the Paulistas complained that the impoverished Emboabas whom they had befriended, later turned on their generous benefactors, so the Pernambucans alleged that the ragged Mascates to whom they had given employment and hospitality on their arrival as penniless immigrants, later repaid them with the basest ingratitude.[7]

The ill-feeling between Pernambucan sugar planters and Mascate merchants was reflected in the rivalry between the provincial capital of Olinda and its neighboring seaport of Recife. Olinda, built on hills like a miniature and tropical Lisbon, was dignified by massive churches and convents, and by the stately town houses of the planters of the *Várzea*. Recife, despite the expansion and improvement it had undergone during and since the Dutch occupation (1630–1654), was still in some respects an ill-built and overcrowded shantytown huddled on the swampy land around the harbor. Admittedly, Olinda had not fully recovered from the eclipse it had undergone during the "time of the Flemings," but the sugar-planting oligarchs jealously guarded its preëminence as the metropolis of the captaincy and seat of the senate or municipal council. Recife, although far more prosperous and thriving a place than Olinda, had not even the status of a town (*villa*), but was a mere appendage of the latter. Then again, whereas the sugar planters of Olinda and the *Várzea* found it almost impossible to keep out of debt, owing to the violent fluctuations in the price of sugar and the steady increase in the cost of Negro slaves, the *Mascates* of Recife often speculated successfully in these and other commodities, thus becoming the exigent creditors of the feckless oligarchs. As Manuel dos Santos noted: "The dwellers of Recife were never indebted to the sugar planters, whereas rare indeed was the sugar planter who did not owe them a considerable sum."

Since those who have economic power are seldom contented without exercising political power, the inhabitants of Recife naturally chafed at their legal and social subordination to the municipal councillors of Olinda. They repeatedly petitioned the Crown to grant Recife the status of a township, with a municipal council of its own. For a long time the Crown resisted these appeals, despite the fact that they were usually supported by the governors of the captaincy, who, more often than not, preferred to spend most of their time in Recife instead of at Olinda as they should have done. They were supposed to reside at Recife only during such time as the annual homeward-bound sugar fleet was loading its cargoes in the harbor, a process which usually took two or three months. In fact, they found the company of their Recife compatriots more congenial, and their mercantile connections more profitable, than residence among the sugar planters and friars who constituted the élite of Olinda.

The merchants of Recife, who had to pay the taxes decreed by the Senate of Olinda, vainly sought to secure representation on this body. They were excluded on the grounds that muncipal councillors could only be drawn from the class of sugar planters and others who were "living nobly" (*vivendo à lei da nobreza*), that is, in manor houses and with "servants, slaves, weapons and horses" at their disposal. Merchants, however wealthy, were specifically excluded. When the Mascates appealed to the Crown for a definition of the term "merchants," the royal reply of May 8, 1705 stated: "The word 'merchants' is applicable only to those persons in an open shop who are actually engaged in measuring, weighing, and selling any kind of merchandise to the people." [8] This ruling effectively excluded the Mascates from the municipal council, since even the wealthiest of them were engaged in retail trade on the side.

There was also keen rivalry between the two groups over the membership of their respective lay brotherhoods. The planters, though regarding themselves as aristocrats, were anxious to be admitted to the plebian but wealthy Jesuit confraternity of the Mascates at Recife. Another source of discord was the annual procession of the Franciscan Tertiaries on Ash Wednesday. The Mascates wanted their own procession in Recife, whereas the municipal councillors insisted that they should come to Olinda. The former got their way in the end, but the sense of grievance remained. Finally, the merchants of Recife claimed that the planters should come to their port for discussions when the annual

sugar prices were fixed prior to the lading of the fleet. In this
instance the Crown upheld the contention of the planters that
there was no need for them to do anything of the sort, "since it
is just as easy for the merchants of Recife to go to the city of
Olinda, which is only a short distance away and easily reached." [9]

The repeated rebuffs sustained by the inhabitants of Recife
when petitioning for the grant of municipal status, did not
discourage them from renewing their efforts, and eventually the
Crown gave way. It could hardly have done otherwise, since the
port now had a population variously estimated at anything between ten and sixteen thousand souls, and was undeniably of much
greater demographic and economic importance that the thinly
populated and half-ruined city on the neighboring hills. A royal
decree of November 19, 1709, enjoined that Recife should be
raised to the status of an independent township; but it left the
ticklish problem of the delimitation of its municipal boundaries
to be settled by the governor of Pernambuco, Sebastião de Castro e
Caldas, in consultation with the regional *Ouvidor* or Crown
Judge, Dr. José Ignacio de Arouche. This judge was a partisan of
the planters and wished to limit the new town's boundaries as
narrowly as possible; whereas the governor favored the Mascates
and wished to include three neighboring parishes in the new
municipality. The Crown's avowed hope in the decree of November, 1709, that the erection of Recife into a *vila* would "prevent
the disputes which there are now between the inhabitants of
Olinda and those of Recife" was destined to be rudely shattered. [10]

The governor, wishing to forestall any forcible objection of
the planters to the official inauguration of the new municipality,
acted with what can only be termed clumsy cunning. Without
informing them of the decree he had received from Lisbon, he
ordered a makeshift *pelourinho* [11] to be secretly prepared in one of
the forts at Recife, and had it erected in the principal square on
the night of February 14–15, 1710, replacing it with a proper
one on March 3 following. Although the appearance of the first
pelourinho was immediately followed by an inaugural ceremony

and the installation of a municipal council, yet its clandestine erection gave the citizens of Olinda an excuse to say that the whole business was obviously unauthorized by the Crown.

This action made Castro e Caldas even more unpopular with the planters. He was soon told by the priests, "who had learnt it under the seal of confession," that plots were being hatched to murder him. In view of these warnings, he took a number of precautionary measures, of which the most unpopular was a general ban on the carrying of firearms by civilians. This edict was naturally received with consternation by the planters, particularly as life was chronically insecure in Pernambuco and most free men went about heavily armed at all times.[12] Moreover, a French attack was possible, even probable, at any moment, and it seemed the height of folly to deprive people of their muskets. If the disgruntled planters had not been actively plotting to remove Castro e Caldas—and the evidence on this point is conflicting—they certainly began to do so now.

On October 17, 1710, when Castro e Caldas was on his way to church, he was shot at and slightly wounded by a group of masked men who fled immediately and were never identified. Failing to catch the real culprits, the governor began to make a series of arrests among the planters and their adherents whom he suspected of complicity. These arrests provoked some of the bolder spirits to act decisively before it was too late. The example was given by Pedro Ribeiro da Silva, who seized the military officer sent to arrest him. Most of the other planters now took up arms, allegedly in self-defense; and the troops sent against them either fraternized with them or else retreated to Recife after some token skirmishing. Encouraged by their preliminary successes, the leading planters now called out the militia, which was largely composed of *lavradores* or share croppers, and mustered their slaves for a general advance on Recife. Castro e Caldas, completely demoralized and unable to rely on what was left of the garrison, hurriedly embarked in a schooner with a few of the principal Mascates and set sail for Bahia on November 7.

Planters and Peddlers

The triumphant insurgents—for such they now were—advanced unopposed on Recife, threatening death and destruction to the upstart town and its hated inhabitants. The latter persuaded the Vice-Rector of the Jesuit College, Padre Manuel dos Santos, to go and intercede with the approaching attackers. Throwing himself with his crucifix at the feet of those leaders who were most eager for vengeance, he persuaded them to content themselves with milder measures. Entering tumultuously into the town, they overturned the *pelourinho,* deposed such of the senators as had not fled with the governor, and released the prisoners from the jail. They neither killed anyone nor looted private property; but before proceeding to Olinda, they ordered that on pain of death the inhabitants of Recife should surrender all "the insignias of the posts which they occupied by virtue of royal letters-patent." [13]

Masters of the situation, the planters and their principal followers met in a general conclave at Olinda on November 10, 1710, to decide who should succeed the fugitive governor. Accounts of what transpired at this meeting differ widely, but it seems that the bolder spirits, led by Bernardo Vieira de Mello, suggested that Pernambuco should become an independent republic "like that of the Venetians." [14] They are also said to have advocated that if the worst came to the worst, the Pernambucans should accept the suzerainty of the French king rather than yield and "serve the coarse, uncouth, and most ungrateful Mascates." These allegations were made by the Mascates, and were later indignantly denied by the Pernambucans. It is, however, more than likely that something of the sort was suggested, as it had been at the beginning of the Pernambucan revolt against the Dutch in 1645, when King John IV hesitated to support the insurgents for fear of involving Portugal in a war with the United Provinces.

Be that as it may, the majority were not yet ready for such a dramatic break with the mother country. After much discussion, it was decided to offer the interim governorship to the Bishop, Fr. Manuel Alvares da Costa. This prelate, who had only recently arrived in his diocese, was absent on a pastoral visit to Paraíba when the trouble broke out. Though a Portuguese born and bred, he was notoriously ill-disposed to Castro e Caldas, and had shielded the pro-Olinda judge, Dr. Arouche, from arrest by the governor's emissaries. This decision gave a certain appearance of legality to the planters' position, since the Bishop was in the authorized direct line of succession to the governor. The Pernambucans formulated a number of demands, to which the Bishop acceded on assuming the governorship on November 15, when he granted a formal pardon in the king's name to the victors. Several versions of these demands exist in print, and one of the more interesting stipulations was the demand for direct (if limited) trade with Dutch and English ships.[15]

The planters exploited their triumph by lording it over the crestfallen Mascates for seven months, but they were then taken completely unawares by a sudden and successful rising of the townsmen of Recife. The Pernambucan accounts allege that this outbreak was the result of a carefully hatched plot by the Mascates. "And so cautiously did they behave, that, although many of them were in the secret, yet none of the sons of the soil knew anything about it."[16] It was further alleged that the Mascates had secretly accumulated a six-month supply of provisions, concealing manioc flour in sugar chests so as to avoid suspicion. They were also said to have bribed the soldiers of the garrison of Recife and various senior authorities, such as the governor of the neighboring captaincy of Paraíba, João da Maia da Gama. Finally, they were said to have spread unfounded reports that the Pernambucans were ready to call in the French if the new governor expected from Portugal did not bring the royal confirmation of the episcopal pardon granted on November 15, 1710.

The Mascates, on the other hand, claimed that the outbreak was entirely spontaneous and unpremeditated. They alleged that it arose out of a street brawl between soldiers of the Recife garrison and those of Bernardo Vieira de Mello's Paulista regiment over a mulata prostitute. The garrison soldiers, fearing they would be arrested and punished by Vieira de Mello, rose in arms and proclaimed their loyalty to King John V and to their ex-governor at Bahia. The excitement quickly spread, and the oppressed Mascates made common cause with the soldiers to overthrow the tyrannous rule of the Pernambucan planters and their Paulista supporters. As evidence of the truth of this version, Manuel dos Santos pointed out that far from having an adequate stock of provisions in hand, the inhabitants of Recife were compelled to subsist mainly on shellfish gathered daily at low tide for the first few weeks of the ensuing siege.

So much hard lying is involved in this conflict of evidence, that the exact truth is probably unascertainable, nor does it greatly matter. What is certain is that on June 18, 1711, the soldiers of the garrison and the Mascates of Recife rose in arms against the Pernambucan planters and the Paulista auxiliary troops. Bernardo Vieira de Mello, who happened to be visiting the town, was only saved from being lynched by the intervention of the *Ouvidor,* Dr. Valenzuela Ortiz, who (though secretly sympathizing with him) placed him in close confinement together with eighteen Paulista soldiers who were rounded up in the streets. The Bishop, who was likewise visiting Recife at this juncture, was compelled to adhere to this movement for a few days, and to publish a circular that everything which had happened up to date would be forgiven and forgotten. The ink was hardly dry on this document (June 19), when the Bishop made his way to Olinda two days later, together with Dr. Valenzuela Ortiz. According to his own account, he was only able to make his escape by the use of guile and subterfuge; but the Mascate version alleged that they freely let him leave on his giving his word of honor that he would return after pacifying the planters at Olinda.[17]

On reaching the city, the Bishop came out openly against the Mascates, stating that he had only signed the circular of June 19 under duress. He summoned the Mascates to yield, and ordered that all supplies and reinforcements should be prevented from entering Recife from Paraíba or elsewhere. The Mascates refused to surrender and elected one of the officers of the garrison, João da Mota, as their leader. Seeing that recourse to force was inevitable, the Bishop resigned his governorship on June 27 to a junta composed of Dr. Valenzuela Ortiz, Colonel Christovão de Mendonça Arraes (another Paulista, incidentally), and the municipal councillors of Olinda. This junta acted with speed and decision, mobilizing all the regional militia units and laying siege in form to Recife before the month of June was out.

The siege—or blockade as it might more aptly be termed—of Recife lasted for just over three months. It was, of course effective only on the landward side, since the Pernambucans had no shipping to attack the place from seaward. The besieged were far better supplied with artillery than were the besiegers and this proved the decisive factor. The Pernambucans had only a few cannon of small caliber dragged from the coastal batteries at Itamaracá and Nazaré, whereas the defenders had the full use of the local forts. This disparity accounts for the fact that whereas the besieged fired more than 5,400 cannon shot during three months, the besiegers responded with fewer than 450. Moreover, the Pernambucans were so short of ammunition that sometimes they employed broken bricks and even unripe fruit as projectiles![18] Fortunately, the casualties on both sides were more commensurate with the last-named type of munitions than with the round shot so freely expended by the defenders. The Mascates' loss was limited to one Negress slave killed, and the Pernambucans acknowledged only three wounded.

A few sallies were made by the besieged but the fatal casualties suffered in the ensuing skirmishes were not much more numerous than those inflicted in the bombardment. In one of these halfhearted actions, however, the Pernambucan field commander, Christovão de Mendonça Arraes, was taken prisoner with a number of his men (August 19, 1711) after what can only be described as a token resistance. The victor on this occasion was the Amerindian chief, Camarão, nephew of one of the heroes of the Dutch War. He had joined the Mascates together with his colored col-

league who commanded the local regiment of Negro militia—
Henriques as they were called after another paladin of the "Time
of the Flemings," Henrique Dias.[19] The besieged were less successful in subsequent sorties and eventually gave them up altogether, since the soldiers of the garrison showed no enthusiasm
for these ventures. The Pernambucans, on the other side, realizing
the futility of their bombardment, several times discussed the possibility of risking everything on a general assault, but nobody was
forthcoming to volunteer for the van. This mutual caution helped
to keep the casualty lists on both sides to modest figures. The
Mascates admitted to a loss of only twenty-five men all told;
and although the Pernambucan casualties are not reliably recorded, they cannot have been much heavier.

If the "War of the Mascates" was hardly deserving of this
title judging from the size of the casualty list, in other respects
it had deeper and wider repercussions. Each side believed its
own propaganda that the other party was anxious for French assistance and was composed of actual or potential traitors. Each
side accused the other of mistreating its prisoners, or those of the
rival party who were in their power; and these allegations, unlike
the first, certainly had some substance. All these stories, whether
true or false, lost nothing in the telling and inevitably embittered
the existing enmity. It may be added that although both sides
wrote to Lisbon and Bahia giving their respective version of
events, the authorities in Portugal were at first inclined to give
more credit to the Mascates, who had many agents at Court,
whereas those at Bahia were better informed and paid little attention to the complaints of Castro e Caldas.

As mentioned above, the besieged could count on the support
of João da Maia da Gama, the governor of Paraíba, though there
is no need to believe the Pernambucan allegations that the
Mascates had bribed him with 14,000 *cruzados*. He was, however, unable to march to their relief as he had originally intended,
since his own captaincy would have risen behind him had he done
so, and did in fact contribute a small force to the besiegers. Maia

da Gama had to rest content with dispatching some boat loads of supplies for Recife, and with engaging in a lengthy and acrimonious correspondence with the Pernambucan leaders in a vain attempt to dissuade them from pressing the siege.[20] On the other hand, the governor-general at Bahia, Dom Lourenço de Almada, to whom both sides appealed for sympathy and support, showed himself on the whole more favorable to the Pernambucans. He sent a small shipload of provisions to the defenders of Recife but scornfully rejected the Mascates' allegations that the planters were actual or potential traitors; and he prevented Castro e Caldas from returning to Recife by imprisoning him in a fortress. He also severely reprimanded João da Maia for his pro-Mascate attitude.

It may be added that the division between Mascates and Pernambucans, though wide and deep, was not necessarily automatic in individual cases. We have seen that the Portuguese Bishop supported the "sons of the soil," whereas the Mascate leaders included Dom Francisco de Sousa, member of one of the leading planter families and colonel of a local militia regiment. It was mainly through his influence that the Amerindian and Negro auxiliaries had rallied to the defense of Recife, instead of joining the Brazilian-born planters alongside whom they had been born and bred. The two judges who supported the "sons of the soil" were also European-born Portuguese, and other exceptions could be mentioned.

While still smarting from their humiliating reverse at Camarão's hands near Serinhaem, the drooping spirits of the besiegers were revived by the appearance of a heavily armed contingent of the local clergy. Each priest was accompanied by "two, three, or more slaves, very well armed, and very fit for any enterprise," and a smaller reinforcement of forty Negroes and mulattoes came from Paraíba.[21] Though welcoming the aid of these colored men, the Pernambucan planters professed great scorn for the Mascates who were prepared to take orders from the leaders of

the Amerindian and Negro militia regiments. They also denounced the menial origins of another Mascate leader, Miguel
Correia Gomes, "who yesterday brought us water to wash our
hands in, and our Negro slaves lodged him in their huts." All
the more humiliating for the proud planters was it, therefore,
when the prisoners captured near Serinhaem were paraded half-
naked through the streets of Recife on September 11, to the accompaniment of jeers and catcalls (and more solid tokens of contempt) from the rabble gathered to watch them on their way to
jail.[22]

The disturbances of June–October, 1711 were not entirely confined to Recife and its immediate vicinity. The fortress of Taman-
daré was likewise unsuccessfully besieged by the planters and
their adherents, and serious rioting took place at Goiana where
both factions were strongly represented. But both sides realized
that the struggle for Recife was the vital factor, since without
the possession of this port the planters' movement had no chance
of growing into a full-scale revolution against the mother country, whatever incipient feelings of independence some of the Pernambucans may have entertained.

For most of the siege, the inhabitants of Recife subsisted mainly
on a diet of shellfish and sugar. The former were gathered at
low tide in the neighboring mangrove swamps by slaves who were
often waylaid and kidnapped by the besiegers. More than three
hundred are said to have been captured in this way. As has been
known to happen in other emergencies before and since, the
meager diet to which the defenders were reduced did more good
than harm to those wealthier members of the community who
had been accustomed to overindulgence in the pleasures of the
table. Manuel dos Santos, himself a physician, recounts that the
general health of the citizens was never better than during this
time. "And some people, who normally suffered from daily ail-
ments, which none of the many and varied remedies which they
took could ever cure, found that only during the time of the siege

were they completely free of their bodily ills, . . . for many of these people, once the siege was over, found that their aches and pains returned as before." [23]

In due course, the besieged equipped some armed boats to go out and purchase provisions along the coast at places not sufficiently controlled by the rival faction. The food thus secured was at first inefficiently distributed, "some stealing and others concealing it; the infantry complaining that the citizens engrossed everything, and the citizens complaining that the soldiers ate everything." In order to avoid these demoralizing disputes, it was decided that the garrison and the townspeople should make separate arrangements for purchasing their own food supplies on these expeditions. Francisco Cazado de Lima, one of the richest and most active Mascates, lent the garrison commander more than 6,000 *cruzados* free of interest to enable him to purchase food for his men, and in this way harmony between soldiers and civilians was restored.[24]

The stalemate into which the siege had subsided was finally resolved by the appearance of the annual fleet from Portugal on October 6, 1711 with a new governor, Felix José Machado de Mendonça, on board. He brought with him a royal pardon, dated June 6, 1711, couched in general terms and confirming that granted by the Bishop to the Pernambucans in the previous November. Both sides hastened to send their emissaries to him before he had time to disembark, but his first actions were correct and impartial enough. He refused to take over the government from anyone but the Bishop, who was accordingly reinstated in office for this purpose and accepted by both sides. The siege of Recife was raised, the planters' contingents dispersed, the prisoners on both sides were released, and all seemed set fair for a general reconciliation. Felix Machado was duly installed as governor both at Recife and Olinda, with festivities which included theatrical performances in his honor. On November 4 he promulgated an edict prohibiting the use of "opprobrious and offensive words" by both sides, and enjoining unity on the erstwhile contenders as "being a Catholic and Christian people, and all alike loyal vassals and faithful subjects of the same king." [25] Unfortunately, this good beginning had a bad ending so far as the Pernambucan planters were concerned.

Recife was again—and this time definitively—erected into a town by the formal erection of a pillory on November 18; and shortly afterwards it became apparent that the Mascates had forgiven and forgotten nothing and that they had won the governor and the new *Ouvidor,* Dr. João Marques Bacalhau, over to their side. Disregarding the general terms of the royal pardon, these two authorities began to arrest those whom they regarded as the ringleaders of the original revolt against Castro e Caldas, and even the Bishop was deported to a remote part of the captaincy. These punitive measures took still more sweeping and rigorous forms when a conspiracy against the governor's life was allegedly discovered in February, 1712. None of the "sons of the soil" felt safe from arrest, and many of them fled to the bush in order to escape capture.

To round up the fugitives, the governor reinforced the regular Amerindian and Negro auxiliaries with a band of 360 ruffians, mostly mulattoes and crossbreeds whose color ranged from pure white to jet black. Their participation now gave events the aspect of a class struggle, for these unemployed and vagrant types were only too glad of the opportunity to revenge themselves on the haughty planters and sharecroppers, who had formerly treated them with the greatest contempt and aversion. These vagabonds all had criminal records, and were led by a certain Manuel Gonsalves who was nicknamed *Tunda-Cumbé.* This was an Angolan term indicating that he had once been beaten up by outraged Negro slaves, with the result that he had a twisted body and mind ever since. The *Tunda-Cumbés,* as they were called after their leader, pillaged the houses of the planters of everything of value and killed and ate all the livestock, and ill-treated the women and children. So outrageous were their excesses, that even the Amerindian auxiliaries were horrified by them. They told the fugitives concealed in the woods, "that they would never reveal the hiding place of any of them," and they proved as good as their word. At one time some 400 men were hidden in the bush and many dramatic escapes were recorded. One man spent nine days in a hollow tree, and an old gentleman of seventy-one lay concealed in a chest for five days.[26]

Those who were arrested, or who voluntarily gave themselves up in order to save their friends and families from molestation, had a singularly harrowing time of it, if contemporary Pernambucan accounts are to be trusted. They were dragged through the streets of Recife, tied with cords or loaded with chains, and subjected to every kind of insult and contumely by the triumphant Mascates and their Negro slaves. No distinction was made between those of gentle and those of plebeian birth. Most of them were herded into the subterranean dungeons of Fort Five Points (*Cinco Pontas*), already occupied by mulatto and other common criminals. Sanitary arrangements were conspicuous by their absence, "and they all had to make in public the secret operations of nature, just as if they were animals." Only if their friends or families bribed the head jailer could they receive adequate rations or get some of their heavier irons replaced by lighter chains.[27]

The same accounts depict Felix Machado as a chronic cacophilist and a monster of depravity and vice. Some of the stories which they relate in this connection are virtually unprintable, and it is difficult to believe that they are not grossly exaggerated.[28] Even so, there is sober evidence enough to show that the governor was one of the worst with which the unfortunate colony was ever afflicted, and his memory is execrated in Pernambuco to this day. Although the Crown sent another pardon in March, 1713, which specifically amnestied those concerned in the "war" of 1710–1711 (though not those accused of attempting to assassinate Felix Machado), the governor evaded implementing this act of clemency on one pretext or another. Felix Machado and his minions strove to intercept and confiscate all letters addressed to Lisbon and Bahia which complained of this reign of terror and which besought the intervention of the Crown and the governor-general.

The first chance that the oppressed Pernambucans had of stating their case to a sympathetic high official, who was in a position to intercede for them, was when António de Albuquerque passed through Recife bound from Rio de Janeiro to Lisbon in December, 1713. He stayed for eighteen days in the harbor, and since he had some relations and friends among the persecuted planters, they found ways and means of informing him of what was really happening. Albuquerque was horrified by what he heard and he promised to intercede for them to the Crown after his arrival at Lisbon. This he did, but he was lucky to reach Lisbon safely. The ship in which he sailed, the *Nossa Senhora do Carmo e Santo Elias,* was attacked by three sail of Algerine pirates off the bar of the Tagus, and only entered the harbor after a hotly-contested action lasting two days (March 6–7, 1714).[29]

Realizing rather belatedly that the governor of Pernambuco was behaving with unjustifiable and unauthorized severity, the Crown sent him fresh orders in April, 1714. He was severely reprimanded for arresting so many people who had been covered by the terms of the two previous royal pardons, and he was told to release them at once, with restitution of their confiscated goods and estates. Those allegedly concerned in the attempt on his life were to be sent to Lisbon for trial. The ships bearing these dispatches reached Recife on June 3, 1714, when the first batch of prisoners had already been sent to Portugal. The remainder, including sixty men who had been hoisted "in chains, and like chests or pipes," aboard a vessel which was just ready to sail, were released at the moment when they had least expected it. Of those already sent to Lisbon, Bernardo Vieira de Mello and his son died in jail, others were sentenced to terms of exile in India, and a few were released. Meanwhile, the Bishop was allowed to return to his see, being received at Olinda with great rejoicing.[30]

The Pernambucan planters' "time of troubles" was now virtually over; although they did not really feel secure until their implacable enemy, Felix Machado, had been succeeded as governor by the affable and easy-going Dom Lourenço de Almeida (June 1, 1715). This fidalgo's mild and beneficent rule "mellowed their sufferings not a little," but the bitterness engendered by the Mascates' victory and the tyrannical conduct of Felix Machado remained latent for many years. Manuel dos Santos, writing in 1749, testified to and deplored its existence then. Many families of note had been completely ruined, and were forced to intermarry with the hated Mascates or be reduced to abject poverty. Intensely proud of their real or alleged noble blood, the surviving planter families never forgot the humiliations endured at the hands of the plebeian Mascates or at those of the colored scallywags of Camarão and *Tunda-Cumbé*. Colonel Leonardo Bezerro Cavalcanti, one of the few who survived deportation to India and who eventually returned to Brazil, wrote repeatedly from his final exile at Bahia to his relatives in Pernambuco: "never cut a single *quiri*-tree in the woods. Try and keep them so that when the time comes you can break them on the backs of the sailors." "Sailors" (*Marinheiros*) was another insulting epithet applied to the Mascates; and it is still used (or was until a few years ago) as a derogatory word to describe the Portuguese immigrant who has failed to achieve success in Pernambuco.[31]

Much ink has been expended by Brazilian historians in discussing whether the "War of the Mascates" represented a genuine independence movement—"the first in the Americas," as the more enthusiastic supporters of this thesis claim—or whether it was merely a sectional squabble between progressive Recife and decaying Olinda. As indicated above, I feel that although there probably was some loose talk among the planters of separating from the mother country in 1710–1711, Bernardo Vieira de Mello was the only important person who seriously proposed such a move. He was overruled at the Olinda conclave on November 10, 1710; and since he was imprisoned by the Mascates at Recife during the siege of the following year, he was not able to act as the leader of an embryo independence party then, as otherwise he might, perhaps, have done. Once the leadership of the planters was assumed by the Bishop, there was no question of a decisive break with the mother country, only a determination to secure some political and economic concessions from the Crown. On the other hand, the savage repression of the planters by Felix Machado, and the insolence displayed by the Mascates in their hour of victory, did undoubtedly contribute to exacerbate and prolong the bitterness between the "sons of the soil" and the Portuguese immigrants. To this extent, these factors stimulated the growth of national consciousness, which was inevitable in any case, and which was manifested a century later in the abortive revolution of 1817.

VI. BAY OF ALL SAINTS

THE FAMOUS BRAZILIAN sociologist, Gilberto Freyre, is the author of a small work on Bahia which is humorously entitled, "Bay of All Saints and of nearly all the sins," [1] and in truth the city's reputation for both sanctity and sinfulness was not undeserved. As is the way with mankind the world over, sinners rather than saints predominated in the capital of colonial Brazil; but colorful manifestations of both the sacred and the profane in the daily life of the city are recorded by many observant travelers. On the one hand were the numerous and richly decorated churches—popularly if erroneously supposed to number three hundred and sixty-five, one for every day in the year—crowded with worshipers, whose real or apparent devotion impressed even prejudiced Protestant visitors. On the other hand were the daily— or rather, nightly—deaths by murder most foul, and the sexual license typified by the richly dressed mulata prostitutes. The multitude of Negro slaves, on whom the life of the city and the cultivation of the neighboring sugar and tobacco plantations depended, formed a perpetual reminder that Brazil had an African soul.[2]

The City of the Savior (*Cidade do Salvador*) was the capital of Brazil from 1549, when it was founded on the southeastern shore of the Bay of All Saints (*Bahia de Todos os Santos*), until

126

1763, when the seat of the colonial government was moved to Rio de Janeiro. Though Salvador was the name of the city, the looser designation of Bahia was usually employed instead, even in official correspondence. The term Bahia was also applied to the vast captaincy of that name, which confined roughly with the River São Francisco on the north and west, and with the captaincies of Ilheus and Minas Gerais on the south. Since bay, city, and captaincy alike were indiscriminately termed "Bahia" for centuries, it will, I hope, be apparent from the context to which one I am referring hereafter.

As mentioned in Chapter i, Bahia had long since outstripped "Golden Goa" to become the second city in the Portuguese empire, being surpassed only by Lisbon in population and in importance. An Italian visitor in 1699 estimated the population of the city and its environs at 700,000 souls. This is certainly a great exaggeration, and about 100,000 would seem a more reasonable figure, although we have insufficient data for anything more than very rough estimates.[3] It was the seat of the governors-general and viceroys, and, from 1675 onward, of the only archbishopric in Portuguese America. It was a thriving entrepôt of trade with Portugal and West Africa, the chief whaling station in the South Atlantic, and boasted a shipbuilding yard of some importance. It was also the seat of a *Relação* or High Court; and if it did not possess a university, as did several cities in Spanish America, this was because the citizens' petition that the local Jesuit College should be raised to that status was rejected by the Crown on the advice of the University of Coimbra.[4]

The city was built, like Lisbon and Porto in the mother country, or like Luanda in Angola, Macao in China, and Rio de Janeiro and Olinda in Brazil, on very uneven and hilly ground, running steeply into the sea. The commanding heights were occupied by churches, convents, public buildings, and the town houses of the gentry. The long narrow waterfront contained the commercial quarter with warehouses, stores, shops, and the like. There was thus an upper and a lower city, connected by narrow, tortuous, and steep streets and alleys, which made wheeled traffic virtually impossible. Slaves and (to a lesser degree) pack horses or mules were used for the transport of goods, and litters were employed by the gentry and merchants instead of coaches or carriages. In other words, it was a typical Portuguese city, medieval in its lack of planning and in its haphazard growth, forming a strong contrast to the methodically laid-out Spanish-American towns.

One of the best descriptions of Bahia at the end of the seventeenth century, is that by William Dampier, who stayed there in April and May, 1699. His description is worth reproducing in full, although he does not mention the great windlass which was used for hauling heavy goods between the upper and lower towns, and which was the forerunner of the electric elevator that is such a prominent feature of the city today. His description of the streets is evidently rather flattering; but the general accuracy of his observations is attested by comparison with those of Ramponi and others who were there about the same time.[5]

The town itself consists of about 2,000 houses; the major part of which cannot be seen from the harbour; but so many as appear in sight, with a great mixture of trees between them, and all placed on a rising hill, make a very pleasant prospect. . . . Here lives an Archbishop, who has a fine palace in the town; and the governor's palace is a fair stone building, and looks handsome to the sea, though but indifferently furnished within. Both Spaniards and Portuguese in their plantations abroad, as I have generally observed, affecting to have large houses; but are little curious about furniture, except pictures some of them.[6] The houses of the town are two or three stories high, the walls thick and strong, being built with stone, with a covering of pantile; and many of them have balconies. The principal streets are large, and all of them paved or pitched with small stones. There are also parades on the most eminent places of the town, and many gardens, as well within the town as in the outparts of it, wherein are fruit trees, herbs, salladings and flowers in great variety, but ordered with no great care nor art.

Nearly all visitors to eighteenth-century Bahia were deeply impressed by the number and magnificence of its convents and churches. Even Mrs. Nathaniel Edward Kindersley, who felt that "no Protestant ever saw a monastery, without reflecting as I do now, on the indolence and inutility of a monastic life, and the folly of its mortifications," felt constrained to admit that the convents at Bahia were "handsome buildings." She was still more complimentary about the churches. "Some of them are large and superb," she wrote, "and by being unencumbered with pews, the double rows of pillars have a very fine effect, and give the whole choir an open airy appearance which our churches can never have: they are kept in the greatest order, and adorned, particularly the altars, with carving, paintings, and gilding; with candlesticks and ornaments of gold and silver to a vast expence." [7]

Roman Catholic visitors were naturally even more enthusiastic, and one of them considered that the sacristy of the Jesuit church might "passe pour une des plus belles du monde, tant pour la grandeur que pour les peintures exquises dont elle est ornée, & ou ces Peres ont employé des plus celebres Peintres d'Italie." [8] It would be easy to multiply such quotations, and there is overwhelming evidence to support the assertion of contemporary Portuguese writers that their countrymen were particularly distinguished for the lavishness and generosity with which they endowed and maintained their religious establishments throughout their overseas empire. An outward-bound Jesuit missionary, after visiting the island of Mozambique in 1691, observed that: "The churches are beautifully clean, even the smallest hermitages. If God still keeps us in India, it is because of the grandeur, magnificence, and ostentation with which the churches are maintained and the divine worship celebrated. The smallest village church here can put to shame those of the best towns in Portugal." [9] Similarly, richly decorated churches and monumental monasteries were not confined to the capital of colonial Brazil, but their ruins, or their restored originals, are to be found in many decayed towns and in rural solitudes today.

The Bahian churches which aroused the admiration of foreign visitors, were built, for the most part, in the century 1650–1750. These churches, like their Portuguese prototypes, were characterized by a persistent preference for low rather than tall buildings, and for stable rectangular forms. The most important surviving monument of this period is the actual cathedral of Bahia, formerly the Jesuit Church, and built between 1657 and 1672. In plan and elevation it is of late Renaissance—now more often called Mannerist—conception, with emphasis upon verticality and many rectilinear divisions. Entirely divorced from the spatial and plastic concepts of the Italian baroque, it belongs to the architectural tradition established by the Jesuits in Portugal, and brought by them to Brazil. Hence the term "Jesuit style" is frequently applied to all the late seventeenth- and early eighteenth-century Brazilian churches, irrespective of their real designers and constructors. Although the term "baroque" is also applied to these Luso-Brazilian churches, there was, in reality, little Portuguese baroque; and what little there was, had a delayed impact in Brazil owing to the belated persistence of Mannerism. Despite the claims made for these colonial churches by some of their more fervent admirers, it is doubtful if they attained the standards of their richer and more imposing Spanish-American counterparts.

The attention of eighteenth-century visitors to Bahia, as of twentieth-century tourists, was concentrated chiefly on the churches and convents, which, whatever their defects, were certainly more spacious and imposing than the public buildings and private houses. The upper city at Salvador, however, did possess some important mansions, built after the style of the old palaces of the Alfama region at Lisbon. The principal apartments were on the top floor, the ground floor being reserved for the accommodation of slaves and of merchandise or heavy goods. The chief attraction of these old Bahian houses is their elaborately carved doorways, made for the most part of local stone. This coarse sandstone was not, incidentally, of good building quality. Hence the churches were sometimes built, in whole or in part, with *pedro-lioz,* a cream-colored and rose-veined pseudo-marble, imported from Portugal.[10]

Although there were some selfless and even saintly men among the secular clergy, the general standard seems to have been deplorably low. French visitors, such as Le Gentil de la Barbinais in 1720, were particularly scathing in their denunciation of the laxity and immorality of the Bahian clergy. As regards the Religious Orders, the Jesuits and the Capuchins were generally respected for their high standards, but the representatives of the other Orders were mostly on a par with the secular clergy. The sense of a religious vocation was not strongly implanted among the Brazilian-born Portuguese; and the missionary spirit was conspicuously lacking for the reasons explained by a French friar who knew the country and the people well.

Premierement, il y en a tres-peu qui se veuillent donner la peine d'apprendre la langue, sans quoy neanmoins il est impossible de les catechiser comme il faut, pour en faire de bons Chrêtiens. 2. Ils ont presque tous un extrême mépris pour les Indiens, ils les traitent de chiens, & les traitent en chiens. 3. Ils sont interessés encore qu'en d'autres occasions ils soient liberaux jusqu'à la prodigalité. 4. Etans nés dans un Païs tres-chaud, et vivans dans l'oisiveté, & dans une grande liberté parmy les esclaves des deux sexes presque tous nuds, dont ils disposent à leur volonté. Il est tres-difficile que changeant l'état Laïque dans Ecclesiastique ou Regulier, qu'ils soient bien chastes.[11]

The Jesuits were also seriously worried by the great difficulty of finding suitable Brazilian-born candidates for admission to their Society. They noted that the Iberian conviction of the essential indignity of manual labor was carried to such lengths in Brazil that, with very rare exceptions, nobody would become a lay brother.[12] They also blamed the enervating tropical climate and the lax upbringing of boys in slave households for the dearth of true religious vocations; but neither they nor Fr. Martin de Nantes mentions another factor which must have contributed to the prevailing low standard of the clergy. This was the Portuguese practice, explicitly recommended by Dom Francisco de Mello in his classic *Guide for Married Men,* that a father should not keep his bastard boys at home, but ship them off to India or make them take the tonsure.[13] All things considered, it is not surprising that the official correspondence of the period abounds with complaints of lax and simoniacal clergy, or that many priests seemed to be following a mercantile rather than an ecclesiastical calling.[14] Instances of clerical concupiscence were likewise relatively common; although few of them attained the notoriety achieved by a canon of Bahia Cathedral who lived openly with a planter's wife by whom he had a child.[15]

The frequent complaints of the misdemeanors of many of the colonial clergy did not alter the fact that as a body they were most powerful and influential, being held in awesome regard by the majority of the laity. The Portuguese had a deep-rooted tradition of respect (amounting to veneration) for the Cloth, though some contemporaries claimed that it was less noticeable in Brazil than in the mother country and in Portuguese Asia. Be this as it may, it was a common theme in classical Portuguese literature that the worst priest was superior to the best layman.[16] Nuno Marques Pereira, who is not sparing in his criticisms of the Luso-Brazilian clergy, explains that nevertheless the Roman Catholic priesthood is superior to all other human callings and even to that of the angels. "With five words they can bring God Himself down into their hands; and with another five they can open the gates of heaven to a sinner and close those of hell: the first five words being those of consecration, and the second five those of absolution." [17]

This emphasis on the sacramental and sacerdotal aspects of religion helps to explain why the Portuguese priesthood enjoyed such exceptional consideration, a fact noted by all foreign travelers in Portugal and her overseas possessions. There were, of course, other contributory reasons, such as the superior education of the clergy as compared with the laity, and the exemption of the former from most forms of taxation, which greatly enhanced their social position and prestige. I think it safe to assert that the Portuguese regular and secular clergy, whatever their shortcomings as individuals, were more highly regarded as a body throughout the Portuguese-speaking world than their colleagues in any other country—with the possible exception of the Philippines and some parts of Spanish America. During the two centuries which elapsed between the time of King João III and that of Pombal, Portugal was probably the most priest-ridden country in Christendom, and only exceeded elsewhere in this respect by Tibet. Admittedly, Nuno Marques Pereira was not alone in asserting that Brazil was less devout in this respect than the rest of the Portuguese empire. If this was so, the difference was not great enough to impress foreign visitors, whose accounts confirm the testimony of Fr. Martin de Nantes that the Portuguese of Brazil "ont beaucoup de respect pour les Religieux, & encore plus pour les missionaires." [18]

It may be added that the Religious who were worthy of this respect were not so few as the accounts of many visitors to Bahia would imply. They were chiefly to be found among the Jesuits, their exemplar being the long-lived Alexandre de Gusmão (1629–1724), who ended his days in the odor of sanctity in the seminary which he had founded at Belem da Cachoeira. He was a prolific educational and ascetic writer, but it is to be feared that his *Arte de crear bem os filhos na idade da Puericia* (Lisbon, 1685), did not find many adepts in Bahia. Another admirable ecclesiastic was the Archbishop, Sebastião Monteiro da Vide, whom even the hostile Le Gentil de la Barbinais described as a "saint vieillard" in 1717. One of his predecessors, D. Fr. Manuel da Ressureição, earned the commendation of Nuno Marques Pereira for his efforts to secure better treatment for the slaves. Unfortunately, the example of these and of other conscientious clerics had no apparent effect on the bulk of the clergy.

However much Protestant observers might deplore the all-pervading prevalence of "Popery" at Bahia, they could not deny the devotional fervor displayed by all classes of the population. No respectable man was to be seen in the streets without a sword at his side and a rosary in his hand, and with another, as often as not, round his neck. At the sound of the Angelus bell, passersby knelt down in the streets and said their prayers. The churches were thronged with worshipers of all classes, and even the censorious Mrs. Kindersley felt bound to commend "the warm and steady devotion of the common people here." She was particularly impressed by the piety of the converted Negro slaves. "They are all made Christians as soon as bought, and it is amazing to see the effect the pageantry of the Roman Catholic religion has upon their uninformed minds; they are as devout as the common people in our cities are profane; constant at their worship, obedient to their preceptors without scruple, and inspired with all the enthusiasm of devotion; the gilded pomp, the solemnity of processions, the mysterious rites, the fear as well as the admiration of their ghostly fathers, all conspire to render them so." [19]

The religious processions which took place on many of the feast days of the Church were indeed a striking feature of life at Bahia, blending the sacred and the profane together in the most intriguing way. Portuguese Catholicism has always tended to concentrate on the external manifestations of the Christian cult, and the large African element at Bahia undoubtedly strengthened this tendency. Popular amusements were few, and the gaily dressed and richly decorated religious processions, with their masqueraders, musicians, and dancers, served social needs which are nowadays supplied by the dance-hall, the theater, and the cinema. They afforded the sole opportunity for the mingling of all classes on terms approaching equality, even if they sometimes ended in rioting and disorder. A French voyager in 1718 was astonished to see the elderly and dignified viceroy dancing before the high altar in honor of São Gonçalo d'Amarante,[20] just as if he had been a choirboy in Seville Cathedral on the Feast of Corpus Christi. Le Gentil de la Barbinais added that a Brazilian Portuguese was quite capable of spending his whole year's income on celebrating his patron saint's feast day. "Si on ôtoit aux Portuguais leurs Saints et leurs Maitresses," he concluded, "ils deviendront trop riches."

These colorful religious processions were organized by the lay brotherhoods or confraternities (*Irmandades*), which were voluntary associations of the faithful for charitable and pious ends. Much of the social work that would be done nowadays (if at all) by the government or by the Church, was then performed by the brotherhoods. The principal Religious Orders each had their own affiliations of such laymen, and there was often considerable rivalry between them. Their social status varied from those restricted to pure whites of good family to others whose members were composed solely of Negro slaves. As a rule their composition was on racial lines, whites, mulattoes, and Negroes each having their own *Irmandade;* but a few made no distinctions of class or color, or between bond and free. Some brotherhoods were devoted to purely pious ends; others had a guild character, their membership being limited to a particular trade or calling; and others combined social and religious activities in about equal proportions.[21]

The first half of the eighteenth century saw the full flowering of these brotherhoods in Brazil, where some of them amassed very considerable wealth. Childless members, who had made their money in mining, mercantile, or other pursuits, often bequeathed their entire fortune to their brotherhood. The palatial hospice for respectable women attached to the Misericordia at Bahia was built with a legacy of 80,000 *cruzados* left by João de Mattos. Even those with family responsibilities often bequeathed a considerable sum, and smaller legacies were an almost daily occurrence. The Tertiary Order of St. Francis, despite its founder's fame as an exemplar of holy poverty, was particularly celebrated for its wealth and exclusiveness, and membership thereof was eagerly sought by the richest and most powerful.[22] Originally these brotherhoods had been content to build or endow chapels in existing churches for the devotion of their members; but with increasing prosperity they often financed the building and maintenance of imposing churches of their own. Sometimes, indeed, their ambition outran their resources. In the second half of the eighteenth century they were often compelled to ask the Crown for money to complete churches which they had begun in more spacious days. All the brotherhoods made a point of celebrating the feast day of their patron saint with special splendor, and the money spent on these occasions sometimes ran the more extravagant members heavily into debt.

The most famous brotherhood was that of the Holy House of Mercy (*Santa Casa da Misericordia*), a charitable institution primarily concerned with the relief of orphans, widows, prisoners, and the sick. The Misericordia maintained hospitals in many towns, and often provided food and drink for prisoners who would otherwise have perished in the noisome and ill-found jails. The rules of the original Misericordia elaborated at Lisbon in 1498 provided for a brotherhood of three hundred members, of whom half were gentry and half *mecanicos* or plebeians. The branches that were founded by the Portuguese from Brazil to Japan were sometimes severely selective, admitting only those of gentle birth, or those who could pass themselves off as such. On the other hand, when the Crown authorized the establishment of a Misericordia at Villa Rica de Ouro Preto, Minas Gerais, in April, 1738, it expressly stipulated that there should be no discrimination between "nobres" and "mecanicos" in that institution.

The funds that supported the Misericordia were also derived from private charity and from legacies in mortmain. The accumulated capital was not supposed to be invested or given out on loan, save under the most rigorous safeguards, but abuses inevitably occurred. The viceroy, Count of Sabugosa, complained to the Crown in 1729, that the Misericordia at Bahia was in serious difficulties owing to prolonged maladministration by the board of guardians. They had made a practice of loaning money from the Misericordia funds to their friends and relatives on inadequate security. They had also, he alleged, misappropriated much of the money which had been left by testators for the celebration of masses for their souls, sending it to Portugal instead of spending it at Bahia. He severely criticized the way in which elections to the board of guardians were "rigged," with the object of electing persons who would be complacent about the granting of loans on flimsy collateral. Similar complaints were voiced at this period about the Misericordias of Luanda and Recife; but all these institutions have survived the vicissitudes of centuries to function at the present day, albeit in an emasculated form.[23]

Membership of these brotherhoods was naturally confined to men, but women were at least allowed to watch their processions, which was one of the very few diversions permitted them in colonial days. Even the Spaniards made fun of the jealous seclusion in which the Portuguese of all classes kept—or strove to keep—their wives and daughters. The Portuguese themselves were not ashamed of this, save for a few eccentrics like Thomé Pinheiro da Veiga, whose *Fastigimia,* written in the early seventeenth century, is full of mordant criticism of his compatriots' habit of secluding their women. The more general attitude was exemplified by the proverb that a really virtuous woman left her house only thrice during her lifetime: for her christening, for her marriage, and for her funeral. The harem-like seclusion in which nearly all upper-class women were kept, inevitably gave their menfolk an unenviable reputation as husbands abroad. A Portuguese envoy in London, Dr. António de Sousa de Macedo, observed in 1642: "The English women are so convinced of the subjection in which Portuguese women are kept, that it would be very difficult for a Portuguese man to find anyone willing to marry him here," although he slyly added, "there are many women who would like them as lovers." [24] All travelers in the Portuguese empire were equally uncomplimentary about the rigorous seclusion of Portuguese women, from Huighen van Linschoten in sixteenth-century Goa to Maria Graham in nineteenth-century Bahia.

This misogynistic attitude is attributed by some authorities to the influence of the long Moorish occupation during the Middle Ages, and by others to the Roman Catholic Church. Admittedly this latter body was certainly no advocate of the equality of the sexes, but Luso-Brazilian custom went too far even for those prelates who took a Pauline view of women. We find the Archbishop of Bahia complaining in 1751 that the local girls could not be induced to attend the lessons given in the Ursuline Convent,

137

owing to the opposition of their parents. These latter, "despite the continual complaints of prelates, missionaries, confessors, and preachers, kept their daughters in such strict seclusion that they rarely let them go out to hear Mass, much less for any other reason." The Archbishop added that this practice was not confined to white women, but was imitated by colored girls, "and by any others who can make confession at home." [25] This attitude did not help to enliven family life in colonial Brazil, which the great Brazilian historian, Capistrano de Abreu, characterized as "taciturn father, obedient wife, cowed children."

However tedious the lives of the Bahian ladies may have been, their lot was in most ways more enviable than that of their slaves. Something has been said about the mistreatment of slaves in the first chapter and more will be said in the next, but a few observations will not be out of place here. A royal dispatch of March 1, 1700, denouncing the barbarity with which many slaveowners of both sexes treated their slaves, stated that these atrocities originated on plantations in the interior, but had lately spread to the cities and towns. The Crown condemned as particularly shameful the practice of lady owners living on the immoral earnings of their female slaves, who were not merely encouraged but forced into a life of prostitution.[26] This practice was a reprehensible extension of the more common habit whereby women slaves were allowed to work on their own account as cooks, seamstresses, or street hawkers, provided they paid their owners a fixed sum out of their daily or weekly earnings. Similarly, male slaves who were skilled laborers were often allowed to work as journeymen, on condition that they paid their masters an agreed proportion of their wages.

Miserable though the life of Negro slaves often was, they were not entirely without legal means of redress, though practice in this matter usually seems to have fallen far short of precept. A Crown decree of November 5, 1711, ordained that as a result of representations made by the Bishop of Rio de Janeiro on the cruelty with which slaves were treated by their owners, the governor was to appoint a solicitor through whom slaves could sue for redress. The salary of this official was to be a charge on the Crown, and the governor was enjoined "to take every care in ascertaining whether the ill-treatment of slaves continues, and to use all means to ensure that it does not, so that the clamorous plaints of these poor wretches may cease on this account." The activities of this slaves' advocate or solicitor have not left any trace in such documents as I have seen, nor do I know whether similar appointments were made in other cities, though it would seem quite likely *a priori*. Twenty-two years previously the Archbishop of Bahia had intervened to compel a cruel lady slaveowner to sell "for a just price" the slave girl she was mistreating, and the Crown upheld his intervention.[27]

A curious set of documents in the Bahia archives shows that on occasion the complaints of maltreated slaves were personally and sympathetically considered by "The Magnanimous King." These documents concern the case of a Negro slave, António Fernandes, who complained that he had been savagely tortured to extract from him a confession of something he had not done. Dom João V ordered the viceroy at Bahia personally to investigate the truth or otherwise of these allegations, meanwhile suspending all judicial proceedings against the accused. The evidence given at the subsequent viceregal enquiry was somewhat conflicting, though the viceroy ends up his report by admitting that if the allegations were true, "this case was the most serious, the most cruel, and the most tyrannical which has happened in Brazil since the discovery thereof."

The witnesses who were heard included two delegates of the Misericordia, a priest and a layman, who were present at the torturing of the accused, in order to see that this was not excessively severe. They deposed that the victim had fainted and seemed in a bad way, "but we cannot affirm whether this was entirely due to the torture, or partly to dissimulation." The doctor and the surgeon, who were likewise present at the torture by virtue of their respective functions, declared that the amount applied was not excessive and that the prisoner's reactions after two applications were normal, although they had forbidden a third bout. The surgeon added revealingly: "in the upshot, the accused was left sound and unmarked, which was not the case with many others whom I saw when I was acting as surgeon to the municipal hospital, for they had been maimed for life by the treatment they received." [28]

The frequency of slave prostitution and of other obstacles in the way of a sound family life, such as the double standard of chastity as between husbands and wives, all made for a great deal of casual miscegenation between white men and colored women. This in turn produced many unwanted children, who, if they lived to grow up, became criminals and vagrants, living on their wits and on the margin of society. Brazil, like all European colonies, was then used as a dumping ground for undesirables and as a place of banishment for those who fell foul of the law in the mother country. These factors, complicated by the periodic deportation of gypsies from Portugal to Brazil, presented the authorities at Bahia and elsewhere with a problem that caused them constant concern.

One of the ways in which they tried to mitigate this evil was by conniving at the unauthorized return of deportees to their place of origin, but this was a procedure which cut both ways. In 1698, for example, we find the Crown complaining that many convicts exiled to Brazil were returning to Portugal before completing their sentences. Thirty years later, we find the viceroy at Bahia complaining still more forcibly that criminals whom he had exiled to Angola and Benguela were constantly returning to Brazil owing to the culpable negligence of the West African authorities. He asked the Crown to reprimand the governor of Angola for this, and to ensure that such exiles were sent into the interior of the colony and that all ships leaving Luanda were rigorously searched. The Crown complied with these requests, but similar complaints recurred at frequent intervals. Just as there was a triangular traffic in bullion, sugar, and slaves between Portugal, Brazil, and Angola, so there was a three-way interchange of criminals and vagrants, and not always in the direction which was intended. [29]

The task of keeping law and order with a large and shifting criminal element in the urban population was not an easy one. Ramponi observed after his visit to Bahia in 1699 that anyone who went out in the streets of Salvador after nightfall did so at considerable risk. Every morning the corpses of twenty-five or thirty newly murdered people were found lying in the streets, despite the vigilance of the soldiers who patrolled the streets at night. This number may be exaggerated, but there is plenty of independent evidence to show that the streets of eighteenth-century Bahia were exceedingly unsafe after dark.[30]

The garrison of Bahia made a favorable impression on William Dampier at the close of the seventeenth century. "Here are about 400 soldiers in garrison. They commonly draw up and exercise in a large parade before the governor's house; and many of them attend him when he goes abroad. The soldiers are decently clad in brown linnen, which in these hot countries is far better than woollen; but I never saw any clad in linnen but only these. Besides the soldiers in pay, he can soon have some thousands of men up in arms on occasion." [31]

These regular soldiers were part of the permanent garrison of two infantry regiments, called respectively the Old and New, with a nominal strength of eight hundred men each. As can be gathered from Dampier's account, they were never up to strength; owing to the "inexplicable repugnance" of the inhabitants of Brazil to volunteer for military service, as successive viceroys bitterly complained.[32] Their colleagues in Spanish America, incidentally, made similar complaints about the extreme reluctance of Mexicans and Peruvians to serve as soldiers, for the American-born did not take kindly to military discipline. Opportunities of earning a more profitable and a less constrained living were easily available, and a soldier's pay was wretchedly small and usually in arrears. Moreover, the empty spaces and huge distances of South America greatly facilitated desertions. Drafts sent out as reinforcements or replacements from Portugal tended to abscond to the gold fields soon after their arrival, and the wastage from disease was also high. It proved impossible to maintain an adequate garrison in the southern outpost of Colonia do Sacramento, where service was particularly unpopular and where desertion was particularly easy.

Soldiers being difficult to recruit and hard to retain, extreme measures were taken to keep them in the service. Even a private soldier could only be discharged with the personal approval of the king, and the promotion and posting of sergeants overseas was a matter for consideration by the Crown. Two instances of the former practice will suffice. In April, 1730, the king ordered the viceroy to investigate a petition which the Crown had received from a veteran soldier of the Bahia garrison. This man asked for his discharge on compassionate grounds, "since he could not live on his slender pay" as a private soldier, being a married man with several small children. The viceroy in his reply vouched for the accuracy of the facts stated by the petitioner, who, he added, "is so poor that he has not even a single slave to serve him" in the little allotment which he cultivated when not on duty. He was accordingly discharged so that he could seek a more lucrative occupation. A mulatto soldier who petitioned for his discharge in the following year, in order to support his widowed mother, was not so fortunate. The Count of Sabugosa advised the Crown that the petitioner "has no physical defect which might excuse him from the royal service, nor is his mother one of those widows who are eligible under the law, since she is a colored woman; wherefore I advise Your Majesty to withold your consent."[33]

White and colored soldiers served alongside each other in the ranks of the two regular infantry regiments; but the militia units were organized on a color basis, each company being commanded by officers of the same hue as the men. Despite the reluctance of the local whites to serve under or alongside men of color in the Bahia militia, the Crown ordered that they should do so in 1730. The Conde de Sabugosa began to implement this order, but I do not know to what extent he was successful.[34] By the end of the century the four militia regiments were again organized on a differential color basis.

With a view to stimulating recruiting and to eliminating desertion, the Crown ordered in 1731 that soldiers who volunteered for service in Brazil need only stay in the colony for ten years. They could then apply for a transfer to Portugal, if they wished, and provided that they had not married in the meantime. As regards Angola, which really was a "white man's grave," the tour of duty had previously been reduced to six years, although this concession was likewise limited to unmarried men.[35] Needless to say, enough volunteers were never forthcoming, and the garrison of Angola was supplemented by drafts of convicts from Brazil throughout the eighteenth century.

One of the perennial difficulties of the Bahia garrison was the supply of uniforms. This was on a contract system, but whereas the contractors wanted to be paid in money, the Crown preferred to pay in sugar.[36] There were endless disputes over the quality of the material, and whether the uniforms should be supplied ready-made, or tailored at the soldier's expense from the material supplied by the contractor. The municipal council was responsible for paying the contractor and also for providing a basic ration of manioc flour. This body was often in arrears with its obligations, which led to a mutinous demonstration by the garrison in October, 1688. Much more serious was the mutiny of the Old Regiment in May, 1728, which was directed against a judge who specialized in giving stiff sentences to soldiers accused of theft. The Count of Sabugosa suppressed this outbreak in the manner which was almost invariably employed by Portuguese colonial governors in similar crises, a classic example of which will be given in the next chapter. Briefly, the viceroy promised the redress of grievances and gave the men an unconditional pardon in the king's name. Then, soon after they had returned to duty and all was quiet, he seized the ringleaders by a mixture of force and guile, and had them summarily tried and executed.[37]

Despite the cruelty with which he acted on this and on a few other occasions,[38] the Count of Sabugosa can be termed one of the best viceroys Brazil ever had. The captaincy of Bahia in particular was much indebted to his energetic and enlightened administration. The representatives of the Crown had supervised (rather than governed) Brazil from the city of Salvador since 1549, but, though they had a wide discretion in the infliction of capital punishment, their other powers were never so great as those of the Spanish viceroys of Mexico and Peru. Moreover, as was the case in Spanish America, the viceroy of Brazil's writ was only effective in inverse proportion to the distance of the remoter settlements from the capital at Bahia. The governor of each captaincy corresponded directly with the Crown through the Overseas Council, and the viceroy only exercised a very loose supervision over most of them, when he had any control at all. In 1722, the Crown, at Sabugosa's request, ordered the governors of the other captaincies to keep the viceroy at Bahia fully informed of what transpired in their respective spheres, and to obey his orders so far as these did not conflict with those which they received directly from the Crown; but ten years later Sabugosa complained that this admonition had had little effect on most of the recipients and none at all upon the governor of Minas Gerais.[39]

Unlike their Spanish colleagues, the great majority of the Portuguese colonial governors were professional military men, with no experience of the law or of administration until they received their first governorship. Vasco Fernandez Cezar de Menezes was no exception to this rule. Born in 1673, he served in the War of the Spanish Succession, and as viceroy of Portuguese India from 1712 to 1717. His health was none of the best when he was appointed Viceroy of Brazil in 1720, and his long tenure of office was handicapped by alternating periods of unseasonable droughts and heavy rains. Nevertheless, his conduct in this responsible and exacting post gave such satisfaction to the Crown that he was created Count of Sabugosa in 1729, and only relieved of the office six years later, after repeatedly requesting a successor on the grounds of ill health. His official correspondence with Lisbon during these fifteen years shows that he was a man of great force of character who never hesitated to write frankly to his royal master. His dispatches also show with what skill he contrived to strike a balance between the selfish interests of the Crown and those of the citizens of Salvador and the planters of the *Reconcavo*.[40]

Like other viceroys and governors-general who could be mentioned, the Count of Sabugosa was not always on the best of terms with his senior (and largely nominal) subordinates. He was often at odds with the senior crown judge (*Ouvidor Geral*) at Bahia, and he carried on a veritable vendetta with Dom Lourenço de Almeida, the governor of Minas Gerais from 1721 to 1732. The latter returned his dislike, and the way in which these two fidalgos denounced each other in their respective correspondence with the Crown must by turns have amused, angered, and, perhaps, bewildered the king and his advisers. Beyond periodically enjoining these two governors to coöperate amicably, the Crown did nothing to resolve this feud, obstinately refusing to dismiss either of them. This, no doubt, was because such a state of affairs, though it did not make for administrative harmony, fitted in with the colonial system of checks and balances, which ensured that the misdeeds or mistakes of any one governor would speedily be reported by a disgruntled colleague.[41]

The wealth increasingly derived from the Brazilian gold fields in the early eighteenth century accentuated the desire of the Crown to control the colonial administration and expenditure more closely. This tendency was further strengthened by the wish of Dom João V to emulate Louis XIV, and inaugurate a golden age of royal absolutism. Dom João V is usually represented as being the most sluggish and the most superstitious of the Portuguese kings, active only in his amours and in his prodigal expenditure on churches and music. He certainly was a drooling bigot by the time he died in 1750, but he was a very different character before the epileptic stroke which crippled him six years earlier. Lord Tyrawly, who knew him well, considered he had "a piercing intelligence," and was "extremely quick and lively" in the apprehension and dispatch of official business.[42] The staunchly Protestant Tyrawly was never unduly complimentary about Roman

Catholics, even if they were crowned heads. His estimate of D. João V is confirmed by a study of the voluminous papers of the Overseas Council which were submitted to him for his approval. These papers frequently bear marginal annotations in the king's hand, proving that he did not sign them without reading them, and that he did not always accept the advice of his councillors. If further proof of Dom João V's capacity is required, the reader will find it in the richly documented studies of Jaime Cortesão and Eduardo Brazão, which are listed in my bibliography.

The greater the desire of the Crown to tighten its control of the colonial administration at Lisbon, the greater became the amount of paper work, which was already formidable at the beginning of the reign. It soon became impossible for the king to cope with the flood of documents from all quarters of the Portuguese empire, ranging from pathetic petitions by obscure widows to matters of high policy adumbrated by viceroys and archbishops. The issue of a copper coinage for Angola, the terms of a whaling contract at Bahia, the treatment of nautch girls at Goa, the activities of smugglers in Minas Gerais, and the ecclesiastical complications of the Chinese Rites were all alike grist to the Crown's mill, and all final decisions concerning them had to be made by the king himself.

In an effort to reduce this intolerable burden and the vexatious delays in the dispatch of all business, an edict was promulgated in 1713, whereby many matters which hitherto had been submitted to the king for his personal decision could now be dealt with by one or another of the royal councils in his name. Nevertheless, many categories were still reserved for his personal decision, including "all grants, of whatever nature they may be, which have to be paid from my exchequer." Since this clause involved the overwhelming majority of awards, appointments, postings, and promotions, not to mention the recipients of an ever growing pension list—the so-called *filhos da folha,* or "sons of the ledger" —the king's working day was still a very full one. His task was not lightened by the fact that his Overseas Councillors, though evidently conscientious, were also exceedingly prolix on paper.

They clearly had not mastered the art of summarizing the lengthy dispatches from overseas governors which they laid before the king. Consequently, routine business still took a long time to transact at the Portuguese Court, although not so long as it was to do in the next reign. King Joseph's dictatorial minister, the Marquis of Pombal, insisted on handling everything himself, often with delays of anything from two to ten years.[43]

A similar state of affairs prevailed on the other side of the ocean. Several viceroys at Goa and at Bahia complained of the excessive paper work with which they had to contend. Both Sabugosa and his successor explained to the king that the clerks of the Bahia secretariat were overworked and underpaid. Wrote the Count of Galveas in 1736: "their poverty is such that they cannot appear respectably dressed in Government House . . . and their work is so excessive that it often lasts day and night, Sundays and holidays, not leaving them any time in which to find some other occupation that might help them." Almost identical observations came from Minas Gerais, where the governor complained that he often had to help the secretary to write his dispatches after office hours.[44]

One of the matters which had been left to the decision of the Brazilian viceroys or governors-general by a decree of 1693 was the creation of new townships in the interior, provided that the expense of erecting a council house, jail, and municipal buildings was borne by the local inhabitants. The more capable and energetic administrators, such as Dom João de Lencastre, the Marquis of Angeja, and the Count of Sabugosa made full use of their powers. They were rightly convinced that the erection of such townships was the best means of civilizing and developing the rough settlements of the *sertão*. When the Overseas Councillors claimed prior consultation on this matter, the Marquis of Angeja tartly observed that if the viceroy at Bahia was not competent to make such decisions on his own responsibility then the king should not have chosen him to govern Brazil.[45] This reproach seems to have had the desired effect, at any rate for a time.

The Count of Sabugosa was particularly active in founding

townships in the *Reconcavo*. On erecting that of Maragogipe in 1724, he pointed with pride to the precedent of Jacobina. No fewer than 532 persons had been murdered with firearms in that unruly mining camp between 1710 and 1721, when he promoted it to a municipality, complete with a town council, magistrate, and militia. In the three years which had elapsed since that date, only three murders had been recorded, and these were unpremeditated affairs with knives and swords. Similarly, Maragogipe, which was described as a "den of thieves" (*covil de ladrões*) in 1716, became a model municipality in 1724, when the grateful townsmen offered the viceroy an annual contribution of 2,000 *alqueires* of manioc flour for the Bahia garrison's basic ration.[46]

The municipal councillors of these new towns were sometimes inclined to wax fat and kick. Those of Cachoeira requested the Crown to grant them the same privileges as were enjoyed (theoretically at any rate) by the citizens of Salvador. These privileges in turn were based on those of Oporto, which had been extended to the colonial capital in 1646. The Oporto privileges, incidentally, had already been granted to the much smaller and poorer city of São Luís do Maranhão, and were subsequently extended to Rio de Janeiro and São Paulo. The most cherished of these privileges was that of immunity from judicial torture, save only in the exceptional circumstances (high treason and the like) when this could also be inflicted on noblemen and gentlemen. The aldermen and officials of the Bahia municipal council were also "recognized and acknowledged as being gentry," as were their children. They and their sons were exempted from military service, save in times of great danger, or when the Crown expressly ordered otherwise. They were also exempted from certain statutory liabilities, such as having soldiers billeted in their houses, or having their dwellings, storehouses, horses, carts, and boats confiscated for the use of civil and military officials on government business.[47]

Apart from these enviable privileges, a seat on the municipal council naturally gave the occupant a chance of forwarding his own interests and those of his friends and relatives. On the other hand, the position of councillor involved him in many duties, some of them onerous at times, though the Salvador Council only met twice weekly, on Wednesdays and Saturdays. As noted above, the council had the thankless task of collecting and disbursing on behalf of the Crown the funds for the pay and clothing of the garrison, and the revenue allotted for this purpose was not always sufficient. The council was also responsible for the upkeep of the council house, jail, roads, bridges, fountains, and similar public works. It was concerned, too, with keeping the city clean, preventing profiteering by middlemen, supervising the prices of sugar and other commodities, as well as with organizing festivities and illuminations on such occasions as a royal birth or marriage.[48]

Brazilian historians differ on whether the municipal councils were genuine representatives of the people, or merely of a self-perpetuating and selfish oligarchy. They also argue over whether the councils were largely autonomous or were merely rubber stamps for governors and viceroys. The answer, I think, depends largely on the time and the place. The distant *Camara* of São Paulo (which has been the most publicized, since its history is the best documented in print) was in a much stronger position regarding the central authority at Bahia before 1720, than was the Senate of Salvador in the shadow of the viceroy's palace. A senior Crown official in Minas Gerais in the late 1730's, accused the town councillors of that captaincy of acting as if they were "seditious parliamentarians" in England, adding that they were openly hostile to any extension of the authority of the Crown. Such a truculent attitude was not possible at Bahia. But even the Bahia council had a will of its own during the period with which we are dealing, and its members not infrequently differed from so powerful a personality as the Count of Sabugosa.

The sugar planters of the *Reconcavo* had their representatives on the council but they did not necessarily dominate it. On the other hand, planters, council and viceroy sometimes made common cause against the Crown. A royal edict of 1687 forbade the council to fix the prices of sugar and ordered that this commodity should be sold freely. Ten years later this policy was reversed, and the Crown ordained that the annual sugar prices should be fixed by agreement between two representatives of the planters and two of the local merchants, under the supervision of the municipal council of Salvador. All sugar chests were to be inspected, graded, and weighed in accordance with certain specifications before they were shipped to Portugal. Planters who adulterated their sugars were to be fined and exiled from Bahia for two years. Another edict of 1698 fixed the maximum weight of a loaded sugar chest at forty *arrobas,* "including the wood." Experience had shown that the Lisbon stevedores could not cope with heavier chests, "with the result that many of them left their jobs and absented themselves for fear of imperiling their life and health with a weight which was more than they could bear." With the connivance of the *Camara* and of successive governors, the Bahia planters systematically evaded compliance with these edicts for more than thirty years, and the Crown was only able to call them to order in 1732.[49]

Since sugar was for so long the mainstay of the Brazilian economy, the *senhores de engenho* (as the planters were termed) came to be recognized as the rural aristocracy and were awarded corresponding privileges and immunities. Gubernatorial and royal decrees exempted their sugar mills, technical equipment and slaves, from being seized or distrained for outstanding debts. Their creditors were only allowed to take a portion of the cane ground at harvest time. These privileges were later extended to the *lavradores* or copyholders who cultivated smaller fields and had their cane ground by the planters. The production of sugar in the *Reconcavo* varied greatly in the first half of the eighteenth century owing to the fluctuating demand in Europe and to periods of unseasonable weather in Brazil. A good harvest, such as that of 1725–1726, produced between 12,000 and 13,000 chests for export to Portugal, which may be compared with the corresponding figure of 14,000 chests in Antonil's day.[50]

An important by-product of the sugar industry was the distilling of rum and sugar-cane brandy. These fiery spirits found a big export market in the slave trade with West Africa, being in great demand by the Negroes of Angola and Guinea. On the other hand, their excessive consumption by soldiers, slaves and sailors in the coastal towns of Brazil and Angola, led to increased mortality from drunken brawls and alcoholism. Their sale in these places also adversely affected the demand for wine from Portugal and the Atlantic Islands. For these reasons, periodic attempts were made to restrict, or even to ban, the sale of rum and sugar-cane brandy in Brazil and Angola, but these efforts soon had to be abandoned as impracticable. Disadvantageous as these spirits were in many ways, the slaves could hardly have endured the back-breaking labor of the sugar and tobacco fields without this solace. Even white children, it was insinuated, would wilt and die without the fortifying warmth of the *agoardentes da terra,* as these spirits were called.[51] Rum and brandy distilleries accordingly flourished, and their owners more than once petitioned for the same fiscal privileges as those enjoyed by the sugar-planting aristocracy.

As Antonil had observed on the threshold of the eighteenth century, Brazilian tobacco was even more profitable than sugar. Alleged to be the finest in the world, it was eagerly sought by the Manchu monarchs at Peking and by the dusky potentates of Dahomey. The best variety of leaf came from the Cachoeira region, which in 1726 produced some 20,000 choice rolls, "and as much again of inferior quality for export to the Mina Coast." The harvest was graded in three qualities, the finest being reserved for export to Portugal, and the lowest for export to Guinea, but this regulation was often evaded in practice. Dampier had observed in 1699 that the Bahia tobacco was exported "either in roll or snuff, never in leaf that I know of," and this practice continued throughout the first half of the eighteenth century. The tobacco growers were, for the most part, men in a smaller way of business than the sugar planters, working with only a few slaves each, and occasionally participating in the curing of the tobacco themselves. In 1729 they petitioned the Crown for the same privileges and fiscal immunities as those granted to the sugar planters and copyholders, this petition being supported by the Count of Sabugosa.[52]

The consumption of tobacco in Brazil itself was also very considerable, and Antonil noted disapprovingly that many men could not live without the "holy herb" (*herva santa*) as they called it. Tobacco was usually taken in the form of snuff, but pipe smoking and quid chewing were scarcely less common. Antonil states that tobacco addicts were numerous, "not only among sailors and manual workers of all kinds, whether bond or free, who are convinced that tobacco alone gives them energy and vigor," but among the idle nobility and gentry, among soldiers on guard duty, and "not a few ecclesiastics, clergymen, and religious." While conceding that in moderation it was probably an excellent antidote for indigestion, constipation, asthma, and toothache, he reminded his readers that successive popes had forbidden its use and mastication in churches.

Though sugar, rum, and tobacco were the staples of the Bahia export trade, the production of gold in the hinterland of the captaincy was far from being unimportant. The mining districts of Jacobina and Rio das Contas were discovered at the beginning of the eighteenth century, but for nearly twenty years the Crown forbade their exploitation on the grounds that this might encourage foreign attacks on Bahia and deprive the sugar and tobacco fields of their slave labor. This prohibition remained a dead letter, being even more impossible to enforce than the closure of the São Francisco River route to Minas Gerais. In 1727 rich strikes were made in the region of Araçuahi and Fanado, and these districts were placed under the supervision of the viceroy of Bahia for many years, though they were eventually transferred to Minas Gerais. All these workings were of the placer variety.

The pattern of development in these mining districts closely paralleled that in Minas Gerais. The first strikes were followed by a rush of adventurers of all colors and both sexes, Paulista pioneers being prominent in the early stages. Life in the turbulent mining camps which they established was nothing if not dangerous, and Paulistas and Emboabas were constantly murdering one another, especially in the Minas Novas of Araçuahi. Only when these camps were transformed into towns and provided with clergy, magistrates, and militia, did some semblance of order come out of the chaotic anarchy in which they had lived for so long. This pacification was largely the work of two men, Pedro Barbosa Leal and Pedro Leolino Mariz. The latter not only established a smeltery at Araçuahi in the teeth of local opposition, but had previously contrived to arrest the redoubtable Manuel Nunes Viana and send him to Bahia.[53]

It was alleged in 1795 that these mines in the jurisdiction of Bahia had never yielded the Crown sufficient profit to cover the cost of collecting the royal fifths. The establishment of smelteries and the maintenance of officials to supervise the collection of the fifths was certainly a costly business, but such incomplete statistics as we possess indicate that in some years at any rate large amounts of gold were remitted to Bahia.[54] Doubtless the amount of contraband gold was even greater, and not all of it was smuggled to the Guinea coast to buy slaves, or sent to England in exchange for manufactured goods. Much of it remained in the city of Salvador, as attested by the profusion of gold decoration in the churches which so impressed foreign visitors, and by the massive gold jewelry worn by the Bahia ladies which aroused Mrs. Kindersley's envy.[55]

As was true in Minas Gerais, most of the actual mining was done by Negro slaves under the supervision of their owners. If the figures for the matriculation of slaves in 1734 are any guide, there must have been about 13,500 employed in the three Bahian mining regions, about half of them in the Minas Novas of Araçuahi and Fanado.[56] As also in Minas Gerais, slaves from the Guinea coast were found to be far stronger and better adapted for this work than those from Angola and elsewhere. This led to a great boom in the Mina slave trade, which, during the first half of the eighteenth century was mainly concentrated between Whydah and Bahia. The local Ardra ruler had offered to let the Portuguese build a fortified factory there in 1698; but though the Bahian slavers frequented that port subsequently, the "Fortaleza Cezaria de São João Baptista d'Ajuda" was only founded in 1721 by the Count of Sabugosa on his own responsibility.

The Brazilian slavers which visited Whydah, and, to a lesser extent, the neighboring port of Jaquin, had continual difficulties with the Dutch governors of Elmina. The Dutch kept patrol vessels cruising in the vicinity with the object of forcing the Brazilian ships to call at Elmina and pay duties, since the Netherlanders claimed suzerainty of this part of the Slave Coast. This branch of the slave trade was also financed in part by contraband Brazilian gold, which was used not only to purchase slaves, but also manufactured goods from the Dutch and English traders in the Bight of Benin.[57] For these reasons, the Crown more than once thought of banning the trade altogether, or, alternatively, of putting it under the control of a monopolistic company with headquarters at Lisbon. These projects aroused intense opposition at Bahia, where viceroy, merchants, planters, and commonality, were alike agreed that the Whydah slave trade was the life line of Brazil in general and of Bahia in particular.

Arguing against the Crown's proposals in 1731, the Count of Sabugosa stressed the complete dependence of the Brazilian economy on the West African slave trade, and especially on that with Whydah. He estimated that between 10,000 and 12,000 slaves were imported yearly into Bahia alone from Whydah, adding that even this number was not enough for the mines and plantations. Angola provided about six or seven thousand slaves annually, and these were distributed between the three ports of Rio de Janeiro, Pernambuco, and Bahia. The Bantu from Angola were inferior to the Sudanese from Ardra and Dahomey; nor was there any possibility of acquiring additional slaves in Angola if the trade with Whydah was stopped. Other slave markets in Upper Guinea, Senegal, Gambia, Loango, and even Madagascar and Mozambique, had all been tried and found wanting for one reason or another, so that slaves from Whydah were irreplaceable.[58]

The viceroy tactfully forbore to dilate on the contraband gold trade with Whydah (some of it via São Tomé), but he emphasized that Ardra and Dahomey provided an indispensable outlet for Bahian tobacco, sugar, and rum, which were in greater demand there, relatively speaking, than in Europe. All classes in Bahia participated directly or indirectly in this slave trade, and its cessation or transference to a monopolistic company at Lisbon would ruin the citizens of Salvador. The Crown would suffer equally, since the bulk of its revenue at Bahia was derived from the heavy duties levied on the slaves coming from Whydah, and on the sugar, rum, and tobacco exported thither. The profits of this branch of the slave trade paid in great part for the upkeep of the churches and the fortifications, the pay of the garrison, and for the entire official establishment and pension list (*filhos da folha*) of the island of São Tomé. His arguments were repeated with minor variations seven years later by his successor, the Count of Galveas, who reminded the Crown that neither mines nor plantations could function without slave labor. A slave's life, he added, was usually a short one; and Whydah was the best source of supply for slaves, both in quantity and quality.[59]

The contraband trade in gold and tobacco which worried the Crown so much was not confined to Whydah. As mentioned in Chapter i, smuggling with Lisbon reached alarming proportions, despite all the efforts of the Crown to check its growth by means of stringent orders, threats of dire punishment, and rigorous inspection of all shipping and cargoes. When Dom João de Lencastre proudly informed the Crown that he had stopped all possible sources of smuggling in the Bahia fleet in 1699, the secretary of state retorted by sending him a list of the confiscated contraband tobacco, showing that in "this fleet, in which your worship thought all possible irregularities were prevented, there was found more than ever before." [60] The preamble of an edict against smuggling promulgated in 1711, stated that in the previous year "there were four warships and four East Indiamen, all English, in the Bay of All Saints, and others in Rio de Janeiro; and all these ships were smuggling merchandise from Europe and Asia into the said ports, and taking from Brazil much gold and tobacco." [61]

Homeward-bound Portuguese East Indiamen, which regularly called at Bahia on their voyages from Goa and Macao, were among the worst offenders. A Frenchman wrote of Brazil in 1730 that "les marchandises de la Chine s'y vendroient beaucoup plus avantageusement que par tout ailleurs," and there is plenty of contemporary evidence to indicate that this was true.[62] All efforts to stop this flourishing contraband trade failed, because the military guards placed on board the Indiamen to prevent smuggling, "are those who most shamelessly and scandalously smuggle the goods ashore from the Indiamen and foreign ships." [63] Disregard of the anti-smuggling laws was also prevalent in the highest places. The celebrated French seaman and colonial administrator, Mahé de la Bourdonnais, sent a consignment of Indian textiles for sale at Bahia in 1729, on board the homeward-bound Portuguese ship *Nossa Senhora da Apparecida,* with the consent of the viceroy of Goa. This particular consignment was sold "tant bien que mal," but this was apparently the fault of the French pilot to whom La Bourdonnais had entrusted the goods, and the incident is characteristic of the active trade carried on between Goa and Bahia despite all the prohibitions against it.[64]

One of the arguments adduced in favor of maintaining Bahia's trade with Whydah was that this was about the only branch of overseas trade in which the profits remained in Luso-Brazilian hands. Trade with Europe, the Counts of Sabugosa and Galveas pointed out, was to a large extent controlled by English and other foreign merchants operating through Portuguese agents in the Brazilian ports. This opinion was shared by the above-quoted Frenchman, who wrote of the Brazil Fleets in 1730: "Les principaux intéressés sur ces flottes, tant à l'allée qu'au retour, sont d'ordinaire les Etrangers: les Portugais, excepté un très-petit nombre, n'y ont quasi d'autre part que leurs commissions." [65] These gloomy views were doubtless somewhat exaggerated, but they contained a great deal of truth. The way in which much of the wealth of Brazil was channeled through Lisbon to England was a continual source of irritation to the Portuguese and of complacent satisfaction to the English. The London newspapers regularly chronicled the arrival of large consignments of Brazilian gold, and this indiscreet publicity provoked Lord Tyrawly to a characteristic outburst in a dispatch to the secretary of state: "It is a most miserable thing, that there is no stopping the mouths of our news writers, these paragraphs that Mr. Hayes quotes from them do infinite hurt; they set down the gold they hear, or dream, we extract from Portugal, with just as little caution, as they do the oats and barley that are sold at Bear Key." His lordship added wistfully: "If these people could be confined to the accounts of highwaymen, and horses stolen or strayed, their papers would be every bit as diverting and instructive to the generality of their readers." Exactly how much gold reached London is uncertain, but there are good grounds for thinking that between half and three quarters of the gold which entered the Tagus in an average good year (1,200 *arrobas* or 38,400 lbs., avoirdupois), soon found its way to England.[66]

Under a series of treaties concluded with England and the United Provinces in the second half of the seventeenth century, the Portuguese government had been compelled to allow four merchant families from each of those two nations to reside at Bahia and at Rio de Janeiro. This forced concession was much resented by the Portuguese Crown, and its representatives were always on guard against any attempt to expand it. Even the possibility that heretics among these privileged families might seek to convert their slaves to Protestantism did not escape unfavorable comment.[67] Any attempt to increase legitimate foreign trade with Brazil at once aroused antagonism at Lisbon and Bahia. When the English Royal African Company sounded the British ambassador at Lisbon about the possibility of getting a slave-trading contract with Brazil, Lord Tyrawly promised to help but wrote to Lord Newcastle: "We, on this side of the water, must nevertheless go on with that caution, that all business requires, that in any wise relates to the Brazils, which they are very jealous here of admitting foreign nations into any part of, though ever so remote." [68]

Regarded with resentful suspicion by the local authorities, these few privileged foreign families at Bahia had little chance to flourish and take root socially, whatever material profits their trading interests might bring them. Dampier remarked that at the time of his visit to Bahia, a Mr. Cock was then the sole English resident merchant. "He had a patent to be our English Consul, but did not care to take upon him any public character, here having been none in eleven or twelve years before this time." Nevertheless, though all foreign visitors to eighteenth-century Bahia comment on the extreme jealousy and suspicion with which outsiders were regarded, a number of strangers did enter Brazil and remain there. Many of these were sailors from ships in the Brazil fleets, for there were always plenty of foreign mariners on board these vessels, as Fr. Martin de Nantes observed in 1671. Most of them were or became converts to Roman Catholicism; but there were even a few heretics in official employment, such as the French Huguenot engineer officer, Jean Massé, who came to Bahia with the Marquis of Angeja and remained in Brazil for the rest of his life. [69]

As is apparent from this chapter, it was gold, sugar, and tobacco that occupied the minds of educated laymen at Bahia rather than literature, art, or music. Nevertheless these latter manifestations of the spirit were not neglected, even if they did not normally reach very high standards. The chief focus of culture was inevitably the local Jesuit College, where instruction was not confined to actual or potential members of the Society, and whose library contained in 1694 some 3,000 volumes "by every kind of writer who could be desired." [70] The Jesuits had many lay brothers and priests who were professional painters, sculptors, woodcarvers, and metalworkers. Though much of their work has disappeared, enough survives to show that in woodwork particularly they often attained more than a merely mechanical skill. There were also numerous goldsmiths and silversmiths in Bahia, but such of their works as survive do not indicate that they possessed more than mediocre abilities.[71] The local school of military engineering (*aula de fortificação*) produced some competent practitioners: perhaps the best-known graduate of this school was the locally born engineer, José Antonio Caldas, whose lavishly illustrated topographical and statistical survey of Bahia in 1759 is a model of its kind.

Poets and poetasters abounded at Bahia, as everywhere and always in the Portuguese-speaking world; but the only one of outstanding merit, the satirist Gregorio de Mattos, died in 1696, just when our concern with Bahia begins. His verses were too pungently critical to be printed in his lifetime and for long afterwards, but they circulated in manuscript during this period. Such lines as:

> Só sei que deste Adão de massapé
> Procedem os fidalgos desta terra

must have given as much offense to the more snobbish of his fellow citizens, as the oft-quoted verse

> Que os Brasileiros são bestas,
> E estarão a trabalhar
> Toda a vida por manterem
> Maganos de Portugal

would have done to any Portuguese officials who may have heard it.[72]

Historical studies received an impulse when the Count of Sabugosa was commanded by the king to collect information that might be useful for the Royal Academy of History. This body had been founded at Lisbon in 1720, and was entrusted with the task of compiling a history of the Portuguese empire in all its aspects. The royal order stimulated the viceroy to found an academy at Bahia, whose members decided, with what was obviously mock modesty, to call themselves "The Forgotten" at their inaugural session in March, 1724. The "Academia dos Esquecidos" only flourished for a short time, during which period the forty-four members limited themselves to exchanging poetical effusions, laudatory speeches, and dissertations on trivial themes, in the manner of similar literary academies which waxed and waned in Portugal. Sabugosa's initiative was not entirely wasted, however. The corresponding members of the Academy included Pedro Leonel Mariz, who spent most of his life in the turbulent mining camps of the Bahia *sertão,* and this indicates that some of the graces of life may have penetrated there.[73] The only production of a Bahian academician that achieved the dignity of print during its author's lifetime was Sebastião da Rocha Pitta's *Historia da America Portuguesa,* published at Lisbon in 1730. Though scornfully dismissed by Robert Southey as being "a meagre and inaccurate work which has been accounted valuable, merely because there is no other," the *Historia* does not deserve this censure. For all its Gongoric turgidity, it contains some valuable and authentic information, being on some points more fair-minded and accurate than Southey's better written but more prejudiced work.

The indefatigable Count of Sabugosa was also responsible for the establishment of the first secular theater in Bahia, with the object of "acting comedies on occasions celebrating royal festivities." This theater was built at his own expense as an adjunct of the municipal hall, but it was pulled down in 1733 by order of his pet aversion, the Royal Judge, Dr. Joseph dos Santos Varjão, which led to an acrimonious correspondence between those concerned.[74] During the few years it lasted, this comedy theater may have provided a welcome change from the Jesuit tragicomedies or religious operas which they staged on occasional high days and holy days. Early eighteenth-century Bahia also witnessed the flowering of the *modinha,* which was later transplanted to Portugal and described by William Beckford in glowing terms: "Those who have never heard this original sort of music, must and will remain ignorant of the most bewitching melodies that ever existed

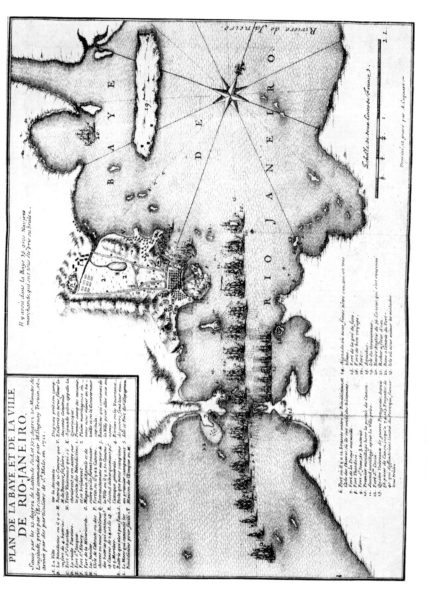

DUGUAY-TROUIN FORCES THE BAR OF RIO DE JANEIRO IN 1711

THE FEAST OF SÃO GONÇALO D'AMARANTE AT BAHIA IN 1718

Within the oval frame border:
FREIRE DE ANDRADA · SARGENTO MOR DE BATALHA · GOMES

Arte regit populos bello præcepta ministrat
Mavortem cernis milite pace Numam

O. Cor Sculpsit 1747

GOMES FREIRE DE ANDRADA

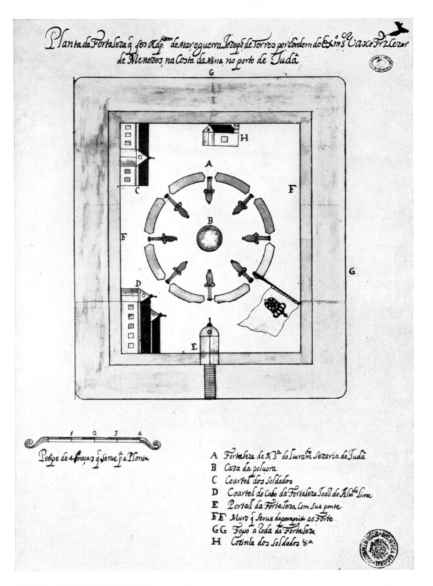

PLAN OF THE FORTIFIED FACTORY AT WHYDAH, DAHOMEY, IN 1722

VIEW OF THE TOWN OF BOM JESUS DE CUIABÁ
IN THE EIGHTEENTH CENTURY

Prospecto de Villa Boa tomada da parte do Norte para o Sul no anno de 1751.

1 *Matriz.* 2 *Consistorio da Irmand.ª do S.ᵗ dos Passos.* 3 *Consistorio da Irmand.ª do S.ᵐᵒ Sacram.ᵗᵒ* 4 *Capella de N. Sr.ª da Boa Morte.* 5 *Cadêa.* 6 *Caza da Camara.* 7 *Passo do S.ᵗ dos Passos.* 8 *Cazas da Real Intendencia.* 9 *Cazas da Rezidencia do General.* 10 *Capella de N. Sr.ª da Lapa.*

THE TOWN OF VILLA BOA AS SEEN FROM THE NORTH IN 1751

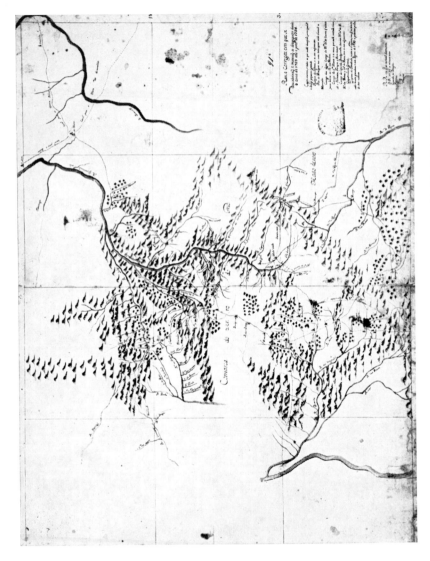

MAP OF THE DIAMOND-PRODUCING DISTRICT IN 1729–1734

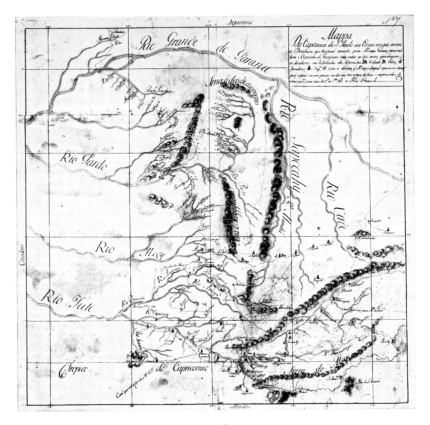

MAP SHOWING THE TRAILS FROM SÃO PAULO TO MINAS GERAIS AND
GOIÁS IN THE FIRST HALF OF THE EIGHTEENTH CENTURY

Goyana

Igara

Olind

Recit

Hum dos especiaes favores q tem receb⁰ esta freg.ᵃ de Igaraſſu do
te, aq̃. chamàram males que infestàram à todo Pern.ᶜᵒ eduzàraõ m͂ᵗᵒˢ a̅nnos cc
o a toda esta de Igaraſſu deixaram intacta, porque ſebẽm 2 ou 3 peſſoas
noͭᵗʳ.º Ep͂ᵃ memoria ſepòs este quadro no anno de 1729, e

PRINCIPAL TOWNS OF PERNAMBUCO AT THE TIME
OF THE YELLOW FEVER EPIDEMIC, 1685

Ittamaracá

qaraſſu

tinda

eciffe

ũ dos ſeos Padroeyros S. Cosme e S. Damiàm, ſoy o deſenderem à da peſ
os começando no de 1685, e ainda q paſsàraõ à Ooyana e à outras freg.ᵃˢ adiante,
roas ôs trouceram do N.ᵉ nellas ſeſindàram ſem paſsar à outra, o que tudo hê
29, e o deo de esmolla M.ᵈˡ Frr.ᵃ de Carv.º

NEGRO SLAVES WASHING FOR DIAMONDS IN THE SERRO DO FRIO

NEGRO SLAVES MINING IN THE SERRO DO FRIO

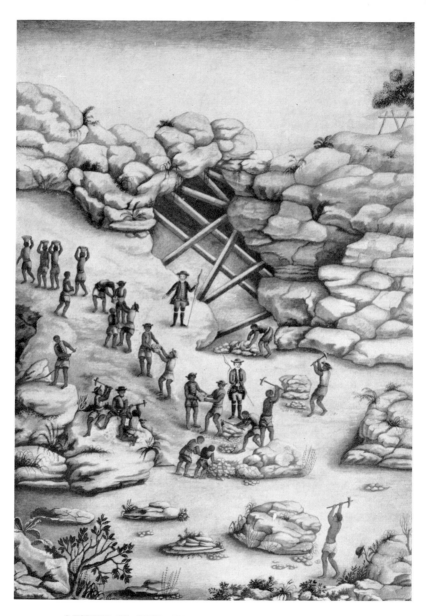

MINING OF GOLD AND DIAMONDS IN MINAS GERAIS
IN THE EIGHTEENTH CENTURY

CHAPEL OF THE ROSARY OR OF PADRE FARIA,
VILLA RICA DE OURO PRETO, MINAS GERAIS

CHAPEL OF NOSSA SENHORA D'O, SABARÁ, MINAS GERAIS

CHINOISERIE DECORATION IN THE CHAPEL
OF NOSSA SENHORA D'O, SABARÁ, MINAS GERAIS

FAÇADE OF SÃO FRANCISCO DE ASSIS, SALVADOR, BAHIA

since the days of the Sybarites." [75] But despite the popularity of the *modinha,* the introduction of African musical influences through the slaves, and the initiative of the Count of Sabugosa, the culture of the educated élite at Bahia remained preponderantly a clerical one, as it did elsewhere and as we shall have occasion to see again in the next chapter.

VII. RICH TOWN
OF BLACK GOLD

I F THE CITY OF THE SAVIOR as the capital and chief
port of Brazil attracted the commerce and the comments of foreigners for so long, the less accessible Rich Town of Black Gold
in the highlands of Minas Gerais was perhaps a more important
and was certainly a more curious place. The gold-mining camp
transformed into a township by António de Albuquerque in July,
1711, had been christened by him with his own surname (p. 82
above), but the Crown considered this to be bordering on lese-
majesty and restored the original place name. Villa Rica de Ouro
Preto was not the only town of its kind, but it represented the
quintessence of that peculiar *Mineiro* civilization which flourished
during the first half of the eighteenth century and which it is our
purpose to consider here. This civilization waxed and waned in
the gold-mining regions scattered over the vast captaincy of Minas
Gerais, and it was reflected elsewhere in similar settlements in the
hinterland of Bahia and in the remoter captaincies of Goiás
and Mato Grosso. But it was in the mining towns along the flanks
of the Serra do Espinhaço that this civilization attained its finest
flowering, and more particularly in Villa Rica, for reasons explained by the author of the *Triunfo Eucharistico,* in 1734.[1]

"In this town live the chief merchants, whose trade and impor-

tance incomparably exceed the most thriving of the leading mer-
chants of Portugal. Hither, as to a port, are directed and collected
in the Royal Mint the grandiose amounts of gold from all the
Mines. Here dwell the best educated men, both lay and ecclesiastic.
Here is the seat of all the nobility and the strength of the military.
It is, by virtue of its natural position, the head of the whole of
America; and by the wealth of its riches it is the precious pearl of
Brazil." The citizens of Mexico City or of Lima would certainly
not have agreed that Villa Rica de Ouro Preto was the chief city in
all America; but they would not have disputed another contem-
porary writer's description of this Brazilian mining town as a
"golden Potosí." [2]

The author of the *Triunfo Eucharistico* further alleged that
"although it is difficult or impossible to satisfy the covetousness
of the human heart, and in this respect the Portuguese more so
than any other nation," yet even his fellow countrymen were satisfied with the extent, wealth, and fertility of the newly discovered
lands in Minas Gerais. This panegyric was written at a time when
the production of the gold mines seemed likely to increase rather
than to diminish, but it was not merely a piece of baroque bombast.
In the upshot, the amount of gold produced did not satisfy either
the cupidity of the Crown or slake the *auri sacra fames* of its
vassals; but it did make many people's fortunes, and it affected
not only the economy of Portugal and Brazil but that of England
as well. The gold of Minas Gerais thus played a far from insignificant role on the eighteenth-century world stage, and we may
here consider in more detail some of the men and women who
mined, spent, and handled the coveted yellow metal.

The early governors of Minas Gerais were generally emphatic
in their condemnation of the white men over whom they ruled,
describing them as a race of base-born and truculent rogues, liable
to break out into open revolt at any monent. One of the more
popular and sympathetic governors, Dom Lourenço de Almeida,
explained to the Crown in 1722 that most of these men were young
and unmarried, a large proportion of them being recent immi-

grants from Portugal. Since they had nothing to lose, "as their worldly wealth is of little bulk, consisting only of gold, they are not only emboldened to disobey your Majesty's laws and justices, but they likewise frequently commit the most atrocious crimes." A similar accusation was made twelve years later by Martinho de Mendonça, who averred that the original inhabitants of this unruly captaincy were either "Paulistas, accustomed to violence and independence, or else Portuguese of the lowest and most ignorant class." The Count of Assumar, who governed Minas Gerais from 1717 to 1721, was even more uncomplimentary, describing the Mineiros as the scum of the earth, "even the so-called great ones being bred in the milk of servitude." [3]

Much of this abuse can be discounted, but the fact remains that the overwhelming majority of the immigrants from Portugal were poor and lowly if able-bodied and enterprising young bachelors from the province of Minho e Douro. This overwhelmingly male preponderance was, of course, the nub of the trouble, as both the Crown and the governors realized, if only somewhat belatedly. As Dom Lourenço de Almeida admitted, if these men could marry women of their own kind and settle down, they would soon become respectable and reliable citizens, but the acute shortage of white women prevented the great majority from doing so. The position was aggravated by the fact that the parents of the relatively few white girls in Brazil, who were mostly living in the coastal towns, preferred to send their daughters into convents at Bahia or (better still) in Portugal, rather than let them marry in Minas Gerais or elsewhere. Other adverse factors included the paucity of clergy to celebrate marriages, and the high fees which they demanded for officiating.

Writing on this subject to the Crown ten years later, Dom Lourenço de Almeida declared that the situation had improved somewhat in the last decade, as "a fair number of married people" had emigrated into Minas Gerais from other parts of Brazil and from the Atlantic Islands. "However," he added, "this number is still far from sufficient for such a vast colony." He further stated that in any case parents who could afford to do so, still preferred to send their daughters to Bahia or Portugal to take the veil, "for it is typical of low-born people to want their daughters to become nuns. Most of these girls," he averred, "would like nothing better than to find husbands in Minas Gerais," and he advised the Crown to prohibit the passage of white women from Brazil to Portugal. Similar advice had been tendered to the Crown from Bahia and elsewhere, and in March, 1732, legislation was enacted prohibiting women from leaving Brazil for Portugal without first obtaining the sanction of the Crown.[4] This draconic measure was modified a year later to enable wives to return with their husbands without seeking prior permission. It can be regarded, in a way, as the corollary of the decree of March, 1720, which drastically limited emigration from Portugal to Brazil, although the decree of 1720 was not so strictly observed.

Given the perennial shortage of white women, and what an exuberant North American writer has termed "the Lusitanian Libido on the loose,"[5] a vast increase in the mulatto population of Minas Gerais was the inevitable result. "Necessity is the mother of invention and the father of the Eurasian" was a saying in John Company's India, and necessity would equally have produced a large and increasing class of Brazilian mulattoes. But even when marriageable white women were available, the Portuguese male frequently preferred to live with a mulata or with a Negress, as the scandalized Le Gentil de la Barbinais noticed at Bahia.[6] Quite apart from this double sexual urge, there was a third reason which applied in Minas Gerais, where the Negro slaves exported from Whydah were believed to have a peculiar gift for discovering new gold-bearing deposits. "For this reason," wrote the governor of Rio de Janeiro in July, 1726, "there is not a Mineiro who can live without a Negress from Mina, saying that only with them do they have any luck." Finally, there was the widespread practice of letting out colored women slaves for prostitution, against which the Crown and the governors legislated in vain.[7] Since more than three-fifths of the virile Portuguese immigrants came from the province of Minho e Douro, the result of these factors was that after a few generations anybody who was not either pure black or pure white had a dose of Minhoto and of African blood in his or her veins.

The fact that most white men had mulatto children, whether legitimate or otherwise, posed an administrative as well as a social problem for succeeding generations. In law, Negro blood was a bar to the holding of any civic or official position, such as a seat on the local municipal council, but this color bar was often surmounted. In 1725, the Overseas Councillors urged the Crown to forbid colored men from holding municipal posts, and to enact that only the husband or the widower of a white woman could do so. This would encourage white men to marry white women, and to have children by them instead of by Negress and mulata concubines; "seeing that otherwise neither they nor their descendants will be able to attain high office in the regions where they live." Such legislation was largely futile. Provided that the aspirant was not of too dusky a hue, it was wealth rather than color which remained the chief criterion for municipal office in Minas Gerais, as Gomes Freire de Andrada noted many years later.[8]

Apart from those men of color who succeeded in passing as white, there were, in the course of time, many others who became persons of substance and property, by exercising such professions as painting, music, and the law. In the mid-eighteenth century these men petitioned the Crown for the right to wear swords at their side, like any white gentleman, and their request was warmly supported by Gomes Freire de Andrada, who, in this as in some other respects, was a man in advance of his time.[9] Insofar as Minas Gerais was concerned, the Crown granted this request in 1759, but mulattoes were for long afterwards still regarded with a good deal of mistrust by the government, and they had to wait until the next century for their complete emancipation.

Although European and African blood predominated in the

racial cauldron of Minas Gerais, the Paulista and Amerindian strains were by no means negligible. It will be recalled that Albuquerque had ordered that Emboabas and Paulistas should be equally represented on the councils of the newly founded towns (p. 83), but this measure was not implemented for long. Similarly, a Crown injunction of 1715 to favor the Paulistas rather than the Emboabas came too late to be effective. From 1710 onwards the Paulistas were heavily outnumbered by the newcomers, save in a few places like Pitanguí, whither they had "hived off" after pushing westwards. The Paulistas had the wanderlust almost as much as the Bedouin, and apart from their congenital dislike of an urban life, they suspected (no doubt rightly) that the Emboabas regarded their backwoods' habits and customs with contemptuous aversion.[10] Nevertheless, a certain amount of intermarriage between the two groups did take place, and some Paulista families were absorbed in the general population after a generation or two. A perusal of the slave lists in the archives of Minas Gerais also reveals the presence of numerous Amerindian slaves. Mostly designated under the generic name of "Carijó," no doubt the majority were men, but some must have been women and their blood doubtless mixed with that of their owners' families.[11]

The fact that so many people of both sexes and of several colors lived in Brazil "à lei da Natureza," as the viceroys, bishops, magistrates, and missionaries were constantly deploring, gave rise to a swarm of homeless beggars, vagrants, and vagabonds, who were nowhere more of a problem than to the authorities in Minas Gerais. The problem was not confined to Brazil, for it was general throughout the Portuguese empire in one form or another—a fact which is discreetly ignored by those twentieth-century apologists who laud the Portuguese to the skies as colonizers *par excellence* of the tropics. So, in some respects they were, such as in the admirable tenacity with which they hung on, once they were established, in the face of a hostile human and geographic environment. But they had the defects of their qualities, and if they regarded poverty as no crime, they also regarded it as something to be apathetically endured rather than as an incentive for hard work and self-betterment.

The Brazilian-born Jesuit, Padre Francisco de Sousa, who spent most of his life in the Asian mission field, wrote feelingly of "the rabble who abound in all our strongholds, to their ruination," [12] and his complaint was echoed by many others from the Maranhão to Macao. "To beg, I am ashamed" was seldom an Iberian motto, and manual labor was usually regarded as more degrading than either begging or stealing. *Trabalho é para cachorro e Negro,* "work is for a cur or a Nigger," as the Brazilian saying runs. The governor of Rio de Janeiro wrote to the Crown in 1726: "the mines certainly cannot be worked except by Negroes, both because they work harder as because the whites and Portuguese immigrants, even if they were bred with a hoe in the hand, no sooner do they set foot in Brazil than they refuse to work; and if God does not give them some lawful means of existence, they usually maintain themselves by thieving and cozening." When the Count of Assumar, whom we shall frequently meet in this chapter, became Viceroy of India in 1744, he found an indigent and delinquent population on his arrival at Goa. "For as nobody wants to work nor practice any handicraft, many of them live either by begging or by stealing." [13] The author of the "Calamidades de Pernambuco," writing at Recife in 1749, observed that the population of that town then amounted to 30,000 souls, "the greater part as poor as the beggars who go from door to door." A Franciscan friar residing at Macao in the years 1742–1745 declared that the population of the City of the Name of God in China was little more than a mass of paupers, since both sexes would rather beg their bread in the streets than do a hand's turn of manual labor. [14]

I do not mean to suggest that the Portuguese were the only people afflicted with the problem of poverty. Sir George Clark has recently reminded us that in the year 1688 it was estimated with a fair degree of probability that out of an English population of some five and a half millions, no fewer than one and a quarter million were classified as "vagrant poor." [15] Spain and Italy, to say nothing of wealthy countries like France and the United Provinces, also had similar troubles in varying degrees. But one gets the impression from both official correspondence and the accounts of trustworthy travelers that the incidence of poverty in the Portuguese empire was even greater than in those of the Dutch, English, French, or Spaniards. On the other hand, as pointed out by Caio Prado Junior, the loose living which produced this swarm of pauper vagrants in Brazil had one good result in the long run. It brought about a relatively peaceful fusion of the three races, European, African, and Amerindian, which were very different from one another in their ethnic characteristics and in the relative positions which they occupied in the social organization of the colony. [16]

Contrary to what is sometimes asserted, the Crown and the colonial authorities made various attempts to grapple with this problem, but their efforts were more in the nature of palliatives than of cures. They realized that marriage and a good home was the real answer, but the bachelors of Minas Gerais (and elsewhere) found a life of dissipation more congenial, and suitable wives were hard to find for the reasons outlined above. In 1721 the Crown urged the local authorities to provide a school and a couple of schoolmasters in each town, one man to teach Latin and another the three R's, these teachers to be paid by the pupils' parents. [17] Something seems to have come from this suggestion, as we find elementary schools functioning in Minas fifteen years later (p. 198 below), but the instruction given therein obviously did not go beyond the primary stage. When the first Bishop of Mariana in 1753 asked for permission to secure four Jesuits to teach in his recently opened seminary, since the one already there could not cope with the work and the inhabitants of Minas were most anxious to have their sons educated, Gomes Freire de Andrada, who was nothing if not frank, wrote to the Crown: "Between the evils of keeping the sons of Minas less educated than those of the other captaincies, and permitting Religious Orders or colleges here, the first evil seems to me the lesser of the two. Your Majesty will decide." [18] King Joseph gave temporary sanction to a few Jesuits teaching at Mariana, but reversed this stand a few years later under the influence of Pombal and out of jealous fear for the royal fifths, as is explained below.

One method of coping with the undesirable products of miscegnation in Minas Gerais was to deport the worst offenders to Angola, a course which, as we have seen, was also favored elsewhere in Brazil. Another favorite expedient was to enlist free mulattoes, Negroes, Amerindians, and half-breeds, into armed bands under the so-called *capitães do mato* ("bush-whacking" captains), who scoured the countryside in search of runaway Negro slaves. The *capitães do mato* in Minas Gerais were rewarded by gold payments for each Negro they apprehended, the rewards being calculated on a sliding scale in accordance with the distance and the length of time in which they had to operate away from their home base. When caught, the Negroes were placed in the local jail and turned over to their masters after the latter had paid the stipulated reward. The standing order or *Regimento* of 1722 enjoined the *capitães do mato* not to use unnecessary cruelty in the capture of runaway slaves, but this injunction was often disregarded. Complaints were also made that the *capitães do mato* were likely to seize innocent Negro slaves who were going about their own or their masters' lawful business, and only surrender them on payment. They were also alleged to keep slaves whom they recaptured working for themselves for a long time, before informing the rightful owners of their apprehension.[19]

Save when engaged on punitive and "bush-whacking" expeditions of this kind, free Negroes, mulattoes, and Amerindian half-breeds were forbidden to carry lethal weapons. This law naturally proved impossible to enforce, despite the savage punishments periodically inflicted on transgressors, a hundred lashes for the first offense, and two hundred for the second. The laws forbidding the employment of mulattoes in government positions were, of course, largely responsible for the perennial problem of unemployed or under-employed half-breeds, but this was something that the Crown and the colonial officials would never face squarely. In 1733 the governor of Minas Gerais was told to make secret enquiries about the existing numbers of Negro and mulatto freemen, as the latter, in particular, were alleged to be enjoying "excessive liberty." Service in the militia subsequently gave these men some employment and an outlet for their superabundant energy; but by and large, as remarked above, the colonial authorities never ceased to regard proletarian members of this class with dislike and suspicion. A very similar situation prevailed in Spanish America, where penal and restrictive legislation was frequently enacted against mulattoes and persons with Negro blood.[20]

One of the chief duties of the *capitães do mato* was to find and destroy the *quilombos, or* settlements of fugitive Negro slaves, that were established in the bush. Usually situated in places difficult of access and remote from the towns and highways, *quilombos* were often the size of large villages with several hundred inhabitants. Periodically the occupants would sally forth to ambush convoys of passengers and goods along the roads, or to raid outlying farms and plantations in search of new recruits and of women. They usually grew enough crops and raised sufficient livestock for their own needs, and they were, of course, a magnet for all slaves who wished to desert. Some of these *quilombos* lasted for years before being discovered. A punitive expedition which destroyed several in 1759 found children of twelve years old who had been born and bred therein.[21] Nevertheless, they were all tracked down and destroyed sooner or later, those Negroes who resisted arrest being decapitated and their heads exhibited by the *capitães do mato* to substantiate their claims for reward.

Runaway slaves remained a major problem in Minas Gerais throughout the eighteenth century. In March, 1741, in response to representations from the Mineiros, the Crown ordained that all Negroes "who were found to be living voluntarily in *quilombos* should be branded with an **F** on the shoulder," a branding iron for this purpose to be kept by each town council. Those who were caught after deserting a second time, had an ear cut off, and death was the usual punishment for a third offense of this kind. Desertions still continued on a large scale, however, for many Negroes preferred to take the risk of being hunted down and killed to a life of toil under the lash. Indeed, it was alleged that they were proud of their branded **F**, regarding it as a badge of honor rather than of infamy. It was therefore proposed that all Negro slaves who deserted and who were subsequently recaptured should have the Achilles tendon severed in one foot, thus preventing them from running but not from hobbling about to work. The author of this infamous proposal boasted that after four or five hundred runaways had been mutilated in this fashion, no other slave in Minas Gerais would dare to desert. He also advocated the large-scale employment of "Tapuya" Amerindians instead of the free mulattoes, to hunt down the Negro fugitives, since the former were far better backwoodsmen and much more dreaded by the Negroes.[22]

The suggestion of cutting the Achilles tendon was warmly welcomed by the city councillors of Mariana in 1755, and they petitioned the Crown to sanction its adoption forthwith. They also urged that slaves should no longer be able to buy their freedom if they could find the necessary money, as the law allowed, but should only be manumitted voluntarily by their owners, "out of pure charity, or in return for services rendered." The Crown submitted these suggestions to the Viceroy, Count of Arcos, at Bahia for his comments. It is to be hoped that King Joseph and Pombal had the grace to blush when they read them, for the Count did not mince his words. He stigmatized the proposal to cut the Achilles tendon as "a barbarity unworthy of men who call themselves Christians, and who live at least outwardly as such. They deserve to be severely reprimanded for daring to make such a request, and for insinuating that Your Majesty was a king and ruler capable of allowing them to exercise such tyranny.

The greater part of these slaves run away because their owners do not feed nor cloth them, nor treat them with compassion and charity as they ought to do, both in health and sickness. And besides ill-treating them as regards food and clothing, they likewise inflict a thousand cruelties and unheard-of punishments on them." He urged the Crown to reject the representations of the Mariana town council out of hand, and his remarkably outspoken humanitarian plea seems to have had the desired effect.[23]

Apologists for slavery, who still exist in surprising numbers, commonly claim that allegations of ill-treatment must be exaggerated, since owners would not willfully reduce the value of their own property by working their slaves to death in a few years, or by deliberately starving them. This, however, is just what many proprietors did do, in the belief that it was more profitable to get everything out of adult slaves in a few years and then replace them by *Negros boçais* or raw hands. The common belief that the Brazilian was an exceptionally kind master is applicable only to nineteenth-century slavery under the Empire, and is contradicted for the colonial period by the testimony of numerous reliable eyewitnesses from Vieira to Vilhena, to say nothing of the official correspondence between the colonial authorities and the Crown. Here it will suffice to quote the evidence of Luís Gomes Ferreira, a doctor-surgeon who lived for more than twenty years in Minas Gerais during the first half of the eighteenth century, and who wrote a fascinating book about his experiences there after his return to Portugal.[24]

In the *Erario Mineral* he admonishes the slaveowners of Minas Gerais to treat sick slaves kindly, to house them warmly and well and generally to take a personal interest in their welfare. "In this matter slaveowners commonly sin greatly, for which they will have to account to God . . . and thus for their own profit as from a sense of duty, they should treat their slaves well when they are healthy and better when they are sick, not depriving them of what they need. In this way the owners will do what is right, they will be well served, they will have fewer diseases, more

profit, fewer losses, and they will have a smaller debit balance
in the Day of Judgment." Elsewhere in this book he denounces
the masters for their cruel treatment of slaves, "whom they ought
to cherish as their children." Naturally, there were some humane
owners, and several of them figure honorably in the pages of the
Erario Mineral, but they were clearly the exception rather than
the rule.

Given the hard work and the short commons which were usually his lot, a slave's working life was likely to be nasty, brutish,
and short. An Italian Capuchin missionary who visited Bahia in
1682 was told that "their labor is so hard and their sustenance so
small, that they are reckoned to live long if they hold out seven
years." [25] Martinho de Mendonça, after making exhaustive enquiries in Minas Gerais in 1734, stated that the owners did not
normally expect to get more than twelve years work out of the
slaves they bought as young men. He added that their reproduction rate was very low, "owing to the small fecundity of the
women who are commonly prostitutes, and to the infirmities and
diseases among Negro children in their infancy." [26] The low fertility rate of the slaves in the mines and on the plantations was remarked by Burton a hundred and thirty years later, when their
treatment had vastly improved. This relative barrenness contrasted with the fecundity of the Negress and mulata mistresses
of white men in town and country houses and needs no elabora-
tion here.

A good idea of the number of able-bodied slaves in Minas
Gerais can be ascertained from the figures of the capitation tax
returns for adult slaves of both sexes between 1735 and 1750. The
first return of 1735 gave a total of 100,141 slaves and the last
return of 1749 a figure of 86,797. These totals are, of course, rather
on the low side, since tax evaders naturally strove to make false
returns when they could, but this was not easy save in very remote
regions. Other estimates range between 80,000 and 150,000 slaves,
but the latter figure was given by the author of the tendon-cutting
project in 1751 and is obviously exaggerated. It is probably safe

to say that the figures given in my Appendix IV are an approximately reliable guide. Judging by the slave lists for 1718–1719, it would appear that the wealthier proprietors in Minas Gerais possessed between thirty and fifty able-bodied slaves; but the majority of people seem to have had about half a dozen, and many owners had only one or two.[27]

Since their death rate was so high and their reproduction rate so low, a rapid turnover of slaves resulted. This in turn made great demands on the resources of the slave trade with West Africa. We have seen above that the Mineiros preferred "Minas," exported principally from Whydah, both because they were stronger and more vigorous than the Bantu, as because they were believed to have almost magical powers of discovering gold. Dr. Luís Gomes Ferreira adds that they were also much more courageous and resistant to disease. "When they do finally admit that they are ill, they are already half dead, as I have often observed." The Bantu, he averred, quickly became demoralized when attacked by any illness, and soon gave up the ghost. The demand for "Minas" is also reflected in the taxation rolls for slaves, whether for payment of the fifths or for capitation, which are still preserved in considerable numbers in the archives of Minas Gerais. In those for the years 1714–1740 which I have cursorily examined, "Minas" appeared to be the most numerous, closely followed by slaves from Angola and Benguela. Amerindians, or "Carijós," for some years occupied the third place, though I doubt whether many of these were used in mining. Among the categories which bring up the rear we find "Luango" (= Loango), "Congo," "Cabo Verde," "Moçambique," "Crioulo do Reino," "Crioulo do Rio," "Bastardo," and even the odd Chinese.[28]

The term "Mina(s)," as employed at this period, was an exceedingly vague one. The *Costa da Mina,* or Mina Coast, of the Portuguese included what the English termed respectively the Ivory, Gold, and Slave coasts. It may be taken as extending roughly from Cape Palmas to the Cameroons. However, as mentioned above, the bulk of the slaves exported to Brazil from this region

were purchased at Whydah. The incessant wars connected with
the fall of Ardra and the rise of Dahomey in the early eighteenth
century guaranteed a good supply of slaves, even though the fighting often interrupted the trading. Dahomey itself, however, never
extended for much more than 120 miles from north to south, and
had a coast line of only about 35 miles, but it was frequented by
Dutch, English, and French slave traders as well as by the Luso-
Brazilian. The bulk of the slaves classified as "Minas" were evidently of the Yoruba linguistic group, being Nagos and Geges; but
the term also included the Twi-speaking Fanti-Ashanti from further west and the Calabar or Yefik from further east.

The Dahomey monarchs were mostly irresponsible and savage
despots with a penchant for human sacrifice, but in their milder
moods they were as anxious to sell their defaulting subjects and
prisoners of war as the European traders were to buy them. The
Portuguese never had the least political power in this blood-
stained realm, and their weakly garrisoned fort at Nossa Senhora
da Ajudá was very much at the mercy of the Dahomean rulers.
These latter did not hesitate to expel the Portuguese directors from
Whydah when it suited them, as happened on more than one
occasion. The Portuguese were powerless to resent these and other
insults, since their periodic threats to withdraw from Whydah
altogether were only bluff, as the Dahomeans very well knew.
Even more troublesome than the caprices of these Negro kings,
was the aggressive attitude of the Dutch who were based on Elmina. As mentioned previously, they hampered the Luso-Brazilian
slave trade in the Bight of Benin for most of the eighteenth century. Nevertheless, though the volume of trade declined somewhat after about 1740, it continued to flourish until well into the
nineteenth century for it was fundamentally attuned to the needs
of both Brazil and Dahomey.[29]

The mixture of races among the Negroes in Minas Gerais and
elsewhere was the chief safeguard of their masters against the
slave revolts which were planned at various times and places.
The Count of Assumar notified the Crown in 1719 of one par-

ticularly widespread plot which envisaged a general massacre of all the whites on Good Friday when they were expected to be attending church and off their guard. The plot was given away at the last moment because the Minas (West Sudanese) and Angolas (Bantu) could not agree about which of the two races should supply the king they intended to proclaim after the extermination of their masters. This perennial rivalry between Sudanese and Bantu was likewise the prime reason for the failure of similar slave conspiracies in later years, of which those in 1724 and 1756 were potentially the most dangerous. The fear of a Negro rebellion on the scale of the Palmares in Pernambuco was a perpetual nightmare to the authorities of Minas Gerais. As early as 1718 the Count of Assumar had advised the Crown to adopt the more summary and informal methods of justice inflicted on this "indomitable canaille" in Spanish America, but humaner councils seem to have prevailed at Lisbon.[30]

One of the few redeeming features in the life of slaves in Minas Gerais—or elsewhere in Brazil for that matter—was the possibility of their buying or being given their freedom at some time, a contingency which was much rarer in the French and English American colonies. Moreover, by the nature of their work in searching for placer gold it was often relatively easy for them to secrete gold dust and even small nuggets, apart from the fact that some masters allowed their slaves to seek gold for themselves after working a fixed number of hours for their owners. In this way a fair number of slaves were able to buy their freedom, and the hope of so doing was given to many more. The story that the church of Santa Efigenia was mainly built from the proceeds of the gold dust washed out of their hair by Negress devotees in the font may be apocryphal, but it is symptomatic of what could happen in Minas Gerais. The Negro *Irmandades,* whether bond or free, sometimes amassed considerable wealth, as instanced by the "Black Brethren of the Brotherhood of Our Lady of the Rosary" of Ouro Preto. They sponsored the publication of the *Triunfo Eucharistico* at Lisbon in 1734, and took a leading part in organizing the costly festivities which that book describes. They were also one of the more genuinely democratic brotherhoods, admitting people of all colors and both sexes in accordance with their *Compromisso* of 1715.

The author of *The Triumph of the Eucharist* rightly stresses the penchant of the Portuguese for the outward splendors of the Roman Catholic cult, and nowhere did they have a better chance of gratifying this inclination than in Minas Gerais. It is true that the gold they so freely expended for this purpose was lavished on the interior decoration rather than on the external appearance of their churches; presumably on the principle that the interior of a church, symbolizing Our Lord's soul, should be richer than the exterior symbolizing His body. It was on the carving, decoration, and gilding of the altars, retables, reredos, and pillars, that the sculptors and artists concentrated with a lavish use of gold leaf. The original churches and chapels were nearly all built of wood and *taipa* (tamped earth), or else of *pau-a-pique,* with thatched roofs. The great majority of those which the visitor admires today were rebuilt with stone walls and tiled roofs in the years 1750–1850. The larger buildings nearly always had twin-tower façades, and were treated in the Mannerist fashion. Of the few that survive in something like their original form, both outwardly and inwardly, the chapel of Nossa Senhora d'O at Sabará is perhaps the most beautiful. Its rich interior decoration is entirely in the flamboyant style of Dom João V, including some interesting panels imitating Chinese motifs in red and gold lacquer.[31]

In the building of these churches the brotherhoods played a great role, whether they were exclusively white or limited to Negro slaves. Sometimes an *Irmandade* would build a church or chapel entirely from its own resources, but more often they clubbed together (not always amicably in the upshot) to build the larger parish churches. One such example is the *Matriz* or mother church of Catas Altas, founded in 1703 or soon afterwards. Originally a small thatched adobe chapel, it was rebuilt on an impressive scale between 1730 and 1750, at a cost of 70,000 *cruzados* for the edifice alone. The entire cost was defrayed by the local brotherhoods and a levy on the townspeople.[32] It was a similar story elsewhere in Minas Gerais, the Crown only contributing tardily and occasionally, although it carefully collected the tithes which it was in theory supposed to spend on the stipends of the clergy and the construction and upkeep of churches.

If the Crown neglected its bounden duty in this respect, the local clergy more than made up for this omission by the extortionate fees which they charged their parishioners. Writing to the Crown at the request of the town councils of Minas Gerais in June, 1716, the governor, Dom Braz Balthazar da Silveira, gave a schedule of the fees which they charged. These included one dram of gold from each person who communicated and half a dram from anyone who did not do so. They charged sixteen drams for a sung Mass, four for a burial service, three for reading marriage banns, one for baptism (apart from the offering), and twenty for a sermon. Since the number of clergy was very small—there were fewer than thirty parish priests in 1712—and the population very numerous, these sums came to a vast amount of money in the aggregate. Dom Braz added that nearly all the clergy were appointed by the Bishop of Rio de Janeiro, "and the majority of them lead a very licentious life, being brought up in Brazil, their bad example being the main reason why people in these Mines live without fear of God." This representation seems to have had little effect beyond an admonition from the Crown to the Bishop of Rio de Janeiro enjoining that prelate to choose his clergy more carefully. On the other hand, we find the Bishop of Rio complaining to the Crown in 1726 that the exemplary parish priest of Ribeirão do Carmo had been violently expelled by his parishioners owing to his denunciation of their sexual irregularities.[33]

The appointment of a bishop to the see of Mariana (as Ribeirão do Carmo was renamed in 1745) did not ease the financial burden on the faithful, if an anonymous report of about 1750 is to be believed. The writer, who was clearly well informed, states that the bishop received as offerings when officiating at christenings and confirmation a sum amounting to 2,600 *cruzados* a year in gold and wax, "which he sent to be sold as soon as he got it and for a good price." The same authority estimated the total annual revenues of the bishopric as worth more than 21,000 *cruzados*. The Crown, which had farmed out the tithes of Minas Gerais since 1714, now received much more than this sum, but spent most of the money on other things. It has been argued that many of the complaints of the rapacity of the clergy in Minas Gerais, which continued throughout the colonial period, would not have been made if the Crown had allotted adequate stipends to the clergy from the substantial sums it received in tithes. Be this as it may, the fact remains that despite the greed and laxity of most of the clergy in the captaincy, Minas Gerais is still today the most Catholic region of Brazil.[34]

Another handicap from which the Church suffered during this period was the adamant refusal of the Crown to permit the establishment of any of the Religious Orders in Minas Gerais. This anticlerical attitude was something quite unprecedented for the kings of Portugal, who were, by and large, the most priest-ridden monarchs in Christendom. They usually gave lavish support to these same Orders elsewhere in their dominions, Minas Gerais being the only region where they were rigorously banned. As regards the Mendicant Orders, this prohibition did not matter very much, since their standards in colonial Brazil were, for the most part, notoriously low; but the rigid exclusion of the Jesuits was undoubtedly a grave handicap to the education of youth in this captaincy. The first Bishop of Mariana founded a seminary which had chairs of Latin, moral theology, and philosophy, in 1749; but, as we saw on page 169 above, when he attempted to broaden the curriculum and increase the pupils and the teaching staff, the governor gave him no and the Crown only temporary encouragement. The ban on the Religious Orders was repeated at frequent intervals throughout the eighteenth century, which shows that its enforcement left something to be desired. It was a Carmelite friar

who introduced raffles into Minas Gerais (for his own benefit), and the legislation of the period contains numerous enactments against other and more unedifying sons of Holy Mother
Church.[35]

If raffles were frowned upon by the colonial authorities as a
diversion for the people, they enthusiastically supported, when
they did not promote, the religious processions and the *festas
reais*, or celebrations staged to commemorate royal births, betrothals, and marriages. The religious processions, in particular,
were the favorite diversion of the populace of Minas Gerais, as
elsewhere in the Portuguese-speaking world. Perhaps the most
ambitious of these rejoicings were those organized to mark the
transference of the Blessed Sacrament from the Church of Rosario
to that of Pilar in May, 1733, of which the *Triunfo Eucharistico*
gives a colorful account. These festivities lasted more than a week,
and they included elaborately staged processions with the participants on foot, on horseback, and in triumphal cars, wearing
fancy dress and bearing allegorical devices. There were also equestrian sports, including tilting at the ring (the rings being of solid
gold), bull fights, and dancing in the streets to the music of
flutes, bagpipes, and guitars.

Triumphal arches were erected in the principal streets, and
householders hung out of their windows costly carpets, tapestries,
oriental damasks, and silks. Father Diogo Soares, the eminent
Jesuit cartographer whom we shall meet again in a later chapter,
acted as pageant master; and he also arranged the nightly fire-
work displays which aroused great enthusiasm. A makeshift open-
air theater was erected for the performance of three Spanish
comedies, *El Secreto a Vozes, El Principe Prodigioso,* and *El Amo
Criado.* These plays were likewise well received, and it is to be
presumed that the acting was of a higher standard than that in
La Monja Alferes, which Le Gentil de la Barbinais saw "acted
by the worst actors in the world," at Bahia in 1718. People of all
colors and classes shared in these diversions, whether as spectators
or participants, while the Governor, André de Mello de Castro,

Count of Galveas, "kept a most splendid table for all the gentry and persons of distinction, secular and ecclesiastical." He had acquired a well-deserved reputation for regal hospitality when ambassador at Rome in 1718–1728, and no doubt the crumbs which fell from this rich man's table at Villa Rica in May, 1733, were well worth having.

These particular celebrations were probably the most prodigal ever staged in Minas Gerais, but some of the *festas reais* were on a hardly less lavish scale. Those commemorating the successive betrothals and marriages between Portuguese and Spanish princes and princesses in 1723–1729, likewise included fancy-dress processions, bull fights, equestrian sports, and comedies staged in open-air theaters. Musical performances were also given on these occasions, many of the pieces being specially composed for the event. The remarkable school of mulatto professional musicians who flourished in Minas Gerais during the second half of the eighteenth century, and whose works have been recently discovered and revived for us by Professor Curt Lange, presumably originated in the first quarter of that century, though little is yet known of its origins.[36]

The gold which paid for these jousts and junketings, as for the necessities of daily life and the splendid decorations of the churches, was still mined for the most part in the ways described by Antonil at the beginning of the eighteenth century and by John Mawe a hundred years later. Since the latter's account is in English, it will be simplest to reproduce it here, with the caveat that the bowls he terms *gamellas* were usually called *bateias* in earlier days.

Suppose a loose gravel-like stratum of rounded quartzose pebbles and adventitious matter, incumbent on granite, and covered by earthy matter of variable thickness. Where water of sufficiently high level can be commanded, the ground is cut in steps, each twenty or thirty feet wide, two or three broad, and about one deep. Near the bottom a trench is cut to the depth of two or three feet. On each step stand six or eight Negroes, who, as the water flows gently from above, keep the earth continually in motion with shovels, until the whole is reduced to liquid mud and washed below. The particles of gold contained in this earth descend to the trench, where, by reason of their specific gravity, they quickly precipitate. Workmen are continually employed at the trench to remove the stones, and clear away the surface, which operation is much assisted by the current of water which falls into it. After five days' washing, the precipitation in the trench is carried to some convenient stream, to undergo a second clearance. For this purpose wooden bowls are provided, of a funnel shape, about two feet wide at the mouth, and five or six inches deep, called *gamellas*. Each workman standing in the stream, takes into his bowl five or six pounds weight of sediment, which generally consists of heavy matter, such as oxide of iron, pyrites, ferruginous quartz, &c. of a dark carbonaceous hue. They admit certain quantities of water into the bowl, which they move about so dexterously, that the precious metal, separating from the inferior and lighter substances, settles to the bottom and sides of the vessel. They then rinse their bowls in a larger vessel of clean water, leaving the gold in it and begin again. The washing of each bowlful occupies from five to eight or nine minutes; the gold produced is extremely variable in quantity and in the size of its particles, some of which are so minute, that they float, while others are found as large as peas, and not infrequently much larger. This operation is superintended by overseers, as the result is of considerable importance.[37]

When the rivers and their banks had been thoroughly exploited, these placer mines, "more fitly to be denominated washings," as John Mawe observed, were sometimes supplemented by more ambitious works, which involved driving shafts and tunnels into the hillsides for considerable distances. Luís Gomes Ferreira claims that some of these underground galleries penetrated for a distance of more than six or seven hundred spans, but this type of subterranean mining was the exception rather than the rule. Apart from the fact that the gold of Minas Gerais was mainly of the alluvial variety, the rocks of the region were for the most part either too friable or else too hard to be tunneled effectively by the primitive processes then used. Some of the mining techniques were apparently of West African origin, for the Portuguese evidently knew less about mining than did some of their slaves from the Western Sudan.

Most of the mining was done by Negro slaves, but many "poor whites" engaged in prospecting and mining on their own. These were the so-called *faiscadores,* who are still found in Minas Gerais today. Working individually or in small groups, they roam the countryside prospecting, washing, and digging for gold in remote places, seldom finding more than a few grains to earn their daily bread. As regards the more substantial miners, few of them owned more than a dozen slaves; but they were continually petitioning the Crown to grant them similar immunities from distraint for debt as those enjoyed by the large-scale sugar and tobacco planters. After much hesitation, the Crown decreed in 1752 that miners who had thirty or more slaves working for them, would be exempted from having these slaves or their mining equipment distrained for debt. This measure was opposed on the grounds that since virtually all business was done on credit in Minas Gerais, merchants and shopkeepers would be reluctant to extend credit facilities to customers on whom they could not foreclose. Nevertheless, this law remained on the statute book for many years, and in 1813 was extended to all miners without qualification.[38]

Whether working in gold-washings or in subterranean galleries, the miners' toil was often long, arduous, and conducive to disease. Wrote Luís Gomes Ferreira: "There they work, there they eat, and often there they have to sleep; and since when they work they are bathed in sweat, with their feet always in the cold earth, on stones, or in water, when they rest or eat, their pores close and they become so chilled that they are susceptible to many dangerous illnesses, such as very severe pleurisies, apoplectic, and paralytic fits, convulsions, pneumonia, and many other diseases." The resultant mortality was particularly heavy among the Negro slaves, who, as Gomes Ferreira noted disapprovingly,

were mostly badly treated, poorly housed, and worse clothed. He
mentions as one of several exceptions, a slaveowner who brought
him a slave for further treatment, "because he was a good slave,
and he wanted him cured, even though what he had already spent
on him amounted almost to his original price."

Among the common illnesses which afflicted both Black and
White in Minas Gerais, as elsewhere in Brazil, were bacillary
dysentery, intestinal worms, and venereal diseases. Gomes Ferreira gives us many graphic case histories of these and other sick-
nesses, together with his own often avowedly empirical methods
of treating them. Acute dysentery was very liable to result in
ulceration of the lower intestine and rectal gangrene. This was
the dreaded *mal do bicho,* which Gomes Ferreira correctly diag-
nosed, and which he noted was particularly prevalent in the São
Francisco River valley. Prevention being better than cure, he
recommended bodily cleanliness and the daily bath as the best
safeguard, another being a dose of brandy or of *cachaça* first thing
in the morning. This last habit has survived on both sides of the
south Atlantic, whence the name of *mata-bicho* in Brazil and
Angola. The mortality from intestinal worms was also very heavy,
and many of his observations on the incidence of this scourge
are applicable to the poorer parts of Brazil today. Venereal diseases were likewise widespread and by no means confined to
the lower orders of society. Some of Gomes Ferreira's cures were
painfully drastic, but he records appreciatively the wealthy landowner who gave him five hundred drams of gold after under-
going a successful course of treatment.

Luís Gomes Ferreira was a skillful surgeon as well as a quali-
fied physician, and the unruly population of Minas Gerais gave
him plenty of practice in blood staunching and bonesetting. He
records some astonishing cures of severe gunshot, sword and
knife wounds, many of his patients being clearly as tough as they
come, even in an age when pain killers were unknown. He was
often called upon to treat Negro slaves in mining accidents, and
he gives a particularly vivid account of one such disaster in 1711,

which was the worst that occurred during his twenty years in Minas. Understandably enough, chronic alcoholism was widespread among the Negro slaves, who found that they could best endure their work and forget their misery when fortified by the "white girl" (*moça branca*) as *cachaça* was commonly called.

Our surgeon doctor was in many ways in advance of his time, and his *Erario Mineral* forms a fascinating prologue to a modern *Manual of Tropical Medicine*. Unlike most of his contemporaries, he was very sparing with bleeding and purging, and he frequently denounces the excessive use which his countrymen commonly made of these two sovereign remedies.[39] He explained that ignorant patients, such as Negro slaves, must be cross-examined carefully and kindly, in order to elicit their real symptoms; "for since they are a rough and volatile people, they will first of all say one thing and then, when asked again, they will say something else." As mentioned above, he was insistent on the importance of personal hygiene and a daily bath, in an age when the average European regarded washing as a luxury and when Dr. Johnson could avow that he was not fussy about clean linen.

While angrily denouncing the *curandeiros* or quack doctors, both male and female, who were so popular in Minas Gerais, Gomes Ferreira realized that many of the native herbs and plants had better medicinal and curative properties than did the costly drugs and powders imported from Portugal. He particularly praised the Paulistas for their knowledge of "roots, herbs, plants, trees, and fruits, since they wander in the interior for years and years, curing their illnesses with these things alone, and because they are so closely connected with the Carijós, from whom they have learnt useful matters." Some of his own prescriptions, incidentally, included tea and Chinese ink, both of which (he states) were readily obtainable in Minas. This affords incidental testimony to the demand for Chinese wares in Brazil, which was mentioned on page 156 above. Of course, he had his own pet fallacies, such as a firm belief in the prophylactic qualities of urine, but he clearly lived up to his boast—"I, in this climate, have always cured my patients more by common sense and experience than by printed authorities," in contrast to those numerous doctors who still regarded Galen and the classical authorities as "the Tablets of the Law." [40]

The Mineiro who survived the *mal do bicho* and other hazards of life in Minas Gerais, had also to struggle against the high cost of living and the exigencies of the tax collector. The minutes of the Villa Rica town council teem with references to the undesirable activities of monopolists and engrossers, and the efforts of the councillors to combat them. The worst offenders were those who hoarded imported provisions, such as dried fish, olive oil, vinegar, wheaten flour, and cheese, selling them at famine prices in times of (often artificially induced) scarcity. Profiteering by the owners of neighboring farms (*fazendas*) and allotments (*roças*) was also not uncommon, and Assumar complained in 1718 that a carpenter got two drams of gold a day. Even the governors came under suspicion at times. These functionaries, and all civil and military officials down to the rank of captain and its equivalent, had been strictly forbidden to engage in any form of trade or commerce, directly or indirectly, "upon any pretext whatsoever," by a royal decree of August, 1720. Militia officers were later excepted from this ruling, but their colleagues in the regular army often took little notice of it. In September, 1723, Dom Lourenço de Almeida, the governor of Minas Gerais, publicly complained that "monopolists, or persons of evil conscience, enemies of the public peace," were spreading rumors that he was buying up maize through third persons—an allegation which he indignantly denied. His denials would be more convincing if we did not know that he speculated heavily in contraband diamonds, as we shall see in the next chapter.

The high price of foodstuffs meant that most people who could afford to do so had a farm or allotment on which they raised vegetables, poultry, pigs, and the like, for themselves and their slaves, selling the surplus at a good profit for consumption in town. For example, Dr. Luís Gomes Ferreira, apart from his extensive practice as a physician and surgeon, was also the proprietor of a fine *fazenda,* São Miguel do Bom Retiro de Itacolomí. The high cost of living in Minas Gerais is amusingly reflected in an anecdote reported by Martinho de Mendonça to a friend at Lisbon in 1734. "A Paulista one day asked an Emboaba, or Portuguese, if the king had a *roça* to maintain his family. When the latter replied 'no,' the former muttered, 'well, I'm not surprised that his majesty needs all the gold we pay him if he has to buy his food at retail prices.'"

In reversal of their attitude at the beginning of the century, when the Crown strove to check the influx of labor from the plantations to the mines, the authorities now legislated with the object of favoring mining at the expense of agriculture in Minas Gerais. These efforts met only with a limited degree of success, as necessity forced some people and profits tempted others to make a living from the land.[41]

One reason why prices remained so high in Minas Gerais was the vexatious and crippling network of imposts, tolls, and taxes, which bore even more heavily on necessities than on luxuries. Duties were levied on all merchandise, slaves, provisions, and cattle entering Minas Gerais along the three legal trails from Rio de Janeiro, São Paulo, and Bahia. The *dizimos reais,* or royal tithes were levied on a wide range of agricultural and industrial products in the four *comarcas* (counties) of Villa Rica, Rio das Mortes, Sabará (Rio das Velhas), and Serra do Frio, into which Minas Gerais was administratively divided. Tolls were levied at the principal river crossings on all travelers and beasts of burden. The *quinto,* or royal fifth, was levied on the production or the circulation of gold in various ways which are briefly described below. Most of these taxes were originally introduced for some specific purpose, such as the payment of the salaries of military officers and civilian officials, or for the upkeep of ecclesiastical establishments; but they were soon taken over by the Crown, and the surplus remitted to Lisbon with the royal fifths. In addition, the Crown "asked" periodically for *donativos,* or voluntary contributions to defray extraordinary expenses. These included the dowering of royal princesses and subsidies for the War of the Spanish Succession, or for the relief of the colony of Sacramento. On top of all these exactions by the Crown, the Mineiros also had to pay local dues levied by the town councils for the upkeep of roads and bridges, and other municipal services. The taxes levied by the Crown were normally farmed out to contractors, who, in return for an agreed cash payment or series of payments, collected the dues in the Crown's name and were entitled to keep the surplus (if any) after the needs of the local administration had been satisfied. Contracts were usually on a triennial basis and might be operated by one individual or by a syndicate. Finally there were the *propinas* or "rake-offs" from official salaries which officeholders had to pay to the Crown or its nominees, as well as those which contractors had to pay to certain officials connected with the administration of their contracts.

Tithes, as collected in Brazil during the first half of the eighteenth century, were real, mixed, or personal. Real tithes comprised the tenth part (or its equivalent in gold) of agricultural products such as manioc, maize, rice, sugar, tobacco, vegetables, and fruits. They also included, theoretically at least, the tenth part of other products of the land, such as wood, whether raised naturally or through cultivation. Mixed tithes were those collected on livestock and fowls, beehives, honey, wax, cheese, and building materials; as also on the products of sugar mills and rum distilleries, bread ovens, and so on. Personal tithes were the tenth part of the net proceeds of any office, trade, or business. These were not collected by the Crown, but paid directly to the clergy, usually in the form of *conhecenças* or "acknowledgments," at Eastertide. The King of Portugal collected colonial tithes in his capacity of Grand Master of the Order of Christ, which was theoretically responsible for the upkeep of the Church overseas; but by this time that privilege had become in effect a *regalia* of the Lusitanian Crown and the tithes were termed *dizimos reais*.[42]

The duties levied on merchandise entering Minas Gerais,

whether on horses, mules, or slaves, were calculated on a basis of dividing all goods into two classes, wet (*molhado*) and dry (*secco*). The former included foodstuffs, such as wine and olive oil, and the latter comprised agricultural implements, workmen's tools, textiles, clothing, furniture. The duties, which remained fixed from 1714 onwards, bore most heavily on vital goods and foodstuffs, for they were calculated on a basis of weight. For example, salt, which was a royal monopoly and paid heavy duties at Brazilian ports, cost 720 *reis* the *alqueire* at Rio de Janeiro, and had to pay another 750 on entering Minas Gerais. When costs of packing, carriage, and insurance, not forgetting the contractors' profits were added to this, it is not surprising to learn that the inhabitants of Minas Gerais had to pay 3,600 *reis* for an *alqueire* of salt by the time it reached the market. On the other hand, luxury articles such as silks, which were included in the "dry goods" category, were relatively much cheaper. Goods which were worth 100 *moedas* a *quintal* paid exactly the same tax as those worth ten times that valuation, thus putting a virtual premium on luxury goods.

The duties on goods, slaves, merchants, and travelers entering Minas Gerais were collected by posts established at convenient sites such as narrow defiles and river crossings. These posts were called *registros,* and everyone had to stop there and submit to a customs inspection by the contractor's representative, who was likewise a Crown official. The way in which these *registros* functioned can be gathered from the following entry in the 1716–1717 ledger for the post established on the Rio Grande. It has the added interest of containing the only known physical description and autograph signature of one of the makers of eighteenth-century Brazil.

"Let pass Manuel Nunes Viana, a man of medium height, round faced, dark eyes, black hair, with his pack-train of 23 loads of wet goods. Rio Grande, 14 May 1717. [signed] *Manuel Nunes Viana."*

Having paid the required duty and been given a receipt, the

traveler was then allowed to proceed on his way. Similarly, on the outward journey from Minas Gerais, everyone had to stop at these *registros* and secure a clearance for whatever gold and slaves he was taking along. The traveler also had to pay the royal fifths unless he could produce a certificate proving that he had already done so elsewhere.[43]

Onerous as most of these manifold exactions were, it was the collection of the royal fifths which gave the most trouble throughout the colonial period in Minas Gerais. Generally speaking, the Mineiros did not object to the *real quinto* in principle, but to the various ways in which it was collected, for a satisfactory method was never evolved. The Duke of Newcastle told Lord Tyrawly in 1739 that "the King of Portugal is absolute master in his own dominions, and consequently can exact or excuse the payment of any duties that he pleases within them," [44] but this was an exaggeration. Although Dom João V was in theory and by inclination an absolute monarch, his representatives in Minas Gerais had to tread as delicately as Agag before the Count of Assumar terrorized Villa Rica in 1720—and even after that they had to watch their step until Pombal's ruthless energy made itself felt in Brazil. The checkered history of the *quinto* shows this clearly enough.

The system established by Albuquerque in 1710 of collecting the fifths by imposing a tax of ten drams of gold dust on each *bateia* (p. 82 above) did not work satisfactorily. It amounted in effect to a capitation tax on slaves employed in the mines, and meant that miners who found little or no gold in their washings paid as much as those who struck it rich. Albuquerque's successor, Dom Braz Balthazar da Silveira, therefore made an agreement with the representatives of the town councils in December, 1713, that they would pay the Crown yearly a tax of thirty *arrobas* (440 kgs) in commutation of the *quinto*. To raise the amount, they taxed not only the miners' slaves, but organized the system of *registros,* whereby transit dues were levied on slaves, goods, and cattle coming into Minas Gerais as explained above. But the Crown refused to sanction this agreement and ordered Dom Braz to denounce it and to revert to the original system of *bateias*. This he tried to do by playing off the *Camaras* against each other; but the people of Caeté and Morro Velho rose in revolt and the disturbances showed every sign of spreading. Since Dom Braz had no regular troops to support him, and the militia was on the side of the rebels, he was compelled (in his own words) "to pass under the Caudine Forks" and revert to the global contribution of thirty *arrobas* yearly.

The Crown accepted the rebuff for the time being, but when a new governor, Dom Pedro de Almeida, Count of Assumar, came out to relieve Dom Braz at the end of 1717, he was instructed to secure somehow an increase in the Crown's share of the gold. In March next year he made an agreement with the *Camaras* whereby their contribution was reduced to twenty-five *arrobas,* but the Crown took over the operation of the *registros* which levied duties on incoming and outgoing traffic. This was an astute move, for after the collection of these duties was farmed out to contractors by the Crown they yielded an annual return of thirty-one *arrobas* of gold by 1750.

The Crown was dissatisfied with the reduction of the *quinto* by the agreement of March, 1718, considering that in view of the increase in population and in the production of gold, the fifths ought rather to be augmented. A royal decree of February 11, 1719 enjoined the establishment of one or more smelting-houses in Minas Gerais, to which all gold intended for export from the captaincy must be taken for casting into bars, stamping, and payment of the royal fifths.[45] Gold dust was still permitted to circulate in Minas Gerais itself, for the purpose of ordinary payments and purchases, but it was not to be taken to any other part of Brazil on pain of very severe penalties. Two companies of dragoons, formed almost exclusively of men from the north of Portugal, were sent to Minas in the same year, to give the Count of Assumar the backing which previous governors had lacked.

On receiving these instructions, the Count of Assumar published a proclamation on July 18, 1719, announcing that smelting-houses for the reception and quinting of gold would be opened on July 23 of the following year at Villa Rica, Sabará, São João d'El Rei, and Villa do Principe. This proclamation was quickly followed by wild rumors, "mixing many lies with a few truths, whose seeds still survive today in these mines, where the doctrine of Machiavelli rather than that of Christ is taught in the schools." [46] Apart from these inspired rumors, many Mineiros knew they would have to travel long distances over difficult country to reach the nearest smelting-house, where they could expect to endure further delays and expenditure at the hands of an inefficient and corrupt bureaucracy. Instigated by the *poderosos da terra,* or "great ones of the land," and by the renegade friars against whom Assumar was simultaneously taking drastic measures, the Mineiros began armed demonstrations and disturbances in various districts. The earlier riots were suppressed by the dragoons without much difficulty, but a far more serious movement broke out at Villa Rica on the night of June 28–29, 1720.

The ostensible reason for this outbreak was the great unpopularity of the local ouvidor (royal judge), who narrowly escaped being lynched by a mob which broke into his house just after he had received timely warning and fled. After sacking the judge's house, raping his mulata concubine, and maltreating his servants, the crowd began to demonstrate against the proposed establishment of a mint and smelting-houses by the Crown. Three days later, some two thousand men marched on the neighboring town of Ribeirão do Carmo, where the Count of Assumar found he could count on only forty dragoons (the remainder being away sick or on detachments) and the distinctly lukewarm loyalty of the local inhabitants. The rioters presented him with an eighteen-point ultimatum demanding among other things the abandonment of the smeltery project and the formal granting of an unconditional pardon under the royal seal. After some discussion,

Assumar assented to all this, "since they still asked for it [the pardon] with some show of submission," and the rioters returned triumphantly to Villa Rica.

Assumar had no intention of fulfilling an agreement that he had made under duress and only to gain time to rally the loyal elements to his side. These included the townspeople of São João d'El Rei and the bulk of the Paulistas in the vicinity, the latter perhaps being moved by a desire for revenge on the Emboabas. Dissensions among the rebel leaders soon gave him the chance to strike. The movement had originally been inspired mainly by Pascoal da Silva Guimaraes, a Minhoto immigrant who had made a large fortune from trading and from the gold diggings on the *morro,* or hill, which was called after him and which overlooked the town of Villa Rica.[47] Another ringleader was the retired *ouvidor,* Manuel Mosqueira da Roza, who was largely actuated by intense dislike of his successor. Once the movement had started, its direction was largely taken over by a Minhoto muleteer, Felipe dos Santos, who, with a few others, seems to have contemplated killing or expelling the governor and making Minas Gerais independent of the Crown in all but name. This was a good deal further than most people were prepared to go, and the townspeople of Villa Rica were becoming nervous of the armed bands of Negro slaves whom Pascoal da Silva and the others maintained to keep them up to the mark.

Feeling himself strong enough to strike, the Count of Assumar left Ribeirão do Carmo at the head of a column of 1,500 men at first light on July 14. He occupied Villa Rica without resistance, rounded up several of the ringleaders, paraded them through the streets, and subsequently sent them in chains to Rio de Janeiro for deportation to Lisbon. Felipe dos Santos evaded arrest on this occasion but was seized shortly afterwards when trying to raise the countryside. Assumar being resolved to make an example of him, he was summarily tried, sentenced to death without due process of law, and executed by garrotting. His head was exposed on the pillory at Villa Rica and his dismembered limbs by the roadside. With the same object of terrorizing the townspeople, the Count had previously ordered the houses of Pascoal da Silva and his adherents to be fired one windy night on the Morro. In the darkness and confusion, many other dwellings became involved, and the Negro slaves had a glorious time getting drunk on stolen brandy. The formerly populous site was laid completely waste, and has ever since been termed the *Morro da Queimada* ("Hill of the Burning").[48]

It is clear from Assumar's subsequent correspondence with the Crown and from the polemically defensive tone of the "Discurso Historico-Politico," that he had something of a guilty conscience over the summary trial and execution of Felipe dos Santos. The governor had no authority to inflict capital punishment on a freedman on his own responsibility, but only after consultation with the royal judges. The *Ouvidor* of Villa Rica was then a refugee on his way to Rio, and Assumar pleaded lack of time to consult those of the other *comarcas,* apart from the need of making a drastic example forthwith. The Crown accepted his arguments, though not without some misgivings, and the consensus of later official opinion was that Assumar's severity had the desired effect. The *poderosos* no longer kept Minas Gerais in turmoil with their bands of armed Negro slaves, and the Mineiros realized that "the yoke of civil obedience was better than that of licentious liberty."[49] Indeed, so cowed was the populace of Villa Rica that when the Count of Assumar some months later arranged for a pseudo summons calling on the people to rise, nobody ventured to do so. More people married and settled down on the land to rear respectable families, and better behaved immigrants came out from Portugal. Martinho de Mendonça reported of the Mineiros in 1734: "It can be said, much to the credit of those who govern them, that the king has not got more obedient vassals, nor ones who more readily sacrifice great wealth in the royal service, and that the ministers of justice in the Mines are treated with great respect, and are not merely obeyed but feared"—and this despite the fact that some of these ministers behaved very badly.[50] Similar sentiments were expressed by the Count of Galveas, who told the Crown that the last instalment of the *donativo* in 1733, had been paid by many impoverished Mineiros "with the gold, jewelry, and petticoats of their wives." [51] Admittedly, discordant voices were not entirely lacking. Diogo de Mendonça Corte-Real, King John V's principal Secretary of State, stigmatized the inhabitants of Minas Gerais as being mostly vagrant Negroes and mulattoes, who enjoyed too much freedom in the spacious wilds of America, but this elegant old gentleman had never been in Brazil.[52]

Although the Count of Assumar had won the final round at Villa Rica and imposed the royal authority once for all, he did not venture to establish the smelteries, but retained the old system of collecting the fifths by an annual contribution of thirty *arrobas* supplemented by the taxes, tolls, and imposts levied under contract at the *registros*. The Crown, on its side, rather reluctantly confirmed the pardon given by him to the rioters in July, 1720, and thus accepted the rebuff to its plans for the moment. But only for the moment. Acting on Assumar's earlier advice, Dom João V now separated the unwieldy captaincy of São Paulo and Minas Gerais into its two component parts, thus giving formal sanction to what was already in some ways an accomplished fact. As the first governor of the new captaincy in succession to Assumar, the king appointed Dom Lourenço de Almeida, a man whose mild and conciliatory disposition had been evinced so successfully at Pernambuco (p. 124 above). He was ordered to do his best to secure a substantial increase in the royal fifths by whatsoever means he deemed best, but preferably by the establishment of a mint and smelting-houses, as envisaged in 1719.

Dom Lourenço found the people of Minas Gerais still hostile to the proposed smelting-houses, although the town council of Villa Rica had promised Assumar to build a mint at its own expense, by way of reparation for the revolt of 1720. To avoid instituting either of these establishments, the united representatives of the town councils offered to raise the contribution of the royal fifths from thirty to thirty-seven (and later fifty-two) *arrobas* yearly. Dom

Lourenço accepted this offer and warmly commended it to Lisbon; but the Crown had now screwed its courage to the sticking point and ordered him to enforce the establishment of a mint and four regional smelting-houses. More fortunate or more tactful than his predecessor, Dom Lourenço managed to secure the opening of a mint and smelting-house at Villa Rica in February, 1725, by a mixture of persuasion and guile. Two other smelting-houses were established at Sabará and at São João d'El Rei, respectively, in July, 1734, but the fourth does not seem to have materialized.[53] The fifths were now collected at these smelting-houses, being cast into bars after the payment of an additional five per cent for seigniorage and brassage. The mint (*Casa da Moeda*) at Villa Rica also accepted gold for casting into coin after payment of these dues. In May, 1730, Dom Lourenço lowered the payment of the *quinto* from twenty to twelve per cent, which resulted (as expected) in a great increase in the amount of gold turned in, but this experiment was of short duration as the higher limit was restored in September, 1732, by order of the Crown.

This system worked fairly well from the Mineiros' point of view —at any rate in retrospect—although there were numerous complaints about the time and money they wasted in taking their gold dust to Villa Rica from outlying parts of the captaincy before the establishment of the two other smelting-houses in 1734. The Crown, however, was far from satisfied, since the increased yield did not match its sanguine expectations, while smuggling and frauds of every description flourished for the reasons explained below. The problem was long and anxiously debated at Lisbon, Dom João V himself carefully considering the various alternative methods that were suggested. After much discussion, and after consulting ex-governors of Minas Gerais, such as the Count of Assumar and Dom Lourenço de Almeida, it was finally decided to adopt a capitation tax on the lines proposed by Alexandre de Gusmão, the Brazilian-born private secretary of the king.[54]

A specially selected official, Martinho de Mendonça de Pina de Proença, was sent out in 1733 to enforce the new system after due consultation with the governor and *Camaras* of Minas Gerais, all of whom were strongly opposed to it. So much did the Mineiros dread the advent of a capitation tax, that in March, 1734, they offered instead to raise the annual contribution of the *quinto* to a minimum amount of 100 *arrobas,* any surplus accruing from the gold brought to the smelteries to remain with the Crown. The Count of Galveas accepted this offer and warmly commended it to the king, since he felt certain that the amount produced yearly would easily exceed 100 *arrobas.* Martinho de Mendonça, on the other hand—or so it was alleged—"went throughout these Mines, persuading the people to accept what oppresses them so sorely today [1750]. To make matters more confused, he visited the schools and asked the boys to write their names because he wanted to see which one of them wrote best. With the signatures he secured in this way, he returned to this town [Villa Rica] and did the same thing in the schools there. And after this, he called a meeting in which he said that the common people of all the Mines wanted the capitation, as could be seen from their signatures." [55] After some shilly-shallying on the part of the Crown, the Count of Galveas' advice was rejected and a slightly modified version of the capitation tax was inaugurated in Minas Gerais as from July 1, 1735, by the new governor, Gomes Freire de Andrada.

One of the Crown's reasons for imposing this new form of taxation was that it was fundamentally fairer than the old method of the fifths, since it was applied to a very much wider range of people and not to miners and *faiscadores* alone. All slaves of both sexes over the age of twelve were taxed at a flat rate of 4¾ drams of gold a head, even those who were too old or infirm to do any useful work. Moreover, free Negroes, mulattoes, and mixed bloods who had no slaves of their own, had to pay an identical capitation tax on themselves. Craftsmen and workmen paid the same amount, while shops, stores, and inns, were divided into three categories, their owners paying twenty-four, sixteen, and eight drams respectively. The smelting-houses were closed and the circulation of coin prohibited in Minas Gerais, though gold dust was allowed to circulate freely there. The capitation tax had to be paid in two instalments, due on March 15 and September 15, respectively. Defaulters were fined as soon as they were in arrears for a day, and if a few weeks passed without their being able to find the necessary sum in gold, their slaves, goods, or personal belongings were liable to seizure for the value of the amount outstanding.

The capitation tax proved highly unpopular, for the following reasons among others. The tax bore more hardly on the poor than on the rich, since miners whose slaves were lucky in washing for gold paid the same amount on each slave as did those miners whose slaves earned them little or nothing—and these last were in the great majority. Similarly, the owners of unprofitable shops, stores, or inns, paid the same rates as those owners who were making large profits from their establishments. Farmers and cultivators had to pay not only the tenths (*dizimos*) on their crops, but the fifths (*quintos*) on their slaves as well, thus being liable in effect to double taxation. Numerous mulata and colored girls were compelled to resort to prostitution in order to raise the gold for their capitation tax; "others, with more tears than words, give some small piece of gold from their pathetic finery." The incidence of tax on all slaves more than twelve years old was manifestly unfair, since it included even the slave employed by a blind beggar to solicit alms.

Worst of all, however, was the drastic distraint for debt on those who could not pay or who were unavoidably in arrears with their tax on the stipulated dates. The whole system of trade and commerce in Minas Gerais was founded on long-term credit, "for whatever is offered for sale there, is not sold for ready gold but on trust for years; in such wise that the merchandise which arrives from one fleet is not paid for until after four or five years have passed. This is why the people of Minas owe such large sums of money to merchants at Rio de Janeiro, Bahia, and Pernambuco." To pay their capitation tax on time, most people were forced to borrow still more gold, or else to sell their own plate or their wives' and daughters' jewels. Slaves were all bought on long-term credit, and miners who could not pay their capitation tax often had their slaves seized by the Crown officials before they had paid for them in whole or in part. This sort of thing in its turn had adverse effects on the trade with the ports, where merchants became increasingly shy of extending credit to Mineiros.[56] All these protests eventually had the desired effect, and Martinho de Mendonça complained that he was regarded as "the executioner of the people" (*algoz do povo*). Despite Alexandre de Gusmão's able defense of his brain child, the Crown finally gave way and abolished the hated capitation tax by an edict of December 3, 1750. The smelteries were reopened in the following year and the system based on a guaranteed minimum of one hundred *arrobas,* which the Count of Galveas had provisionally accepted in March, 1734, was restored.

One of the reasons why the Crown retained the capitation tax for so long despite its extreme unpopularity, was the alarming way in which the smuggling and falsification of gold flourished during the decade 1725–1735. It will be recalled that António de Albuquerque had prophesied in 1710 that three-fifths of the *reais quintos* would never be collected by the Crown, whatever precautions were taken to prevent smuggling and embezzlement (p. 82). Referring to the conditions that prevailed before the imposition of the capitation tax, Alexandre de Gusmão asked rhetorically in 1750: "is it to be expected that anyone would voluntarily deprive himself of a fifth part of his capital, when he can save it with a little risk and trouble?" And so it proved. The obligation to pay twenty drams of gold out of every hundred to the royal treasury and another five per cent for seigniorage and brassage in the smelteries, was in itself sufficient to explain the widespread prevalence of fraud and evasion. This was rendered all the more tempting by the wild and mountainous terrain of the mining regions, the fewness and badness of the roads, the bureaucratic delays involved at the smelteries, and the venality of many of the poorly paid Crown officials. Last not least, the Crown would only pay for gold at the fixed rate of 1,200 *reis* the *oitava,* whereas it was worth from 1,350 to 1,500 on the open market.

Gold was smuggled out by unfrequented rivers and paths through the bush to Bahia and Rio de Janeiro, whence much of it was again diverted illegally to the Mina Coast, to the Azores, to Buenos Aires, and even to French Guiana. Still greater quantities were smuggled out in the annual fleets to Lisbon and in homeward-bound East-Indiamen, "in barrels and chests and faggots of sugar, and also concealed in the cabins and the hulls" of those ships. The Crown gave the most stringent orders to prosecute offenders and threatened the severest penalties for those who were convicted. Large numbers of small fry were caught, but nobody dared to give evidence against the powerful people who were smuggling on a colossal scale, and who, as often as not, were working in collusion with the legal officials who should have been enforcing the law against them.[57]

The governor of Rio de Janeiro told the Crown in July, 1730, that he was not worried about 500 or 600 drams of gold which a poor man might be tempted to smuggle on board ship, "because the regal grandeur of Your Majesty should not heed such petty infractions, since the like can occur in any private household." But he drew the line at recent developments, when business companies were being formed for the sole purpose of defrauding the royal fifths—and there were even some theologians who were prepared to justify such robbery. Luis de Vahia Monteiro's warning was justified quicker than he had, perhaps, expected. In March of the following year, an informer betrayed a clandestine mint and smeltery which had been installed in a remote part of the Serra de Paraopeba in Minas Gerais. This was operated by a gang of coiners under Inacio de Sousa Ferreira, an unscrupulous but cultured adventurer who had been successively an Oratorian friar and captain of an East-Indiaman before his arrival in Brazil. The gang included experts formerly employed in the smelteries and more than thirty well-armed Negro slaves. The building included a farmstead, storehouses, and chapel—the spiritual needs of this self-contained criminal community being cared for by a resident Dominican friar.[58]

Inacio de Sousa had a strongly developed quarter-deck mentality and enforced a most rigid code of discipline on his subordinates. They were forbidden to indulge in drink or gambling on pain of severe penalties, in which no distinction was made between white and black offenders. His chief agent at Villa Rica was Manuel de Afonseca, secretary to Dom Lourenço de Almeida, and therefore a man who was in the best possible position for giving them timely warning or information. The gang also had their agents at Rio de Janeiro and Lisbon, a strongly rooted tradition affirming that the Infante Dom Francisco, King John V's scapegoat and sadistic brother,[59] was involved in this criminal organization. That the gang had powerful protectors at court was shown by what happened after the *Ouvidor* of Sabará, Dr. Diogo Cotrim de Sousa, surprised and stormed their stronghold at daybreak one wild March morning. Some of the miscreants escaped, but Inacio de Sousa and others were captured and sent in chains to Lisbon for trial. Though caught *in flagrante delicto* with ample proof of the heinousness of their offense in the shape of the coining machines and Inacio de Sousa's standing orders for the gang, they were released after a few years, and some of them returned to Minas Gerais.

Of course, not all criminals were equally lucky or equally well protected. The Count of Sabugosa caught two Portuguese-born coiners at Bahia in 1732, both of whom he had burnt to death, in accordance with the statutory punishment for their offense. Other arrests for coining bars or money were made at Tijuco and at São Paulo in the years 1732–1733, but I have not been able to ascertain what happened to the culprits.[60] In any event, the smuggling of gold and the falsification of gold bars continued for the rest of the colonial period, but seem to have reached their high-water mark during the 1730's. It was at this period, too, that the illicit production of diamonds provoked savage countermeasures by the authorities. Whatever the severity of the measures taken by the Crown to prevent gold smuggling and falsification in Minas Gerais, they were far exceeded by the ruthless way in which the mining of diamonds was controlled. If gold smugglers were chastised with whips, diamond smugglers were chastised with scorpions.

VIII. DIAMOND DISTRICT

A STUDY of the published and unpublished records relating to colonial Brazil shows that the claim made by successive kings of Portugal that they behaved more like fathers than like liege lords toward their vassals was by no means unfounded.[1] Individual complaints usually received a careful and conscientious hearing in the royal councils, even though, as we have seen, pressure of business and bureaucratic red tape might delay a decision for years. The Crown's anxiety to see that justice was done is evident from the trouble it took to hear both sides of any given case and the care with which it sifted conflicting evidence before giving a final verdict. (Admittedly, this procedure was sometimes due to a desire to procrastinate for as long as possible where an eventual and substantial payment by the royal exchequer was envisaged). If the Crown squeezed a great deal of gold out of its vassals through the fifths, tithes, salt gabelle, and other vexatious monopolies, it also made innumerable payments and maintained an enormous pension list wherein figured widows and orphans in remote colonies as well as parasitic courtiers at Lisbon.

The Crown frequently reversed its previous decisions when confronted with convincing evidence that the people were suffering as a result of the enforcement of a particular policy. The abolition of the capitation tax in 1750, in deference to public opinion in Minas Gerais, is an example of this; and the reader will recall that the tax had only been imposed in the first instance after two years of conscientious consultations, in which the king himself took a leading part. Another such instance was the appeal made by the peasant women of Minho against a tax on the regional lace industry, which was likewise abolished after a delegate had visited Lisbon on their behalf in 1749.[2] But there was one object and one region to which these qualifications did not apply, and where the Crown displayed a calculated ferocity in upholding its rights and in squeezing its vassals in a way which a tyrannical oriental despot might have envied. This was the Diamond District of Minas Gerais—the one region where, whenever the interests of the Crown and of its subjects conflicted, the former prevailed unhesitatingly, even in defiance of moral and economic laws. The Crown might—and did—tolerate considerable relaxation and backsliding elsewhere, but not in the *Distrito Diamantino*. Harsh and oppressive laws could often be circumvented with relative ease and impunity in the backlands of Brazil, but not in the bleak and forbidding region of the aptly-named Serro do Frio.

This region had been traversed by the *bandeiras* of Fernão Dias Pais in the 1670's and 1680's (p. 35 above), but the Paulistas were then looking for silver and emeralds, not for gold and diamonds. These last were only known to exist half a world away, in India and Borneo, whereas the belief that Brazil was rich in emeralds had a basis of ascertained fact as well as of hoary tradition. The upper reaches of the river Jequitinhonha and its tributaries were found to be rich in gold during the early days of the "rush"; and despite the inhospitable terrain of this savage region, mining camps were soon established in many places. The principal *arraial* was made a township under the name of Villa do Principe in 1714, and it was at an unascertained date in the ensuing decade that a few discerning people first recognized diamonds for what they really were.

These stones had been turned up in great quantities by miners and their slaves who were washing the *cascalho* of the river beds for gold; but they were thought to be merely some kind of crystals. They were used as counters and scoring points in card games, and changed hands freely for many years. When someone—tradition differs on whether it was a friar or a judge—who had been in India finally recognized their real nature, the discovery was kept secret by this man and his cronies, who quietly secured all they could without arousing suspicion. In 1726, some of these stones came into the hands of Dom Lourenço de Almeida, the governor of Minas Gerais. He likewise pretended that he did not know what they were, though in point of fact he identified them at once, since he had become a connoisseur of these gems during his long residence at Goa, which was then a center of the diamond trade.[3] Dom Lourenço also collected as many diamonds as he could from the unsuspecting miners, but someone at Villa Rica soon gave the game away. Crowds of adventurers with their slaves turned from gold to diamond washing, penetrating to the remotest parts of the Serro do Frio.

Dom Lourenço had now no alternative but to tell the Crown what was happening, which he did in an ingenuously worded dispatch of July 22, 1729. Adopting a skeptical tone, he reported that "some little white stones" had been found in the Serro do Frio, but local opinion differed about what they really were. Being uncertain of their value, he had not hitherto notified the Crown of their discovery, but he now forwarded six of these stones for examination by jewelers at Lisbon. Pending the Crown's reply, he promulgated an edict suspending all gold washing and mining in the district where these stones had been found, and he canceled all *datas* previously granted for the former purpose. Replying on February 8, 1730, the Crown severely censured Dom Lourenço for not reporting the discovery sooner, since diamonds had been arriving regularly from Brazil with passengers on board the fleets of the last two years. Dom Lourenço was told to consult local opinion as to the best means of levying the royal fifths on diamonds and then to institute this tax forthwith.

On June 26, 1730, Dom Lourenço accordingly promulgated the first regulation (*Regimento*) concerning the extraction and disposal of diamonds. A capitation tax of five *milreis* was levied on each slave or miner employed in searching for diamonds, and the Crown Judge (*Ouvidor*) of Villa do Principe was appointed to superintend the redistribution of *datas* in that region. No shops, taverns, or booths were to be established within a distance of two leagues of any place where mining was carried on. Nobody was allowed to buy any diamonds from slaves, and the superintendent was ordered to expel any friar who might be found in the diamond district. The limits of this area were very vaguely defined, and as the capitation tax was a relatively modest one, the search for diamonds continued apace. The most flourishing mining camp (*arraial*) was that of Tijuco, which soon became a bustling center surpassing Villa do Principe in population and importance, though not in official status.

The Crown did not approve of Dom Lourenço's moderation, and on March 16, 1731 enjoined him to limit the diamond mining (or, rather, washing) to the rivers Jequitinhonha and Ribeirão do Inferno. *Datas* could only be secured for a minimum payment of sixty *milreis* a square fathom, being granted to the highest bidder over that sum, and the best sites were to be reserved for the Crown. Everyone not actually engaged in searching for diamonds was to be expelled from these two valleys, even if they had been well established with their families for years. By way of excusing these draconic measures, the Crown claimed that even severer measures were taken by the Great Moghul in the diamond mines of Golconda.[4]

Dom Lourenço attempted to enforce these restrictive measures in January, 1732, but, impressed by the volume of complaints, protests, and petitions which followed, he took upon himself the responsibility of moderating this system for a trial period of one year as from the end of December. The inhabitants of Tijuco had offered to pay a capitation tax of fifteen *milreis* if the Crown regulations were not enforced; and Dom Lourenço agreed to allow diamond mining to continue throughout the Serro do Frio region in return for a further increase to twenty *milreis* a head. One clause in the regulations of January, 1732 was retained. This was that all free Negroes and mulattoes of both sexes should be expelled from the diamond district, leaving only free Whites and Negro slaves to operate there. He further ordained that no Negro or mulatto in Minas Gerais, whether bond or free, should carry any defensive weapon, "not even a staff," on pain of receiving two hundred lashes. This in a country where brigands and robbers abounded, to say nothing of dangerous wild beasts and snakes, and where virtually everyone went about armed to the teeth!

The Crown and its councillors at Lisbon were still dissatisfied with Dom Lourenço's relative moderation, although they realized that diamonds were, if anything, more readily concealed and smuggled than gold. The Count of Galveas, who took over the captaincy of Minas Gerais from Dom Lourenço on September 1, 1732 brought with him instructions to raise the capitation tax to forty *milreis*. This was not so much to increase the yield of the royal fifths, as to limit the numbers of people engaged in diamond mining and hence (it was hoped) to lower the production of diamonds and so maintain their value. Two years later Tijuco was made the administrative center of the Diamond District, which was now carefully demarcated for the first time. The original boundaries measured about fifty leagues in circumference, but the area was subsequently enlarged to include neighboring places where diamonds were discovered. The control of this district was exercised by an intendant with far-reaching judicial, fiscal, and administrative powers. He was to a great extent independent of the authority of both the governor of Minas Gerais and the viceroy at Bahia.[5]

The first intendant of the Diamond District was Dr. Raphael Pires Pardinho, a Crown lawyer with a long and creditable record of service in Brazil, principally in the captaincy of São Paulo. His colleague in the demarcation of the district, Martinho de Mendonça de Pina e de Proença, was one of Dom João V's most trusted advisers and an exceptionally cultured and intelligent man. Belonging to the group known in Portugal as the *Estrangeirados* ("foreignized") he had served under Prince Eugene against the Turks and had spent some time in England, where he had become a great admirer of the works of John Locke. He had been sent out to Brazil to help enforce the capitation tax on both gold and diamonds in accordance with the plan elaborated by Alexandre de Gusmão, as mentioned on page 197 above. The choice of these two eminent civilians by the Crown was something of an innovation in Portuguese America, where, as we have seen, military governors were the almost invariable rule.

The Portuguese judiciary at this period had an unenviable reputation for corruption, as anyone familiar with the official correspondence must admit. The matter was put as amusingly and succinctly as usual by Lord Tyrawly, who wrote in a dispatch of February 14, 1738: "The Portuguese, more than any other people, adhere to that rule of Scripture, that a gift maketh room for a man, and it is incredible how a present smooths the difficulties of a solicitation; nay, they even expect it, and though the presents necessary are not considerable, since a few dozen bottles of foreign wine, or a few yards of fine cloth will suffice, yet this often repeated amounts to money." Unlike the majority of their colleagues, Pires Pardinho and Martinho de Mendonça had an enviable reputation for complete honesty and integrity, recalling in this respect some of the great Spanish *Oidores,* on whom the Kings of Castile so often relied for the detection and rectification of abuses in their American empire. Gomes Freire de Andrada, a military martinet who governed some or all of the southern captaincies of Brazil between 1733 and 1763, adopted at times an almost deferential tone in his correspondence with these two civilians, whom he treated as colleagues rather than as subordinates.[6]

The unexpected—and for several years unofficial—influx of Brazilian diamonds into Lisbon in the early 1730's inevitably led to a sharp decline in their market value, which at one time was only a third of the pre-1730 price. Some contemporaries, including the Count of Sabugosa, as well as some recent writers have attributed this fall mainly to the machinations of Jewish financiers in England and Holland. Admittedly, the Jewish merchants of London and Amsterdam, who originally handled most of the trade in Indian diamonds from Bengal and Golconda, were greatly upset by the sudden influx of Brazilian diamonds, but it is unnecessary to place the whole blame on their efforts to corner the market. Long and anxious consultations were held at Lisbon concerning the best means of raising prices by restricting output, and in these debates the representations of John Gore, one of the leading diamond merchants in London, carried great weight.[7]

Since successive increases in the capitation tax from five to forty *milreis* had failed to discourage diamond miners in the Serro do Frio, the Crown finally resolved to ban the mining of diamonds altogether for some years until prices recovered. This decision was implemented by an edict of the Count of Galveas in July, 1734, which likewise prohibited gold mining and washing in the Diamond District. Anyone, bond or free, henceforth found in the sites of former washings and mines would be summarily arrested, even if no diamonds were actually found on him. Slaves apprehended in this way were to be flogged and sold; and free men were to be fined, imprisoned, and subsequently expelled from the District. No one living there was allowed to possess any mining instruments. Later orders increased the severity of the punishments inflicted on real or suspected diamond diggers, smugglers, and traders, nor was any appeal allowed from the judicial authority exercised by the Intendant.

In vain the wretched inhabitants of the Diamond District protested against these draconic measures, which deprived many of them of their means of livelihood, and which plunged the once thriving *arraial* of Tijuco into a severe economic depression. The most they could obtain was a grudging concession from the Crown that the governor of Minas Gerais (Gomes Freire de Andrada since March, 1735) and the Intendant of the Diamond

District could, after joint consultation, allow at their discretion gold mining to be resumed in certain localities where diamonds had never been found. Since diamonds had never yet been found save where gold also occurred in the *cascalho,* these places were all old workings which had already been vainly sifted for both diamonds and gold. The concession was, therefore, of little or no practical value.[8]

These drastic measures and the thoroughness with which they were carried out by the dragoons of Minas Gerais under the personal supervision of Dr. Rafael Pires Pardinho, soon had the desired effect. The flow of diamonds from the Serro do Frio dwindled to a thin trickle of illicit gems, and the price in Europe began to rise. Encouraged by this turn of events in 1736-1737, the Crown resolved to renew the mining of diamonds on a strictly limited scale and on a monopoly-contract basis. The Count of Sabugosa had urged that the diamond mines should be operated directly by the Crown in 1732, and five years later his successor, the Count of Galveas, was equally emphatic in advocating this method as the only satisfactory solution. He pointed out as precedents, the Austrian Emperor's profitable monopoly of the Hungarian copper mines, the Catholic King of Castile's tobacco monopoly, and the Duke of Bavaria's monopoly in beer. "Is it possible," the viceroy asked rhetorically, "that all these princes have vassals who loyally and honestly administer such vast and important undertakings for them, and that His Majesty cannot find two honest men to do as much for him?" He deplored the traditional Portuguese *má lingua* which spread this notion of Portuguese dishonesty and inefficiency among foreigners, "who thus look upon us as inept and incapable of serving our prince." Martinho de Mendonça and others on their part complained of the congenital incapacity of the Portuguese to form and operate great commercial companies, like those of the English and Dutch; but the Crown always favored the contract system as we have seen in the case of salt and other essential commodities. This method was inaugurated on January 1, 1740, by a contract signed in June of the previous year with João Fernandes de Oliveira in partnership with Francisco Ferreira da Silva.

This contract was for the four-year term, January 1, 1740–December 31, 1743. The search for diamonds was thereby limited to the bed of the river Jequitinhonha with its banks and immediate neighborhood. Not more than 600 slaves were to be employed by the contractors in the actual mining, for each of whom an annual capitation tax of 230 *milreis* was paid to the Crown. Any of the contractors' slaves found washing or digging for diamonds outside the allotted area would be confiscated to the Crown, as would any slaves over and above the permitted 600 who were found in them. All diamonds mined by the slaves were kept in the Intendant's safe, and were only handed over to the contractor for remission to headquarters at Lisbon. Contractors were empowered to recover debts due to them by distraining the property or imprisoning the persons of their debtors. The local Crown officials, from the Intendant downwards, were ordered to afford the contractors all judicial and adminstrative facilities in the execution of their contracts. If the contractors suspected anyone of mining, buying, or selling diamonds, they could inform the Intendant secretly of their suspicions. He in his turn was authorized to expel from the district any individual accused in this way, nor could the accused appeal against this decision.

All protests of the inhabitants of the Serro do Frio against this arbitrary despotism were either ignored or contemptuously dismissed. For instance, when the municipal council of Villa do Principe once ventured to remonstrate against all shopkeepers and traders being rigorously—and vainly—searched in their property and persons at the behest of the diamond contractor, Dr. Pires Pardinho gave them short shrift. He observed that he himself, or the contractor, or the commanding officer of the dragoons were entitled to carry out these searches whenever they felt inclined. If the inhabitants did not like this treatment, they could easily avoid it by emigrating from the District and going to live elsewhere. He added that they were all tarred with the same brush, whether black or white in the color of their skins, since the latter acted as receivers of the diamonds stolen by the former. He ended by saying that the "feeble-minded" municipal councillors "should carefully consider that His Majesty would not have maintained a ban on the production of diamonds for four years at great expense without some very good reason, and that he would rather see the Diamond District entirely depopulated than that its inhabitants should renew their former trading in diamonds." [9]

For enforcing these restrictions on an unwilling populace, the authorities relied chiefly on the dragoons of Minas Gerais. As mentioned on page 192 above, the original two companies were formed of sixty picked men each, recruited from the north of Portugal. A third company was formed in 1733 and a fourth in 1746, eighty men being always on duty in the Diamond District. In later years some of the rank and file were recruited locally, but the officers were always sent out from Portugal. The Count of Sabugosa also raised a company of dragoons in 1729 for service in the Minas Novas and to police the trails leading to the Diamond District from that mining region. The principal duties of the dragoons were to arrest smugglers of contraband gold and diamonds, and to prevent the establishment of virtually independent bailiwicks by leading cattle ranchers and other "great ones of the earth" in the remoter parts of the *sertão*.

Travelers in eighteenth-century Portugal and her overseas possessions were usually very scathing about the ragged and undisciplined appearance of most of the Portuguese soldiery, but the dragoons of Minas Gerais were a noteworthy exception and always maintained a high standard of dress and discipline. The first company arrived in 1719 under the command of Captain Joseph Rodrigues de Oliveira, a veteran of the War of the Spanish Succession. He was warmly praised by the Count of Assumar for the "ceaseless diligence and efforts" with which he brought his men and horses over the precipitous trails from the coast to Villa Rica in the height of the rainy season. Moreover, he had so disciplined his men that they "had not given the least vexation to the countrymen, paying promptly for everything which they took." The Count added that this exemplary discipline had greatly contributed to the respect with which everyone in Minas Gerais now regarded the dragoons. The second company, under Captain João de Almeida, arrived some months later, and Assumar reported regretfully that this officer did not exercise such effective control over his men on the line of march.[10]

The suppression of the revolts at Pitanguí and Villa Rica, in which the dragoons played a decisive part, did not contribute to their popularity among the inhabitants of Minas Gerais, by whom they were henceforth feared as much as they were respected. On the other hand, they did break up the private armies of the *poderosos* who terrorized large areas at times, as instanced by the "mutinies in the backlands" (*motins do sertão*) of the São Francisco River valley in 1736.[11] The original system of billeting these soldiers on private householders was also resented, and this formed one of the chief complaints of the rioters at Villa Rica in 1720. This particular grievance was partly remedied by the construction of barracks at Ribeirão do Carmo and Villa Rica a few years later, though it was a long time before quarters were built at São João d'El Rei and elsewhere. The dragoons were not paid and clothed directly by the Crown but on the usual contract system, and the same applied to their hospital and medical services.[12]

These dragoons continually patrolled the trails of Minas Gerais, only a small detachment being usually left in reserve at their barracks. They were authorized to stop and search anyone they met for contraband gold and diamonds, receiving a reward proportionable to such seizures as they made. They atoned for the smallness of their numbers by their vigilance and activity, particularly in the Diamond District. Their patrols were usually supplemented by bodies of swashbuckling mulattoes and half-breeds under the local "bushwhacking captains," or *capitães do mato*. These men knew the *sertão* even better than the dragoons and could guide the regular soldiers to the remotest parts of the bush.

Despite the severity of the laws, the vigilance of the dragoons and the monopoly exercised by successive contractors, it was, of course, impossible to stop illicit diamond mining and trading. The wild and rugged terrain rendered concealment easy in many places, nor did smuggling diamonds out of the District present an insuperable problem to such adepts in contraband trade as itinerant merchants and muleteers. *Garimpo* was the name given to illicit diamond mining, and persons who practiced this calling, whether whole or part time, were called *garimpeiros*. Many people who had been ruined by the decrees prohibiting general mining in the 1730's inevitably became clandestine miners and smugglers, but the *garimpeiros* were not robbers or bandits. Working alone or in small groups, they never attacked the dragoons or molested their fellow countrymen; but when surprised and assaulted by the soldiers or the militia they resisted courageously. Captured *garimpeiros* never betrayed their comrades, and they were never accused by their captors of robbery, rape, or any form of violence save that of resisting arrest. Though hunted night and day like wild beasts by the forces of the Crown, the *garimpeiros* continued their activities throughout the rest of the colonial period. The diamonds found and smuggled by these men were, incidentally, often better than those found in the official diggings.

The *garimpeiros,* whether white or colored, were free men. They should not be confused with the runaway Negro slaves or *calhambolas*. These latter naturally also indulged in illicit diamond and gold mining when they could; but they often had to kill cattle and domestic animals in order to keep alive, and hence they could be classified as bandits and robbers. Whereas the *garimpeiro* usually had his family in a neighboring camp or village, and could double the roles of lawful worker and illicit miner, the fugitive Negro's hand was often against every free man, and he had no sure refuge outside the *quilombo*. As the Intendants and contractors constantly complained, there was no lack of buyers for clandestine diamonds, despite the fact that (since June, 1745) nobody was allowed to enter the Diamond District without written permission from the Intendant.[13]

For the first ten or fifteen years after the discovery of diamonds, the methods of washing and mining for them were essentially the same as those originally used for obtaining gold in Minas Gerais. The chief instrument was the bowl (*bateia*) in which the gravel (*cascalho*) from the river bed or the banks was washed and sifted. An eyewitness report of 1735 noted that: "There is no certain sign to indicate that there are diamonds in the gravel. But it is an infallible sign that there are none if there is no particle of gold in the *bateia;* and it is likewise sure that the more gold there is, the more diamonds there are. The size of the gold is also in proportion to that of the diamonds; so that when the gold is extremely small, so are the diamonds." The Brazilian diamonds were usually found in a rougher state than those in India and Borneo, and they also lost far more in weight and size when they were being cut.

The bowls were later replaced by sieves, and these in their turn by a more complicated system of troughs, sluices, and conduits in the second half of the eighteenth century. The rivers were in flood during the rainy season between October and April, so these months were used to sift the piles of gravel which had been excavated from the river beds in the (relatively) dry season. As with the gold workings, it was often necessary to build dams of considerable strength and size in order to divert the waters from a given stretch of the river even during the favorable season. Disasters when the dams broke and the Negro slaves were drowned in the ensuing flood were not unknown.[14]

Although the Negro slaves were closely watched while mining or washing for diamonds, and rigorously searched when the day's work was over, they still contrived to steal many of the best gems. "Ten whites are not enough to watch one Negro," wrote the anonymous eyewitness of 1735. "For this reason," he explained, "the Negroes give very few large diamonds to their masters, for they all prefer to give them to the Negresses, who then sell them in the taverns to whites who buy them secretly. The Negroes only give the small diamonds to their owners, and this is one of the reasons—and not the least of them—why it is not much use employing Negroes in this work." As in the gold fields, the authorities were—rightly or wrongly—convinced that the mulatas and Negresses who sold food and drinks to the miners were the chief intermediaries in the smuggling game. This accounts for the severely worded edicts forbidding these colored women to hawk their wares—or their persons—in places where mining was in progress.[15]

The writer of 1735 alleged that when diamond mining was still open to all who could afford to pay the capitation tax, as many as 18,000 Negro slaves were employed mining for diamonds in the Serro do Frio. This was certainly a gross exaggeration, the real number being between eight and nine thousand, as we know from the capitation figures of the years 1736–1740. One of the objects in limiting the number of working slaves to 600 under the contract system was to reduce the risk of their stealing or smuggling diamonds. Thenceforward there was usually one white (or mulatto) factor to supervise every eight Negro slaves, but the latter still found means of cheating their employers, though only allowed to wear the equivalent of a loincloth or G string when they were actually working.[16]

The slaves had to work in a stooping position facing their overseer, so as to sift the *cascalho* in the troughs and throw away the gravel while picking out the diamonds. They frequently had to change places with each other so as to prevent them from finding again some diamonds they might have concealed in a heap of stones or earth. Even so, they could sometimes identify the exact spot where they had hidden a diamond, and return under cover of night to secure it. The first thing that old hands among the slaves taught the *moleques* or new arrivals was how to steal diamonds. "For this purpose they practice on them with beans, or grains of maize, which they throw from a distance into the mouth, and in this way they teach them to catch them in the mouth and swallow them." They also practiced sleight of hand and other tricks which enabled them to hide a diamond between their fingers, or in the palm of the hand, and convey it to the mouth unseen. By dint of practice, they could even pick up a diamond with their toes, "concealing it between them for hours on end, and walking with it in this way to the slave quarters." Another favorite trick was to push the diamond up a nostril when taking snuff, or when pretending to do so. The slaves also let their nails grow long, so as to conceal small diamonds behind them, and they had recourse to many other ingenious methods, too complicated to describe here. Swallowing the diamond seems to have been their favorite device. When a slave was suspected of this practice, he was locked in a strongroom and given a violent purge of Malagueta pepper.[17]

When a Negro found a diamond which he saw no chance of concealing, he stood upright, clapped his hands, and then extended his arms upwards and sideways, holding the gem between the forefinger and thumb. The overseer then took it from him and put it in a bowl which was kept ready to hold all the diamonds found in the course of a day's work. In Mawe's time, the slaves received a bonus according to the size of the diamonds which they turned in. Thus, the lucky finder of a diamond which weighed an *oitava* (17½ carats) was "crowned with a wreath of flowers and carried in procession to the administrator, who gives him his freedom, by paying his owner for it. He also receives a grant of new clothes, and is permitted to work on his own account. When a stone of 8 or 10 carats is found, the Negro receives two new shirts, a complete new suit, with a hat and a handsome knife. For smaller stones of trivial amount, proportional premiums are given." Despite these incentives, Mawe noted that the Negro slaves' fare was poor and scanty, "and in other respects they are more hardly dealt with than those of any other establishment which I have visited." Their masters, on the contrary, lived high, dining daily "on a profusion of excellent viands, served up on fine Wedgewood ware, and the state of their household generally corresponded with this essential part of it."[18]

Mutatis mutandis, these conditions were applicable to the early period with which we are dealing. The *Arraial do Tijuco* in its heyday (say, 1730–1753), was celebrated for the ostentatious magnificence of those who made good money out of the diamond mining in one way or another. As at Bahia, Rio de Janeiro, Ouro Preto, and elsewhere, a considerable proportion of their wealth was spent upon the local ladies of easy virtue, whose flaunting of their persons was vehemently denounced by the Count of Galveas in an admonitory edict of December 2, 1733. This edict stigmatized the "great number of dishonest women who live in the mining camp of Tijuco, leading such a dissolute and scandalous life, that not content with going about in chairs and litters accompanied by slaves, they are brazen enough to enter irreverently into the house of God, wearing rich and gorgeous dresses which are utterly unfitted for persons of their sort." His Excellency ordered that all these light women were to be notified to leave the district of the Serro do Frio within eight days, failing which they would be imprisoned and all their wealth confiscated. The Crown Judge and the commanding officer of the dragoons were specifically charged to see that these orders were enforced without fail.

The result of this morality campaign is not recorded, but judging by what happened after similar edicts had been promulgated elsewhere, it probably had only a passing effect. At any rate, one of the most celebrated figures in the history of the Diamond District is Francisca da Silva, or Xica da Silva as she is commonly called to this day. Originally a mulata slave, she became the mistress first of a local gentleman and then of the millionaire diamond contractor Dr. (of laws) João Fernandes de Oliveira, who flourished during the second half of the eighteenth century. He showered on his mistress—whom her original owner had freed at his request—everything that her whims required. Since she had never seen the sea, and expressed a wish to know what a ship looked like, Fernandes de Oliveira built an artificial lake and a large model ship with masts, sails, and rigging, which was manned by a crew of ten and could manoeuvre on the water. He also built for her a large country house, the site of which is still called *chácara da Xica da Silva,* where he gave Lucullan banquets, nocturnal balls, and amateur theatricals in her honor. Needless to say, nobody else could afford the same extravagances as the millionaire contractor, who was also a generous builder and endower of churches; but those who made fortunes at Tijuco, dressed in the height of European fashions and imported luxurious clothes, weapons, household goods, and furniture from Lisbon regardless of cost.[19]

The diamond monopoly during the period when it was operated on a contract basis was exercised by the following principals.[20]

1) 1.i.1740–31.xii.1743   João Fernandes de Oliveira and Francisco Ferreira da Silva.

2) 1.i.1744–31.xii.1748   João Fernandes de Oliveira and Francisco Ferreira da Silva.

3) 1.i.1749–31.xii.1752   Felisberto Caldeira Brant and his three brothers.

4) 1.i.1753–31.xii.1758   João Fernandes de Oliveira.

5) 1.i.1759–31.xii.1762   João Fernandes de Oliveira and his lawyer son of the same name.

6) 1.i.1763–31.xii.1771   Dr. João Fernandes de Oliveira.

During this period the following results were obtained:

CONTRACT	DIAMONDS DUG (in carats)	SALE PRICE (in *milreis*)	PAID TO THE CROWN
First	134,071	1,606,274$037	575,864$438
Second	177,200	1,807,742$837	755,875$726
Third	154,579	1,438,015$987	609,526$465
Fourth	390,094	3,625,586$888	914,921$424
Fifth	106,416	929,476$750	329,329$972
Sixth	704,209	6,108,570$163	1,458,663$563
TOTAL	1,666,569 carats	15,515,403$662	4,644,181$588 [21]

Apart from the diamonds illicitly secured by the *garimpeiros* and *calhambolas,* all these contractors were guilty of defrauding the Crown to a greater or lesser extent. Although the number of slaves working at one time was strictly limited to six hundred, many others were employed in looking for diamonds under the pretext that they were really engaged in clearing the ground, chopping wood, transporting provisions, and so forth. It was alleged by critics of the system that as many as four thousand slaves were employed in this way, but this is certainly an exaggeration. The authorities, as a rule, were both competent and strict, and it is doubtful if the contractors could have employed half that number without being detected. Another illegal device of which the contractors were guilty, though again not on the scale which was alleged, was that of mining for diamonds in brooks and rivulets which were not included in the limits assigned to them. Finally, they were also accused of buying illicit diamonds from the *garimpeiros,* and even from their own slaves in the official diggings.

From the point of view of the inhabitants of the Diamond District—though not of the Crown—the best years were those of the Caldeira brothers' contract. Felisberto, the eldest and most enterprising, evidently acting on the principle that "dog does not eat dog," turned a blind eye to the activities of the smugglers, when he did not actively coöperate with them. During these years the Intendant and the Chief Judge were both old and inefficient valetudinarians, very different from the equally elderly but austerely capable Dr. Rafael Pires Pardinho, and this led to unprecedented laxity in the administration. The Caldeira Brants belonged to a Paulista family, and being Brazilian-born they were more considerate of their countrymen than was the Portuguese-born João Fernandes de Oliveira, the elder. Tijuco accordingly witnessed a recrudescence of prosperity as the wealth accruing from diamonds, however obtained, was more widely distributed.

The elder João Fernandes de Oliveira, although guilty of the same malpractices as was Caldeira Brant and, indeed, associated with him for part of the third contract, basely intrigued at Lisbon against the latter and eventually encompassed his ruin.

Felisberto was arrested on suspicion of defrauding the Crown in 1752 and deported in chains to Lisbon for trial. His case was still pending when the great earthquake of All Saints' Day 1755 laid his prison and most of the city in ruins. Finding himself unguarded—though still fettered—in this holocaust, he dramatically presented himself before the all-powerful minister Sebastião José de Carvalho (later Marquis of Pombal), and demanded justice and a speedy trial. He did not secure either of these; but at least he was not re-imprisoned, being allowed to go to the thermal spring of Caldas da Rainha, where he died shortly afterwards. His unscrupulous rival who thus secured the fourth contract, also ended his life in obscure poverty many years later; but his son and partner in the fifth contract, the protector of Xica da Silva, contrived to make the best of both worlds, being reputedly the wealthiest subject of the Portuguese Crown when he died in Lisbon at the end of the century. The dramatic rise and fall of the Caldeira family was for long remembered in the Serro do Frio as exemplifying the proverbial uncertainty of worldly bliss.[22]

The Caldeira Brant episode led to another tightening of the screw by the Crown in 1753. In August of that year a decree was promulgated whereby the king—or rather the future Marquis of Pombal in his name—announced that he had taken the contract and commerce of diamonds "under my royal and immediate protection." This ominous preamble was followed by eighteen clauses containing the following enactments among others. Nobody could mine, buy, sell, transport, or deal in uncut diamonds in Portugal and its overseas dominions without a written permit from the contractor who was granted the exclusive monopoly. In cases where this law was infringed, no distinction was to be made between principals and accessories, but they would all receive the same punishment, whether this involved perpetual imprisonment, or ten years' exile to Angola, or something equally severe. Informers were guaranteed that their evidence would be kept strictly secret. Slaves informing against guilty persons would receive not only their freedom, but a sum of money to enable them to start life afresh. Any trader or merchant wishing to enter or leave the Diamond District would have to submit to a rigorous customs inspection and find a substantial surety for the limited time he was allowed to remain there. This provision likewise applied to debtors seeking to recover what they were owed. Nobody could continue to reside in the District who was not publicly known to have a permanent job there; and the Intendant was again authorized to expel anybody against whom the contractor might have the slightest suspicion. Only persons of unblemished character would be licensed to operate inns, taverns, shops, and other commercial establishments within the Diamond District and for a radius of five leagues around it. These licenses could be withdrawn and the holder expelled at any time by the Intendant. No judge or legal tribunal could take cognizance of any case involving the diamond contracts, anything concerning them being reserved for the direct consideration and decision of the Crown.[23]

The effect of these measures was still further to accentuate the isolation of the Diamond District. It was virtually a colony within a colony, cut off from the rest of Brazil by a legal and administrative barrier, more effective in its way than the stones and bricks of the Great Wall of China. Even so, the Crown was still dissatisfied with its share of the profits, although the younger João Fernandes de Oliveira had no reason to complain of his gains as contractor. In 1771, Pombal took the final step of abolishing the contract system and thenceforth the diamond mines were operated directly on behalf of the Crown. This final step was the most oppressive of all, being symbolized by the *Livro da capa verde* ("Book with the green binding") which contained the printed *Regimento* or standing orders for the administration of the Diamond District.[24] Though considerably attenuated after the proclamation of Brazilian independence in 1821, the last vestiges of the *Real Extracção* as this Crown monopoly was called, were not abolished until fourteen years later.

Under both the contract system and the *Real Extracção* the diamonds stored in the coffers at Tijuco were sent annually under convoy of a detachment of dragoons to Rio de Janeiro, where they were embarked in warships for Lisbon. Here the best and biggest gems were reserved for the Crown, and the remainder were sold in lots and at carefully regulated intervals so as to avoid upsetting the market. The official buyers were representatives of the leading London and Amsterdam merchant houses. From 1753 to 1755 the export contractors were Bristow, Ward & Co., who bought 121,814 carats of diamonds valued at 1,188,348$425. From 1757 to 1760, John Gore and Josua Van Neck, 115,659 carats valued at 1,067,-198$850; from 1761 to 1771, the Dutchman Daniel Gildermeester, 925,589 carats valued at 8,144,165$537. From London and Amsterdam the diamonds were distributed throughout the world, Turkey and Russia being apparently the principal purchasers toward the end of the eighteenth century.[25]

Estimates of the number and value of the Brazilian diamonds exported to Europe vary widely. Apart from those produced licitly and illicitly in Minas Gerais, they were also mined at certain times and places in the captaincies of Goiás, São Paulo, and Bahia. Only the production in Goiás ever vied with that of the Serro do Frio, and then for a few years only. There is no means of calculating the amount of diamonds smuggled out of the country, for both buyers and sellers had every reason to keep their transactions secret. Admittedly, John Mawe, writing in 1812, affirmed that "there is strong presumptive authority for stating that, since the first discovery of the mines, diamonds to the amount of two millions sterling have thus found their way to Europe, exclusive of what the contractors accounted for." Mawe's guess may be as good or better than another's, but in the absence of any proof, his "strong presumptive authority" does not amount to more than an unsupported assertion.

Nor are such other figures as we possess conclusive. John Gore alleged that the Brazil fleet of 1732 had brought to Lisbon 300,000 carats of diamonds worth five million *cruzados*. He added that the fleet of 1733 had brought about the same quantity, "which is four times the amount that usually çomes from India." During what may be termed this "free for all" period, before the prohibition of mining and the institution of the contract system, overproduction in Brazil caused diamonds of excellent water to be sold for 2,400 *reis* the carat. If we turn to the official figures of the legal diamond remissions to Lisbon, we find that the total of those exported from Brazil during the contract period was 1,166,569 carats, and during the *Real Extracção* was 1,354,770 carats. Unfortunately, there is no reliable check on these figures, since the original *Livros das Entradas dos diamantes para o cofre* or entry books kept at the Tijuco headquarters are apparently no longer extant.[26]

There is, therefore, no way of accurately estimating the total production of the Brazilian diamond fields in the eighteenth century (or nowadays, for that matter). But since prices did not fall again to the low levels prevailing between 1731 and 1735, it may be said that the iron regime of the Diamond District at least partly achieved its avowed purpose of keeping smuggling down and prices up. That this was achieved at the cost of the unfortunate inhabitants of the Serro do Frio is abundantly proved by the accounts of Mawe, Saint-Hilaire, and all the other observers who were able to enter that forbidden and forbidding land. This artifically isolated region was not so much an example of "the world which the Portuguese created," as of a world whose creation the Portuguese could not prevent.[27]

IX. CATTLE COUNTRY

Gold and diamonds were the most famous products of Brazil during the eighteenth century, and both were major factors in the conquest of the *sertão,* but cattle made an equally important if less spectacular contribution to the westward advance of the colonists. Sugar was mainly responsible for the settlement of the littoral; gold and diamonds formed the principal lure in the settlement of Minas Gerais and Mato Grosso; the search for Amerindian slaves, silver, and emeralds impelled the Paulistas ever deeper into the interior; but the drovers and stockmen opened up most of the rest of Brazil (as distinct from the Maranhão). Cattle raising and ranching did not take the same forms everywhere from the island of Marajó in the Amazon estuary to the northern bank of the Rio de la Plata, but the limits of this chapter do not permit detailed discussion of regional variations. I will therefore confine myself principally to three key regions in the penetration of the Brazilian hinterland: the São Francisco River valley in the center, the region of Piauí in the north, and that of Rio Grande in the south. Before considering each of these in turn, a word may be said about the system of land holdings and the position of latifundian landowners in the *sertão.*

One of the most famous laws in medieval Portugal was the

Cattle Country

Lei das sesmarias, or law for the redistribution of lands, enacted by King Dom Fernando I in 1375. The object of this law was to improve agricultural production by redistributing lands, which were not effectively occupied nor adequately cultivated by their owners, to other persons who would till them properly.[1] In due course, the system of *sesmarias* was transplanted to Brazil in 1549, when the coastal belt was administratively divided into a number of captaincies, some of which (such as Bahia) were held by the Crown, and others (such as Pernambuco) by *donatários* or lords proprietor. The first governor-general's *regimento* (standing instructions) specified that a man should not be given more land "than you consider he will be able to cultivate properly," but this restriction remained a dead letter from the start. The framers of the original act of 1375 had envisaged relatively small grants of land which could be tilled adequately by a man and his family, or by a small landowner and his hired hands; and they had discouraged the use of more cattle than were strictly necessary for the plough and the ox-cart. In Bahia and Pernambuco, on the other hand, *cartas de sesmaria,* or title deeds of landholdings, were frequently given by the colonial authorities to latifundian landowners in the coastal towns, who claimed huge areas in the hinterland on which they allowed their cattle to run almost wild. These landowners can be divided into three main types. The first, among whom we may include the Ravasco family which held the secretaryship of the government of Brazil for two generations, spent all or nearly all their time in the coastal towns, and never set eyes on their more distant estates. The second, of whom Francisco Dias d'Avila (p. 229, below) may be taken as a typical representative, divided their time fairly evenly between their headquarters in (or near) a coastal city, and their estates in the far interior. The third type spent virtually all their lives on their estates or in pioneering expeditions in the *sertão,* and hardly ever visited the coastal region.

The penetration of the interior by the gradual establishment of cattle ranches along the São Francisco River valley, had begun

from the *Reconcavo* of Bahia by way of Sergipe and the right
bank of the great river before the Dutch war. It was accompanied
by a similar but slower movement of cattle along the left bank
from the direction of Pernambuco, the São Francisco forming the
boundary between the two captaincies. Both these movements
were greatly accelerated in the second half of the seventeenth
century, and by 1700 they had met and mingled with the Paulistas
who were coming down the São Francisco from the region of
the Rio das Velhas. Shorter trails had also been opened from the
Reconcavo via Cachoeira and Jacobina to Juazeiro and other
points along the river. One of the most important junctions of
these trails was the *Arraial de Mathias Cardoso,* named after
a Paulista pioneer and cattle baron, which place is identical with
the modern town of Morrinhos. As we saw in Chapter ii, the São
Francisco Valley route, and the trails connecting it with the
Reconcavo of Bahia, were of vital importance in the gold rush to
Minas Gerais.

It was just at this time that the Crown began to realize dimly
what was happening in the backlands of Brazil, and strove to
remedy the situation by legislation. A royal decree of December
27, 1695 stipulated that in future a single individual should not
be given a grant of land measuring more than four leagues long
by one league wide. *Sesmarias* of greater extent which had already
been granted, would not, however, be revoked if they were being
properly utilized. Two years later, another decree (December 7,
1697) reduced the maximum area of a *sesmaria* to three leagues
in length by one in width, with a space of one league between
each *sesmaria*. These measurements were maintained in a third
and more forceful decree promulgated on January 20, 1699.[2] In
terms recalling the original *Lei das sesmarias* of 1375, this enact-
ment threatened landowners with the expropriation of such lands
as they could not or would not cultivate, in favor of those persons
who could and would do so. The preamble to this decree stated
that one of the chief reasons why the backlands of Brazil were
inadequately populated or cultivated was because of the dog-in-

the-manger attitude of the great territorial landowners—*os poderosos do sertão*. These magnates only cultivated a fraction of their vast estates, but they would not let anyone else develop the empty lands, save only those who would bear all the expense of doing so and pay an annual rent in addition.[3] We learn from Antonil that such plots of land as were grazed in this way measured a league in extent and yielded an annual rent of 10 *milreis*.

Another edict promulgated at the same time (January 19, 1699) referred to "powerful individuals in the backlands oppressing the poor and lowly, who are too frightened to dare to complain." The Crown ordered the governor-general to investigate this matter carefully and to take swift action against territorial magnates who were guilty of such practices, forcing them to make restitution of whatever they had unlawfully acquired.[4] It was not, incidentally, only the poor and lowly who complained of the tyrannical conduct of the *poderosos do sertão,* "the great ones of the earth." Jesuit and Capuchin missionaries also had plenty to say on this subject, particularly with reference to the greatest latifundian landowners of Bahia. They were the family of Dias d'Avila, the House of Torre (*Casa da Torre*) as they were collectively called from their castellated stone mansion some thirty miles north of Salvador. This was probably the most imposing building of its kind in Brazil, judging by its impressive ruins at the present day.[5]

How ineffective the Crown legislation proved in curbing the land hunger of the cattle barons, can be seen not only from its vain and frequent repetition throughout the eighteenth century, but also from Antonil's classic account of 1711.[6] The Jesuit was reliably informed that there were then more than five hundred large ranches along the banks of the river São Francisco and its affluents. The hinterland of the captaincy of Bahia contained more than half a million head of cattle, and the backlands of Pernambuco more than 800,000, "although these are of more use to Bahia than to Pernambuco, since most of the Pernambucan droves are

sent to market in Salvador." Antonil assures us that nearly all
the cattle-raising regions of Bahia and many of those of Pernambuco belonged to the leading latifundian families, the Dias d'Avila
of the House of Torre, and the Guedes de Brito of the House of
Ponte. The reader may here recall that Manuel Nunes Viana rose
to fame and fortune as the agent or administrator of the cattle
ranches belonging to the heiress of António Guedes de Brito in
the São Francisco River valley. Antonil must have been exaggerat-
ing somewhat, for we have met or shall meet other proprietors
who had extensive estates, such as João Peixoto Viegas, Mathias
Cardoso, and Domingos Affonso Mafrense. But the lands belonging to the houses of Torre and of Ponte were undoubtedly by far
the most extensive and were the ones chiefly envisaged by the
Crown's legislation.[7]

Antonil also informs us that individual ranches contained from
200 to 1,000 head of cattle, and that when these ranches (*currais*)
were grouped together into estates (*fazendas*), a single estate
might contain from 6,000 to 20,000 head. The cattle raised on these
estates provided meat on the hoof for the cities of the littoral,
principally Salvador and Recife, but they were also sent south to
the thriving mining camps of Minas Gerais, and some even went
north to the Maranhão. Cattle were also in constant demand as
draft animals on the coastal plantations, and their hides formed
one of Brazil's major exports. All the rolls of Brazilian tobacco
exported to Lisbon were wrapped in hides (27,500 rolls in an
average good year), apart from a vast quantity of skins exported
for shoe leather. The modern Brazilian historian, Capistrano de
Abreu, reminds us to what an extent the ranchers and stockmen
of the interior lived in what might be termed an Age of Leather.
The doors and beds (when they had any) of their huts, their water-
skins, their saddlebags for carrying food, their leather armor for
riding in the bush, and most other things that they wore or used
were made from hides in whole or in part. Their staple diet was
meat and milk, since the cattle-raising districts were rarely suitable
for the cultivation of manioc or of maize. Coarse and inferior

cheese was made at times, but the ranchers never seem to have made butter.[8]

When a landowner had acquired (legally or otherwise) sufficient land for a ranch, the cattle had first to be accustomed to the new locality, which usually took a little time and involved the employment of several stockmen. Subsequently, one cowboy was usually left in charge of a ranch, though there might be two or more on the larger ones. He had to brand the calves, protect the cattle against the attacks of wild beasts (or of hostile Amerindians), cure their ills, see that they did not stray, and that they had sufficient pasturage and water. This last was not so easy as it sounds, since away from the immediate vicinity of the river, the country was mostly arid scrub (*caatinga*) which grew only small, sparse, and spiny vegetation—except in the rainy season and then it was likely to be flooded. The *vaqueiro* led an arduous if healthy life, and was as a rule unpaid for the first four or five years on a ranch. He then received one out of every four calves that were born, and so could hope in time to start on his own. This he usually did by renting a piece of land from the owner for whom he was working. The *vaqueiros* might be of pure European, African, or Amerindian stock, but mixed bloods greatly predominated. They formed a healthy and self-reliant social group, intensely proud of their special skills and intensely disdainful of townsmen and their ways.

Since the ranches in the backlands of Bahia and Pernambuco were situated hundreds of miles from their markets on the coast, the cattle were driven down to the seaports in droves which were often weeks and sometimes months on the road. A drove might contain from a hundred to three hundred head of cattle, and Antonil gives us a colorful description of those which were sent to the Reconcavo from the region of the river São Francisco. Some of the drovers rode in front singing or chanting, while others brought up the rear and saw that the beasts did not stray. When they came to a river, one of the leading drovers put a hide and horns on his head and then led the cattle across the ford. These men were paid at rates that varied according to the distances they had to go, but they were docked so much a head for any cattle that had strayed. These droves arrived at Salvador almost weekly, "and in some seasons of the year there are weeks in which droves arrive daily." Although the cattle, after their long and exhausting journey across the arid *catinga,* could be fattened in pastures near the city, in practice this does not seem to have happened very often. Complaints of their scrawniness are very frequent, and Dampier wrote of them at Bahia in 1699: "It being Lent when I came hither, there was no buying any flesh till Easter Eve, when a great number of bullocks were killed at once in the slaughterhouses within the town; men, women, and children flocking thither with great joy to buy, and a multitude of dogs, almost starved, following them; for whom the meat seemed fittest, it was so lean." [9]

Among the perils of a *vaqueiro's* life was the danger of attack from hostile Amerindians, particularly in the frontier regions which had not been properly pacified, or where the missionaries were not firmly established. These attacks were not very frequent at the turn of the seventeenth century in the backlands of Bahia, for the missionaries had been working there for a good many years previously. When they did occur, they were usually provoked by famine, or else by the greed of the cattle barons, who even coveted the lands set aside by the Crown for the maintenance of friendly Cariri tribes and of the missionaries who ministered to them. Fr. Martin de Nantes gives us a graphic narrative of the difficulties of the Capuchin missionaries with Francisco Dias d'Avila, the head of the House of Torre (1645–1695). On one punitive expedition this man massacred some five hundred Amerindian prisoners who had surrendered two days previously on promise of their lives being spared. This atrocity was not the only one of its kind, and the missionary accounts are full of complaints against the conduct (or, rather, misconduct) of the Dias d'Avila family. The dislike was mutual, and in 1696 the "ladies of the House of Torre" set at naught the authority of the Crown and the prestige of the Church by ordering their *vaqueiros* violently to expel the Jesuits from their missions along the river São Francisco.[10]

Despite the excesses of the Dias d'Avila family and of other *poderosos* whose misdeeds are chronicled by the missionaries, relations between the settlers and the Amerindians were frequently quite amicable in the São Francisco River valley at this period. If the *vaqueiros* sometimes mistreated the aborigines and filched their lands, many Amerindians found employment on the ranches. They often acted as drovers for the cattle sent on the long trek to the market at Salvador,—though admittedly they were not always paid the rate for the job. Their women were often taken as concubines and less often as wives by the cowboys, and social relationships between the white man and the red were frequently quite friendly. Fr. Martin de Nantes, who never spared his criticisms of Portuguese misconduct, tells us that at the church weddings of converted Amerindians, "il se trouve toujours dans toutes ces occasions bon nombre de Portugais, qui apportent des guitarres et violons pour la solemnité, et qui chantent des motets, et qui tirent même plusieurs coups de fusils pour une plus grande réjouissance." The chief religious festivals, such as those in Holy Week, were also well attended by devout and well-behaved crowds of both races.[11]

Where inter-racial tension was more serious, and where the bloodletting was worse, was in the frontier region of Piauí.[12] This country of gently rolling hills had been penetrated and perhaps traversed by a few roving bands in search of Amerindian slaves and precious metals in the first half of the seventeenth century, but these transient adventurers had left no trace of their passage. The region between the rivers Parnaíba and Gurgueía was first penetrated with a view to settlement by the Paulista, Domingos Jorge Velho, in 1671. A celebrated fighter and hunter of Amerindians, who later took the leading part in the distruction of the runaway-Negro settlement (*quilombo*) of the Palmares, he was described by the Bishop of Pernambuco in the following unflattering terms. "This man is one of the worst savages I have ever met.

When he came to see me, he brought an interpreter with him, for he cannot even converse; nor does he differ from the most barbarous Tapuia otherwise than in calling himself a Christian. And notwithstanding that he married a short time ago, he has seven Indian concubines with him, and from this can be judged how he behaves in any other way."

The Paulista pioneer, after his participation in the campaigns of 1687–1697 against the rebellious tribes of Açu and the Negroes of the Palmares, settled with his immediate followers in the latter region and did not return to Piauí. The pacification—temporary as it proved—of most of Piauí from 1682 to 1710, was the work of Domingos Affonso, variously surnamed Mafrense and Sertão. The first appellation was derived from the fact that he was born near Mafra in Portugal, and the second from his spending most of his life in pioneering, fighting, and cattle raising in what was then the Brazilian Far West. He first comes into prominence in 1671, when we find him, although a recent immigrant, asking for *sesmarias* in the south of the captaincy of Bahia. In the mid-1670's he was associated with Francisco Dias d'Avila in the punitive expeditions (or slave raids) against hostile tribes of the river São Francisco. Here he established himself in the *fazenda* of Sobrado, between Sento Sé and Juazeiro, whence he penetrated to the upper reaches of the rivers Piauí and Canindé.

By the time of his death in June, 1711, he had dominated or driven away most of the tribes in the region of these two rivers, and his ranches had spread westward to join with those founded by Domingos Jorge Velho between the Gurguéia and the Parnaíba. In his last will and testament, Domingos Affonso proudly declared that he was "lord and owner of half the lands for which I asked in Piauí with Colonel Francisco Dias d'Avila and his brothers; which lands I discovered and peopled with great danger to my person and at great expense, with the help of my associates; and without these latter, I also fought many lawsuits that were brought against me over these lands." The ranches which had cost so much in blood, treasure, and litigation he bequeathed to the Jesuits of the College of Bahia as his sole heirs. There were thirty of these Jesuit estates in 1739, containing nearly a hundred leagues of land, on which were pastured 30,000 head of cattle and 1,500 horses, with 164 stockmen to look after them.[13]

We have a detailed description of pioneer Piauí in 1697, from the pen of a secular priest, Miguel de Carvalho, who claimed to have traversed the whole of the settled region within the previous four years. He lists by name and with the number of occupants, 129 ranches, all of which were situated along various rivers and streams, and which contained a total of 441 persons, including "whites, Negroes, Indians, mulattoes, and half-breeds." Apart from these, there were a number of individuals living near isolated water holes, lakes, or swamps, and an encampment of Paulistas with their domesticated Amerindians. All these categories together constituted a community of 940 Christian souls. Out of nearly 150 ranchers who are listed by name, only one white man was married, and very few women of any race are mentioned.

All the land was owned (or claimed) by two persons, Domingos Affonso Sertão and Leonor Pereira Marinho; but most of it was let to individual ranchers at an annual rental of ten *milreis* per *sitio*. There was usually a distance of two or three leagues between each ranch, and few ranchers had more than two or three colored men to assist them, many having only one. When a man left a ranch to set up on his own, he had to hand over to the owner the same number of cattle as he had found on arrival, keeping for himself one out of every four of the surplus, after paying tithes. Ranchers and stockmen alike lived mainly on meat, milk, and wild honey. "They usually roast the meat, as they have no cooking pots. They drink water from wells and lakes, always turbid, and impregnated with nitrate. The climate is very stormy and rather unhealthy, so that these wretched men live dressed in hides and look like Tapuyas." Padre Carvalho criticized the ranchers for not making better use of the land, which he considered was potentially very fertile. He cited the example of one enterprising Paulista, who had grown manioc, rice, maize, beans, bananas, and potatoes in abundance. The devastating droughts (*seccas*) which plagued northeast Brazil at frequent intervals from the last quarter of the eighteenth century onwards, do not then seem to have been as bad in Piauí as they subsequently became. There was no town or even a village as yet; but a small adobe parish church was built in February, 1697, at a place named Brejo da Mocha (also spelt Moicha, Moxa, etc.). This site was chosen by the ranchers as the most conveniently situated, "at equal distances from, and with trails leading to, all the streams and inhabited parts." [14]

After the death of Domingos Affonso Sertão, a leading role in the pacification and development of Piauí was played by Bernardo de Carvalho de Aguiar. Mentioned in the vicar of Mocha's report of 1697 as living with four Negroes on a remote ranch (Bitorocara) in the far north of Piauí, we find him in 1716 styled Camp Master of the Conquest of the State of Maranhão and the Captaincy of Piauí—a rank which he retained until his death in 1730. A considerable part of Piauí was still unpacified in 1712–1713 when a general revolt of the "Tapuyas of the North" involved not only many of those previously subdued in this region but numerous tribes of the border districts of Maranhão and Ceará as well. Two large and well-armed detachments of settlers and soldiers were cut to pieces by the savages, whose most dangerous leader was an ex-convert of the Jesuits called Mandú Ladino. Out of over four hundred ranches that existed in this region when the revolt began, more than a quarter were destroyed or had to be evacuated. After much severe fighting, Mandú Ladino was killed and the back of the revolt broken by the end of 1716, although some pockets of resistance lingered on in the remoter districts for several years. The suppression of the revolt was largely due to the loyalty of the Jesuit mission Indians of the Serra de Ibiapaba in Ceará, who were much more effective than the whites in bush warfare. Bernardo de Carvalho was anxious that these Indians should be detached from the captaincy of Ceará and included in the State of Maranhão, but this suggestion was strongly opposed by the Jesuit missionaries and by the Ceará settlers.[15]

The Jesuits claimed that the rebellion of 1712–1713 was caused primarily by the atrocities committed by the *vaqueiros* of Piauí against both subdued and dissident tribes, of which they gave numerous instances. On one occasion, a number of captive Indians were released one by one from a stockade, "and were then ridden down on horseback, as if they were bulls in a bullfight, being killed with sword cuts amid much laughter and jeering." One Portuguese officer, who prided himself on his fleetness of foot, preferred to run after the unarmed fugitives and cut off their heads when he overtook them. The missionaries also alleged that Bernardo de Carvalho had done little serious fighting, but was merely seeking to prolong the war so that he could increase the number and extent of his ranches, cattle, and slaves. These were already numerous, and he sent droves of cattle not only to Bahia but as far as Minas Gerais. The Jesuits further claimed that the Tapuyas spared the lives of such priests as they captured, with the exception of one who had taken an active part in the fighting against them. They had released the others, telling them that they had no grudge against them, but only against the settlers and stockmen who had oppressed them beyond endurance. Even when the savages burnt the churches, they took care (so the Jesuits said) not to destroy the images, but laid them carefully on the ground away from the fire. There was obviously a good deal of truth in the Jesuits' allegations; but the fact remains that some of the dissident tribes did eventually submit voluntarily to Bernardo de Carvalho, apart from others who were exterminated, and some who responded to the peaceful persuasions of the padres.[16]

Despite the Indian wars which marked its turbulent pioneer days, Piauí made definite if erratic progress during the first half of the eighteenth century. This can be seen from a comparison of the account of the ex-governor of the Maranhão, João da Maia da Gama, who visited Mocha in November, 1728, with that written by Padre Miguel de Carvalho slightly more than thirty years earlier. Maia da Gama saw that the border region with Maranhão was being rapidly resettled, and the bush being cleared for the establishment of new ranches. He found that Mocha now had 120 houses, including a stone jail and council house under construction. He thought that the further development of the town was prejudiced by its being situated in a singularly arid and sterile region, with no timber anywhere near. He therefore suggested the construction of a new center at the junction of the rivers Parnaíba and Potí—a suggestion which duly materialized in the present-day city of Teresina. He praised the vicar of Mocha for his work in pacifying the local Indians, and the district magistrate for arresting one of the most pernicious of the *poderosos do sertão*. Maia da Gama denounced the Dias d'Avila family as the worst offenders in this respect. He stated that they habitually secured local magnates as their representatives (*procuradores*), and that these men then intimidated the ranchers into paying rent for land claimed but never cleared or developed by successive members of the House of Torre. He was surprised to find Mocha well-stocked with European provisions, but noted that these were priced at from 200 to 300 per cent above their cost in the Maranhão. It is clear from this account that Bernardo de Carvalho and the Jesuits were now on friendly terms, and Maia da Gama paid warm tributes to both parties for their work in pacifying the dissident tribes.[17]

According to Rocha Pitta and Southey, Piauí contained at this time about four hundred extensive *fazendas,* from which Bahia received much, and Minas Gerais most, of their supply of cattle. Ten or twelve men sufficed for managing an average estate, part of their duty being to destroy the wild cattle and horses, so that these should not lead the tame beasts astray. If the owner (or tenant) had no slaves, he could easily secure the services of mulattoes, mamelucos, and free Negroes, who hated any other kind of labor but were passionately addicted to this way of life. They served for five years without pay, but then received the fourth of the herd every year and hoped in due course to establish *fazendas* of their own.

Before taking leave of Piauí for the region of Rio Grande in the far south, a word may be said about its peculiar administrative situation. Though first settled and colonized from the captaincy of Bahia, Piauí nominally came under the administration of Pernambuco, which, it will be recalled, comprised all the territory hitherto discovered on the left bank of the river São Francisco. In practice, title deeds to land (*cartas de sesmaria*) in Piauí were issued by both the governor of Pernambuco and by the governor-general at Bahia, though more usually by the former. In 1715–1718, when Mocha was elevated to a township, the Crown subordinated Piauí administratively to the State of Maranhão, but the Bishop of Pernambuco, from his see at Olinda, continued to exercise ecclesiastical jurisdiction over Piauí. To make matters more confusing, judicial appeals from the decisions of the crown judge (*ouvidor*) at Mocha were heard in the high court (*relação*) of Salvador in Bahia.

The droughts (*sêcas*) which have periodically afflicted the northeastern regions of Brazil with such devastating results in the last two centuries do not seem to have been quite so bad in the first half of the eighteenth century. They certainly existed, and João da Maia da Gama, writing of his journey from the Maranhão to Pernambuco in 1728–1729, through the captaincies of Piauí, Ceará, Rio Grande do Norte, and Paraíba, noted the damage done by "the terrible and continuous seven years of drought which burnt and destroyed" all the region he traversed. Nevertheless, one gets the impression even from this account that this drought, serious as it undoubtedly was, did not have such deadly effects as some of the later ones, such as the "great drought" of 1791–1793 when seven-eighths of the cattle are alleged to have perished.

The third cattle-raising area with which we are now concerned, São Pedro do Rio Grande, though it took much longer to develop in the moving frontier regions of the extreme south, eventually proved to be the best in Brazil.[18] Its origins and early growth were closely connected with the vicissitudes of the Colonia do Sacramento, the isolated Portuguese outpost established on the north bank of the Rio de la Plata, opposite Buenos Aires, on January

20, 1680. These vicissitudes are briefly related elsewhere (pp. 246ff), but the need to occupy the empty lands between Sacramento and Laguna (the southernmost settlement in Brazil, which was founded in 1684), became apparent after the Spaniards had reluctantly returned the site of Sacramento in accordance with the provisions of the Treaty of Utrecht. The region between the river Uruguay and the sea, though claimed by both the Crowns of Spain and Portugal, and though traversed occasionally by exploring parties of both nations, was in practice a no-man's land, save for some Spanish Jesuit mission stations, and for some Amerindian tribes. Prominent among these tribes were the Tapes, who had been catechized and largely converted by the Jesuits of the group of mission stations called "Seven Peoples," situated near the left bank of the river Uruguay. These Tapes were admittedly hostile to the Portuguese; but their hostility was to some extent offset by the friendly disposition of the Minuanos, who lived nearer the coast and were mortal enemies to the Spaniards.[19]

Effective penetration of this pampa or prairie-like region began about 1715, with a modest movement down the coast from Laguna, itself a hamlet of only thirty-two households. This was soon followed by the infiltration of Paulista pioneers from the north by way of Curitiba. In January, 1715, the village councillors of Laguna prophetically described the plains of São Pedro do Rio Grande as the best land for colonization in South America, "where the whole of the population of Brazil could be accommodated, without the thousands of inhabitants being noticed therein, owing to its vast and far-ranging prairies." In March, 1718, in reply to a government questionnaire from Lisbon, the governor of Rio de Janeiro reported that the region of Rio Grande de São Pedro was eminently suitable for colonization on a grand scale, "being full of cattle," and "overflowing with everything needful for the increase of the New Colony [of Sacramento]" and for founding numerous cities.[20] The "Continent of Rio Grande" as it soon came to be called by the Portuguese, was mainly prairie land, but it contained sufficient diversity of woodlands, hills, and dales, and was well watered. Apart from the existing herds of wild cattle and horses, originating from runaways from the Argentine pampas and the Jesuit mission stations, it offered every facility for the raising of domestic breeds. These recommendations and subsequent ones to the same effect were accepted in principle by the Overseas Councillors at Lisbon. They periodically urged the Crown to take steps to colonize this region, but nearly twenty years elapsed before this was done.

The decisive step was the establishment of a Portuguese fortified post at São Pedro do Rio Grande in 1737, after the failure of a projected attack on Montevideo and Buenos Aires. André Ribeiro Coutinho, one of the founding fathers of the new settlement, and a military officer with much experience in Europe and India behind him, wrote that this was indeed the land of plenty. "For here is plenty of meat, plenty of fish, plenty of geese, plenty of wild duck, plenty of kingfishers, plenty of partridges, plenty of jacum, plenty of milk and cheese, plenty of pineapples, plenty of hides, plenty of timber, plenty of clay, plenty of balsam, plenty of hills, plenty of lakes, and plenty of marshes. In the summer, plenty of heat, plenty of flies, plenty of motuca, plenty of mosquitoes, plenty of moths, plenty of fleas. In the winter, plenty of rain, plenty of wind, plenty of cold, plenty of thunder; and all the year round, plenty of work, plenty of making fascines, plenty of excellent air, plenty of good water, plenty of hope, and plenty of health." [21]

The nucleus of the population that gradually penetrated into the interior was formed by an amalgam of men and women from many distant regions. Deserters and dissatisfied colonists (some of them originally from Tras-os-Montes) from the struggling colony of Sacramento; soldiers drafted (mostly against their will) from the garrisons of Rio de Janeiro, Bahia, and Pernambuco; vagabonds, prostitutes, and beggars deported from the same places and from São Paulo and Minas Gerais; and, from 1746 onwards, peasant families from the Azores sent out at the expense of the Crown. Some of the earliest pioneers mated with the Minuano women, and in later years Negroes, mulattoes, Carijós, and "bastards" were added to this racial melting pot. The military governors frequently urged that more married families should be encouraged to emigrate, in default of which they were glad to receive single women whether of easy or of proved virtue, from the Brazilian coastal towns. They maintained that the fallen women would soon find husbands and rear respectable families, as some of them undoubtedly did.

Despite the efforts of the colonial authorities—and, after 1746, of the Crown—the population increased rather slowly for the first few years. Military service, always unpopular in Brazil—save in the dragoons of Minas Gerais—was particularly so in the south, despite its temperate climate, and desertions were numerous. Even the Negro slaves resented being sent to this region, although they were fed, clothed, and treated better here than elsewhere, once they had learned to ride and become stockmen, as they soon did. A regiment of dragoons which had been formed with great difficulty for service on this frontier, mutinied in January, 1742, because they had received no pay for twenty months and no uniforms for three years. Being unpaid and ill-clothed—and allegedly ill-treated by their officers—they preyed upon the local populace, who likewise became discontented. Even some of the most ardent advocates of the colony, who had originally maintained that the region was of far greater (potential) use than the exposed and costly establishment of Sacramento, temporarily lost heart and declared that São Pedro do Rio Grande was worse than useless.[22] The crisis was surmounted by 1747, when São Pedro was elevated to a township and the first levies of colonists from the Azores were installed. The coastal region from Laguna to Xuí was now under effective Portuguese control, although the settled districts did not extend inland for more than forty-five miles.

Meanwhile, in the "Continent of Rio Grande" between the rivers Uruguay and La Plata on the one hand and Lakes Mirim and Patos on the other, a new type of man was making his appearance—the *gaúcho*. He seems to have developed soon after 1717, with a variety of Portuguese deserters from the garrison of Sacramento, Spanish smugglers from Corrientes and Santa Fé, and a few fugitives from southern Brazil. These men mated with Minuano and other Amerindian women, and led what was virtually an outlaw's life, revolving around horses and herds of wild cattle. They and their descendants soon became skilled horsemen, and adepts in the use of lasso, *bola* [23] and lance. They lived mainly on fresh meat, tobacco, and *maté* (Paraguayan tea), these last two commodities being acquired from the Spanish and Portuguese settlements in exchange for horses and cattle. Needless to say, the primitive *gaúchos* were even more careless of the way they killed cattle than were the pioneer colonists of Rio Grande, whose wasteful methods were described by André Ribeiro Coutinho in 1740 as follows: ". . . since on the prairie they do not eat the flesh of the bullocks which are killed for the sake of their hides, they kill the cows for meat, and then only eat the most tender portion; and sometimes they kill a cow merely to extract the milk, and they commit other atrocities of this kind." In due course these hybrid *gaúchos* were increased by deserters from the garrison of Rio Grande, and it was many years before the authorities brought them under some sort of control.

The *gaúcho* of the south had some obvious similarities with the *vaqueiro* of the center and north, in that both types spent their lives among horses and cattle, yet there were some striking contrasts between them. In Piauí and Bahia, the *vaqueiro* was either an employee, a tenant, or a squatter on the ranch lands owned (or at least claimed) by territorial magnates of the type of Domingos Affonso Sertão and Bernardo de Carvalho de Aguiar. In the pioneer days of São Pedro do Rio Grande do Sul, the *gaúcho* was either an outlaw or at least completely independent. He either lived a roving life as an individual or else, and more commonly, banded together with a few others of his kind. In Piauí, the Amerindians were disliked and despised, "three or four redskins being bartered for one Negro from Angola." [24] In Rio Grande do

Sul, the Minuano was usually a valued ally and collaborator of the *gaúcho,* though of course clashes between white men and red did occur.

Since Piauí had originally been colonized by stockmen from the São Francisco River valley, the term "Bahiano" was, and has since remained, a synonym for "countryman" in the cattle-raising districts of Piauí and Maranhão. In Rio Grande do Sul, on the other hand, the colonists who came from Bahia were mostly vagrants who had been conscripted from the towns for service in the dragoons. Hence the term "Bahiano" was (and is) contemptuously applied to a man who was ill at ease on a horse and unable to use a lasso. When the first military levies arrived in 1737, Brigadier José Pais and André Ribeiro Coutinho took great pains to teach all the recruits to ride well, and this made the subsequent fusion with the *gaúchos* easier. Since life in Rio Grande do Sul for long revolved almost entirely around horses and cattle, the south, too, had its "Age of Leather." To quote André Ribeiro Coutinho once again on his pioneer days in Rio Grande: "Houses, workshops, gear for carts, baskets for carrying earth, strips for the support of trenches, and innumerable other works" were all made from leather. Despite the great quantity of hides used in this way, he contrived to ship another 19,683 for the account of the royal exchequer at Rio de Janeiro. The export of jerked beef, for which the region later became famous, was of scant importance in the earlier years, but convoys of horses (mostly colts) and mules were soon sent over the Curitiba trail for sale in Minas Gerais.

Hides formed one of the staple Brazilian exports, as Antonil reminded his readers when writing at the height of the gold rush to Minas Gerais. Gold, however, continued to arouse more interest both among his contemporaries and among posterity in general. One of Dom João V's leading advisers, the Duke of Cadaval, urged that monarch to waive his claim to the colony of Sacramento, which the Castilian Crown showed itself anxious to retain during the negotiations which preceded the Treaty of Utrecht. The Duke observed that Sacramento was of little importance, adding that a king "who has dominions which yield gold counted in pounds and hundredweights, should not bother about a few hides, which is all that colony produces." [25] This viewpoint was shared by many people in Portugal and Brazil, though Antonil was not one of them. If cattle formed the impulse behind the moving frontiers of Bahia, Piauí, Rio Grande do Sul, and Sacramento, gold was still the lodestar which drew the pioneers of the Brazilian Far West to the virgin soils of Goiás and Mato Grosso.

X. MOVING FRONTIERS
AND MONSOONS

THE DUKE OF CADAVAL's scornful opinion that
Sacramento was a worthless place, since it produced "nothing but
a few hides" in contrast to the solid lumps of gold from Minas
Gerais, was not altogether correct. It was true that the cost of garri-
soning and fortifying this outpost was always a great burden to the
Crown; but if the king made no direct profit out of the Colonia do
Sacramento, plenty of other people did. Save for times when it was
being closely besieged or blockaded, and sometimes even then,
Sacramento was a smugglers' paradise. Nor were the beneficiaries
of this thriving contraband trade in such varied articles as Peruvian
silver, Brazilian gold, European manufactured goods, and local
hides, confined to obscure *gaúchos* and corrupt customs officials.
Those who profited most were, as often as not, the governors on
both sides of the Rio de la Plata.

Founded by the Portuguese in 1680, taken by the Spaniards in
the same year, returned to the Portuguese in 1683, and occupied a
second time by the Spaniards from 1706 to 1716, the boundaries of
the settlement had never been defined when the Portuguese took
possession for the third time, after the diplomatic haggling which
resulted in the Treaty of Utrecht. The Spaniards claimed that the
Portuguese were entitled to no more land on the north bank of

the Rio de la Plata than the ground which was within range of the cannon of Sacramento. This distance was defined by the Spanish government in 1733 as being the range of a twenty-four-pounder. The Portuguese, for their part, regarded the Rio de la Plata as marking the boundary between Brazil and Spanish territory, asserting that the unoccupied country between Laguna and Sacramento belonged to them. Mainly owing to the inertia or to the connivance of the governors of Buenos Aires, the Spaniards did not attempt to assert their claims forcibly before 1724, and then only to prevent an attempted Portuguese occupation of Montevideo in January of that year. Not until 1735 did another and far more serious armed clash occur; and by this time the Portuguese colony had struck deep roots and had put out strong tentacles toward the north.[1]

Less than seven years after the final Portuguese occupation of Nova Colonia do Sacramento, the official name, their grazing area extended for nearly ninety miles inland. During the next decade the Portuguese continued to consolidate if not to expand their hold, in despite of periodic paper protests by the Spaniards. When the latter finally started hostilities in 1735, the colony comprised more than 3,000 souls, including the garrison of 935 men. The countryside was dotted over with country houses, farmhouses, and cottages, interspersed among ranches, farms, orchards, gardens, and plantations yielding a wide variety of European and American fruits and vegetables. Even vineyards had been planted with success, some of them containing more than 90,000 vines. Windmills, lime kilns, and potteries had been erected to serve this flourishing rural community, where the average family was accustomed to killing a beast a day to provide themselves with fresh meat. This they could easily afford to do, since their livestock included some 87,000 head of cattle, apart from 2,300 sheep and 18,000 horses, mules and asses. In short, the countryside around Sacramento presented an attractive picture of rural prosperity which must have contrasted strongly with the backward state of agriculture and stockbreeding in Portugal itself, judging by the unflattering descriptions given by all eighteenth-century travelers to the mother country.[2]

Considerable quantities of dried meat and of wheat were exported from Sacramento to Brazil, but it is the figures for the export of hides that are really impressive. Between 1726 and 1734, the annual export of this commodity varied between 400,000 and 500,000, most of which, of course, had come from Spanish territory. They were bought with Brazilian gold, or with European manufactured goods, with which Sacramento was plentifully supplied, partly by coastal shipping from Rio de Janeiro and partly by English merchant vessels. Between January and October, 1735, thirty vessels laden with goods for this contraband trade anchored off Sacramento, including four English ships from Lisbon, provided with passes from both the Portuguese and English governments, and sailing under either of these two flags, as they found convenient. This flourishing contraband trade resulted in an alarming drain of Peruvian silver from Buenos Aires, which all the laws and admonitions of the Madrid government were powerless to prevent, mainly because the governors of Buenos Aires had a large personal stake in this illicit commerce.[3]

Since Sacramento was apparently a land of Cockaigne, it is rather puzzling that desertions were so numerous and that official complaints of the poverty and wretchedness of the place were so frequent. Admittedly, Sacramento was virtually a penal settlement for Brazil, and military service there seems to have been only one degree less unpopular than in the deadly climate of Angola and Benguela. A previously quoted memorialist of the 1690's, alleged that "the new colony of Sacramento is only preserved by the grace of God, since it cannot exist without women, for nowhere in the world have new settlements ever been founded without married couples."[4] This was an exaggeration even at the time that he wrote, since a few families had come to Sacramento with Dom Naper de Lencastre in 1690. After the reoccupation of 1716, the settlement of peasant families on the land was encouraged more systematically by the dispatch of married couples with their children from the Azores and Tras-os-Montes; but the complaints still continued, at any rate for some years. In 1719 the governor wrote that both soldiers and civilians were selling the shirts off their backs to buy biscuit from the Spaniards. Three years later, it was officially reported that "entire families" had deserted to Buenos Aires, and that "many soldiers" had fled southwards, as well as northwards to Rio Grande do Sul, "braving the manifold dangers of the *sertão* rather than remain in that wretched stronghold."[5]

The Spaniards were inclined to regard these deserters as the spearhead of a more systematic Portuguese advance into their territories. One governor, with obvious exaggeration, reported that Potosí itself might soon be menaced; and another, with more reason, wrote that if nothing was done to contain Sacramento, the Portuguese there would soon link up with their settlements in southern Brazil. For all their complaints of Portuguese aggression between 1716 and 1735, the Spaniards of Buenos Aires did not do a great deal to checkmate their rivals, probably because the contraband trade was too tempting, and because they thought that if it came to a showdown they could take Sacramento as easily as they had done in 1680. However this may be, they contented themselves with paper protests, and with harassing the Portuguese occasionally with the aid of the Tapes from the Jesuit Reductions of Uruguay. Having foiled the rather feeble attempt of the Portuguese to install themselves at Montevideo in 1724, the Spaniards then proceeded to plant a colony of their own there, mainly formed by levies of peasant families from the Canary Islands.[6]

The Portuguese Crown frequently protested to the Court of Madrid against what it termed Spanish aggression against the colony of Sacramento, but received no satisfaction whatsoever. As one of the Portuguese envoys observed, it would be easier to persuade the Spanish government to abolish the Inquisition "than to cede a single foot of ground in America to any European people, and, least of all people, to the Portuguese." On another occasion, a leading Spanish statesman declared that the loss of Sacramento was a greater blow to the Spanish Crown than the loss of Gibraltar. The Portuguese government was equally obstinate in maintaining its claim to this settlement. Even if other influential people besides the Duke of Cadaval considered that Sacramento was a liability rather than an asset, and would have exchanged it for some other place in America or in Europe, Dom João V assured a new governor of the colony in 1720: "that the stronghold of Sacramento was of such importance for his Crown, that he would not exchange it for the most advantageous equivalent that the Castilians might offer him." [7]

The inevitable clash came in 1735. As a result of the rupture of diplomatic relations between the Crowns of Spain and Portugal, arising out of a trivial incident involving some footmen of the Portuguese embassy at Madrid, the governor of Buenos Aires received orders to take Sacramento by force of arms. He laid waste the fertile and cultivated countryside without any difficulty; but although the fortifications were in a poor state of repair, the Portuguese held firm behind them, under the inspiring leadership of their governor, Dom António Pedro de Vasconcellos, in September, 1735. In response to his urgent appeals for help from Brazil, successive expeditions arrived with reinforcements from Rio de Janeiro, Bahia, and Pernambuco, during the next few months. A successful sortie in October, 1736 drove off the besieging force of Spanish soldiers and Amerindians from the Jesuit Reductions; and although desultory operations dragged on for another year, the place was not again seriously endangered. Dom João V was bitterly disappointed at not obtaining active support from England in this crisis; and after much diplomatic negotiation an armistice was concluded at Paris in March, 1737, ordering the cessation of hostilities in America (they had never broken out in Europe) and the reversion to the *status quo*. The Portuguese soon resumed their commercial and cattle-raising activities at Sacramento; but they would not or could not continue with the agricultural pursuits which had made the place such an enviable sight before 1735. [8]

The setback given to the colonization of the countryside around

Sacramento by the war of 1735–1737, was partly offset by the development of the island of Santa Catarina, which was seriously undertaken in the 1740's. This island, though naturally fertile and of obvious strategic importance, was first settled in 1662 by a small number of Paulistas who established themselves at Desterro. Ten years later this settlement was destroyed by buccaneers; but the survivors and their descendants gained an enviable reputation for friendliness and hospitality to the crews of foreign shipping that touched here for food and water. "For these ships wanting only provisions, of which the natives had great store; and the natives wanting clothes, (for they often despised money, and refused to take it) which the ships furnished them with in exchange for their provisions, both sides found their account in this traffic; and their captain or governor had neither power nor interest to restrain it or to tax it." [9]

The tendency of foreign ships to frequent Santa Catarina, and the welcome they received from the islanders, for long caused uneasiness to the colonial authorities. The Crown toyed with the idea of fortifying it in 1717, but the governor of Rio de Janeiro pointed out that it would be very difficult if not impossible to do so adequately.[10] The fighting around Sacramento and the occupation of São Pedro do Rio Grande twenty years later, made it essential for the Portuguese to mend their fences in the weakly held region of Santa Catarina, and the fortification of the island was finally decided on. Brigadier Silva Pais was entrusted with this work in 1739, and he and his chief colleagues on the mainland, Gomes Freire de Andrada and André Ribeiro Coutinho, insisted that it was no use fortifying Santa Catarina unless the island was colonized by people more reliable than freedom-loving Paulistas. Silva Pais specifically suggested that emigrants should be sent from the Azores, where some of the islands had a perennial overpopulation problem, and whence many people had emigrated previously to Brazil (p. 11, above). The Overseas Councillors at Lisbon warmly supported these recommendations; but Dom João V did not implement them until 1746, when he gave his sanction in principle. Evidently under the impulse of Alexandre de Gusmão, the Overseas Councillors then elaborated an admirable plan for the large-scale colonization of Santa Catarina and the neighboring mainland in the years 1746–1748.[11]

Four thousand families were to be sent in successive levies, mainly from the Azores and Madeira, "although families of foreign nationals may also go, provided that they are Roman Catholics and that they do not belong to nations which already have colonies in America whither they can emigrate." Husbands were not to be more than forty years of age, nor wives more than thirty, so as to ensure that the full demographic benefit should be derived from married couples, apart from the children they took with them. Skilled workers and artisans were offered special privileges and inducements, including a cash bonus on their arrival in Brazil. Meticulous instructions were given about the amount of provisions, clothing, and supplies each emigrant family could take, and how much they would receive from the Crown on embarkation and after reaching their destination. Among other things, each family was to receive a musket, two hoes, an axe, a hammer, two knives, a billhook, two scissors, a saw, two gimlets, two *alqueires* of seeds, two cows, a mare, and a year's supply of [manioc?] flour. The governor of Rio de Janeiro and Brigadier Silva Pais (governor of the island of Santa Catarina from 1739 to 1749) received orders to clear the bush and erect housing for the newcomers before their arrival. They had also to arrange for the necessary supplies of farm and draught animals, seeds, and agricultural implements. Instructions were also given for the layout of the actual settlements, the building of chapels, and the supply of parish priests. Nor was the organization of the immigrants into militia companies overlooked, although they were exempt from conscription for service in the regular army.

Brigadier Silva Pais was specifically enjoined "to take every care that these new colonists are well received and treated; and, as soon as he receives this order, he is to choose both in the said island [of Santa Catarina] as on the neighboring mainland from the southern Rio São Francisco to Fort São Miguel in the backlands, the newest places in that region for founding the settlements, taking due care, however, not to give the Spaniards on the adjacent frontiers any just cause for complaint." About sixty families were to be installed in each settlement, and the head of each family was to receive a quarter of a league of land. The plan thus envisaged the colonization of the littoral from the north of the present State of Santa Catarina to the northern region of present-day Uruguay. From the time of the colonists' arrival in Brazil, all their expenses were to be borne by the royal exchequer at Rio de Janeiro, the whole scheme being placed under the general supervision of Gomes Freire de Andrada, although Brigadier Silva Pais was primarily responsible for carrying it out on the ground. Free passages were provided by the Crown in ships that had been specially selected for their seaworthy qualities. The contractor entrusted with transporting the emigrants across the Atlantic was forbidden to use these vessels for any other purpose, including the carriage of commercial cargoes.[12]

One of the more curious stipulations in the instructions for the accommodation of the peasant families on board the emigrant ships concerned the treatment of the female passengers. Whether married or single, they were herded in adjoining but locked cabins, together with the boys less than seven years old, and under the guard of armed men who were relieved every four hours. Their food was cooked and brought them by carefully selected "trusties" from among the more reliable male passengers. Otherwise, the women and girls were to have no contact even with their own husbands, brothers, or sons, save by special permission of the captain, the master, or the leader of an emigrant group (*mandante*), one of whom had to be present when husband and wife, brother and sister, mother and son conversed through a grille in the presence of an armed guard. Even the ship's doctor, or the chaplain, could only visit the women in the event of corporal or spiritual necessity. The only time the women were allowed to leave their cabins was to hear Mass; and then they had to walk between

253

two files of armed guards and remain in a compact body strictly separated from the men while the service was held. Severe penalties were laid down for anyone attempting to speak to any of the women without official permission, and the women's cabins were virtually prison cells. As mentioned previously, the Portuguese habit of secluding their women was almost Muslim in its rigor. The regulations of 1747 which are summarized above, remind one of Alan Villiers' vivid description of the way in which Arab women were cribbed, cabined, and confined aboard the dhow in which he sailed from Aden to Mombasa in 1939.[13]

The projected total of 4,000 peasant families from the Atlantic islands for the colonization of Santa Catarina and Rio Grande do Sul was never achieved, but a large number did arrive in the years 1748–1753, and gave the former island in particular a strong Azorean strain which has remained to this day. These colonists were further reinforced by others who were transferred from blockaded Sacramento, and who received permission to leave for Santa Catarina in 1748. Even if the high hopes with which this ambitious scheme was started were not entirely fulfilled, sufficient families did emigrate to give the inhabitants of this region a far higher proportion of white blood than those of the rest of Brazil, as observed by Saint-Hilaire and other nineteenth-century travelers.[14]

While the southern frontier regions were experiencing the vicissitudes outlined above, much more striking and dramatic events were being enacted in the Brazilian Far West. A band of Paulistas who had lost their lands in Minas Gerais as a result of the "War of the Emboabas," or who were merely gratifying their traditional wanderlust in searching for Amerindians to enslave, accidentally discovered alluvial gold on a dazzling rich scale in the region of the river Cuiabá in 1718. One of these groups, working with three slaves for a month and a half, secured 900 drams of gold, "being forced to use the barrels of their muskets for digging, in default of any proper iron tools." These pioneers reported that the country through which they had passed was occupied by a great "multitude and diversity" of Amerindian tribes, but that most of them were friendly and offered no resistance. These good relations did not last very long. In November, 1721 the Paulista pioneers of Cuiabá elected one of their number, Fernando Dias Falcão, as their leader against the local tribes who had already killed a number of white men and their Negro slaves.[15]

When news of the gold strikes on the rivers Cuiabá and Coxipó reached the settled regions of Brazil, another exodus began which recalls Antonil's description of the gold rush to Minas Gerais twenty-five years previously. "From Minas Gerais, Rio de Janeiro, and the whole captaincy of São Paulo," wrote Joseph Barbosa de Sá, "flocked many people, leaving their houses, goods, wives, and children, pouring into these backlands as if they were the Land of Promise or the hidden Paradise in which God placed our first parents." As with the gold rush to Minas Gerais, the adventurers who came to Cuiabá also included many deserters from the garrison towns (in this case São Paulo) and many unbeneficed clergymen. The country through which these pioneers had to pass, presented even·greater obstacles than did the primeval forest and wooded hills of Minas Gerais. Whereas the journey to Minas Gerais over the Paratí trail from Rio took only about three weeks, seven months were often required for the river voyage from São Paulo to Cuiabá in the early years.[16] This voyage was made in fragile canoes, usually by way of the rivers Tieté, Pardo, Coxim, Taquarí, and Paraguay, with portages at frequent intervals. Many canoes were lost in trying to negotiate the swirling rapids, since pilots who knew every stretch of the rivers did not yet exist. Many people died of starvation and others of disease, or were devoured by ounces and other wild beasts. These pioneers "did not yet have mosquito nets, which were only invented many years later, as were many such things which experience and necessity taught them," and those who reached Cuiabá did so only after enduring the most appalling hardships. "There was a convoy in which everyone perished, those who came later finding the canoes with the goods spoiled inside them, dead bodies lying along the river banks, and hammocks slung with their owners lying dead inside them." This disaster occurred in 1720, when not a living soul reached Cuiabá. As had happened in the mining camps of Minas Gerais, famine conditions resulted in fantastic prices being paid for food of any kind. One adventurer who had lost all his slaves and goods on the journey, "was forced to barter a little mulatto boy whom he looked upon as a son, for a fish called *Pacú,* in order to save his life." [17]

As had also happened in Minas Gerais, many miners made little or no profit, while a few lucky ones struck it really rich. Among these last were a Paulista named Miguel Sutil and his Portuguese partner, João Francisco. One day, when engaged in planting a *roça* on the Cuiabá river bank, Sutil sent two of his Carijós into the forest to collect some wild honey. The Amerindians returned long after dark without any honey; but when Sutil began to upbraid them for wasting their time, the more intelligent of the two savages cut him short by asking: "have you come to look for gold or honey?" Suiting the action to the words, the Carijó than handed his master twenty-three grains of gold weighing 128 drams. So excited were Sutil and his partner at their good fortune that they could not sleep that night for talking about it. At first light next day the two Carijós guided them "to the place which is now this town of Cuiabá, which was then densely wooded with enormous trees." The gold was so near the surface that they could scoop it up with their hands, and when they returned to their camping place at nightfall, Sutil had secured half an *arroba* of gold and his partner more than 600 drams. News of the discovery naturally spread very quickly, and within a few days the locality was teeming with miners and their slaves. More than 400 *arrobas* of gold were mined in a month, without the miners having to dig deeper than four spans at the most. The Cuiabá diggings, it may be added, were uniformly shallower than those of Minas Gerais and consequently they were more quickly exhausted.

Living conditions in the mining camp of Bom Jesus de Cuiabá, which was elevated to a township on New Year's Day, 1727, continued to be difficult for several years. The mortality was particularly heavy in 1723, when many people perished on the long journey to the mines and many others died of malnutrition or of fever in the encampment. The maize crop failed, and a Negro slave was bartered for four *alqueires* of that cereal. A fish sold for seven or eight drams of gold, and the only redeeming feature was that the first pigs and chickens reached Cuiabá in that year. Conditions were as bad, or even worse, in 1724, and half a pound of gold was given for a flask of salt in 1725. Malarial fevers were endemic, and rats and locusts assumed the proportions of the Plagues of Egypt in those years. The first pair of cats which reached Cuiabá sold for a pound of gold in 1725, but their progeny thrived exceedingly and "there were soon so many that they lost their value." Clouds of mosquitoes tormented the inhabitants by day and night. Sleep was only possible under a mosquito net after dark, and everyone carried a fan in his hand during the daytime.[18] Even when the physical living conditions improved, prices still remained very high in Cuiabá for everything (and the word includes most things) imported from outside. As elsewhere in the gold-mining districts, everyone lived on credit and payments were often years overdue. Hence merchants and retailers charged enormous prices for goods on which they had already.paid heavy import duties.

Despite these privations and others that will be mentioned, the population of Cuiabá comprised some 7,000 souls, of whom about 2,600 were Negro slaves, in 1726. There is no way of knowing the proportion of Paulistas to Emboabas among the white members of the community; but although the former were indisputably the pioneers, the latter, as in Minas Gerais, probably soon outnumbered them. When the first municipal council was installed (January 1, 1727), four of the six councillors were Paulistas and the other two were Portuguese with Paulista wives. The early buildings were all of *pau-a-pique,* including the prison which was built in 1724. Food crops were limited to allotments of maize, beans, pumpkins, and bananas. Manioc does not seem to have been planted, or only tardily and on a very small scale. This was a mark of Paulista influence, since these men never took to manioc in the same way as did the northern Brazilians and the Portuguese—pork and beans, lightly cooked and sprinkled with maize flour, seems to have been the staple Paulista dish. The crops suffered heavily from a terrible drought in 1725–1726, when not a drop of rain fell during the two years. The inhabitants were afflicted with all the physical symptoms of malnutrition until the establishment of sugar-cane brandy distilleries in 1728, if José Barbosa de Sá is to be believed. As mentioned previously (p. 151) the consumption of this brandy was regarded with very different feelings by the colonial officials and by the populace of Brazil, but our chronicler was in no doubt of its virtues.

Referring to the establishment of these distilleries by an enterprising Paulista, he wrote: "This was when people began to enjoy good health and disease declined, and when they began to have wholesome complexions, having hitherto had those of the dead. Dropsies and swellings of the bellies and legs likewise declined, as did the mortality among the slaves which had been experienced up to now, they being buried in heaps daily. This goes to show how useful brandy distilleries are in these backlands, chiefly for the preservation of the slaves who are employed in mining; but nowadays the distilleries are nearly all abandoned, owing to the numerous taxes which have been imposed on them." [19]

As in the gold-mining districts of Minas Gerais, one of the major problems in Cuiabá was the collection of the royal fifths. The original system, which the pioneers voluntarily imposed upon themselves, was an annual payment of 2½ drams of gold per *bateia,* being thus equivalent to a capitation tax on each person mining or rather washing for gold. The authorities claimed that this was insufficient, and in 1724 the tax was raised to three drams per miner, and supplemented by other imposts ranging from two to seven drams of gold, levied on taverns, shops, and drinking booths, on peddlers, and on all slaves and merchandise entering the mining district. These taxes were arranged on a sliding scale similar to, but not identical with, the duties levied in the same way in Minas Gerais. Although the gold production of Cuiabá was soon on the decline, the duties were none the less raised again, and it is far from certain how much they actually yielded to the Crown. The lowest estimates for the period 1724–1728 are as follows:

1724	3,805 drams
1725	8,953 drams
1726	16,727 drams
1727	35,210 drams
1728	14,263 drams [20]

From 1728 onwards the gold of Cuiabá was remitted to the smelting-house at São Paulo for extraction of the fifths there, this change in the system of collection coinciding with one of the most sensational frauds ever perpetrated in colonial Brazil. When the royal fifths from Cuiabá reached Lisbon, via São Paulo and Rio de Janeiro, at the beginning of 1728, the chests containing them, though securely locked and with the official seals unbroken, were found to contain only lead instead of gold. This naturally caused the greatest consternation at Court, and the Crown ordered the most stringent investigations to be made. Various people in high places were implicated, including the governor of São Paulo, Rodrigo Cezar de Menezes, who was visiting Cuiabá at the time when the royal fifths were being collected and dispatched, but nothing was ever definitely proved against any of them.[21]

During his lengthy stay in Cuiabá (November 15, 1726 to June 5, 1728) Rodrigo Cezar published a number of edicts which give us some glimpses of life in this isolated mining region. Slaves who were employed in mining and who sold some of the gold they found to taverners, merchants, and free Negroes or Negresses, incurred the savage penalty of four hundred lashes at the public pillory. Buyers or receivers of this stolen gold were liable to a fine of twice its value and a prison sentence of six months in chains, followed by deportation from Cuiabá if they were colored people.

The governor did, however, realize that many of these thefts were committed by the slaves in revenge for the cruel treatment or gross neglect that they received from their owners and overseers. He, therefore, peremptorily ordered these masters to mend their ways, and to ensure that their slaves received adequate food and clothing, on pain of otherwise incurring his severe displeasure.

As in Minas Gerais and the Diamond District, the authorities at Cuiabá displayed particular animosity against the Negresses— whether bond or free—who acted as itinerant vendors of food and drink to the miners. Rodrigo Cezar published a draconic decree against these wretched creatures, who continued nevertheless, here as elsewhere in Brazil, to make themselves quite indispensable. Jewelers and goldsmiths formed another favorite target for legislators in eighteenth-century Brazil, and Rodrigo Cezar did not forget to include them in his admonitions. Suspected of being one of the chief means of evading payment of the royal fifths, they were ordered to close all their shops or booths forthwith, and to seek some other means of livelihood. Runaway slaves and their protectors were likewise threatened with severe penalties; but conditions being what they were, it is not surprising that many did flee from the mines to take their chance with the mostly hostile Amerindians in the bush. Slaves and free Negroes who were caught carrying weapons were also subjected to savage punishments, of which a hundred lashes were the least.[22]

One of Rodrigo Cezar's minatory edicts ordained the closure of the pioneer route from São Paulo by way of the Anhandui and Aquidauna rivers, skirting the northern edge of the region known as the *Vacaria* or "Cow Country." The frontier between Brazil and Paraguay had never been delineated in the huge region which comprises the modern State of Mato Grosso, and which the Portuguese then considered part of the captaincy of São Paulo. Whites who infringed this edict were threatened with a fine of 2,000 *cruzados* and deportation to Angola; free Negroes and Amerindians being awarded four hundred lashes (evidently Rodrigo's favorite punishment) instead of the fine. This particular edict was first enacted by the governor at São Paulo in 1722, but was reiterated after his arrival at Cuiabá. The original reason had been the risk of defrauding the royal fifths by sending gold along this route which bordered on (if not actually in) Spanish territory; but in any event this way became exceedingly dangerous after 1724, owing to the attacks of hostile Amerindians.

Even apart from the risk of attack by Redskins, the annual river journey or "monsoon" from São Paulo to Cuiabá was a major adventure for the rest of the eighteenth century. The term "monsoon" was apt in more ways than one, for the fresh-water voyage to Cuiabá often took from five to seven months, which was as long as a passage from Lisbon to Goa round the Cape of Good Hope. Owing to the numerous rapids that had to be negotiated, and the numerous portages that had to be undertaken in places where rocks rendered the rivers unnavigable, the canoes employed were all of very shallow draught and often very fragile. The earliest were like the primitive Amerindian pirogues and were made from the bark of trees. Later types were more substantial, being hollowed out of tree trunks, and the largest of these dugout canoes could take up to three hundred *arrobas* of cargo. Even so, they had no keel and were difficult to steer in the swirling waters of rapids and whirlpools. A canoe of this type was sharply pointed at both ends, and carried a maximum of eighteen persons, including the crew. Many canoes were much smaller, taking only fifty or sixty *arrobas* in weight, including three or four persons altogether, according to Rodrigo Cezar writing in 1724. The cargoes shipped in the pioneer canoes were completely unprotected against the rains, and often reached Cuiabá in a ruinously sodden condition, but this was remedied after a few years by the provision of awnings.[23]

The crews were enlisted voluntarily and otherwise from Paulistas accustomed to navigating the Tieté and other rivers. After a few voyages, many of them became exceedingly skillful in shooting the rapids and negotiating the intricate channels of the river route to Cuiabá. The crew of one of the larger canoes comprised

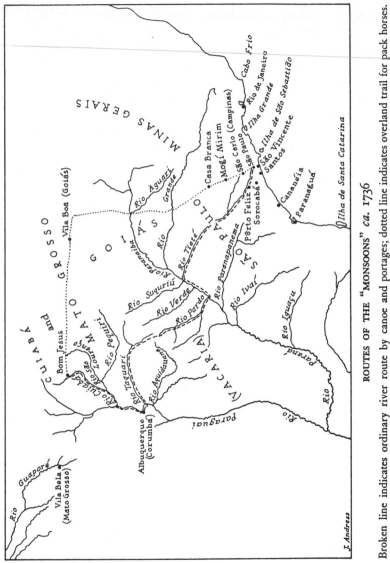

ROUTES OF THE "MONSOONS" *ca. 1736*

Broken line indicates ordinary river route by canoe and portages; dotted line indicates overland trail for pack horses. From Sergio Buarque de Holanda, *Monções* (Rio de Janeiro, 1945), p. 126A.

eight or nine men, including the pilot, assistant pilot, lookout man (*proeiro*), and five or six rowers. These men were stationed in the forepart of the canoe, the cargo being stowed in the middle, and the passengers huddled uncomfortably aft. The crews were often difficult to control and prone to desertion, being recruited from that more or less vagrant section of Brazilian society which had no fixed employment and lived from hand to mouth. They worked naked from the waist up, and sometimes smeared their bodies with grease, so as to make it difficult for anyone to grab them if they tried to run away. The daily run was usually from 8:00 A.M. to 5:00 P.M., when camp was pitched on shore for the night, and guards were often mounted to prevent the crews deserting. With the traditional fecklessness of their deep-sea counterparts, these fresh-water sailors often preferred to spend their leisure hours in singing, dancing, drinking, and brawling, rather than in getting an adequate night's sleep before the next day's work.

More than a hundred rapids had to be negotiated between Porto Feliz, the point of departure on the river Tieté (some eighty miles west of the town of São Paulo), and the mining center of Bom Jesus do Cuiabá. The amazing skill of the lookout men in shooting these rapids, "all differing not only from each other, but each one in itself, according to whether the river water is high or low," aroused the admiration of many passengers. The pilots and *proeiros* developed a phenomenal facility for gauging the depth of water at any time; but sometimes their pride in their skill led them to attempt the impossible, with the resultant loss of their canoe and all on board. The original route was by way of the rivers Tieté–Paraná–Pardo–Anhandui–Aquidauna–Paraguay, and Cuiabá. After 1725, this route was neglected in favor of that by the Tieté–Paraná–Pardo, and thence, with a portage of some ten miles at Camapoã where the canoes were transported by oxcarts, via the Coxim–Taquarí to its junction with the Paraguay near the modern Cormubá.[24]

The annual "monsoon" convoy of canoes usually left Porto Feliz between March and mid-June, since the rivers were then in flood and the rapids easier to negotiate. On the other hand, this was the unhealthy season of the year when fevers were endemic, so some convoys preferred to leave between June and October. Convoys on the return voyage usually left Bom Jesus do Cuiabá in June, taking only a couple of months to travel the distance which took from five to seven months on the outward journey. This difference was partly due to the fact that whereas the outward-bound canoes were heavily laden with people, and with large cargoes of manufactured goods and provisions of all kinds, those returning to Porto Feliz carried little more than gold and essential provisions. They also carried fewer passengers as a rule, and being less heavily laden they did not have to be unloaded in whole or in part in order to negotiate the shallower rapids, as frequently happened on the outward journey. The number of canoes and people in a convoy varied greatly. One of the largest was probably that which accompanied Rodrigo Cezar de Menezes in 1726, when he left Porto Feliz with a fleet of 305 canoes carrying more than 3,000 souls.

Manifold as were the dangers of the river "monsoon" voyages from such natural hazards as canoes capsizing in the rapids, malarial fevers, venomous insects, and man-eating fish (*piranhas*), they paled into insignificance compared to the peril presented by the attacks of the Paiaguá and Guaicurú Amerindians. The Paiaguá first made their appearance in 1725, on the upper reaches of the river Paraguay and its marshy affluents, which overflow in the rainy season on the swampy meadowlands (*pantanais*) bordering them. They had never previously been seen or heard of;[25] but they proved to be a river people, far more at home in or upon water than on land. They handled their canoes with extraordinary skill and could not only swim like fish but could catch fish with their hands under water. Lurking in backwaters and creeks while their scouts watched the approach of a canoe convoy, their main body as a rule never attacked until they were quite sure of taking the voyagers by surprise. The attack when it came was terrifying and was pressed home with reckless courage. The Paiaguá fought in small canoes containing eight or ten warriors, launching their assault with demoniacal yells that often unnerved many of their adversaries. They used bows and arrows, but their favorite weapons were short spears which could be used for both throwing and stabbing, like assagais. On coming to close quarters, they tried to wet the muskets of the white men, and thus prevent them from using their most effective weapons.

On the occasion of their first appearance in 1725, these savages annihilated a convoy of some six hundred people, only one white man and one Negro escaping to tell the tale. For the next ten years not a "monsoon" passed without the Paiaguá taking a greater or lesser toll of the voyagers, although canoes never traveled between Cuiabá and Porto Feliz except in strongly armed and escorted convoys. The Paiaguá scored their most spectacular success in 1730, when the convoy commanded by the outgoing Royal Judge (*Ouvidor*) of Cuiabá, Dr Lanhas Peixoto, was annihilated on the river Paraguay after a battle lasting from 9 A.M. to 2 P.M. Four hundred Christians, "including Whites, Negroes, and Amerindians," perished on this occasion, when the Paiaguá lost only fifty men.[26] The victors also captured sixty *arrobas* of gold, some of which they later traded to the Spaniards of Asunción, where one lucky Don received six pounds of gold in exchange for a tin plate. Three years later the Paiaguá cut up another large convoy, when only the Paulista commander, his mulata mistress, and a herculean Negro from Benguela showed any fight. These three sold their lives dearly. Even after the Negro had been disarmed, he practically tore some of his assailants apart with his bare hands! Such at least was the sworn testimony of the four men (two white and two black) who survived this terrible disaster.[27]

Even such experienced backwoodsmen as the Paulistas seem to have been nonplussed by the tactics of these aquatic warriors. Time and again in José Barbosa de Sá's chronicle we read of victories won by the Paiaguá against white men who offered little or no resistance. The earliest attempts to organize punitive expeditions against these dreaded savages were ludicrous failures, and many settlers thought that the Paiaguá were invincible. An expedition mounted immediately after the Lanhas disaster achieved less than nothing, save to earn for itself the derisive epithet of "Bandeira of the Emboabas," since it was commanded by a veteran of the wars in Portuguese India who had no use for the Paulistas. The latter scored their first great success in 1734, when they surprised a Paiaguá encampment at dawn, killing or capturing about a thousand of their opponents, with the loss of only two Negroes and a mulatto. This victory marked the turning of the tide of war, but the Paiaguá were far from finished. A determined attack on the Cuiabá-bound convoy in March, 1736, was only repulsed after heavy fighting in which a mulatto married couple greatly distinguished themselves.[28] The Paiaguá attacks gradually became less frequent after the period with which we are concerned, but neither Portuguese nor Paulistas ever succeeded in dominating this ferocious people. Their decline and virtual extinction were chiefly due to the onslaughts of the Guiacurú, with whom they were for long allied but with whom they fell out in the second half of the eighteenth century.

Whereas the Paiaguá were essentially an aquatic race, the Guiacurú were preëminently nomadic horsemen, the Portuguese often giving them the alternative name of "cavaliers" (*gente cavaleiro, Indio cavaleiro*). They had long been a menace to the Spaniards of Paraguay, raiding as far as the gates of Asunción in the 1620's; and they were also familiar to the Paulista pioneers who reached the river Paraguay by way of the Vacaria. They do not figure in José Barbosa de Sá's chronicle and in other eighteenth-century sources to quite the same extent as do the Paiaguá; but they became a major peril to the settlers and travelers in Cuiabá and Mato Grosso during the 1730's. First allied with the Paiaguá and then fighting against them, the Guiacurú alone are said to have accounted for the lives of 4,000 Paulistas and Portuguese before the year 1795,[29] by which time the former tribe was nearly extinct and the latter had ceased to be a great danger. It is no exaggeration to say that these two tribes between them gave the Portuguese more trouble than all the rest of the Brazilian Indians put together. One might even claim that only the Araucanians of Chile, who for centuries successfully defied the efforts of the Spaniards to subdue them, proved themselves tougher enemies of the White man in the New World.

The eternal wanderlust of the Paulistas was not satisfied with the discovery and exploitation of the placer mines of Cuiabá. As the crown judge of this town wrote to the governor of São Paulo in 1736: "These Paulistas only concern themselves with making new discoveries so as to live free from the justices. And when they see that these follow them, they continue to make other discoveries in remote regions where one cannot pursue them owing to the great distance." The municipal councillors of São Paulo said as much with a rather different emphasis when they assured the Crown in June of the same year that the local government officials so oppressed the Paulistas that these latter preferred to seek freedom from their exactions "in the remotest regions of the backlands." A third and equally valid reason was given by the anonymous author of the "Annals of Vila Bela," writing about 1759. He observed that the Paulistas ranged the backlands in search of Amerindians, "whose enslavement they value even above gold; and for this reason they went on discovering and settling the far interior of Brazil, and in this way originated the discoveries of the mines." [30]

The triple stimulus of personal freedom, greed for gold, and the desire for Amerindian slaves, was responsible for the discovery of the mines of Goiás in 1725, and for those of Guaporé (Mato Grosso) nine years later. The first named were found in romantic circumstances by an elderly Paulista, Bartolomeu Bueno da Silva, nicknamed "Anhangüera," or "Old Devil," like his father, another great backwoodsman. His *bandeira,* a mixed and quarrelsome group of Paulistas, Emboabas, Negroes, and Amerindians, left São Paulo on July 3, 1722, in search of a gold-bearing locality that Bueno vaguely recalled having seen when a boy on an expedition with his father and namesake to the west of the river

Paraná. Nothing more was heard of these men at São Paulo city for more than three years.[31] They had been given up for dead, when the "Old Devil" reappeared there on October 21, 1725, with the few remaining members of his *bandeira*. He announced that he had finally found what he sought in the region of Goiás, and produced a quantity of alluvial gold (8,000 drams according to one account) to prove it. The "Old Devil" was evidently looking for gold rather than for Amerindians in this particular instance; but the reverse seems to have been true of the Paulista brothers, Pais de Barros, who discovered the gold placers of Guaporé in 1734.

The gold rushes which followed these two rich strikes took much the same forms as those previously described in Minas Gerais and Cuiabá. The Paulista pioneers were first on the spot, but were speedily followed and outnumbered by hordes of Emboaba adventurers and of Negro slaves. Many, perhaps most, of the white men were penniless, and they had perforce to acquire Negro slaves and provisions on long-term credits at high rates of interest. Everything had to be imported over undeveloped country for enormous distances, and this was another reason why prices quickly rose to astronomical heights. Very few people could (or would) ever pay all they owed; and a "boom and bust" economy prevailed, with the emphasis on the "bust." The Crown officials promulgated their usual (and largely ineffective) edicts concerning the collection of the royal fifths, and the closing of all trails into the newly discovered mining regions, save one or two that could be (as they thought) easily policed. Equally ineffective bans were placed on sugar-cane brandy distilleries, on prostitutes, on goldsmiths, on unbeneficed clergy, and itinerant vendors of food and drink. Sanitary conditions in the turbulent mining camps left everything to be desired, disease was rife, and the mortality was very great, especially among the ill-fed and worse clothed slaves. The inevitable jealousy between Paulistas and Emboabas led to serious rioting between the two groups at Goiás in 1736. This enmity was less in evidence at Cuiabá and Mato

Grosso, presumably because unity was essential in the face of the formidable menace presented by the Paiaguá and Guiacurú.[32]

A striking feature of life in the mining region was the chronic instability of most prospectors and miners. Ever on the lookout for new strikes, they packed their few possessions in a satchel or a bag and moved into the jungle or bush whenever they heard rumors of a "better 'ole." José Barbosa de Sá relates how in September, 1737 there were only seven white men and a few slaves left in the town of Bom Jesus do Cuiabá, almost the whole population having migrated to Mato Grosso after reports of rich finds there.[33] This may have been an extreme case; but mining camps were likely to appear suddenly, to flourish briefly, and to vanish overnight. All the gold was of the placer variety, and mining techniques were even more primitive than they were in Minas Gerais. An eyewitness of 1802 affirmed that the most ignorant miner in Minas Gerais was more skilled than the most expert miner in Goiás, and that the most ignorant in Goiás knew more about mining than the most intelligent in Mato Grosso.[34] *Mutatis mutandis,* the comparison was probably valid for the period 1725–1750.

Miscegenation and more of it was the general practice in these remote regions. Few white women penetrated the depths of Goiás and Mato Grosso, where the settlers inevitably lived in concubinage with colored women on an even greater scale than elsewhere in Brazil. The men often abandoned these women with the same facility as they left their makeshift habitations on the news of a gold strike elsewhere in the bush. The children of these temporary and illicit unions, if they lived to become adults, swelled still further the already extensive vagrant proletariat—the *plebe infima* of contemporary chroniclers—of Brazilian society.

Despite all the factors promoting change and decay in a tropical environment that was unfavorable for white settlement in any case, certain solid achievements were evident by the year 1750. Not all the mining camps disappeared completely, but some survived to vegetate as towns awaiting a better future in modest obscurity. There is no way of knowing the actual amount of gold produced in Mato Grosso and Goiás; but Calógeras has calculated with some degree of probability that the total production of these two regions may have been rather more than a third of that of Minas Gerais. The huge captaincy of São Paulo, whose theoretical boundaries ran through much unexplored or little known country, was dismembered in 1748, when two new captaincies, Goiás and Mato Grosso, were carved out of most of its approximately two and a half million square kilometers, the remainder being placed under the supervision of Gomes Freire de Andrada, who was virtually governor-general of southern Brazil. The frontier with Spanish America had been pushed many hundreds of miles westward, into the heart of the South American continent. Last not least, a series of outstanding journeys, beginning with that of the Portuguese Manuel Felix de Lima, had brought the most westerly outposts of Portuguese America into direct contact with each other by way of the rivers Guaporé, Mamoré, Madeira, Tocantins, and Amazon.[35] Contact between Brazil and the sister state of Maranhão-Pará in these far western regions had been forbidden by a royal decree of October 27, 1733, for fear of collision with the Spanish mission stations to the east of the Andes. But the Paulista and Portuguese pioneers who blazed the river trails between Vila Bela and Belem do Pará in 1742–1750, ignored these orders and thus gained this huge region for the Crown of Portugal largely in despite of itself.

XI. MISSIONARIES AND
SETTLERS IN AMAZONIA

O RIO-MAR, the River-Sea, was one of the early Portuguese names for the Amazon, greatest of all rivers on the surface of the globe, with a length, including windings, of nearly four thousand miles. The mouth of its delta measures nearly two hundred miles from shore to shore, and the river is navigable for large liners as far as the confluence of the Marañon and the Ucayale. Nearly all the Amazon's tributaries are navigable to a great distance from the main stream, and the region affords an extent of water communication unequaled in any other part of the world. From July to December, wind and current are usually opposed to each other, so that in days of sail a vessel could make her way up or down the river by utilizing either the one element or the other. The influence of the tides is felt four hundred miles above the mouth of the Amazon, and the river current is distinctly perceptible for more than two hundred miles out at sea. For most of its length the river and its affluents are bordered by tropical rain forest for a depth of many miles, but clearings of low grassy plains and of mud banks are not infrequent.

Seen from an aeroplane, "the great river is always uncertain of its course and itself describes fantastic shapes. Sending out feelers in every direction, it spreads its influence over an area of almost boundless dimensions. The larger of these are reminiscent of any river, such as the Mississippi, which runs through a level plain, describing in its course those long graceful curves which give the name to the host of oxbow lakes which it spawns. Other long slender ribbons of water cut directly across the landscape as if hurrying to a goal. Finally, intermingled with it all is a varied labyrinth of puddles, ponds, lakes, bayous, and rivers, which seemingly try to achieve the maximum shore line, and in so doing give rise to almost every pattern from the serpent to the genealogical tree. One of the interesting features this country has in common with the *pantanal* of Mato Grosso is the manner in which a circle of brown (i.e., fresher) water throws a protecting arm around the darker and more stagnant ponds which lack close connection with the flowing currents. In its indecisive manner of travel even during the dry season the river makes millions of acres more water than land." [1]

There are no violent oscillations of temperature in the Amazon region such as occur frequently in other parts of Brazil, in Minas Gerais and São Paulo for example. Almost the only difference of temperature is that between day and night, the latter being always agreeable. The so-called summer is the season when the flood waters recede, the winter being when they drown the surrounding countryside to an extent which gives the river-sea the appearance of an ocean. In such a watery environment fish formed the basic diet of Amerindians, missionaries, and colonists. The river is singularly rich in edible fish, some of the larger varieties of which are comparable in weight with a pig. This fish diet was supplemented to a greater or lesser extent with manioc flour, and with the products of the chase and the fruits of the forest. A man-made product which soon became indispensable to masters and slaves alike was the regional *cauim,* or sugar-cane brandy, which even the missionaries soon came to regard as a necessity rather than a luxury.[2]

Roads there were none in this water-world, and canoes were the universal means of transportation. Padre António Vieira, S.J., in a famous passage gives us a picturesque and enthusiastic description of how Dame Nature (under God) supplied everything that was necessary for the organization of an expedition up-river, irrespective of whether three hundred or three thousand men were involved. The canoes were hollowed out of tree trunks, the oakum was made from bark, the ship pitch and tar from resinous sap of various trees. The sails were made either of cotton or of matting made from very thin and pliable wood. The awnings were made from osiers and a certain kind of large leaves (*ubi*), "so sewn and joined together that there is nothing which affords better protection from the sun, nor from the rain no matter how hard or continuous this is; and they are so light that they weigh hardly anything in the vessel." The shrouds and rigging were made from tough tendrils which could be stripped from the trees almost anywhere. "Provisions are found with the same facility, for first of all the drinking water is below the keel, and wherever or whensoever it is needed it is always fresh and very good." When camping for the night, the canoes were hauled ashore, and some of their Amerindian rowers dispersed in the forest to find game and fruit for themselves and for their masters. The others busied themselves in erecting leafy shacks, "and when there is a troop of Portuguese on the expedition, they are made so large and fine that they look more like dwelling places than shelters for a few hours." The river was thus the storehouse from which anything could be secured as and when it was required; "which is something truly worth giving thanks for to the providence of the Divine Creator," the Jesuit observed devoutly.[3]

The ease with which communications could be maintained by water along the Amazon and its affluents at all seasons of the year contrasted strikingly with the difficulties of coastal communications in days of sail. For obvious geographical reasons, the Maranhão-Pará littoral was often called the "East-West Coast," in contrast to the trend of the shore from Cape São Roque to the Rio de la Plata, which was termed the "North-South Coast." Owing to differences in the prevailing winds and currents of those two coastal regions, sea communication between them was extremely difficult for ships sailing from the former region to the latter. Wrote Padre António Vieira, S.J., from the river Amazon in 1661: "As regards Brazil, even though one can easily sail from there to the Maranhão, the voyage from the Maranhão to Brazil is almost impossible nowadays. For example, out of eight ships which have left for Brazil since our arrival in this [Maranhão-Pará] mission, only one reached Pernambuco. All the others were forced back to port after many months of costly and futile struggle, and one ship was even driven to leeward as far as the Spanish West Indies." Communication by land between the two colonies was also far from easy, as can be seen from the hardships experienced by João da Maia da Gama and his companions on their adventurous journey from Tutoía to Paraíba in 1728–1729. The voyage from Lisbon to São Luís averaged only about five weeks, so that communications between Maranhão-Pará and Portugal were much easier than those between the "East-West Coast" and the "North-South Coast" of Portuguese America.[4]

The radical differences between the Amazon region with the East-West Coast on the one hand, and the rest of Brazil on the other, led to the combination of the two captaincies of Maranhão and Grão-Pará in the separately administered state of that name which was formed in 1623–1626. At its greatest extent, this state included the area covered by the present-day states of Ceará, Piauí, Maranhão, Pará, and Amazonas. However, Ceará and Piauí were for most of the time only nominally connected with the Maranhão; and for practical purposes the term "Amazonia," as used here, may be taken as coterminous with the old state of Maranhão and Grão-Pará, as it existed from 1626 to 1775. The capital of the state was established at São Luís do Maranhão, but from the seventh decade of the seventeenth century the governors tended to spend more of their time at Belem do Pará, which was the more important commercial center during the period with which we are dealing—a state of affairs not unlike that which obtained between Olinda and Recife at the turn of the same cen-

tury. The governor of Maranhão-Pará was directly subordinated
to Lisbon, and the viceroy of Brazil at Bahia exercised no jurisdiction over him. Similarly, the bishopric of Maranhão, which
was established in 1677–1679, had no connection with the archiepiscopal see of Bahia, but came under the ecclesiastical jurisdiction of the archbishop of Lisbon.

Although the Maranhão and Grão-Pará were only colonized
effectively by the Portuguese from the second decade of the seventeenth century, glowing reports of the actual and potential riches
of the Amazon region were soon in circulation. Some of them are
strongly reminiscent of the more exaggerated claims made for
the fertility and wealth of Brazil. Whereas most modern accounts
of the Amazon stress the insignificance of man's presence in the
vast tropical rain forests, the seventeenth-century panegyrists discreetly forbore to mention this aspect. The archetype of these
enthusiastic accounts was Estacio da Silveira's *Relação Sumaria
das cousas do Maranhão* (Lisboa, 1624), which asserted among
other things that the local Amerindians were very suitable for
all kinds of hard labor, that the region was very rich in gold and
silver mines, and that the Maranhão produced a better quality
sugar cane than did Brazil. Such tendentious statements did not
deceive everybody;[5] but the extent to which they influenced some
people in high places, is reflected in King John IV's proposal
(1647) to abdicate the Crown of Portugal and Brazil in favor of
a French prince who would marry his daughter, when John would
content himself with retaining sovereignty over the Maranhão
and the Azores alone.

At the time when this astonishing proposal was made, the entire
white population of Maranhão-Pará was less than a thousand
souls, and there were probably only about double that number by
the beginning of the eighteenth century. The economy was primitive, to say the least. Money was virtually unknown before the
year 1749, when gold, silver, and copper coins were first minted
at Lisbon for circulation in the colony. Until then, the normal
means of exchange were the natural products of the region, prin-

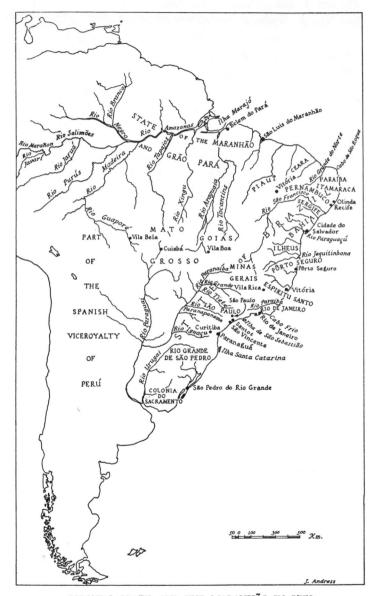

COLONIAL BRAZIL AND THE MARANHÃO IN 1750

Based on the map in Myriam Ellis, *O Monopólio do sal no Estado do Brasil,*
1631–1801 (São Paulo, 1955), p. 24.

cipally cotton, but also sugar, tobacco, cocoa beans, and vanilla.[6] Housing was equally simple, although by the end of the seventeenth century tamped earth and adobe houses with tiled roofs had largely replaced the thatched timber shacks which had previously formed the average town dwellings. As late as 1733, the streets of São Luís had no fixed names but were familiarly called after some prominent man who lived in them, or according to whither they led,—"street leading to the gallows," for example. The settlers were in general much too poor to buy Negro slaves and depended entirely on Amerindian labor. As Padre António Vieira, S.J., observed in 1661: "For a man to obtain manioc flour he has to have a small holding, and, in order to eat meat he has to have a hunter, and, in order to eat fish, a fisherman, and, in order to wear clean clothes, a washerwoman, and, in order to go to mass or anywhere else, a canoe and rowers." Hence, added the Jesuit, "enslaving Indians and drawing the red gold from their veins was always the mine of that State." [7]

The Jesuits alone among the Religious Orders in Brazil had a consistent tradition of upholding the freedom of the Amerindians against all the efforts of the colonists to enslave and exploit them. This made the Society of Jesus extremely unpopular not only with the colonists but with the friars of the Mendicant Orders, with whom, as Vieira wrote, the Jesuits waged "continual and cruel war," over their disregard of the Red Man's interests. The colonists, supported intermittently by the friars, reacted vigorously in kind, alleging that the Jesuits merely wished to deprive them of their Amerindian laborers in order to exploit them for their own purposes. The Crown, by and large, sympathized with the Jesuits' stand, but could not afford to ignore entirely the protests of the colonists and the friars. The laws which were framed at Lisbon to protect the Amerindians were thus inevitably of a compromise character which satisfied none of the parties to the dispute. The Jesuits reluctantly accepted them as better than nothing, though Vieira once declared that it would be a lesser evil for the whole colony to collapse rather then exist on Amerindian slave labor. On an earlier occasion he advanced the scarcely less heretical view that the colonists should perform the necessary manual labor themselves rather than rely on their Amerindian "hands and feet" as they called them. "For it is better to live by the sweat of one's own brow," he wrote, "than by another's blood." [8]

Whether the essential services of the Amerindians were secured by fair means or by foul—and in practice it was mostly by the latter—the mortality of these children of the Stone Age who were transplanted from the forest to the sugar plantations, tobacco fields, and households of the white man was very heavy. "The State is miserably poor," wrote a Jesuit missionary in 1673, "with nothing worth while of its own. Those who have a hundred slaves today, will not have six left a few days later. The Indians, who are anything but robust, have an incredibly high death rate. Any attack of dysentery kills them, and for any small annoyance they take to eating earth or salt and die." [9] These losses from overwork and disease were swelled by the casualties inflicted on those tribes who resisted domestication, or who otherwise incurred the wrath of the white man. Vieira alleged that Portuguese mistreatment of the Amerindians in Amazonia had resulted in the death of more than two million of them in forty years. His exaggerations in this respect recall those of his Spanish precursor, Fr. Bartolomé de Las Casas, O.P., but there is no doubt that the Portuguese often exterminated whole tribes in a singularly barbarous way. [10]

In addition to the employment of Amerindians as field hands and domestic servants, there was another way in which they were used or (as Vieira would say) abused. This was in the expeditions (*entradas*) which periodically went up the Amazon and its tributaries to collect cacao, Brazilian cinnamon (*cravo*), vanilla, cassia, and sarsaparilla from the dense forests which lined the river banks. The Amerindian as *filho do mato,* "son of the woods," was far better able to find the so-called *drogas do sertão,* or "spices of the backlands," than was either the white man or the black—quite apart from the red man's superiority in the handling of canoes. The importance of the Amerindian as a gatherer of the products of the forest was freely acknowledged by officials, settlers, and missionaries in the Maranhão-Pará, but this did not prevent the colonists from abusing their authority over the natives. As mentioned in the first chapter of this book (p. 22), Vieira complained that many of the Amerindians employed in these expeditions up-river perished from overwork and harsh treatment, and similar allegations recur throughout the period with which we are dealing.[11]

The perennial disagreements between the Jesuits and the colonists over the treatment of the Amerindians in Amazonia, twice resulted in the forcible expulsion of those missionaries in a manner which gave some justification to Padre António Vieira's characterization of Maranhão-Pará as Portugal's La Rochelle.[12] On the first occasion (1661/62) the Jesuits were expelled from the whole state, but on the second (1684) from the Maranhão only, Belem having declined to follow the lead of São Luís, owing to the increasing rivalry between the two cities. Deprived of the support of Pará, the Maranhão was easily subdued on the arrival of a new governor, who executed two of the ringleaders in November, 1685. Abortive as it proved, the revolt of 1684 helped to convince the Jesuits that they must compromise with the colonists' need for forced labor to a greater extent than they had done hitherto. The result was embodied in the *Regimento das Missões do Estado do Maranhão e Grão-Pará,* promulgated by the Crown in 1686. With certain alterations and modifications introduced between 1688 and 1718, this *Regimento* formed the basic charter for missionary work and for the supply of Amerindian labor in the State of Maranhão-Pará until the secularization of the missions by the Crown in 1750–1755.[13]

One of the principal provisions of the law of 1686 was that in future Amerindian labor would be increasingly supplanted by a regular supply of Negro slaves from Guinea, by means of a slave-trading company which was formed for this specific purpose. In the upshot, this company was stillborn, and the need for Amerindian labor remained paramount. As envisaged by the final decree

279

of 1718, this labor was to be secured in two ways: peaceful and forceful. The peaceful expeditions were to be organized by the missionaries, who would seek out the unsubdued tribes in the jungle and try to convince them that they would be better off living as "rational men" in mission villages (*aldeias*) under the superintendence of the Jesuits, or of the other Religious Orders, and in the vicinity of the white settlements. Those who freely consented to this course were to be brought down from the interior, but they were not to be enslaved on any account, and were to receive regular and adequate wages, in addition to their keep and clothing for any work they performed for the colonists. Once settled in the *aldeias,* they were to be taught the rudiments of Christianity and civilized ways for two years, before being made available for employment by white men.

The second, or forceful method, was to be employed against those savage tribes who went completely naked, recognized no king nor form of government, and who persistently indulged in unnatural vices such as incest and cannibalism. These barbarians, so the Crown was assured by learned theologians, could be forcibly settled in mission-villages on two conditions. Firstly, that only the necessary minimum of force should be used, and then only after peaceful persuasion had failed and the savages had resorted to arms to defend their bestial way of life. Secondly, those who were forcibly settled in the *aldeias,* but who subsequently fled back to the jungle to resume their uncivilized life, could be pursued and recaptured, but they were not on any account to be killed. Expeditions made under such conditions were entitled justifiable and defensive wars; but they were not to be undertaken without the prior approval of the representatives of the Religious Orders as well as of the senior Crown authorities. Unauthorized raiding by the colonists was categorically forbidden.[14]

The mission-villages as they developed in the early eighteenth century after the Jesuits and the Franciscans of the Province of Santo António had been joined by the Franciscans of the Province of Piedade, the Carmelites, and the Mercedarians, were grouped into four main categories. First, those that were organized solely for the service and benefit of the Religious Order to which they were assigned. Second, those of the Crown, whose inmates provided labor for the public works such as fortifications, shipbuilding, salt pans, and fisheries. Third, those termed of the *Repartição,* which provided labor for the colonists who needed hands for their houses, plantations, sugar mills, and canoes. Fourth and last were the purely mission-villages in the far interior, remote from any contact with white laymen, where the missionaries' only object was to convert and civilize the Amerindians. All these types of *aldeias* were, in principle, economically self-supporting, and all were directly supervised by a couple of missionaries from the Order to which they belonged. No laymen could visit a mission-village without permission from superior authority, and all requests from the colonists for a supply of free Amerindian labor had to be referred to the missionaries of the locality concerned.

Regulations for the conduct and administration of the Jesuits' *aldeias* were drawn up by Padre António Vieira, S.J., about the year 1660, and they lasted substantially unchanged until the secularization of the mission-villages nearly a century later.[15] I do not know whether the corresponding regulations for the Franciscan, Carmelite, and Mercedarian missions have been published; but I presume they do not differ materially from those elaborated by Vieira, which dealt with a wide range of spiritual and temporal concerns. Among other things, the Jesuits were reminded of the importance of daily prayer, and of frequently practicing the "Spiritual Exercises" instituted by the founder. They were told that suitable opportunities for such pious meditations and for the reading of devotional literature were afforded by the frequent voyages they had to make along the quiet rivers and backwaters in canoes. These canoes were usually supplied with a portable altar, hourglass, and a little bell; but firearms could be taken for use in self-defense when voyaging through dangerous districts.

The two missionaries normally resident in an *aldeia* were to make every effort to go to confession at least once a month. In the houses where these Jesuits actually lived, "no servant nor Indian will be allowed to sleep; and no house would have more than four or five servants." A hospital or infirmary was established in each of the principal *aldeias,* where the Amerindians were carefully nursed when sick, and provided with the best medicines and remedies, "in so far as our poverty permits." A guest house for travelers in need was attached to each village residency, but ordinary wayfarers were not encouraged to stay overnight, and the hospitality of the missionary's house was reserved for religious and secular "persons of authority." Some of the *aldeias* (termed *de visita*) in the remoter districts did not have missionaries resident in them, but were visited periodically by Fathers from the *aldeias de residencia.* On such occasions, the visit was always to be made by two Jesuits in company, who were not supposed to let each other out of sight during their stay in the village.

The surplus produce of the mission-villages was marketed by lay agents at Belem and São Luís (on a commission basis, presumably). The proceeds were remitted to the village concerned, for the upkeep of the church and the hospital and the like, after paying for such goods as the villagers might require from those two cities. The resident missionaries were forbidden to receive anything worth more than one *cruzado* for themselves; and they were not allowed to incur debts on their own behalf or on that of their *aldeias* for more than ten *cruzados,* without special permission from the Superior.

The daily round began with a morning Mass celebrated for the inhabitants. This was followed by the congregation repeating in a loud voice the Lord's Prayer, the Ave Maria, the Ten Commandments, and a shortened form of the catechism. The majority of those present then went to work in their fields or plantations; but the more promising characters went to the village school, where they were taught reading, writing, singing, and instrumental music besides the full catechism. At sunset, a second service was held, primarily for the religious instruction of the children, who, at the end of their lesson, went in procession round the village square intoning the Creed and the Commandments. Villagers who were particularly stupid or uncoöperative were given additional instruction by their ghostly fathers. By way of relaxation from the daily round of prayer and work, the villagers were allowed to indulge in their traditional dances (and drinking) every Saturday night and on the vigils of saints' days. This merrymaking was permitted until ten or eleven o'clock, when a bell was rung as a signal for them to return to their dwellings and go to sleep. Full registers were kept in each village of all births, baptisms, marriages, and deaths; special care being exercised in marriage between a free Amerindian and a slave woman, "these marriages, under the pretense of matrimony, being one of the means of enslavement which is used in this State."

The missionaries were strictly forbidden to inflict corporal punishment with their own hands, but only through the intermediary of the *principal,* or headman. The regulations stressed that punishment must in all cases be applied with great moderation, in view of the Amerindians' limited intelligence and their very different cultural background. Flogging was to be avoided as far as possible, and under no circumstances to be inflicted on women, "irrespective of what position they may be." When a village headman died, he was succeeded by his son, if he had one of sufficient age and capacity; otherwise, the resident padre would decide on his successor in consultation with the leading villagers. The employment of the mission Indians by the Crown officials and the colonists was hedged about with numerous safeguards, which I have not space to specify here. The missionaries were exhorted "to insist on the proper payment for the sweat of these poor wretches, since the conversion of those who are still heathen depends on the good treatment accorded to those who are already Christians." Rigid restrictions were laid on the employment of women from the *aldeias,* whose services could only be hired on one of the following four conditions: (1) as wet nurses; (2) as elderly maidservants allotted to senior government and ecclesiastical officials; (3) as maids to poor and respectable white women who had no other resource; (4) in limited numbers and with their respective husbands, at the time of the manioc harvest.

Despite the protective nature of the Crown regulations concerning the domestication of savage tribes, and despite the paternal authority enjoyed by the Jesuits and the other Orders administering the labor force of the *aldeias,* abuses in securing and employing Amerindian labor continued throughout the first half of the eighteenth century, though admittedly not on the scale of which Padre Vieira had only too good reason to complain. The principal culprits were, as often as not, the governors of Maranhão-Pará, among whom Christovão da Costa Freire (1707–1718) set a particularly bad example. He not only misused his authority by sending slaving expeditions into the interior on his own behalf, "but likewise gives free license to all others who wish to do so, contrary to the stipulations of Your Majesty's laws." [16] These slave raiders did not, of course, ostensibly act as such. On the contrary, they asserted that they were merely engaged in peacefully persuading the savages to return with them to the vicinity of the white settlements. They did not scruple on at least one occasion to disguise one of their number as an influential missionary! Where such deceitful measures failed, the slavers indulged in aggressive forays against unsubdued (but often inoffensive) tribes, pleading that they were only acting in self-defense to preserve their own lives from the attacks of ferocious cannibals.

Under the regulations of 1688–1691, the official expeditions (*entradas, resgates*) into the interior were supposed to be accompanied by Jesuit missionaries who would ensure that only those savages were captured who had been taken in "a just war," or as "Indians of the cord." The Jesuits were loath to undertake this invidious task, and normally excused themselves on the plea that they could not spare their men from their work in the *aldeias.* Some of the friars proved more complacent, but most expeditions were undertaken without any adequate missionary supervision. The captives secured, whether by fighting or by barter, were treated as slaves, although a formal decision whether they really were so was postponed until the expedition returned to Belem, usually with only about half of those who had been captured. These survivors were then brought before the *Junta das Missões,* or committee of missions, composed of representatives of all the Religious Orders, who then adjudicated upon their classification and disposal.[17] Those whom the Junta declared to be lawfully enslaved were left in the power of the colonists, and those who were declared free were sent to one of the mission-villages. In 1709, the Crown declared that the main objects of "persuading" the Amerindians to come down from the interior and to settle in the neighborhood of the white settlements, were (1) to provide a labor force for the colonists; (2) to provide gatherers of the "spices of the forest"; (3) to help defend settled territory against the attacks of hostile Amerindian tribes.[18]

Apart from the abuses connected with the *entradas* and *resgates,* whether these latter were official or clandestine, the Jesuits had numerous complaints to make about the way the Amerindians from the mission-villages were treated when they were hired out for the service of the Crown officials or of the colonists (*moradores*). Once the natives had been persuaded to leave the jungle and settle in the *aldeias,* both governors and colonists were likely to break the promises concerning the conditions of labor which the missionaries had made on their behalf. Amerindians who had consented to come on condition that they were not conscripted as rowers for official canoes, or for carrying heavy building stone, found that they were soon employed on such hard labor. Whereas the Crown regulations stipulated that the labor force of a village should be divided into two halves, each of which would work for six months in their own fields and for six months in the colonists' service, all the able-bodied men were sometimes taken away for eight or nine months together. The regulations concerning the proper payment of these laborers were often ignored, and the padres sometimes made good the deficiency from their own funds. Another common abuse was connected with the employment of

Amerindian women from the villages as wet nurses in the houses of the colonists. These women were often kept for years on end in the settlers' houses and when they were finally allowed to return to their husbands, they often brought with them children fathered by men of the households wherein they had been employed.[19]

The complaints were not, of course, all on one side. The missionaries—and particularly the Jesuits—were accused by some officials and by many colonists of interfering with the Amerindians who were not included in the temporal jurisdiction which the Crown had granted the Religious Orders over the mission-villages. They were also accused of employing more natives than they were entitled to do in their sugar mills and plantations, in their tobacco fields, in their village industries and in the gathering of the "spices of the forest," while keeping the settlers unduly short of the Amerindian labor they so vitally needed. They were also alleged to shelter military deserters in their up-country missions, and to engage in trade and commerce to an extent which put the local merchants out of business. Apart from these and other complaints of the *moradores,* the Crown also had constant trouble with the Religious Orders over the payment (or non-payment) of tithes on their landed property. Finally, the missionaries were accused of deliberately neglecting to teach their native converts Portuguese, preferring the use of Tupí as a better means of keeping them under their own control and perpetuating the language barrier between them and the settlers. All these complaints were lodged at one time or another against each of the Religious Orders; but it was always the Jesuits who were the main target for hostile criticism.[20] Not for nothing did Padre António Vieira, S.J., compare Maranhão-Pará with Huguenot La Rochelle; but it was not until the second and third decades of the eighteenth century that this bitter criticism of the Jesuits in Amazonia found powerful supporters in government circles at Lisbon.

The extent of the Jesuits' power and influence in late seventeenth-century Portugal is an easily verifiable historical fact.

Closely connected with the restoration of Portuguese independence, and extremely influential at the court of the first two monarchs of the House of Braganza, their position seemed secure in the early years of the reign of Dom João V. He had been educated by the Jesuits, and he had Jesuit confessors in his youth and for the first seven years of his long reign. From the year 1713 onward, however, he made a point of selecting his own confessors from one of the other Religious Orders. He showed particular favor to the Oratorians, whose house of Nossa Senhora das Necessidades he endowed in a fantastically generous manner. It is true that he still retained Jesuit confessors for his heir and for others of his children; and that he likewise endowed the chapel of São João Baptista in the Jesuit church of São Roque in a way which made it the most richly decorated in Christendom. He also often favored individual Jesuits, such as the Italian Padre Carbone, who was one of the principal advisers until his death in 1750, a few weeks before the king's own demise. But his real cronies in later life were Fr. Gaspar da Encarnação and Cardinal da Mota, and he seems to have subsidized the Oratorians' educational activities as a deliberate counterweight to the hitherto overwhelming preponderance of the Jesuits in this sphere. Finally, he resolutely opposed the efforts of the Jesuits of the Maranhão-Pará mission to secure their *aldeias* from episcopal visitation and inspection. His obstinacy on this long-contested point of ecclesiastical jurisdiction caused their principal spokesman, Padre Jacinto de Carvalho, to exclaim angrily, "on this matter, the man is crazy." [21]

The Jesuits' most dangerous enemy was a settler from the Maranhão named Paulo da Silva Nunes. He was patronized by Bernardo Pereira de Berredo, author of the classic *Anais Históricos do Maranhão* (Lisboa, 1749), who governed the state from 1718 to 1722, and who was likewise an ill-wisher to the Society of Jesus. Berredo's successor, João da Maia da Gama, who governed Maranhão-Pará with conspicuous ability and honesty from 1722 to 1728, was an ardent admirer of the Jesuits in general and of Padre Jacinto de Carvalho in particular, and he soon fell foul of Nunes da Silva. After a short spell in jail, the latter made his way to Lisbon, where he became the official representative of the colonists of Maranhão-Pará, and deluged the Overseas Councillors and other influential persons with vicious memorials denouncing the behavior of the Jesuits in Amazonia, until his death in 1746. He was supported originally by Berredo, and later by Maia da Gama's successor in the governorship, a singularly unscrupulous *fidalgo* named Alexandre de Sousa Freire. This man was a bitter enemy of the Jesuits because they had refused him a loan of 4,000 *cruzados* at the beginning of his governorship, when Padre Jacinto de Carvalho politely but firmly told him that the local mission was far too deeply indebted for it to help discharge the governor's private debts.[22]

Paulo da Silva Nunes had the lowest possible opinion of the Amerindians, whom he denounced as "squalid savages, ferocious and most base, resembling the wild beasts in everything save in human shape." He accused the Jesuits of behaving despotically and of usurping the royal authority. They incited colored servants to leave the houses of the whites by whom they had been brought up. They supplied their Amerindian converts with firearms, resulting in the deaths of several Portuguese. In some *aldeias,* the resident missionary built a prison, into which white men were often thrown in chains. The Jesuits obstructed the efforts of the settlers to secure labor from the *aldeias,* as the colonists were legally entitled to do. Their so-called mission-villages looked more like busy customs houses than houses of prayer. Last not least, they had treasonable dealings with the Spaniards along the upper Amazon, with the Dutch along the upper Rio Negro, and with the French along the coast of Guiana.[23]

For some years Silva Nunes' anti-Jesuit propaganda had no great success at Court. His vilification of the Amerindians ran counter to the Crown's conviction (which originated with the Jesuits) that "the security of the backlands and of the very settlements of the Maranhão and of all America, depends on the friendship of the Indians."[24] The support which the colonists' champion received from Pereira de Berredo and from Sousa Freire was more than off-set by the testimony of Maia de Gama, who had no difficulty in exposing the unreliability of his successor's evidence. Padre Jacinto de Carvalho, who returned to Lisbon as procurator of the Maranhão-Pará mission in 1729, was also very active during the next ten years in rebutting the calumnies of Silva Nunes and of his more highly placed backers. A senior official, sent out to investigate the situation on the spot in 1734–1735, reported favorably on the Religious Orders in general and on the Jesuits in particular. He did, however, suggest that the Crown should give the mission-villages direct financial support, and so obviate the need for the missionaries to gather and export "the spices of the forest," in order to get the wherewithal for the upkeep of the *aldeias*. The Crown rejected this recommendation, preferring the existing practice of self-supporting missions—just as previous monarchs had done in the case of the Far Eastern Jesuit missions in the sixteenth and seventeenth centuries. Nevertheless, the seed so pertinaciously sown by the Jesuits' opponents on both sides of the Atlantic did not all fall on stony ground. Some of it came to fruition soon after the death of Dom João V, when the future Marquis of Pombal and his brother, Francisco Xavier de Mendonça Furtado, reaped where Silva Nunes and Pereira de Berredo had sown.

That the allegations of the Jesuits' enemies were either wholly false or else grossly exaggerated, there can be no reasonable doubt. Apart from the evidence of Maia da Gama and other trustworthy Portuguese, we have the testimony of the French scientist, La Condamine, who voyaged down the Amazon from Jaén to Belem do Pará in 1743.[25] He contrasted the prosperity of the Portuguese mission-villages that he visited on his voyage with the poverty of those on Spanish territory. On the other hand, it is equally clear from the same sources, and from eyewitnesses such as the German Jesuit, Samuel Fritz, that the colonists of Maranhão-Pará continued to make clandestine slave raids into the interior, apart from the so-called ransoming expeditions (*resgates*) which were authorized, and indeed encouraged, by the Crown.[26] If the mission-villages were many and prosperous while the colonial towns were few and poor, as the colonists' spokesmen claimed, then the fault was largely with the settlers themselves. In any event, this particular allegation was not universally true. If the city of São Luís was still vegetating in poverty in 1743, La Condamine was surprised to find that Belem was a well-built city in the European style.[27] It drove a thriving trade in cacao, coffee, cotton, and other regional products with Lisbon; and this trade was certainly not all in the hands of the Jesuits, as their enemies insinuated.

Despite the difficulties and setbacks with which the missionaries inevitably had to contend, the first half of the eighteenth century can fairly be termed the golden age of the missions in Amazonia. In 1693–1695 the Crown had apportioned this huge region between the Jesuits, Franciscans, Mercedarians, and Carmelites, each Order being given the exclusive responsibility for missionary work in a specified area. On the whole, this arrangement worked reasonably well for more than half a century. The other Orders were inclined to think that the Jesuits came off best in the allotment of missionary areas, and the Jesuits were inclined to think that the friars were sometimes too complacent about the colonists' slave raids; but the days of the "continual and cruel war," of which Padre António Vieira had complained in 1661 (p. 277), were now succeeded by more coöperative times.[28]

Such few statistics as we possess, reflect the relative prosperity of the missions. In 1696, there were about 11,000 Amerindian converts in the Jesuit *aldeias* alone, a number which had risen to 21,031 by 1730, despite the periodic ravages of smallpox, a disease to which the natives were particularly vulnerable. These Amerindians were divided among some twenty-eight *aldeias,* and we do not have the corresponding figures for the twenty-six mission-villages maintained by the Franciscans, nor for those of the other two Orders. We know that the number of *aldeias* maintained by all of the Religious Orders amounted to sixty-three in 1750; and it seems probable that João Lucio de Azevedo's estimate that these *aldeias* housed an Amerindian population of about 50,000 souls before the great smallpox epidemic of 1743–1750, is reasonably accurate.[29]

The missionaries' labors were not confined to catechizing and civilizing their converts, and to shielding them in so far as they could from the demands of the labor-hungry colonists. The Jesuits, in particular, planted cacao, coffee (introduced from Cayenne in 1727) and cotton on a large scale, and they maintained important cattle ranches on the island of Marajó. They also made serious efforts to transplant and acclimatize East Indian spices, as they had previously done with cinnamon and pepper at Bahia. If the Jesuits, as usual, were to the fore in these practical matters, it was an unknown Carmelite friar who saved thousands of lives by introducing the practice of inoculation into Amazonia about the year 1728.[30]

During the first half of the eighteenth century, Portuguese enterprise, whether in the form of peaceful penetration by the missionaries, or of slave-raiding and slave-trading expeditions by laymen, steadily pushed back the disputed frontier with Spanish territory in the Amazon region. The process was accelerated by the War of the Spanish Succession, when Spain was a battle ground to a greater extent than Portugal, and when Madrid changed hands more than once. The resulting administrative chaos in the mother country made it more difficult than ever for the Spanish Crown to control, or even to influence, events in the depths of South America. The Portuguese had another advantage in that their advance up the Amazon and its principal affluents could easily be supported from Belem do Pará, itself only a few weeks' sail from Lisbon. Their opponents in upper Amazonia, on the other hand, received their supplies and reinforcements (when they received them at all) by a difficult track across the Andes from Quito, itself many months' journey by land and sea from Cadiz.

The boundary line between the Spanish and Portuguese possessions in South America still theoretically coincided with that laid down by the Treaty of Tordesillas in 1494. This line was a meridian drawn 370 leagues to the west of the most westerly of the Cape Verde Islands; but for more than two and a half centuries there was no agreement between the two Iberian powers as to where this line ran between the Amazon and the Rio de la Plata. By 1746 the rulers at Lisbon and Madrid had belatedly come to realize the need for negotiating a boundary settlement which would take account of what had happened in South America and in the Far East during the last two hundred and fifty years. A private exchange of letters between the two royal families having shown that the prospect of concluding such an agreement was now favorable, the diplomatic negotiations were set afoot which resulted in the conclusion of the Treaty of Madrid four years later.

XII. PORTUGUESE AMERICA
IN MID-CENTURY

T HE SELECTION of any given year as a terminal date in a historical work such as this, is bound to be an arbitrary one to some extent, but the year 1750 does in several ways mark the end of an epoch in Luso-Brazilian history. The death of Dom João V (July 31, 1750) and the accession of Dom José were speedily followed by the rise to power of Sebastião José de Carvalho e Mello, who, better known under his later title of Marquis of Pombal, was the virtual dictator of Portugal for more than twenty years. It was in 1750 that the decision was taken to abolish the unpopular Brazilian capitation tax, and it was about that time that the production of Brazilian gold was recognized to be on the decline.[1] The year 1750 also virtually coincides with the end of the Paulista push westwards—the epoch of the *bandeiras*. Last not least, the signature of the Treaty of Madrid (January 13, 1750) formally recognized the fact that Portuguese America had burst the theoretical boundary line of the Treaty of Tordesillas and had attained what subsequently proved to be substantially her present frontiers.

The antecedents of the Treaty of Madrid have been exhaustively discussed in Jaime Cortesão's definitive work, to which the interested reader is referred for details.[2] It will suffice to recall here that the siege of Sacramento in 1735–1737, and the outbreak of

293

the "War of Jenkins's Ear" between England and Spain in 1739, were two of the main reasons which made the Courts of Lisbon and Madrid desirous of reaching an agreement on the boundaries of their South American territories. Another motive which must have weighed on the Portuguese side, though Senhor Cortesão does not mention it, was the highly critical situation of Portuguese India in 1737–1740. During those years the Marathas conquered Bassein and the fertile "Province of the North," and Goa itself only narrowly escaped the same fate. Dom João V had to send each year costly relief expeditions in men and money, and the situation was not really eased until the victories won by Dom Pedro de Almeida, Count of Assumar and Marquis of Castello-Novo (later of Alorna) during his viceroyalty of 1744–1750. The help sent annually to India was on a scale which made it exceedingly difficult, if not impossible, to succour Sacramento adequately at the same time. It was, after all, the English who were deriving the chief benefit from such contraband trade as was still driven through this closely blockaded outpost; the retention of which, as the Viceroy Count of Galveas wrote from Bahia in 1737, was due "more to reasons of prestige than of profit." [3]

The Portuguese objectives in negotiating the Treaty of 1750 may be resumed as follows:

(1) To strike a balance between the boundary claims of Spain and Portugal by allotting the greater part of the Amazon basin to the latter country and that of the Rio de la Plata to the former.

(2) To secure the undisputed sovereignty of the gold and diamond districts for the Portuguese Crown.

(3) To secure Brazil's frontier by the retention of the Rio Grande do Sul and the acquisition of the Spanish Jesuit mission area ("Seven Peoples") on the left bank of the river Uruguay.

(4) To secure the western frontier of Brazil and river communication with Maranhão-Pará by ensuring that navigation on the rivers Tocantins, Tapajos, and Madeira remained in Portuguese hands.

On the Spanish side, the compelling motives seem to have been:

(1) To stop the westward advance of the Portuguese, who had already encroached on much of what was theoretically Spanish territory even though it consisted mostly of virgin jungle.

(2) To secure the colony of Sacramento, which functioned as a backdoor for the illegal Anglo-Portuguese trade with the Viceroyalty of Peru and which rendered Buenos Aires dangerously exposed to foreign invasion.

(3) To undermine the Anglo-Portuguese alliance, and thus eventually to facilitate a union of the two Iberian powers in South America against English aggression and ambition.

Although by 1741 Dom João V had reluctantly come to realize the advisability of exchanging Sacramento for an advantageous territorial equivalent in South America, there still remained one major obstacle to genuine Hispano-Portuguese understanding. "The King of Portugal," wrote Lord Tyrawly in 1740, "hates the Queen of Spain personally as he hates the Devil, and fears her as much." [4] His dislike was returned with interest by the virile Isabel Farnese, and so long as she was at her husband's side, mutual mistrust and suspicion bedeviled relations between the two Crowns, despite the interchange of princes and princesses in the marriage treaty of 1729, and despite the love that these heirs to the respective thrones soon came to feel for each other. The death of Felipe V in July, 1746 abruptly changed all this. His successor, the feeble Fernando VI, was very strongly influenced by his Portuguese consort, Barbara of Braganza. Isabel Farnese went unwillingly into retirement, and the negotiations which culminated in the treaty of January, 1750 began in earnest. Generally speaking, the treaty was framed on the basis of *uti possidetis,* save that the colony of Sacramento was to be handed over to the Spaniards in return for the territory occupied by the "Seven Peoples" of the Jesuit mission stations.

The consequences which flowed from the signing of this treaty lie outside the scope of this book, but the reader may be reminded of three basic facts. Firstly, the implementation of the treaty was surreptitiously opposed by influential people in both Portugal and

Spain, and by the Amerindians of the "Seven Peoples" with arms in their hands. Secondly, Pombal's hatred of the Jesuits and his suppression of their Society in Portugal stemmed from his conviction that their machinations were responsible for the stipulated territorial adjustments not being made in Uruguay and Amazonia. Incidentally, Pombal was one of the critics of the Treaty, and, while blaming the Jesuits for its failure, he was glad of the excuse to keep the colony of Sacramento and return the ruined missions of Uruguay to the Spaniards by the Treaty of Pardo (1761) which formally annulled that of Madrid. The final settlement which was reached at San Ildefonso in 1777 was basically not very different from that envisaged at Madrid twenty-seven years earlier. Portugal had to renounce her claims to both Sacramento and the "Seven Peoples"; but her extensive territorial gains in Amazonia and in the heart of the South American continent were confirmed.

Articles XI and XII of the Treaty of Madrid envisaged the appointment of Spanish and Portuguese boundary commissioners who would demarcate the new frontiers and make accurate maps of those regions. In this regard, the Portuguese were already somewhat ahead of the Spaniards, as Dom João V's interest in Brazil's disputed boundaries had been aroused by the publication at Paris in 1722 of a map of South America by the celebrated French geographer, Guillaume De Lisle. This map showed the northern bank of the Rio de la Plata and the Amazon delta to the west of the Tordesillas Line, and hence, according to the Treaty of 1494, theoretically in Spanish territory.[5] Since French cartography was then far in advance of either Spanish or Portuguese, this publication was, potentially at any rate, very injurious to Portuguese territorial claims and advantageous to those of Spain in South America.

Probably at the prompting of his Brazilian-born secretary, Alexandre de Gusmão, Dom João V resolved secretly to prepare an accurate atlas of Brazil, with lattitudes and longitudes obtained by astronomical observations on the ground. Scientific studies being then at a discount in Portugal, the King recruited two Italian Jesuits for this purpose, Padres Carbône and Capassi, who reached Lisbon in September, 1722. Carbone became a trusted adviser of the King and never left for Brazil; while seven years elapsed before Capassi did so, accompanied by his compatriot's substitute, the Portuguese Jesuit, Diogo Soares. During this interval, the two Italian Jesuits did some cartographical and survey work in Portugal, and they organized an observatory at Lisbon, equipped with French and English instruments. When Capassi and Soares finally reached Brazil, they surveyed between them the Colonia do Sacramento, most of the southern coasts, and much of Minas Gerais. Capassi died at São Paulo in 1736, and though Diogo Soares continued the work alone until his death at Goiás in 1748, he does not seem to have reached the western frontier region, nor did either of the two geographers visit the State of Maranhão-Pará.[6]

Valuable as was the pioneer work done by these two Jesuits, most of it was kept secret for reasons of state. The surveys subsequently undertaken by a number of army engineer officers proved in the long run to be more important. Manuel de Azevedo Fortes, who was appointed Chief Engineer of Portugal in 1719, retained this post until his death thirty years later, and he never ceased to propagate the necessity of fostering mathematical, cartographical, architectural, and field-engineering studies. Although Dom João V did not always provide sufficient funds for such services, and although for this reason Azevedo Fortes' project for preparing a map of Portugal based on triangulation and topographical survey did not progress beyond the initial stages, some remarkable work was carried out by Portuguese military engineers from 1720 onwards.

A hostile French critic of the Portuguese army in the second half of the eighteenth century was constrained to admit that the engineers were the least inefficient branch of the military service,[7] but this left-handed compliment did less than justice to those concerned. In the second quarter of the eighteenth century and for long afterwards Portuguese army engineers not only carried out field surveys in and mapped some of the remotest parts of

Brazil, but they also were the architects of many churches and public buildings, as well as designers of fortifications. Lisbon after the great earthquake of 1755 was largely rebuilt to their plans and under their supervision; in Brazil, Brigadier Alpoim designed the governor's palace at Ouro Preto and at Rio de Janeiro, besides the imposing aqueduct at the latter place and many other monumental buildings. Portuguese military engineers were also active in Africa and in India during this period, though less of their work has survived in the East.

Presumably at the prompting of Azevedo Fortes, Dom João V decreed in 1732 that each infantry regiment should contain one company whose officers were professional engineers. The two existing military academies where instruction was given on fortification and military engineering (Lisbon and Viana do Minho) were supplemented by another two, established at Elvas and Almeida, respectively. Promotion examinations were instituted for all engineer officers below the rank of lieutenant-colonel, the board of examiners being presided over by the chief engineer or his deputy. Even before this regulation, a number of infantry, cavalry, and artillery officers had already specialized in military engineering and architectural courses. As the reader may recall, these versatile officers included José Rodrigues de Oliveira, the first commander of the dragoons of Minas Gerais, and André Ribeiro Coutinho, the colonizer of Rio Grande do Sul. There had been, as mentioned previously (p. 159), a school (*aula*) of fortification at Salvador, and also at Rio de Janeiro and Recife; but the graduates of these *aulas de fortificação* rarely achieved the competence and eminence attained by Alpoim and his colleagues. Ten or fifteen years before the conclusion of the Treaty of Madrid, the key posts in Brazil and Maranhão-Pará were occupied either by engineers or by governors who were closely associated with engineers and cartographers.[8]

The condition of Portuguese America at this period may, perhaps, best be grasped by taking a rapid survey of the various captaincies from north to south. For practical purposes, they can be grouped into four regional blocks, each of which we shall consider briefly in turn. Firstly, the Amazonian State of Maranhão-Pará, which was discussed in more detail in the previous chapter. Secondly, the northeastern captaincies of Pernambuco, Paraíba, and Ceará. Thirdly, Bahia and its backlands, extending as far as the Rio São Francisco. Fourthly, what may be termed the bailiwick of Gomes Freire de Andrada, the martinet who oscillated between Rio de Janeiro and Ouro Preto, and who kept a vigilant eye on what transpired in the immense region covered by the captaincies of Rio de Janeiro, Minas Gerais, and (down to 1748) São Paulo—not forgetting the troublesome Colonia do Sacramento embedded in Spanish territory. The minor captaincies, such as Itamaracá, Ilheus, and Porto Seguro, which were included in one or another of the above four regions, vegetated in such obscurity that they deserve and will receive only passing mention.

As indicated in the previous chapter, Pará was relatively prosperous, whereas the Maranhão was still struggling with economic adversity. This contrast was mainly due to the fact that Belém flourished through the export of the "spices of the forest," collected by skilled Amerindian labor from the jungle bordering on the Amazon and its tributaries. Contrariwise, the sugar, tobacco, and cotton plantations which supplied the bulk of the exports from São Luís were hampered by the shortage of Negro labor, and by the inefficiency (and insufficiency) of the Amerindian field hands. Coffee, which was first introduced from Cayene to Pará in 1727, as the reader may recall, soon became a valuable export crop. So much so, that in 1743 the home government prohibited the importation of coffee into Portugal from elsewhere than Amazonia, thus indicating that the production of Pará was already sufficient to supply the Portuguese market.[9] Cacao was even more important, though this commodity had to compete with the Spanish-American product. On the principle that it is an ill wind that blows nobody any good, the fourth Count of Ericeira noted in his "Diary" for December, 1733 that the price of Maranhão [i.e., Pará] cacao had risen sharply on the Lisbon market owing to news that part of the returning Spanish *flota* had been lost in a storm.[10]

The transplantation and cultivation of cacao, coffee, and of East

Indian spices have been mentioned previously (p. 291), but a word may be said here about a project, which, although it never materialized, shows that the Portuguese government was not invariably (though it was often) obscurantist in commercial and industrial matters. This was a scheme to establish a calico-printing and textile industry in Pará by contracting skilled Indian weavers on the Coromandel Coast and inducing them to emigrate to Brazil with their families and the tools of their craft. They were to be given free passages on Portuguese Indiamen from Goa to Bahia, and they were to be maintained at government expense from the time of their engagement in Coromandel or in Orissa until they were well settled on an island (or on islands) of their own choice in the Amazon estuary. After selecting the site(s) of their future homes, they were to receive the necessary housing, seeds, and agricultural implements at government expense. They were to be allowed to draw up their own regulations for the conduct of their villages and to retain their own dress, manners, and customs, so far as these did not directly offend Christian decorum. No other people were to be allowed to join them in their settlements, unless they themselves spontaneously requested this; but the Indian immigrants could freely visit Belém and other towns for business or pleasure. They were to be accompanied by a missionary from Madura who knew the language, and who would remain with them to act as guide, counselor, and friend, and to serve as a parish priest for those who were Christians. Last not least, these immigrants and their dependents were to be treated on a footing of perfect equality with the existing colonists, and the products of their looms were to be duty free throughout Portugal and her overseas possessions.[11] All in all, these conditions were in some respects more generous than those offered to encourage emigration from the Azores to Santa Catarina during the same period.

One of the laws in Maranhão-Pará which was more honored in the breach than in the observance was the prohibition against mulattoes, mamelucos, and other mixed-bloods participating in the *resgates e entradas do sertão*. As we have had occasion to observe previously, complaints of the misbehavior of these half-breeds were endemic in Portuguese America, particularly in the captaincies of the Northeast, to which we must now turn our attention. A Jesuit missionary of long experience in these regions complained in 1720 that mulattoes and mamelucos were "lords of Ceará," terrorizing the white and Amerindian parts of the population. As usual, one of the chief reasons for their misbehavior, which also applied to the soldiers of the garrison, was the shortage of white women. The men, whether white or colored, took what women they wanted from the Amerindian villages, procreating children of a mixed race who were, for the most part, no better than their fathers. The resultant vagabonds, "sturdy beggars," gipsies and other undesirables, were periodically rounded up and shipped off to Angola, though many contrived to escape the net. From about 1740 onwards, the island of Fernão de Noronha was also used as a dumping ground for such people, after some French intruders had been forcibly removed in the 1730's. These deportations were more of a palliative than a cure and the problem was still unsolved in the year 1750.[12]

The traditional rivalry between rising Recife and declining Olinda continued during the second quarter of the eighteenth century, although it did not degenerate into civil strife as it had done in the "Peddlers' War" of 1710–1711. Precedence in religious processions, such as that celebrated on Ash Wednesday, was one of the principal causes of these internecine disputes. The governor continued to reside in Recife rather than in the nominal capital at Olinda; and the Crown finally recognized the accomplished fact by enjoining the governors to spend at least a few weeks every year at Olinda if they conveniently could. The strongly-worded decree of 1720 which forbade the colonial governors and the senior officials from trading, either directly or through third parties, was no better obeyed here than elsewhere.

Education was virtually limited to the instruction given by the Religious Orders and more particularly by the Jesuits. A printing press which some unrecorded but enterprising individual installed at Recife in the early years of the eighteenth century was quickly destroyed when the authorities at Lisbon heard of its existence in 1706. If the standard of the secular clergy in general remained low, their prestige remained inordinately high. Not content with showering the Patriarch of Lisbon and other high ecclesiastical dignitaries with honors and emoluments in Portugal, Dom João V went out of his way to increase the prestige of colonial bishops. In 1724 the governor of Pernambuco was ordered to give precedence to the local bishop on all occasions, even when visiting him in the episcopal palace. When the prelate passed through the streets, everyone had to go down on bended knees as he went by, and all the convents and churches rang a peal on their bells.

Complaints of poverty were both loud and general, but nevertheless the inhabitants of Pernambuco usually managed to stage colorful and richly decorated religious processions on the frequent occasions when these were called for. One of the most important, which achieved the dignity of being celebrated in print, was staged in September, 1745 in honor of the Eurasian St. Gonçalo Garcia, martyred in Japan in 1597. A comparison of the *Suma Triunfal*, published at Lisbon eight years later in commemoration of this event, with the *Triunfo Eucharistico* which recorded the Ouro Preto festivities of 1733, shows that while the Pernambucan sports and other diversions were not staged with such costly splendor as in Minas Gerais, they were at any rate on a comparable scale.[13]

The sugar planters' perennial complaints of falling prices, poor trade, high taxes, costly and inefficient labor, are not altogether borne out by such contradictory production figures as we have. According to Pereira da Costa, the number of *engenhos* increased from 254 in Antonil's day to 276 in 1750; but the anonymous "Informação" of 1749 gives a total of 230 *engenhos* which were actually working and another fifty which were not in use (*fogos mortos*).[14] Whatever the true figure, it is evident that prices had declined somewhat, but not catastrophically so. By a royal decree of 1713, prices were fixed on the occasion of the annual harvest by a commission composed of two planters and two merchants, presided over by the *juiz-de-fora*. While the planters continually complained that they could not get a fair price for their sugar, the Lisbon merchants alleged that they constantly received chests with short weight, or else containing adulterated or inferior sugars.[15] The trade was admittedly burdened with heavy duties, as it had been in Antonil's day. The most inconvenient was probably the royal tenth (*dizimo real*), which was exacted before the sugar had left the mill.

Apart from the export of sugar, tobacco, and hides to Portugal and West Africa, the numerous ranches in the backlands of Pernambuco drove a thriving trade in cattle and horses on the hoof with Recife, Bahia, and Minas Gerais. There was also a coastal trade of some importance, particularly with the cities of Salvador and Rio de Janeiro. Negro slaves from the coast of Mina were re-exported to this latter place, in addition to hides, dried meat, and leather shoes. Gold dust and coin, whale fins and train oil were the chief returns. The exports to Angola included sugar, sugar-cane brandy, manioc flour, rice, tobacco, tiles, sweetmeats, "some horses," wrought gold, shoes, slippers, boots, "and every kind of European goods." The returns from Luanda were principally in "slaves of the third sort," ivory, wax, mats, and raffia. The most profitable trade was driven with the Coast of Mina, which took the greater part of the Pernambucan tobacco crop, and also sugar, sugar-cane brandy, gold, jaguar skins, hammocks, silk sun hats, Indian calicoes, European linen and "some light silks." The imports were chiefly in slaves and ivory, but included (oddly enough) "a little gold dust." Lisbon and Oporto took chiefly sugar, hides, dye- and other woods, ipecacuanha, "and some tobacco." This trade of Pernambuco was, for the most part, a barter trade, though the droves of cattles sent to Minas and Bahia were sold for money. The local merchants and officials complained that their correspondents in Lisbon often insisted on payment in coin, thus causing recurrent economic crises for want of sufficient specie.[16]

If, despite all the drawbacks of unpredictable harvests, uncertain sales and unavoidable taxes, the sugar industry still flourished after a fashion in Pernambuco, this was still more true of Bahia. The superior quality of the Bahian sugar was reflected in the price scale imposed by the Lisbon government in January, 1751, which assessed the different grades of sugar exported from Pernambuco, Rio de Janeiro, and the Maranhão, at lower rates than those exported from the Bay of All Saints.[17] As noted previously, something between 12,000 and 13,000 chests of sugar was regarded as a good figure for the annual export from Bahia (p. 150), but the fleet of 1748 took between 16,000 and 17,000 chests distributed among forty-three sail. On the other hand, in years of drought and flood—which were unfortunately numerous during this period—the number of chests exported might fall below 5,000. In March, 1736, the viceroy reported that owing to the prevailing drought, the harvest would not produce enough sugar for local consumption; though the planters must have found some compensation in the fact that the little that was available fetched from 2,000 to 3,000 *reis* the *arroba,* according to category and quality.

The fifteen-year viceroyalty of the Count of Sabugosa, which was briefly discussed in Chapter vi, was followed by the fourteen-year term of the Count of Galveas, who, as the reader may recall, had previously served as governor of Minas Gerais to the general satisfaction of the inhabitants. During this period, Bahia's basic problems remained the same. The sugar and tobacco planters complained continuously of the low prices they obtained for their crops and the high prices they paid for their slaves. The Count of Galveas' efforts to induce the planters to grow manioc as well as sugar cane were no more successful than those of his predecessor; and the manioc growers of Cachoeira complained that they could not get a fair price for their product in ordinary years. The power of the municipal council continued to decline, the Count of Galveas on one occasion clapping all the counselors in jail to cool their heels for nine days, in consequence of their having obstructed the building by the Jesuits of a quay on the sea front, which he had authorized.

Other perennial problems reflected in the correspondence of

304

the viceroy with Lisbon, included the insufficiency of the coinage in circulation and the prevalence of false money; the reluctance of the Bahianos to undergo either military service or holy matrimony; the contraband trade with foreign shipping, with Portuguese East-Indiamen, with West Africa, and with the Azores. The farming out of the Crown's sources of income on a monopoly-contract basis also caused endless difficulties and disputes, as did questions of ecclesiastical jurisdiction and immunity from taxation.

The prevalence of false money was rather fatuously blamed by the director of the Bahia mint on the machinations of foreign traders. The real culprits were obviously much nearer home. Apart from those who were active in Minas Gerais and São Paulo, coiners were caught and executed in the city of Salvador itself during the viceroyalties of Sabugosa and Galveas. The reluctance of the Bahianos to serve as soldiers and the high rate of desertion among the garrison, were due in part at least to military pay, rations, and clothing being so often in arrears. Even so, the situation in Bahia was not so bad as it was, for example, in Paraíba, where the garrison had received no pay for four years in 1727. The Count of Galveas, though educated for the priesthood and at one time an aspirant for a cardinal's hat, did not hesitate to criticize the superfluity of priests, friars, and nuns around the Bay of All Saints. Writing to the Crown in April, 1739, he observed that the desire of gentlefolk of both sexes to enter the Church was one of the reasons why only two marriages between "persons of quality" had been celebrated during the four years of his viceroyalty. Marriages among the commonality, he added, were also relatively few in proportion to the population, and they were chiefly due to the bridegrooms wishing to avoid military service. Nevertheless, three new convents of nuns were founded in Salvador during his viceroyalty, one of them through the efforts of the ill-fated Jesuit Padre Malagrida.[18]

The West African slave trade continued to be the chief prop and stay of Bahia during this period, as the Counts of Sabugosa and Galveas repeatedly pointed out in their correspondence with the Crown. If such mortuary statistics as we have are any guide, it would seem that Negroes of Sudanese and of Bantu origin were about evenly represented in the city of Salvador during the 1740's.[19] By the end of our period, however, the trade with Whydah, which had been the most profitable, began to decline, while that with Luanda became more important. The contraband trade in gold with West Africa attained the proportions of an unprecedented scandal in 1734–1735, when the operations of a clandestine company formed for this purpose were uncovered. This illicit organization had influential representatives in Bahia, Pernambuco, Rio de Janeiro, Sacramento, São Paulo, and in the island of São Tomé. Among the leading personalities who were implicated were the Crown Judge (*Ouvidor*) of São Tomé, who seems to have been the principal culprit, and Luís Tenorio de Molina, a veteran of the "War of the Emboabas," who had made a fortune in Minas Gerais and who subsequently became one of the richest and most prominent citizens of Salvador.[20]

If such a widespread conspiracy could function undetected under the noses of the authorities in the cities, it is not surprising that their jurisdiction in the backlands was often far from effective. The enforcement of the law was not, indeed, a simple matter anywhere. Portuguese colonial legislation was a hodge-podge of the Manueline and Filipine codes, amended and supplemented by a mass of *alvarás, cartas-de-lei, cartas-régias, provisões,* and other decrees, edicts, and instructions promulgated by successive monarchs of the Braganza dynasty. Even the most erudite lawyer could hardly find his way about in this paper labyrinth, which was subject to continual modifications, often of a contradictory nature. Anyone with money or influence could therefore spin out legal proceedings inordinately, particularly since the final decision lay with the Crown. The basic codes were themselves an awkward mixture of feudal concepts and usage and of Roman law. They had not, of course, been framed with any reference to the conditions obtaining in South America.[21]

As noted previously (p. 209), Portuguese lawyers had an unenviable reputation for corruption, although there were honorable exceptions; and both the just and the unjust were past masters in the art of procrastination. Since the towns in the backlands were, generally speaking, few and far between, the judicial authorities therein could not cover adequately the enormous tracts of territory which were usually assigned to them. The inevitable result was that the administration (or maladministration) of justice in the *sertão* was largely taken over by territorial magnates of the type of Manuel Nunes Viana, Francisco Dias d'Avila, and Bernardo de Carvalho de Aguiar. These *poderosos* by virtue of their posts as colonels and captain-majors in the militia (*milícia*) and territorials (*ordenança*) exercised not only military but considerable administrative and judicial authority in their home districts. Since they controlled the local armed forces, and were usually the biggest landowners, they had every temptation to use their position to forward their own interests and to consolidate their control of the countryside.

The Crown was not unconscious of the ways in which the *poderosos do sertão* were likely to abuse their authority, and legislation to curb their excesses was enacted at the end of the seventeenth century. These measures, which were supplemented during the next few decades, included the limiting of the local captain-major's term of office (originally granted for life) to three years; the appointment of resident magistrates (*juizes ordinarios*) at intervals of every five leagues, and, as mentioned previously (p. 228), severe restrictions on the size of *sesmarias*. But it was one thing to enact these measures and quite another to enforce them in remote regions where the only individuals powerful enough to do so were precisely those at whom this legislation was aimed. Apart from anything else, it was difficult to find in the *sertão* enough potential magistrates who could read and write. When this was pointed out to the Crown, the authorities at Lisbon compromised rather feebly by ruling that it did not matter if the magistrate was illiterate, so long as his clerk was not. For the most part these laws remained a dead letter and so far as the *poderosos do sertão* were curbed at all, this was done by energetic viceroys such as the Marquis of Angeja and the Count of Sabugosa. These two *fidalgos* summarily executed a number of notorious malefactors without, as Sabugosa admitted, making a lasting impression on others of the same stamp.[22]

What is said above about the *poderosos do sertão* in the hinterland of Bahia and the region of the São Francisco was, of course, equally applicable to the territorial magnates in the backlands of São Paulo and Minas Gerais. All these men were avid for titles, honors, and military rank, for reasons both of power and prestige. The regional governors were well aware of this fact and continually reminded the Crown that the judicious distribution of such rewards was the best and cheapest way of securing what would otherwise be the doubtful loyalty of these powerful men.[23] António de Albuquerque had begun the process in Minas Gerais with a lavish bestowal of the ranks of brigadier, colonel, and so forth in the *ordenanças* during his pacification after the "War of the Emboabas." Although the Crown considered that he went too far in this respect, the practice was continued by his successors, and the "colonel" who never served in the army is a familiar figure in the Brazilian countryside today, where he exercises, overtly or otherwise, a power corresponding in some ways to that of the old-style North American "boss." The distribution of military ranks and titles was not confined to the white colonists in Brazil and Maranhão-Pará. They were often conferred on the converted Amerindian chiefs who functioned as headmen of the *aldeias*. At the other end of the Portuguese empire, the rank of colonel was conferred on a number of ruling chiefs in the island of Timor by the governor António Coelho Guerreiro (who had served in Pernambuco, 1678–1682) at the beginning of the eighteenth century, and lower commissioned ranks were conferred on the *datus* or nobles. This custom has survived down to the present day, and the Timorese chiefs are very proud of their honorific military titles.

On the other hand, the Crown was for long loath to award the coveted habits of the three military orders of Christ, Santiago, and Aviz on a generous scale in Portuguese America; whereas in Portuguese Asia it was remarkably lavish with them, as the soldier-chronicler, Diogo do Couto, complained as early as 1607.[24] The difference was due, as a *carta régia* of 1715 explained, to the fact that fighting against the enemies of the Cross and Crown was virtually continuous in the regions bordering on the Indian Ocean.[25] In South America, once the Dutch and French wars were over—and they only affected a section of the colony—the hostilities were confined to some unofficial fighting with the Spaniards, and to wars against unsubdued Amerindian tribes who were in a different category from the heretic and the Muslim. I may add that the title of "Dom" which was prefixed so frequently to the names of the Portuguese who served in India, to such an extent that the city of Bassein was nicknamed "Dom Baçaim," was very much less common in Portuguese America. The *fidalgos* of Asia were very conscious of this difference. Though many of them had arbitrarily assumed this prefix, they boasted that their degree of gentility was vastly superior to that prevailing in the mother country.[26]

We have seen in Chapter ix that the Crown's efforts to limit the power of the *poderosos do sertão* by restricting the size of *sesmarias* were, on the whole, far from successful. A study of the *sesmarias* issued by Gomes Freire de Andrada during his long tenure of power in Minas Gerais and southern Brazil, shows that these land grants were carefully framed, and that their provisions were at any rate sometimes enforced. All uncultivated land received in *sesmaria* had to be promptly demarcated by amicable agreement with the neighboring landowners within one year, and adequately cultivated within two years. Where a river ran through the property, the banks were to be left uncultivated for the space of half a league on each side, so as to ensure right of way for travelers and transients. Existing trails or footpaths in public use were not to be closed or otherwise interfered with. If gold or other mineral deposits should be discovered on the property, the landowner could not forbid their exploitation by others in accordance with the provisions of the mining code. Land granted in *sesmaria* could not be bequeathed to any Religious Order whatsoever; and if it was leased to any ecclesiastics they would have to pay tithes on it in exactly the same way as laymen. Confirmation of the grant had to be claimed from the Crown through the Overseas Council at Lisbon within four years. If any of the foregoing conditions were not complied with, the grant was to be considered null and void, and the land as available for redistribution.

Gomes Freire de Andrada also enacted a number of other salutary measures, such as restrictions on the indiscriminate felling of trees and rules for the conservation of valuable timber. In the regions where canoes formed the principal means of transport, rules were made that adequate stands of timber for their construction should be left on private property for felling by anyone who needed a new canoe in transit. That all this legislation did not remain on paper is evidenced by the fact that much of Minas Gerais was brought under cultivation at this period. The increasingly hazardous and speculative nature of the mining industry caused many people to forsake this calling for the less glittering but more certain rewards of agriculture and stockbreeding. This change was the more significant because agriculture and stock raising were still regarded as socially inferior pursuits in comparison with gold mining, a fact observed by John Mawe on his travels in Minas Gerais over half a century later. There can be no doubt but that this "back to the land" movement was fostered by the legislation enacted by Gomes Freire.[27]

Although cattle were still imported into Minas Gerais from as far away as Piauí, Martinho de Mendonça stated in September, 1736 that the rate of increase in the backlands was in the nature of 20,000 head a year. Since an annual tithe of one dram of gold had been levied on each head of cattle, whether a bull or a cow, after 1716, this naturally represented a considerable income for the Crown, though tax evasion in the remoter parts of the *sertão* was admittedly widespread before the enforcement of the capitation tax. The growth of horse breeding kept pace with that of cattle in Minas. By the year 1725 packhorses and mules had largely replaced Negro and Amerindian slaves for the carriage of goods between Rio de Janeiro and the gold-mining towns of the Serra de Espinhaço.[28]

The onerous monopoly-contract system, which was briefly sketched in Chapter vii above, continued to function along similar lines in Minas Gerais and elsewhere during the time that Gomes Freire de Andrada supervised southern Brazil. Among the most important of these contracts were those which arranged for the collection of import duties (*entradas*) and for the royal tithes (*dizimos reais*). As the reader may recall, the tithes collected in Minas Gerais were not solely, or even mainly, for the upkeep of the Church and its ministers, but served to pay the salaries of the governor and of the military, judicial, fiscal, and administrative establishments. The reader may also recall that contracts for the collection of tithes were originally made separately for each of the four *comarcas* into which Minas Gerais was divided for administrative purposes. From 1728 to 1734, however, and from 1738 onwards, these regional contracts were farmed out simultaneously to the same contractor, or group of contractors, usually on a triennial basis. This tendency to unify regional contracts was also seen in the salt gabelle which was unified in one contract embracing the whole State of Brazil in 1732, remaining on this footing until the abolition of the monopoly in 1801. Monopoly contracts were not limited to such staple commodities as salt, sugarcane brandy, wine, olive oil, train oil, tobacco, or to items such as duties on slaves imported into Minas Gerais or on hides exported from Sacramento. Even the surgical and medical treatment of the dragoons of Minas Gerais was farmed out to a local doctor in return for an annual cash payment to the Crown. A royal decree of 1706 had ordained that the maximum number of associates who could tender jointly for any colonial contract should be limited to three in small contracts and four in large ones; but this stipulation does not seem to have been strictly observed.[29]

Although the abolition of the hated capitation tax in 1750-1751 was greeted with unfeigned relief by the miners of Minas Gerais, their municipal councillors immediately began to make difficulties about finding the annual 100 *arrobas* of gold which they had offered as an alternative payment in the time of the Count of Galveas, and which the Crown now called upon them to produce. The *Vereadores* of Villa Rica pointed out that economic conditions in the captaincy had greatly changed for the worse since 1734 when the offer was first made. The river gold washings were either quite exhausted or else very nearly so. Where gold was still being obtained from the precipitous mountainsides, this was a costly process involving years of work with hydraulic methods before an adequate return was received. Many miners and their slaves had emigrated to the (temporarily) more promising fields of Goiás and Mato Grosso. The Serro do Frio, which was in full and free production in 1732, was virtually closed to gold diggers and limited to the production of diamonds in 1750. During the same period, the number of Negro slaves imported annually into the captaincy had dropped by four-fifths—or so it was alleged. Trade had slumped badly, "and in this decadence, which is notorious, the miners are those who suffer most, for the obvious reason that nothing whatsoever is exported from this region save only gold. And from the hand of the miner the gold passes to that of the slave dealers, the traders, the shopkeepers, and the craftsmen, and is expended on building materials and so forth," thus leaving the miner worse off than anyone else. Doubtless the worthy aldermen were laying on the dark colors a bit thick, but other evidence is not lacking to indicate that the Rich Town of Black Gold had seen its best days in the time of the *Triunfo Eucharistico* and the Count of Galveas.[30]

In Rio de Janeiro, on the other hand, the impression is one of increasing rather then of decreasing prosperity, for it was to the city of São Sebastião rather than to that of Salvador that the gold of Minas Gerais, Goiás, and Mato Grosso tended to gravitate. A short account of the former city as it appeared in 1748 to an officer of a visiting French warship, *L'Arc-en-ciel* (50), gives us a valuable glimpse of Rio in the days when Gomes Freire de Andrada was just past his prime.[31] Despite all the money which had been lavished on the fortifications since Duguay-Trouin's exploit, our French visitor did not think much of them, opining that "la defense ne peut être fondée que sur la valeur de ses habitans." The regular garrison consisted of about 800 or 900 infantrymen, "assez bien entretenûs, parmi lesquels il y a environ cent grenadiers de bonne mine," though he dismissed their officers as being "en general sans naissance et sans merite, crées par le gouverneur suivant sa fantasie." Priests, monks, and friars abounded, but the Frenchman thought that only about 2,000 able-bodied white men could be raised for service in the militia at a crisis. Negroes were much more numerous, and he saw "une grande quantité de Mulatres," whose daily increasing numbers he ascribed to "la libertinage auquel le climat et l'oisivité rendent les habitans enclins."

He observed that the great numerical preponderance of Negro slaves would be dangerous for their white masters, but for the mutual hatred between the Sudanese and Bantu: "Et la sureté publique est fondée sur cette antipathie." According to him, the Bantu slaves were more highly regarded than the Sudanese, but the Portuguese took care to import them in roughly equal proportions, so as to balance one race against the other. In this he was evidently mistaken. The Portuguese were well aware of the mutual antipathy between the two Negro races; but their purchases were guided more by the kinds of work for which the slaves were required (mining, agriculture, domestic service) and by their relative availability in the slave markets of Guinea, Angola, and Benguela, than by any Machiavellian plan to divide and rule.

Like most foreign visitors to Brazil, our anonymous Frenchman aciduously criticized the laziness and lasciviousness of the Luso-Brazilians. He contrasted these latter unfavorably with their fifteenth-century ancestors, "qui à travèrs mille dangers, se sont fixé le route d'un nouveau Monde et ont donné au reste de l'Europe

le premier example d'y faire des Conquêtes." He professed surprise at the backwardness of the local agriculture, while admitting
that there were prodigious quantities of fruits and vegetables of
all kinds and of excellent quality, "propres à raffraichir les Equi-
pages." Fish were equally varied and abundant, forming the basic
food for slaves, "outre la quantité qu'on abandonne aux Pourceaux."
Beef, mutton, and pork, though easily obtainable, were alike of
inferior quality; whereas chickens, ducks, and geese, were good
and plentiful, though not particularly cheap. He noted the invariable Lusitanian contrast between the frugal eating habits of
the citizens ("une médiocre quantité de farine, de vin de Porto,
et d'epiceries, dont la frugalité Portugaise se content") and their
ostentatious extravagance in dress ("des Etoffes d'or et d'argent,
des Galons, des soyeries, des beaux draps, des toiles fines, et
d'autres Marchandises de gout, tirées pour la plus grade partie
des Manufactures de France"). He described the city as being
somewhat irregularly built in the form of a rough square, with a
circuit of half a league at the most. He considered that the majority
of the houses were "mediocres et inegales: Presque toutes n'ont
qu'une seule etage."

   This succinct French account of Rio de Janeiro in 1748, though
fair enough on the whole, does not do justice in some respects to
the people or to the place. For instance, no mention is made of the
richly decorated churches and the imposing public buildings
which either already existed or else were in course of construction. If many of the citizens were lazy and lascivious, this could
not truly be said of all of them, and least of all of their governor,
Gomes Freire de Andrada, whom the Frenchman admitted was
a polished and intelligent *grand seigneur,* and who was also a
singularly energetic administrator. His tireless devotion to the
royal service is apparent from his vast correspondence and from
his very considerable achievements. His jurisdiction at this period
exceeded that of the viceroy at Bahia and comprised the greater
part of Brazil. At one time or another he traveled through much
of his bailiwick, and he was as familiar a figure in Ouro Preto

and Tijuco as he was in Rio de Janeiro. Whether fitting out expeditions for the relief of Sacramento, or East Indiamen which had put into port in distress; whether superintending the collection of the royal fifths, or supervising the construction of fortifications and of public works; whether signing *sesmarias* in Minas, or dictating dispatches in Rio, Gomes Freire spared neither himself nor others. He often worked through the night at his official correspondence, after spending the daylight hours in the arsenal or at his desk. It is obvious that these long hours involved sleepless nights for others besides himself and his personal staff.[32]

Our French visitor's contemptuous dismissal of the professional abilities of the officers of the garrison is also unfair as regards this time and place. Admittedly, the Portuguese army officers in general were exceedingly inefficient (cf. p. 86); but we have seen that there were exceptions (cf. p. 297), and the garrison of Rio de Janeiro contained a strikingly high proportion of them, some of whom we have met before. André Ribeiro Coutinho, a veteran of the wars in Hungary and in Portuguese India, one of the leading defenders of Sacramento and a pioneer of Rio Grande do Sul, was also the author of a manual of military training which included a critical study of the Battle of Fontenoy.[33] José da Silva Paes, another defender of Sacramento, colonizer of the Rio Grande and of Santa Catarina, was responsible for many major engineering works in Portugal and Brazil. José Fernandes Pinto Alpoim was the author of two technical treatises on motars, siege- and field-artillery, and he was the architect-constructor of many public works in Rio de Janeiro and Minas Gerais.[34] The works of Ribeiro Coutinho and Pinto Alpoim, though written at Rio de Janeiro, were published in Europe, for the Crown refused to allow the establishment of a printing press in Brazil. An enterprising Lisbon printer who emigrated to Rio with his press in 1746, was forced to return to Portugal when this fact was discovered in the following year, before he had been able to print anything but a few pamphlets. All these highly competent professional soldiers—and others who might be mentioned—were friends and collaborators of Gomes Freire, himself a veteran of the wars in Flanders and the Peninsula. Few readers will dispute the justice of Frederick the Great's dictum, "the army means its officers," or that of Napoleon, "there are no bad soldiers, only bad officers." With such an array of talent in the senior ranks of the Rio garrison of the 1740's, it is virtually certain that some units must have been in a high state of efficiency. At any rate, when the Spaniards met Gomes Freire's grenadier detachment in Uruguay a few years later, they seem to have been greatly impressed by the smartness and discipline of those Luso-Brazilian soldiers.[35]

The French account of Rio in 1748 noted that the annual Brazil fleets now left Lisbon in September or October, convoyed by three or four warships, which left the merchantmen successively at Recife, Salvador, and Rio. The return voyage was begun during December or January, when the three fleets were supposed to sail from the Bay of All Saints in convoy; "et n'emportent du Païs, avec leurs matieres pretieuses [gold and diamonds], que du sucre, du tabac, et du coton, qu'il semble produre malgré ses maitres." The Frenchman should have added that hides, dyewoods, and hardwoods were also important Brazilian exports. The last-named commodity was sometimes exported in the form of pre-fabricated houses, which were subsequently re-erected at Lisbon [36]—an interesting reversal of the export of cut *pedra-lioz* stone from Portugal for the churches and public buildings at Bahia.

It should also be added that the Brazil fleets' times of sailing from Lisbon and from Brazil were seldom strictly adhered to. They were changed several times after the decree of 1690, which ordained that the annual fleets should leave Portuguese ports between December 15 and January 20, and Brazilian ports between the end of May and July 20. The Count of Sabugosa observed in 1729 that the Brazilian "midsummer months" of November, December, and January, formed the best season for the fleets to load their cargoes in Brazilian ports and sail for Portugal with fair weather in early February, so as to ensure their arrival at Lisbon by May 10. But the Count-Viceroy also observed in another dispatch three years later, that captains of merchantmen and captains of king's ships both preferred to sail not at the times ordered by the Crown, but at times which suited their private trade and personal convenience.[37] The upshot was that the ships usually sailed from Brazil in detachments instead of as a properly escorted fleet. The convoy system which had been introduced at the crisis of the Dutch war in 1649 had never worked really smoothly. It was finally abolished by Pombal in 1765, to the relief of merchants and shippers on both sides of the Atlantic.

Another royal provision which was not always strictly observed was that all gold exports from Brazil, whether in the form of coins, ingots, gold dust, gold leaf, or gold objects and ornaments, had to be sent in the chests (safes) of the convoying warships, and on no account in any of the merchant ships of the fleet. Diamonds and precious stones were to be treated in the same way, and all these valuables had to pay an extra tax of one per cent for carriage. Captains of warships were ordered to give every facility to induce people to embark their gold and silver valuables in this way. These objects were to be graded according to their categories and placed in separate chests, after proper receipts had been given for them in the presence of three responsible witnesses. On arrival at Lisbon, the gold had to be sent to the mint for coining, the owners receiving in ready money the full market value of their consignments. An exception was made in ships bound for Madeira and the Azores, which were allowed to take thither gold coins received in payment for goods exported to Brazil from those Atlantic Islands. Gold from the Maranhão was exempted from the one per cent carriage tax but had to be sent to the mint to be coined in the same way as that from Brazil.[38]

Gold smuggling still continued on an extensive scale despite these and other enactments, some of the most oppressive and vindictive of which were directed against the numerous goldsmiths and jewelers who worked in early eighteenth-century Brazil. As early as 1698 the Crown ordered that only two or three goldsmiths should be permitted to ply their trade in Rio de Janeiro. The drive against members of this profession was subsequently extended to the whole of Brazil, those of Minas Gerais being particularly harried. They were accused of helping their customers to evade payment of the royal fifths by turning unquinted gold into ornaments, or into such utensils as knives, forks, and spoons. They were also accused of counterfeiting gold coins and quinted ingots; and of melting them down to turn them into other objects. In February, 1719, the Crown ordered the expulsion of all goldsmiths from Minas Gerais and forbade the admission into that captaincy of any new ones. The order was repeated eleven years later, and goldsmiths in the other captaincies were successively placed under increasingly irksome restrictions.

Although some colonial governors, such as the Count of Galveas, spoke up on their behalf and pointed out that not all members of this maligned profession were necessarily black sheep, the Crown paid little or no heed to these remonstrances. After first confining the goldsmiths working in Rio and other towns to ghetto-like quarters, where they could be kept under strict surveillance, the Crown took the final step of banning the exercise of their craft altogether in Brazil in 1766. Working goldsmiths and their apprentices were given the alternatives of enlisting in the army, or taking up some other form of livelihood; the most skilled and experienced among them were given employment in the colonial mints and smelting-houses. The tools and implements of their craft were confiscated (but paid for at their current value), except those belonging to goldsmiths who declared their intention of emigrating to Portugal, where they would be allowed to practice without let or hindrance.[39]

The laws against goldsmiths, oppressive as they were, directly affected only a part of the population; but among the vexatious impositions which were a burden to everyone were the *donativos reais,* or "voluntary contributions" toward the expenses of the royal marriages between the ruling houses of Spain and Portugal which were solemnized in 1729. Two years earlier, the viceroy at

Bahia had been ordered to arrange for the collection of seven million *cruzados* for this purpose and another million for the dowry of the Portuguese Infanta. Payments were to be spread over a period of twenty-five years, and collected by means of regional imposts levied on slaves, cattle, sugar, etc., after due consultation with the principal inhabitants. Pernambuco and the Northeast were to contribute one and a quarter million; Bahia and its subordinate captaincies, three million; Rio de Janeiro, Minas Gerais, São Paulo, and the smaller southern captaincies, three and three-quarter million. Even some of the richer captaincies found difficulty in fulfilling their respective quotas, and some of the poorer, such as Espiritu Santo and Ilheus, found it impossible to do so. In May, 1748, the municipal council of São Jorge de Ilheus petitioned to be relieved of this crushing burden. It alleged that this captaincy was the least developed and the poorest in all Brazil. Much of it was still occupied by unsubdued Amerindian tribes, who raided within a short distance of the town on some occasions, and who prevented the establishment of sugar plantations on any extensive scale. The petitioners concluded their catalogue of woes by stating: "finally, this is a land where there is not a single Misericordia, nor a butcher's-shambles, nor a doctor, nor a surgeon."

In fairness it should be added that the burdensome nature of this so-called "voluntary contribution" was not entirely the fault of the Crown. The viceroy at Bahia reported in 1753 that although far more than three millions of the 1727 assessment had been collected from the inhabitants of that region by the year 1748, yet the total forwarded to Lisbon fell far short of that sum. As the viceroy observed, Bahia's contribution would have been discharged long since, but for the "immense and scandalous frauds" perpetrated by some of the officials who were responsible for its collection, several of whom had embezzled huge sums. Apparently they ordered these things better in the city of Saint Sebastian than they did in that of the Savior, as Rio de Janeiro seems to have discharged its obligation by 1738. As regards the Northeastern contribution, Pernambuco paid the final instalment of its quota in 1751.[40]

Robert Southey, in giving his judgment on the golden age of Brazil, observed in the third volume of his monumental *History* (p. 40) that: "It brought with it no moral melioration, no increase of happiness, and it may be doubted whether it promoted or retarded the progress of the colonies; but it produced a great change in the system of administration, and in the condition and pursuits of the people." The reader who has persevered thus far with this book, may be inclined to feel that Southey's verdict still stands. Moral betterment was hardly to be expected in a slave-owning society which was not unfairly described in 1730 as being "very lax and ignorant [and] where the Ecclesiastics are the most covetous and unbridled." [41] That there was "no increase of happiness" during this period is also very likely, though it is obviously impossible to prove the truth or falsity of this assertion. If the average colonial family can be defined in Capistrano's words as "taciturn father, submissive mother, and cowed children," the frequent religious festivals and processions gave welcome opportunities for breaking the monotony of life in general. The average slave's life must have remained what it always had been—nasty, brutish, and short. The toil and tribulation undergone by the pioneers, whether freemen or bondsmen, who opened up the mining districts of the south, center, and west have been sufficiently indicated in the foregoing pages. Those people who stayed in the coastal cities and plantations also had their share of adversity and suffering if their reiterated complaints as reflected in the governors' correspondence with the Crown are to be taken at even half their face value.

It may also be doubted whether the discovery of gold and diamonds "promoted or retarded the progress of the colonies." Immense amounts of treasure were sent to Portugal; very considerable amounts to West Africa; while far more remained in Brazil than was generally acknowledged then or is generally realized now. Certainly all this treasure was not dissipated on the personal and ecclesiastical extravagancies of Dom João V, although a great deal of it was. Many useful public works and richly decorated churches were erected with this money, both in Portugal and Brazil. Charitable foundations were endowed, pension lists were swelled, widows and orphans were relieved, and some families were raised from indigence to affluence. On the other hand, this wealth did not serve to bring about the rise of a prosperous middle class, or perceptibly to improve the lot of the poor. It was not used to effect any great improvements in agriculture and in industry; nor did it generate a lasting improvement in the quality of the civilian administration or of the fighting services, whether at home or overseas.

The wealth derived from Brazil did, as Southey states, effect some great changes in the administration, condition, and pursuits of the people of Portuguese America. The boundaries of the colony were pushed thousands of miles westwards, and large tracts in the interior of the continent were opened for settlement. The discovery of the gold and diamond mines brought about a great shift of population from the coastal plantations to the *sertão*, and agricultural pursuits were relatively neglected in favor of mining. A new, and in some ways more lasting, impetus to the settlement of the interior was given by the phenomenal expansion of ranching and stock raising, particularly in the regions described in Chapter ix. These changes were reflected in the increasing shift of economic and political power from Pernambuco and Bahia to Minas Gerais and Rio de Janeiro. This shift had been virtually accomplished by 1750, though it was only given formal recognition thirteen years later when the seat of the viceregal capital was transferred from the city of Salvador to that of São Sebastião.

Nevertheless, if Southey's verdict of 1819 still holds good in 1961, there were some other factors which deserve mention here. Although the evidence of foreign visitors and of Luso-Brazilian

321

official correspondence is impressively unanimous concerning the low standards of the bulk of the secular clergy and of the friars in colonial Brazil, there were always some and at times there were numerous exceptions; though these naturally did not attain the publicity achieved by the "frades licenciosos e soltos" whom the authorities never tired of denouncing. The Jesuits, as we have more than once had occasion to observe, should be entirely exempted from these strictures; and their labors in both the missionary and the educational fields can fairly be described as herculean. If they did not achieve more—and they did achieve a great deal—it was through lack of numbers, and not through lack of high standards or of self-sacrificing efforts. Nor should the labors of the Oratorians of Pernambuco, the Capuchins of the São Francisco River valley, and the Carmelites of the middle Amazon be forgotten in this connection; though the work of all these men was almost entirely destroyed a few years later through the secularization of the missions by Pombal.

The relative scarcity of white women in many regions, and the resultant miscegenation between white men and colored women, professedly shocked many foreign observers and provoked much adverse comment from contemporary governors and bishops. This large-scale miscegenation was undoubtedly responsible for the growth of a colored urban and rural proletariat which had no proper upbringing and lived from hand to mouth. This state of affairs led in turn to those social evils—vagrancy, prostitution, disease—which such a state of social insecurity implies. On the other hand, a surprising number of this colored community eventually made good, whether as *vaqueiros* in the cattle districts of the river São Francisco and of Piauí, as mulatto musicians and notaries in Minas Gerais, or in other crafts and callings where skilled persons of color were often to be found—sometimes in defiance of the discriminatory laws. Moreover, as mentioned on page 169 above, the Brazilian racial cauldron, with all its varied stresses and strains, did bring about a more or less peaceful fusion of the three races, European, African, and Amerindian, which otherwise might have had to resolve their cultural and ethnical differences by bloodshed.

Whatever the real extent of the wealth derived from the Brazilian gold and diamond mines, not to mention the sugar and tobacco plantations and the cattle ranches, this wealth was popularly believed to be enormous. This opinion was fostered by the fact that just when the original gold strikes in Minas Gerais began to show signs of exhaustion, new rich strikes were made in Cuiabá, and then came the (official) discovery of diamonds in the Serro do Frio. These discoveries were followed in due course by the finding and exploitation of the gold fields of Goiás and Mato Grosso. The flame of hope that flickers eternally in the human breast was periodically fanned by these successive discoveries whenever the preceding finds seemed to be tapering off in production. The impression was given that the mineral wealth of Brazil was inexhaustible, and that if one mining district became unprofitable another would soon be found in the *sertão* to take its place. Although much of the gold and diamonds of Brazil were expended in payments for imports from northern Europe, or were lavished on the churches and convents of the Portuguese Atlantic world, it was widely (if erroneously) believed that Dom João V was the richest monarch in Europe—a belief that his lavish expenditure did nothing to discourage. This widespread conviction was echoed by John Wesley when he wrote in his *Serious Thoughts Occasioned by the Great Earthquake at Lisbon* (London, 1755): "Merchants who have lived in Portugal inform us, that the King had a large building filled with diamonds; and more gold stored up, coined and uncoined, than all the other princes of Europe put together."

Whatever the shortcomings of Brazilian society, there can be no doubt but that the colony was in most ways more prosperous than the mother country. This was apparent to one of the greatest eighteenth-century Portuguese statesmen, Dom Luís da Cunha, who secretly suggested that Dom João V could not do better than transfer his court to Rio de Janeiro and take the title of "Emperor of the West." The idea of the Portuguese monarch taking refuge in Portuguese America was not a new one, having been canvassed on various critical occasions, notably in 1580 and 1660; and it was actually carried out by Dom João VI, under English pressure, in 1808. But these were occasions when the survival of the dynasty in Europe seemed highly problematical, whereas Dom Luís da Cunha's proposal was made in the piping times of peace. He argued that Rio de Janeiro was much better situated than Lisbon as the metropolis of the Portuguese maritime and commercial empire, while the natural, economic, and demographical resources of Brazil were far greater than those of the mother country. Portugal could not survive without the riches of Brazil, whereas Brazil could survive very easily without those of Portugal. "From which it follows," he wrote, "that it is safer and more convenient to be where one has everything in abundance, than where one has to wait for what one wants." [42]

It is interesting but futile to speculate on what might have happened if Dom João V had transferred the capital of his empire to Rio de Janeiro in 1738. His grandfather had termed Brazil the "milch cow" of the Portuguese crown in the mid-seventeenth century and this was still truer of their relative positions a hundred years later. Although in some respects the golden age of Brazil was anything but golden, and in other respects all that glittered was not gold, yet very real benefits did result to the Luso-Brazilian community on both sides of the Atlantic. Not the least of these was the exceptional purity of the gold coinage which, during all of Dom João V's long reign, suffered no debasement whatsoever and was in high repute all over the world. The stability of the Joannine *cruzado* forms a striking contrast to the disastrous decline in the value of the modern *cruzeiro*. In this respect at any rate the golden age of Brazil was a real one.

There is nothing to indicate that Dom Luís da Cunha's secret memorandum of 1738 was ever seen by Dom João V, for whose eyes it was certainly never intended. But it must have been as obvious to that monarch as it was to his principal advisers that Brazil now counted for more than the mother country. António Rodrigues da Costa, one of the most perspicacious and intelligent of the Overseas Councillors at Lisbon, had pointed out to the Crown just before his death in 1732 that a dangerous situation was developing in Portuguese America, owing to the fiscal and administrative burdens with which that section of the Lusitanian empire was saddled. Apart from the heavy duties on sugar, tobacco, and other colonial products, the *donativo real* imposed in 1727 was particularly resented by the colonists, since the expenses of the royal marriage which had been celebrated two years later did not amount to a fraction of the millions that were being remitted to Lisbon on this account. Rodrigues da Costa added that the longer this system of oppressive taxation continued, the more it would be resented by the colonists, who would eventually be tempted to combine with any ambitious foreign power which would enable them to throw off their allegiance to the Portuguese Crown. "It is obvious," he concluded, "that if Brazil is placed in one scale of the balance and Portugal in the other, the former will weigh far more heavily than the latter; and consequently the larger and richer will not consent to be ruled by the smaller and poorer." [48]

António Rodrigues da Costa proved a true prophet. The break did not come for another ninety years, but the foundations of Brazilian independence were laid willy-nilly by the Portuguese government during the reign of Dom João V.

APPENDICES

CONTENTS

328

Contents

APPENDIX I

"For a horned beast, 80 drams.
For an ox, 100 drams.
For a bundle of sixty spikes of maize, 30 drams.
For an *alqueire* of manioc-flour, 40 drams.
For six cakes of maize-flour, 3 drams.
For a thick sausage, 3 drams.
For an 8-lb ham, 16 drams.
For a small pie, 1 dram.
For a pound of butter, 2 drams.
For a hen, 3 or 4 drams.
For 6 lbs of beef, 1 dram.
For a regional cheese, 3 or 4 drams, according to its weight.
For a Dutch cheese, 16 drams.
For an Alemtejan cheese, 3 or 4 drams.
For a jar of marmalade, 3 drams.
For a 4-lb flask of comfits, 16 drams.
For a 1-*arroba* loaf of sugar, 32 drams.
For a pound of cedrat sweetmeat, 3 drams.
For a little cask of brandy, a slave's load, 100 drams.
For a little cask of olive oil, 2 pounds.
For 4 drams of scented tobacco snuff, 1 dram.
For 6 drams of unscented tobacco snuff, 1 dram.
For a *vara de tobacco em corda,* 3 drams.
For an ordinary baize coat, 12 drams.
For a fine cloth coat, 20 drams.
For a silk waistcoat, 16 drams.
For a pair of fine cloth breeches, 9 drams.
For a pair of silk breeches, 12 drams.
For a linen shirt, 4 drams.
For a pair of silk stockings, 8 drams.
For a pair of Cordova leather shoes, 5 drams.

Appendix I

For a fine beaver hat, 12 drams.

For an ordinary hat, 6 drams.

For a silk bonnet, 4 or 5 drams.

For a cloth bonnet lined with silk, 5 drams.

For a tortoiseshell snuff box, 6 drams.

For an embossed silver snuff box of 8 drams of silver, 10 or 12 drams according to the decoration thereof.

For a plain musket, 16 drams.

For a well-made and silver-inlaid musket, 120 drams.

For an ordinary pistol, 10 drams.

For a silver-inlaid pistol, 40 drams.

For a pointed knife, made like a bayonet, with a curiously carved handle, 6 drams.

For a pen-knife, 2 drams.

For a pair of scissors, 2 drams.

And all the knick-knacks imported from France and elsewhere, are sold for such prices as they will fetch according to the eagerness of the buyers.

For a robust Negro, manly and intelligent, 300 drams.

For a black youth (*molecão* *), 250 drams.

For a black boy (*moleque* *), 120 drams.

For a Brazilian-born Negro (*crioulo*), who is a good craftsman, 500 drams.

For a mulatto who is gifted, or a craftsman, 500 drams.

For a good trumpeter, 500 drams.

For a gifted mulata, 600 drams or more.

For an intelligent Negress cook, 350 drams.

For an old hack, 100 drams.

For a pacing horse, two pounds of gold.

And these excessively high prices which were current in the Mines formed the reason why the prices of other things increased so

* *Molecão*, a Negro youth between eight and fifteen years old; *Moleque*, a Negro boy under eight years old.

much elsewhere, as is experienced in the ports and cities and towns of Brazil, and why many sugar mills lack the necessary slaves; and why the inhabitants suffer from great lack of provisions, which are almost all taken and sold where they give the most profit." (Andreoni-Antonil, *Cultura e Opulencia do Brasil,* Part III, Chap. 7.)

APPENDIX II

REVENUE DERIVED BY THE CROWN FROM THE CAPTAINCY
OF MINAS GERAIS, 1700–1724.

a) Table of the Yield for the Years 1700–1713

Year	Source	Amount (in drams and grains)	Total (in drams and grains)
1700	Royal Fifths	940	940
1701	Royal Fifths	6,640	10,079
	mining claims	3,320	
	confiscations	695	
1702	Royal Fifths	28	2,139
	mining claims	1,442	
	confiscations	669	
1703	Royal Fifths	1,648-57	9,135-57
	mining claims	684	
	confiscations	6,823	
1704	Royal Fifths	2,926-50	8,685-2
	mining claims	604	
	confiscations	4,708-36	
	tithes	445-60	
1705	Royal Fifths	1,637-18	5,270-34
	mining claims	447	
	confiscations	1,640	
	tithes	804-16	
	absentees	742	
1706	Royal Fifths	4,890	9,323
	mining claims	90	
	confiscations	1,182	
	tithes	816-61	
	absentees	3,345	

333

Year	Source	Amount (in drams and grains)	Total (in drams and grains)
1707	Royal Fifths confiscations tithes absentees	4,890 * 2,905-54 1,632-43 ** 2,580-13	9,269-38
1708	Royal Fifths confiscations tithes absentees	1,163-18 7,824-18 1,020-61 110	10,118-25
1709	Royal Fifths confiscations tithes absentees	4,546 2,912 8,329 1,468	9,009-29
1710	Royal Fifths mining claims confiscations tithes	5,682 320 3,542-11 116-61	9,661
1711	Royal Fifths mining claims confiscations condemnations war contribution transit-tolls	13,579 280 6,185 120 17,187 990	38,341
1712	Royal Fifths confiscations condemnations	8,618-36 1,782 100	10,500-36

* 2,151 in the "Extracto" compiled by order of Luís Diogo Lobo da Silva in 1766 (APM, Cod.76,DF).
** 1,600 in the "Extracto" of 1766.

Appendix II

a) Table of the Yield for the Years 1700–1713 (continued)

Year	Source	Amount (in drams and grains)	Total (in drams and grains)
1713	Royal Fifths	2,781-18	
	mining claims	150	
	confiscations	7,106-54	13,924
	transit-tolls	3,886	

Total collected, 146,416 drams, equivalent to 219,623$375 in money." (Biblioteca da Universidade de São Paulo, Lamego MSS, no. 104).

A codex in the Arquivo Publico Mineiro (76, "Delagacia Fiscal"), gives the total income of the Crown from all sources (Fifths, tithes, tolls, etc., etc.) as being

for 1700–1713: 8,895$000
for 1714–1721: 1,196,905$694.

b) Table of the Yield from the Royal Fifths during the Period when the Inhabitants Paid by Commutation, 1714–1724

From	To	Amount in arrobas
20 March 1714	19 March 1715	30
20 March 1715	19 March 1716	30
22 July 1716	21 July 1717	30
22 July 1717	21 July 1718	30
22 July 1718	21 July 1719	25
22 July 1719	21 July 1720	25
22 July 1720	21 July 1721	25
22 July 1721	21 July 1722	25
1 August 1722	31 July 1723	37
1 August 1723	31 July 1724	37
1 August 1724	31 January 1725	18½
		312½

From Visconde de Carnaxide, *Brasil na administração Pombalina* (São Paulo, 1940), p. 244.

APPENDIX III

Some Figures for the Quint and Capitation Taxes in Minas Gerais, 1724–1750

a) *Gold handled by the Mint and by the Three Smelting-houses of Minas Gerais, 1724–1735*

	1	2	3
PERIOD	Weight of gold of various carats, cast into bars from which money was coined. Marcs, ounces, drams, grams.	Quint at 12 per cent taken in coin from the end product of the said gold.	Seigniorage and Brassage from coining money.
26.viii.1724–31.i.1725	19,746-2-6-16	. . . .	138,008U901
February–December 1725	17,617-6-3-30	337,812U021	123,341U024
1726	26,115-4-7-59	511,284U202	151,961U781
1727	25,037-2-5-58	481,855U653	132,463U471
1728	26,163-2-2-24	33,978U273	126,509U935
1729	14,160-5-0-49	. . . .	81,942U305
1724–1729	128,841-0-2-20	1,364,930U149	754,227U417
1730	23,350-7-7-50	230,400U904	158,544U896
1731	39,566-2-7-71	473,361U535	246,837U259
1732	33,093-0-4-36	448,827U940	209,245U681
1733	28,332-1-5-18	568,980U921	184,650U447
1734	6,553-3-6-17	132,005U512	21,325U053
1730–1734	259,737-1-1-68	3,218,506U961	1,574,830U753
January 1735	. . . .	. . . .	. . . .
February 1735	. . . .	. . . .	. . . .
March 1735	. . . .	. . . .	. . . .
April 1735	. . . .	. . . .	. . . .
May 1735	. . . .	. . . .	. . . .
June 1735	. . . .	. . . .	. . . .
January–June 1735	259,737-1-1-68	3,218,506U961	1,574,830U753

"N.B. These last two additional remittances were made in the fleet of 1736, comprising the gold and bars or marcs. It can be seen from columns 1 and 4 of this table that the gold which entered the said houses, after being cast into bars, both for being subsequently coined 'into money as for being handed over in bars, amounts to 50,893 *arrobas*, 1 pound, 7 ounces, 3 drams, 2 grains. The duties of the Quint at 12 per cent, extracted in money as shown in column 2, and those of the seigniorage and brassage as shown in column 3.

"*Table of all the gold that entered the smelting-house and the Mint of Villa Rica of Minas Gerais from August 26, 1724, the day on which the Mint began to function, and from February 1, 1725 for the smelting-house, when the collection of the Quint began; the revenue therefrom; and of everything else pertaining to the Crown Exchequer; remittances made to Lisbon; and likewise the yield of the Quint from the two smelting-houses which were established in the districts of Rio des Mortes and Rio das Velhas, both of which began to function on February 2, 1734.*"

4	5	6	7	8
Weight of gold reduced to bars, which entered to leave in this form.	Quint at 12 per cent taken not only from the gold bars but from some gold which entered to leave in money.	Expenses paid by individuals for the casting of their gold.	Remittances made to Lisbon in money.	Remittances made in gold bars, and some in gold dust.
. . . .	. . . .	6,338U202	408U000	653-4-5-42
9,013-2-2-07	1,802-5-2-0⅖	9,272U638	120,499U455	7,038-5-6-22
8,762-7-3-60	1,752-4-5-40⅘	14,750U597	247,273U462	8,485-0-4-58
11,065-0-1-43	2,213-0-0-23	15,842U727	10,734U054	7,468-6-0-15
7,992-3-5-64	6,344-2-2-27⅕	13,379U471	16,475U081	4,842-0-1-24
5,175-0-4-45	3,697-0-3-67⅗	9,982U033	87,366U447	. . . .
42,008-6-2-03	15,809-4-6-16	69,565U668	482,756U499	28,488-1-2-17
3,996-3-1-34	1,176-5-6-35²³⁄₂₅	13,270U394	16,559U333	2,721-7-1-24
5,618-4-6-58	674-1-6-64¹⁴⁄₂₅	20,978U333	285,784U028	5,520-2-2-48
4,924-2-0-39	649-7-0-43²⁄₂₅	18,184U435	400,005U633	4,449-1-1-29
1,289-7-6-16	257-7-7-46²⁄₅	14,822U638	410,240U000	1,946-3-3-24
33,142-6-3-54	6,628-4-3-68¹⁰⁄₂₅	17,923U917	157U777	5,683-5-6-084
90,980-6-4-60	25,196-7-7-58⁰⁄₂₅	154,745U385	1,595,503U270	48,809-5-1-06⅘
3,122-5-4-32	624-4-2-35⅕	1,491U721	. . . .	. . . .
2,555-3-0-12	511-0-4-60	1,202U683	. . . .	. . . .
3,497-7-5-14	699-4-5-60²⁄₅	1,460U466	. . . .	. . . .
5,339-5-6-02	1,067-7-4-29⅕	2,178U491	. . . .	. . . .
11,085-6-3-54	2,217-1-2-25⅕	4,502U605	273U600	*7,446-7-2-69
835-3-0-48	167-0-4-67⅕	399U315	32,544U850	*2,539-7-6-38⅕
117,417-6-1-06	30,484-3-0-47¹⁴⁄₂₅	165,980U666	1,628,321U720	58,796-3-6-38

as also the charges for expenses as shown in column 6, amount to a total of 12,398,295¾ *cruzados*. The duties of the Quint at 12 per cent extracted in bars, as shown in column 5, amount to 476 *arrobas*, 10 pounds, 3 ounces, 47 grains, and 14 *avos*. The amount remitted to Lisbon in coin, as shown in column 7, totals 4,070,804¼ *cruzados*. The amount remitted in gold, as shown in column 8, totals 918 *arrobas*, 22 pounds, 13 ounces, 6 drams, 38 grains."
(Biblioteca Municipal de São Paulo, Codice Costa Matoso, fol. 180.)

b) *Gold yield of the capitation tax in Minas Gerais, 1735–1749*

"Gold yielded by the capitation tax in this government of Minas Gerais from July 1, 1735 to December 31, 1749."

Matriculation period	Drams	Grains	Equivalent to	Arrobas	Lbs	Drams	Grains
2nd of 1735 and 1st of 1736	517,723	46	"	126	12	91	46
2nd of 1736	279,796	42	"	68	9	116	42
the two of 1737	549,312	28	"	134	3	64	28
the whole of 1738	550,464	60	"	134	12	64	60
the whole of 1739	541,600	00	"	132	7	32	00
the whole of 1740	538,143	00	"	131	12	31	00
the whole of 1741	539,396	00	"	131	22	04	00
the whole of 1742	536,302	00	"	130	29	110	00
the whole of 1743	531,012	00	"	129	20	68	00
the whole of 1744	527,028	00	"	128	21	52	00
the whole of 1745	541,901	00	"	132	9	77	00
the whole of 1746	535,666	00	"	130	24	114	00
the whole of 1747	525,418	00	"	128	8	106	00
the whole of 1748	511,528	00	"	124	28	40	00
the whole of 1749	509,692	00	"	124	13	124	00
Grand total, 1735–1749	7,734,983	32	"	1,888	13	71	32

"The capitation tax on slaves has yielded from July 1, 1735 to December 31, 1749, seven *contos,* 734,983 drams, 32 grains of gold; which are equivalent to 1,888 *arrobas,* 13 pounds, 71 drams, and 32 grains of gold. *N.B.* The capitation tax for the whole of the year 1750 yielded 114 *arrobas* and 907 drams." (Biblioteca Municipal de São Paulo, Codice Costa Matoso, fol. 189.)

For another estimate of the yield from the capitation tax in Minas Gerais from July 1, 1735 to July 31, 1751, see Visconde de Carnaxide, *Brasil na administração Pombalina* (São Paulo, 1940), p. 245.

Appendix III

c) *Gold sent from the Royal Exchequer in Minas Gerais to the Crown in 1750*

"*Table of the gold sent to our Lord the King through his Overseas Council from this* Provedoria *of the Royal Exchequer in Minas Gerais on March 16, 1750, for dispatch in the Rio de Janeiro Fleet of this same year.*"

Drams	Grains		Money
16,099	-24	of gold-dust belonging to this *Provedoria* of the Royal Exchequer in Minas Gerais, sent to Rio de Janeiro on February 19, 1750, included in the two millions, which at 1,500 *reis* the dram is equivalent to	24,149$000
59,264	-04	of gold-dust belonging to this *Provedoria* of the Royal Exchequer in Minas Gerais, also sent for dispatch in the present fleet, which at 1,500 *reis* the dram is equivalent to	88,896$083⅔
26,666	-48	which were remitted from this *Provedoria* in a bill of exchange, which was accepted by the diamond contractor, Captain Felisberto Caldeira Brant, in accordance with his contract	40,000$000
102,030	-04 *Total*		*Total* 153,045$000

Reduced to money		In the following way	Reduced to drams and grains	
	137,877$000	belonging to the balance of the two contracts of the districts of Rio de Janeiro, São Paulo, and Backlands of Bahia and Pernambuco, during one year of the said contracts, totaling 125,610 drams, of which were spent 33,692 drams 28 grains, owing to the non-arrival of the other revenues from the contracts for the tithes, tolls, &c.	91,918-00	
140,495$479	1,882$479⅙	belonging to the 1 (one) per cent for pious Works during one year	1,256-23	93,663 dr. 47 grains
	201$000	belonging to the salaries and allowances of the said period	134-00	
	533$000	belonging to the perquisites of the Overseas Councillors	355-24	

339

Third Parts

6,129$102⅛	4,587$604⅛	belonging to the third parts of the offices from March 3, 1749 until December 31, 1749	3,058-29	4,086-05
	1,541$500	belonging to the third parts of the offices from January 1, to March 10, 1750	1,027-48	
3,009$875	2,412$125	belonging to the new rates from March 1 to December 31, 1749	1,608-06	2,006-42
	597$750	belonging to the new rates from January to March 10, 1750	398-36	
2,140$000	1,715$000	belonging to the contributions of the offices from March 1 to December 31, 1749	1,143-24	1,226-48
	425$000	belonging to the contributions of the offices from January 1 to March 10, 1750	283-24	

(Biblioteca Municipal de São Paulo, Codice Costa Matoso, fol. 193.)

340

APPENDIX IV

THE MATRICULATION OF SLAVES IN MINAS GERAIS, 1735–1750

"Table of the Negroes who were taxed since the beginning of the capitation tax in each of the districts, from 1735 to 1750."

SIX MONTHS OF 1735
(The capitation tax was inaugurated on July 1, 1735)

Place	Slaves	Free
Villa Rica	20,863	316
Mariana	26,892	176
Rio das Mortes	14,400	144
Sabará	24,284	576
Serro Frio	10,102	208

1736 (FIRST MATRICULATION)

Villa Rica	20,904	289
Mariana	26,752	181
Sabará	24,284	483
Rio das Mortes	14,471	159
Serro Frio	8,988	178
Backlands	3,331	94

1736 (SECOND MATRICULATION)

Villa Rica	21,158	870
Mariana	26,828	757
Sabará	23,746	919
Serro Frio	8,329	330
Rio das Mortes	14,629	521

1737 (FIRST MATRICULATION)

Villa Rica	21,405	241
Mariana	26,584	193
Sabará	23,937	813
Serro Frio	8,474	133
Rio das Mortes	14,716	129
Backlands	2,877	34

1737 (SECOND MATRICULATION)

Villa Rica	21,171	227
Mariana	26,684	184
Rio das Mortes	15,083	153
Sabará	27,972	531
Serro Frio	8,274	139

341

The Matriculation of Slaves in Minas Gerais, 1735–1750 (*cont.*)

1738 (FIRST MATRICULATION)

Place	Slaves	Free
Villa Rica	21,012	223
Mariana	26,532	184
Rio das Mortes	15,096	138
Sabará	28,082	516
Serro Frio	8,166	107
Backlands	2,719	38

1738 (SECOND MATRICULATION)

Villa Rica	20,959	208
Mariana	26,432	197
Rio das Mortes	15,532	139
Sabará	29,695	466
Serro Frio	8,198	109

1739 (FIRST MATRICULATION)

Villa Rica	20,883	192
Mariana	26,545	219
Sabará	22,931	288
Rio das Mortes	15,281	128
Serro Frio	8,216	111
Backlands	8,154	36

1739 (SECOND MATRICULATION)

Villa Rica	21,038	206
Mariana	26,171	227
Sabará	22,274	263
Rio das Mortes	15,182	122
Serro Frio	8,266	105

1740 (FIRST MATRICULATION)

Villa Rica	20,667	188
Mariana	26,082	254
Sabará	22,392	243
Rio das Mortes	15,301	170
Serro Frio	8,063	93
Backlands	2,127	20

Appendix IV

1740 (SECOND MATRICULATION)

Place	Slaves	Free
Villa Rica	21,165	187
Mariana	26,131	214
Sabará	22,127	212
Rio das Mortes	15,302	128
Serro Frio	8,166	90

1741 (FIRST MATRICULATION)

Villa Rica	21,171	183
Mariana	26,149	236
Sabará	22,495	209
Rio das Mortes	13,303	125
Serro Frio	8,206	97

1741 (SECOND MATRICULATION)

Villa Rica	21,451	172
Mariana	25,750	239
Sabará	22,369	200
Rio das Mortes	15,328	113
Serro Frio	8,316	86
Backlands	1,498	7

1742 (FIRST MATRICULATION)

Villa Rica	21,492	219
Mariana	25,491	252
Sabará	22,335	217
Rio das Mortes	15,331	111
Serro Frio	8,123	80
Backlands	1,356	19

1742 (SECOND MATRICULATION)

Villa Rica	21,561	247
Mariana	25,425	252
Sabará	22,227	213
Rio das Mortes	15,342	111
Serro Frio	8,135	62

1743 (FIRST MATRICULATION)

Villa Rica	21,673	236
Mariana	25,495	260
Sabará	22,148	216
Rio das Mortes	15,380	117
Serro Frio	8,009	55
Backlands	1,719	7

343

THE MATRICULATION OF SLAVES IN MINAS GERAIS, 1735–1750 *(cont.)*

1743 (SECOND MATRICULATION)

Place	Slaves	Free
Villa Rica	21,746	238
Mariana	24,820	254
Sabará	22,740	221
Rio das Mortes	15,340	121
Serro Frio	7,513	41

1744 (FIRST MATRICULATION)

Villa Rica	21,403	251
Mariana	24,448	248
Sabará	22,146	237
Rio das Mortes	14,923	119
Serro Frio	7,106	57
Backlands	1,349	3

1744 (SECOND MATRICULATION)

Villa Rica	20,488	240
Mariana	23,768	253
Sabará	20,271	219
Rio das Mortes	14,691	111
Serro Frio	6,828	48
Paracatú	5,946	56

In these six months Paracatú was taxed separately for the first time, having been included hitherto in the Backlands *(Sertão)*

1745 (FIRST MATRICULATION)

Villa Rica	20,168	245
Mariana	23,438	232
Sabará	20,253	235
Rio das Mortes	14,420	120
Serro Frio	6,935	50
Paracatú	8,548	81
Backlands	1,604	6

1745 (SECOND MATRICULATION)

Villa Rica	20,036	231
Mariana	23,153	201
Sabará	20,242	254
Rio das Mortes	14,410	99
Serro Frio	6,943	49
Paracatú	7,632	69

344

Appendix IV

1746 (FIRST MATRICULATION)

Place	Slaves	Free
Villa Rica	19,932	235
Mariana	22,891	229
Sabará	20,490	276
Rio das Mortes	13,900	117
Serro Frio	6,952	50
Paracatú	7,581	74
Backlands	1,582	4

1746 (SECOND MATRICULATION)

Villa Rica	19,584	226
Mariana	22,665	240
Sabará	20,706	258
Rio das Mortes	13,662	112
Serro Frio	6,952	50
Paracatú	7,203	71

1747 (FIRST MATRICULATION)

Villa Rica	16,893	221
Mariana	21,866	241
Sabará	20,919	290
Rio das Mortes	13,619	133
Serro Frio	6,968	65
Paracatú	6,620	83
Backlands	1,085	4

1747 (SECOND MATRICULATION)

Villa Rica	19,541	208
Mariana	21,550	253
Sabará	21,094	287
Rio das Mortes	13,518	112
Serro Frio	6,945	49
Paracatú	6,725	67

1748 (FIRST MATRICULATION)

Villa Rica	19,162	208
Mariana	21,331	235
Sabará	20,740	267
Rio das Mortes	13,584	124
Serro Frio	7,005	71
Paracatú	6,412	59
Backlands	1,465	4

THE MATRICULATION OF SLAVES IN MINAS GERAIS, 1735–1750 (*cont.*)

1748 (SECOND MATRICULATION)

Place	Slaves	Free
Villa Rica	19,064	206
Mariana	20,792	233
Sabará	20,183	249
Rio das Mortes	13,518	107
Serro Frio	6,988	65
Paracatú	6,223	58

1749 (FIRST MATRICULATION)

Villa Rica	18,739	189
Mariana	20,539	244
Sabará	20,838	284
Rio das Mortes	13,711	103
Serro Frio	6,980	72
Paracatú	6,019	62
Backlands	1,460	7

1749 (SECOND MATRICULATION)

Villa Rica	18,293	182
Mariana	20,014	230
Sabará	20,819	280
Rio das Mortes	13,715	105
Serro Frio	6,975	51
Paracatú	5,521	60

(Biblioteca Municipal de São Paulo, Codice Costa Matoso, fols. 181–87.)

APPENDIX V

CONTRACTS AND TOLLS IN MINAS GERAIS, 1710–1750

a) *Historical Survey, 1710–1750*

"List of the contracts and revenues which His Majesty has in this captaincy of Minas Gerais; their origin, institution, application and allocation, in accordance with his royal order[s]"

Contract of the highways and entrances.

This contract, which is subdivided into two,—that of the New Road from Rio de Janeiro and of the Old Road from Rio de Janeiro via São Paulo, and that of the road from the Backlands of Bahia and Pernambuco,—was instituted by an assembly of the people of São Paulo and Minas Gerais held on July 17, 1710 by order of the Governor and Captain-General António de Albuquerque de Carvalho, to decide on the best means of establishing and increasing the Royal Exchequer so as to obtain funds for the payment of salaries, wages, and other expenses of the civil and military government personnel which had been authorized by royal decree. This assembly agreed to tax each load of dry goods [*fazenda secca*] which entered these Mines at four drams of gold, and each load of moist goods [*fazenda molhada*] at two*; the slaves at four; the mulattoes at six; and each head of cattle at one. His Majesty being informed of this, was pleased to order by a dispatch of July 24, 1711, the abolition of the small tax on cattle. The King then referred the matter to the same people again in April, 1713, as a result of which the said tax was reduced to the rates which are applicable nowadays, viz; slaves pay two drams of gold each; horses and mules without saddles pay two each; cattle pay one each head; the loads of dry goods are taxed at 1½ drams for every two *arrobas* and each load of moist goods pays ½ dram. . . . The profits from this contract of the highways are not allocated locally; for although it was instituted, as explained above, for the payment of wages, salaries and other government expenses, these payments were subsequently transferred as charges against the revenues of the other contracts, and the whole of this one is remitted through the Overseas Council to our lord the king —excepting only when in an occasional year the profits from the other contracts do not suffice to pay the expenses disbursed by the royal ex-

---

* For an explanation of these terms, see p. 190, above.

chequer, because then the revenue derived from this contract is likewise utilized.**

Contract of the Royal Tithes.

This contract is divided into three, viz., the District of Villa Rica, the
district of the Rio das Mortes, and the combined districts of Sabará and
the Serro do Frio. They derive their origin from those of Rio de
Janeiro, and they were instituted in these Mines in February, 1715, by
virtue of an order signed by the former governor of these Mines, Dom
Braz Balthazar da Silveira in February, 1715 . . .

The proceeds of this contract of the royal tithes are used to pay the
salaries of the governor and troops of dragoons, the salaries and al-
lowances of the ministers of justice, the *Provedor* and other officials
of the Exchequer, of the Vicars, and other expenses to which the Exchequer is liable. However, it is not clear by what order His Majesty
was pleased to make this allocation, but it can be inferred from the
[proceedings of the] assembly and the order which instituted the contract of the highways as mentioned above.

Contract of the tolls of the Rio das Mortes.

This began in 1714, by virtue of a royal order of April 29, 1711 sent
to the Governor, António de Albuquerque, ordering him to give all
support and favor for establishing a monopoly contract to the highest
bidder for exacting tolls at the crossing places of all rivers on the way
to Minas Gerais. This order cannot be found in this *Provedoria,* nor
in any of the others; and it is understood that it is by the governor's
order that tolls over some of the river crossings are nowadays farmed
out to the highest bidder, in the belief that they will yield something
for the Royal Exchequer. In that of this crossing there is usually a
charge of eighty *reis* in money for each person, and 160 *reis* for each
horse . . . The revenue derived from this contract is likewise applied
to all expenses of the Royal Exchequer, in the same way as that of the
royal tithes, without further clarification.

Contract for the tolls of the Rio Grande.†

This contract began in the year 1714, and the usual charge is four
vintens of silver for each person, and half a *pataca* of silver for each
horse, whether a pack horse or a riding horse. Double loads pay two

** See Myriam Ellis, "Contribuição ao estudo do abastecimento das zonas
mineradoras do Brasil no século XVIII," in *Revista de Historia,* Nr. 36 (São
Paulo, 1958), pp. 429–467, for further details on these tolls and taxes.

† There are many Rio Grandes in Brazil, and this particular one may have
been that in the district of the Rio das Mortes.

silver *vintens* extra, and each ox pays half a *pataca* . . . The revenue derived from this contract is applied in the same way as the former.

Contract for the tolls of the River Paroupeba.
This contract began in the year 1724, and each person is charged four *vintens* of gold, or half a *pataca* of silver; each horse is charged half a *pataca* of gold, or a *pataca* of silver; and each load is charged four *vintens* of gold. The revenue is applied in the same way as the foregoing.

Contract for the tolls of the Rio das Velhas, called Santo Hipolito Piedade and Bicudo.
This contract originated in the year 1725, and the usual charge is four *vintens* of silver for each person, and six *vintens* for each horse. A Negro carrying a load pays twenty *reis,* and a pack horse two *vintens.*

Contract for the tolls of Maypendy.
This contract began in 1716 and only lasted for one year, since people gave up using this crossing.

Contract for the tolls of the River Jequitinhonha.
This began in 1725 and likewise was soon dropped for the same reason.

Contract for the tolls of the River São Francisco.
This began on September 29, 1738, being farmed out to Ignacio Fagundes and Ignacio da Costa Neves.

Contract for the tolls of the Rio Verde in the District of the Rio das Mortes.
This began on April 20, 1749, being farmed out for three years to Manuel de Sousa Vieira. The usual charge for each person is eighty *reis* in silver, and 160 for each horse."

[Added in another hand] "The contracts for the tithes since their creation in the year 1728 were always organized and farmed out separately. On August 1, 1728 they were farmed out together for the three-year period ending on July 31, 1731. On August 1, 1731 they were farmed out for another three years, ending on July 31, 1734. From 1734 to 1737 they were farmed out separately again. In the year 1738 they were farmed out for the account of the Crown, the administrator being João Fernandes de Oliveira. And from the year 1739 to the year 1752 they have always remained united without any separation at all." ‡

‡ For further details, see Manuel Cardozo, "Tithes in Colonial Minas Gerais," in *The Catholic Historical Review,* Vol. XXXVIII (July, 1952), pp. 175–182.

(Biblioteca Municipal de São Paulo, Codice Costa Matoso, fols. 325–326.)

b) *Perquisites paid by the contractors of the tolls, 1750*

To the Lord General	1,200	drams of gold
To the *Doutor Provedor*	800	" " "
To the Dr. Procurator of the Crown and Exchequer	200	" " "
To the Scrivener of the Exchequer	200	" " "
To the Treasurer	200	" " "
To his Assistant	100	" " "
To the Porter and Book keeper	50	" " "
To the Bailiff	50	" " "
To his clerk	50	" " "

(Biblioteca Municipal de São Paulo, Codice Costa Matoso, fol. 328.)*

* At fol. 329 of the same codex is another and much more detailed list showing the perquisites paid to government officials at Lisbon and in Minas Gerais by the contractor of the tithes in the latter captaincy on August 1, 1751. The total paid in Lisbon was 2,399$744 and in Minas 6,700$500.

APPENDIX VI

The Cargoes of the Brazil Fleets in 1749

i) "List of the commodities and capital comprising the cargoes of the twenty merchant and two warships of the Rio de Janeiro Fleet, which left there on March 26 and entered this port of Lisbon city on June 23, 1749, commanded by D. Manuel Henriques de Noronha in the flagship *Nossa Senhora das Necessidades.*

137,585   *cruzados* in 55,034U000 in money in the *capitania.**
106,567½   *cruzados* in 42,627U000 in money in the *almiranta.***
1,432,931¾ *cruzados* in 573,172 drams of gold dust in the *capitania.*
1,428,300   *cruzados* in 571,290 drams of gold dust in the *almiranta.*
173,403   *cruzados* in 46,241 drams of gold bars in the *capitania.*
179,062   *cruzados* in 47,570 drams of gold bars in the *almiranta.*

The capital for the account of private individuals in both warships was:

9,971,886 *cruzados* in 3,998,754U411 in money.
1,190,018 *cruzados* in 317,445 drams of gold dust.
479,865   *cruzados* in 127,964 drams in gold bars.

So that this capital in gold totaled 13,784,655 *cruzados* and 294 *reis.*

Diamonds.
2,185   drams, 6 grains, and 6 *avos* in the *capitania.*
2,186¾ drams, in the *almiranta.*

Other commodities.
3,057   chests of sugar.
640   cases of sugar.
247   loaves of sugar.
41,305   untanned hides.
4,746   hides.
1,043   boards.
692   dozens of *Tapinhoen* boards.
1,516   barrels of honey, and of [manioc] flour.
873   ship's timbers.
150   pipes of fish oil.
1,870   elephant tusks.

* *Capitania:* flagship of the "General" (equivalent to the English admiral) of a Portuguese fleet.
** *Almiranta:* flagship of the second-in-command (*Almirante*, "Admiral" in Portuguese, corresponding to the English vice-Admiral).

1,753	jacaranda tree trunks.
663	bales of whalebone.
311	bags of wool.
2,851	tree trunks of brazilwood.
1,191	switches (rods) of mangrove trees for trellises.
860	shafts for coaches.
230	slaves"

(Biblioteca Municipal de São Paulo, Codice Costa Matoso, printed sheet at fol. 505.)

ii) "List of the capital and commodities comprising the lading of the thirty-nine merchant ships of the Fleet of Pernambuco, convoyed by the warship *Nossa Senhora de Lampadoza,* commanded by the *capitão-de-mar-e-guerra* José Gonçalves Lage, which left that place on March 1, 1749, and entered the port of Lisbon on July 20, of the same year.

15,056	*cruzados* in 6,002,400 [*reis*] in money of the *donativo*.†
30,460	*cruzados* and 320 reis in 8,122 drams and 64 grains of gold dust.
2,140	*cruzados,* 220 *reis* in 570 drams and 60 grains in gold bars.
8,512	*cruzados* in 3,404,800 *reis* in money for the Bull.‡
751	*cruzados* in 200 drams and 24 grains of gold dust for the same.

For private individuals.

787,487	*cruzados* in coin for private individuals.
87,900	*cruzados* in 23,440 drams of gold dust.
696	*cruzados* in 199 drams of gold bits and pieces.
50,830	*cruzados* 300 *reis* in 20,232 *reis* in money of the manifest.

The whole being worth 1,013,735 *cruzados*.

In goods.

13,290	chests of sugar.
1,221	cases of sugar.
1,022	loaves of sugar.
98,260	hides.
37,360	tanned hides.
16,251	raw hides.

† Cf. pp. 318–319 of the text for the *Donativos Reais* or forced contributions to the Royal Exchequer.

‡ *Bulla da Cruzada,* Bull of the Crusade, presumably. For an account of this remarkable means of raising money, see [J. Colbatch], *An Account of the Court of Portugal* (London, 1700), Part I, pp. 24–39.

528	deerskins.
553	thick boards.
753	barrels of sweetmeats.
399	barrels of molasses.
359	barrels of [manioc] flour.
4	barrels of *pacaconha*.
7,090	quintals of brazilwood.
45	quintals of violet wood.
60	quintals of *tatajuba*.
128	rods for trellises.
23	shafts for coaches.
25	beams.
140	slaves."

(Biblioteca Municipal de São Paulo, Codice Costa Matoso, printed sheet at fol. 507.)

iii) "List of the commodities comprising the cargoes of the five ships which left the Maranhão and Grão-Pará on June 28, 1749, and which began to enter the port of this city of Lisbon from the 15th to the 20th of August, 1749.

To wit:

48,148	*arrobas* 19 lbs. of cacao.
1,022	*arrobas* 19 lbs. of coarse cloves.
236	*arrobas* 16 lbs. of fine cloves.
2,355	*arrobas* 9 lbs. of garden parsley
2,307	*arrobas* 9 lbs. of coffee.
8,047	*arrobas* 4 lbs. of sugar.
245	*arrobas* 12 lbs. of cotton.
170	*arrobas* 4 lbs. of cotton thread.
20	*arrobas* 20 lbs. of *ourocú* for ink.
2	*arrobas* of chocolate.
5	*arrobas* of medicinal bark.
24	turtle shells.
15	*arrobas* of *quina-quina* (for quinine).
8,000	raw hides."

(Biblioteca Municipal de São Paulo, Codice Costa Matoso, printed sheet at fol. 506. Reproduced in facsimile on the plate opposite p. 177 of Vol. II of Borba de Moraes, *Bibliographia Brasiliana*.)

N.B. Unfortunately, the three printed news sheets giving the cargo lists of the above three Brazil Fleets during the year 1749 do not include that from Bahia. Judging by the amount of gold shipped in the Pernambuco Fleet, however, it is possible that much of this came from Bahia.

APPENDIX VII

PORTUGUESE MONEY, WEIGHTS AND MEASURES, 1700–1750

a) *Money in the reign of Dom Pedro II, 1683–1706*
   (struck in Portugal)

GOLD

Moeda of	4,400 *reis.*	*Moeda*	4,000 *rs.*
½ *Moeda*	2,200 *rs.*	½ *Moeda*	2,000 *rs.*
¼ *Moeda*	1,100 *rs.*	¼ *Moeda*	1,000 *rs.*

SILVER

Cruzado	400 *rs.*	*Vintem*	20 *rs.*
Tostão	100 *rs.*		

(struck in Brazil)

GOLD

Moeda of	4,800 *rs.* (Rio)	*Moeda*	4,000 *rs.* ⎫ (Rio,
½ *Moeda*	2,400 *rs.* (Rio)	½ *Moeda*	2,000 *rs.* ⎬ Bahia,
¼ *Moeda*	1,200 *rs.* (Rio)	¼ *Moeda*	1,000 *rs.* ⎭ Recife)

SILVER

Pataca of	320 *rs.* ⎫ (Rio,
Vintem	20 *rs.* ⎬ Bahia, Recife)

b) *Money in the reign of Dom João V, 1706–1750*
   (struck in Portugal)

GOLD

Dobrão of 5 *Moedas*	24,000 *rs.*	*Moeda* of	4,800 *rs.*
Dobrão of	12,000 *rs.*	½ *Moeda*	2,400 *rs.*
Dobra of 8 *Escudos*	12,800 *rs.*	¼ *Moeda*	1,200 *rs.*
Dobra of 4 *Escudos*		*Escudo*	1,600 *rs.*
(Peça)	6,400 *rs.*	½ *Escudo*	800 *rs.*
Dobra of 2 *Escudos*		¼ *Escudo* (*Cruzado*)	400 *rs.*
(½ Peça)	3,200 *rs.*	*Cruzado novo*	480 *rs.*

SILVER

Cruzado	480 *rs.*	*Vintem*	20 *rs.*
Tostão	100 *rs.*		

Appendix VII
(struck in Brazil)

GOLD

Dobrão of	.. 24,000 *rs.*	(Minas)	*Dobra*	..... 3,200 *rs.*	(Rio,	
Dobrão	.... 12,000 *rs.*	(")	*Escudo*	.... 1,600 *rs.*	Bahia,	
Dobrão	.... 12,800 *rs.*	(Rio,	½ *Escudo*	.. 800 *rs.*	Minas	
		Bahia,	¼ *Escudo*	.. 400 *rs.*	Rio,	
Dobra	..... 6,400 *rs.*	Minas)			Minas)	

SILVER

2 *Patacas*	... 640 *rs.*	(Rio)	½ *Pataca*	.. 160 *rs.*	(")
Pataca	..... 320 *rs.*	(")			

COPPER

Vintem	.... 20 *rs.*	(Bahia, rarely)	10 *Reis* .... 10 *rs.*	(Bahia, rarely)

N.B. At various times in this reign the Lisbon Mint coined *Moedas* of gold of various denominations (4$, 2$, and 1$) and of silver (640, 320, 160, and 80 *reis*) and of copper (20, 10, and 5 *reis*) for the State of Maranhão; of copper for circulation in Minas alone (40 and 20 *reis*), and of copper for circulation throughout Brazil (20 and 10 *reis*). The above tables are derived from the more detailed ones in S. Sombra, *História Monetária do Brasil Colonial* (Rio de Janeiro, 1938), pp. 121, 186–187.

c) *Approximate equivalents in English and French money*

Before 1714 the English Treasury officially valued the *moeda* at 28/- and thereafter at 27/6 (information from Mr. H. Fisher M.A. of Exeter University). The silver *cruzado* of 480 *reis* seems to have been valued at between 2/6 and 3/-, though an anonymous report on Portuguese trade and commerce about 1730 (Brit. Mus., Lansdowne MS, 820) equates 360 *reis* with 2/- sterling, and so 180 *reis* with 1/-. According to John Stevens, writing in 1705, "an hundred *Reys* is eight pence English" (*Present State of Portugal,* p. 79).

A French naval officer who visited Rio de Janeiro in 1748 gives the following table of monetary equivalents:

GOLD

Dobrão of	12,000 *reis* = 80	French *Livres*	
½ *Dobra* of	6,400 *reis* = 40	"	"
¼ *Dobra* of	3,200 *reis* = 20	"	"

355

SILVER

2-*Pataca* of	640 *reis* =	4	"	"
Pataca of	320 *reis* =	2	"	"
½ *Pataca* of	160 *reis* =	1	"	"

COPPER

¼ *Pataca* of	80 *reis* =	10	"	*sous*
Vintem of	20 *reis* =	2.6	"	*denier*
½ Vintem of	10 *Reis* =	1.3	"	"

He added: "Le Reis est ideal, et vaut un denier et demi du Pais, mais il n'y a pas d'espece effective au dessous d'un demi vingtain" (*vintem*) (M. Cardozo, ed. "A French Document on Rio de Janeiro, 1748," in *HAHR,* Vol. XXI, August, 1941, p. 433.)

d) *Table of weights*

quintal = 2 or 4 *arrobas,* according to the region. The Portuguese hundredweight.

arroba = 25 to 32 *arratels,* according to the region. The Portuguese quarter.

arratel = 12 to 16 *onças* (ounces) according to region. The Portuguese pound.

marco = 8 *onças*-4608 *grãos.*

onça = 8 *oitavas* (drams).

oitava = 72 *grãos* (grains).

e) *Measures of capacity*

These were likely to vary widely both in Portugal and in her overseas possessions, but the most common ones were:

almude (liquid) = 26 *almudes* to the average Portuguese pipe of wine (*pipa*).

alqueire (dry) = 1⅗ peck = 13 litres.

canada (liquid) = ¹⁄₁₂ *almude* = 3 English pints.

moio = 60 *alqueires.*

pipa = 25 to 27 *almudes.* About two hogsheads.

Appendix VII

f) *Measures of length.*

légua = league (3755¹⁄₁₅ geometrical paces).

palmo = span, which varied regionally but is usually considered as 22 cm.

vara = yard, measuring 1,096 millimeters as a rule, but varied regionally.

braça = fathom (6 feet).

APPENDIX VIII

a) *Monarchs of Portugal and Brazil, 1641–1822.*

Dom João IV, December, 1640–November, 1656.

Dom Affonso VI, November, 1656–November, 1667 (deposed). Died, 1683.

Dom Pedro II, Regent from November, 1667 to September, 1683. King, September, 1683–December, 1706.

Dom João V, December, 1706–July, 1750.

Dom José, August, 1750–February, 1777.

Dona Maria I, February, 1777–February, 1792 (deposed). Died 1816.

Dom João VI, Regent, March, 1792–March, 1816. King, March, 1816–1826.

(Brazilian independence declared, September, 1822, and recognized by Portugal in 1825.)

b) *Viceroys and Governors-General of Brazil at Bahia, 1694–1750.*

(GG) Dom João de Lencastre, May, 1694–July, 1702.

(GG) D. Rodrigo da Costa, July, 1702–September, 1705.

(GG) Luís Cesar de Menezes, September, 1705–May, 1710.

(GG) D. Lourenço de Almada, May, 1710–October, 1711.

(GG) Pedro de Vasconcellos de Sousa, Conde de Castello Melhor, October, 1711–June, 1714.

(VR) D. Pedro de Noronha, Conde de Villa Verde and Marques de Angeja, June, 1714–August, 1718.

(GG) D. Sancho de Faro e Sousa, Conde de Vimeiro, August, 1718–October, 1719.

Interim government of the Archbishop, D. Sebastião Monteiro da Vide, garrison commander, João de Araujo e Azevedo, and the chancellor, Caetano de Brito de Figueiredo, October, 1719–November, 1720.

(VR) Vasco Fernandes Cesar de Menezes, Conde de Sabugosa, November, 1720–May, 1735.

(VR) André de Mello de Castro, Conde das Galveas, May, 1735–December, 1749.

c) *Governors of Rio de Janeiro, 1697–1763.*

Artur de Sá e Menezes, July, 1697–July, 1702.

Alvaro da Silveira e Albuquerque, July, 1702–April, 1704.

Interim government of the Bishop, D. Francisco de São Jeronimo, and of colonels Gregorio de Castro Morais and Martim Correa Vasques, April, 1704–August, 1705.

D. Fernando Martins Mascarenhas e Lencastre, August, 1705–June, 1709.

António de Albuquerque Coelho de Carvalho, June, 1709–June, 1710, during most of which time he was absent in Minas Gerais and São Paulo, being substituted by the garrison commander, Francisco de Castro de Morais, who was the effective governor from April, 1710 until the French invasion of 1711. António de Albuquerque Coelho de Carvalho reassumed office October, 1711–June, 1713.

Francisco Xavier de Tavora, June, 1713–November, 1716.

Manuel de Almeida Castello-Branco, November, 1716–June, 1717.

António de Brito Freire de Menezes, June, 1717–May, 1719.

Ayres de Saldanha de Albuquerque, May, 1719–May, 1725.

Luís Vahia Monteiro, May, 1725–October, 1732, when he became insane.

Manuel de Freitas da Fonseca, October, 1732–July, 1733.

Gomes Freire de Andrada, July, 1733–January, 1763. The government of Minas Gerais was subordinated to him from March 25, 1735 onwards, and that of São Paulo from December, 1737 to February, 1739. From August 9, 1748, his government comprised the greater part of Brazil, viz., the captaincies of Rio de Janeiro, Minas Gerais, São Paulo, Goiás, Mato Grosso, Santa Catharina, Rio Grande do Sul, and Colonia do Sacramento. During his frequent absences from Rio de Janeiro (which are listed in *PANRJ,* X, pp. ii–iv) the interim government of Rio was exercised by José da Silva Paes, Mathias Coelho de Sousa, José António Freire de Andrada, and Patricio Manuel de Figueiredo.

d) *Captaincy of São Paulo and Minas Gerais, 1710–1721.*

António de Albuquerque Coelho de Carvalho, June, 1710–June, 1713.

D. Braz Balthazar de Silveira, August, 1713–September, 1717.

D. Pedro de Almeida, Conde de Assumar (later, Marques de Castello Novo and Alorna, Viceroy of India 1744–1750), September, 1717–August, 1721.

e) *Captaincy of Minas Gerais, 1721–1752.*

D. Lourenço de Almeida, August, 1721–September, 1732.

André de Mello de Castro, Conde das Galveas, September, 1732–March, 1735.

Gomes Freire de Andrada, March, 1735–May, 1736.
Martinho de Mendonça de Pina e de Proença (acting), May, 1736–December, 1737.
Gomes Freire de Andrada, December, 1737–February, 1752.

f) *São Paulo, 1721–1748.*

Rodrigo Cesar de Menezes, September, 1721–August, 1727.
António da Silva Caldeira Pimentel, August, 1727–August, 1732.
António Luís de Tavora, Conde de Sarzedas, August, 1732–August, 1737.
Gomes Freire de Andrada, December, 1737–February, 1739.
D. Luis de Mascarenhas (later, Conde d'Alva and Viceroy of India), from February, 1739 until the extinction of the captaincy of São Paulo in 1748 and its incorporation into the governorship of Gomes Freire de Andrada.

g) *Pernambuco, 1693–1756.*

Caetano de Mello e Castro, June, 1693–March, 1699.
D. Fernando Martins Mascarenhas e Lencastre, March, 1699–September, 1703.
Francisco de Castro e Morais, September, 1703–June, 1707.
Sebastião de Castro e Caldas, June, 1707, until his flight to Bahia, November, 1709.
The Bishop, D. Manuel Alvares da Costa (acting), November, 1709–October, 1711.
Felix José Machado de Mendonça, October, 1711–June, 1715.
D. Lourenço de Almeida, June, 1715–July, 1718.
Manuel de Sousa Tavares e Tavora, July, 1718–January, 1721.
D. Francisco de Sousa (interim), January, 1721–January, 1722.
D. Manuel Rolim de Moura, January, 1722–November, 1727.
Duarte Sodré Pereira Tibão, November, 1727–August, 1737.
Henrique Luís Pereira Freire de Andrada, August, 1737–January, 1746.
D. Marcos de Noronha, Conde dos Arcos, January, 1746–March, 1749.
Luís Correia de Sá, March, 1749–February, 1756.

h) *Goiás, 1749–1755.*

D. Marcos de Noronha, Conde dos Arcos, November, 1749–August, 1755.

Appendix VIII

i) *Mato Grosso, 1751–1762.*

D. António Rolim de Moura Tavares, Conde de Azambuja, January, 1751–December, 1762.

j) *Maranhão and Grão-Pará, 1690–1751.*

António de Albuquerque Coelho de Carvalho, May, 1690–June, 1701.
Fernão Carrilho (interim), June, 1701–July, 1702.
D. Manuel Rolim de Moura Tavares, July, 1702–September, 1705.
João Velasco de Molina, September, 1705–January, 1707.
Christovão da Costa Freire, January, 1707–June, 1718.
Bernardo Pereira de Berredo, June, 1718–July, 1722.
João da Maia da Gama, July, 1722–June, 1728.
Alexandre de Sousa Freire, June, 1728–July, 1732.
José da Serra, July, 1732–March, 1736.
António Duarte de Barros (interim), March, 1736–September, 1737.
João de Abreu Castello-Branco, September, 1737–August, 1747.
Francisco Pedro de Mendonça Gorjão, August, 1747–September, 1751.

The governors of minor captaincies, such as Paraíba, Ceará, Espirito Santo, have been omitted from this appendix, but their names can be found, together with more details of those given here, in F. A. Varnhagen, "Auxilios chronologicos para verificar as datas e os factos," in *Historia Geral do Brasil antes da sua separação e independencia de Portugal* (3d. ed.; São Paulo, n.d.), Vol. V, 297–388. My own abbreviated list is compiled principally from this source, with a few corrections from the *PANRJ* and other works.

PERSONALIA

Dom Pedro de Almeida Portugal, third Count of Assumar, and successively Marquis of Castello-Novo and of Alorna, was born at Lisbon on September 29, 1688. He served throughout the War of the Spanish Succession, particularly distinguishing himself at the battles of Saragoça and Villa-Viçosa in 1710. When the fighting ended in January, 1713, he commanded the Portuguese troops who returned overland through a hostile and devastated countryside. As governor of the vast captaincy of São Paulo and Minas Gerais in 1717–1721, his name is imperishably connected in Brazil with the suppression of the revolt at Villa Rica, as described in the text. When visiting the *Morro da Queimada* in March, 1959, I met a *faisqueiro* who shook his head over the misdeeds of the *Conde-Governador*.

After his return to Portugal, the Count of Assumar occupied several (sinecure) military commands and was elected a member of the Royal Academy of History in 1733. He had received an exceptionally good education for his age and nation, being well read in Latin, French, Italian, and Spanish, and was genuinely interested in mathematical, philosophical, and historical studies. A contemporary French nobleman described him as being one of the four best educated fidalgos in Portugal, the other two being the fourth and fifth Counts of Ericeira (father and son), and the Marquis of Alegrete. He was certainly conscious of his superior education, for he wrote to the fourth Count of Ericeira from Minas Gerais (April 26, 1718): "Have pity on a man living amongst Kaffirs and send me some of the papers published by the Academy."

Dom Pedro de Almeida thus ranked as one of the *estrangeirados,* or fidalgos who were strongly influenced by foreign ideas, and as such he was regarded by Dom João V with mingled respect and dislike. "I don't like either Ericeira or Assumar," the King wrote to his crony, Cardinal da Mota, when discussing the suitability of various noblemen for the vacant embassy at Madrid in 1739. The reason for D. João V's antipathy to these two men is not altogether clear, but their real or suspected anticlericalism may have had something to do with it. Both were "kicked upstairs" by being appointed viceroys of India, at times when (Ericeira in 1740, and Assumar in 1744) they did not particularly want to go. "I am more afraid of these people than I am of the Marathas," wrote the King of the two Ericeiras in 1740, at a time when the Hindu invaders were carrying all before them in Portuguese India, and in words which anticipated the Duke of Wellington's remark about some of his own generals: "I don't know what effect they will have on the enemy, but by God they frighten me."

Assumar pleaded poverty and the difficulty of providing for his large family when appointed viceroy in succession to the fifth Count of Ericeira in 1744, but D. João V gilded the pill by creating him Marquis of Castello-Novo on the eve of his departure. His six-year viceroyalty (1744–1750) was one of the few bright interludes in the unhappy history of eighteenth-century Portuguese Asia, and both his military and administrative talents were freely acknowledged at the time and gratefully remembered for long afterwards. On the other hand, he was also accused of illegally enriching himself through the sale of Crown offices and by trading through third parties. These allegations, whether justified or not, drew on him a severe reprimand from the Crown in the same year that his marquisate of Castello-Novo was changed to that of Alorna, in order to commemorate his capture of the Maratha stronghold of that name in May, 1746.

After his return to Lisbon in 1751 he was not employed in high office again, although he rendered useful service at the time of the great earthquake in 1755. Some authorities attribute to him on the day of that unprecedented catastrophe the famous remark which is usually credited to Pombal—"bury the dead, succor the living, and close the gates"—in reply to the King's distracted query to those around him as to what should be done. His semi-disgrace was undoubtedly owing to the enmity of Pombal, who already possessed sufficient influence with the new king, D. José I, to induce this monarch to refuse audience to the ex-viceroy until the latter had cleared himself of the charges of corruption laid against him. Since Pombal likewise contrived that D. Pedro de Almeida should have no opportunity of making a judicial rebuttal of these charges, he died a dissatisfied man in 1756. His son and heir, who was imprisoned for eighteen years in the subterranean dungeons of Junqueira on the trumped-up charge of being involved in the alleged plot of his in-laws, the Tavoras, against the life of the King, vainly tried after his belated release to secure a judicial investigation which would clear his father's name.

Brazilians who still execrate the memory of the third Count of As-

363

sumar for his suppression of the revolt at Villa Rica in 1720, may be intrigued to know that twenty-four years later he publicly denounced in Goa the earlier Portuguese cruelties and misbehavior in Asia, in terms which savor strongly of the anti-colonial sentiments of the Enlightenment.

MANUEL NUNES VIANA, after his début in the so-called "War of the Emboabas" described in Chapter iii of this work, retired to his vast estates in the São Francisco River valley, where he held the post of captain-major of that region. According to his friends he was a great civilizing influence there and cleared the district of wrong-doers; but according to his enemies he was the arch-villain of all the unscrupulous *poderosos do sertão*. The former opinion was propagated by the viceroy at Bahia, the Marquis of Angeja, who corresponded with him on friendly and at times almost fulsome terms, and who assured the Crown of Viana's loyalty and integrity. The unfavorable viewpoint was maintained by the Count of Assumar, who denounced Manuel Nunes Viana in vituperative terms—"No worse plague ever came from Hell, nor did God ever inflict a worse punishment on the dwellers in the backlands of Brazil." The Crown and its Overseas Councillors at Lisbon not unnaturally wavered between such diametrically opposed views expressed by the senior authorities concerned, and remained for long undecided how to treat him. In mid-April, 1717, the King finally ordered the viceroy at Bahia to send Nunes Viana back to Lisbon in the first fleet; but he can hardly have complied with this order since in October, 1718 the culprit gave a formal undertaking to Assumar at Villa Rica that he would not interfere with the supply of cattle along the São Francisco trail to Minas Gerais, as he had been accused (unjustly, so he claimed) of doing. In 1724 we find Nunes Viana applying for leave to return to Portugal with the object of placing some of his daughters in a nunnery at Santarem. The Crown granted this request, after some hesitation, in February, 1725; but meanwhile Pedro Leolino Mariz had succeeded in arresting him and sending him to Bahia, where the Viceroy Count of Sabugosa gave him the city of Salvador as his open prison. On July 28, 1725, Nuno Marques Pereira addressed to him here the dedication of the *Compendio Narrativo do Peregrino da America,* which was published in Lisbon three years later, probably at Nunes Viana's expense. It is not clear whether he did in fact return to Portugal, but, as related in the text, he gained his case at Court, allegedly through the intercession of the Infante Dom Francisco, D. João V's scapegrace brother. He was subsequently given official recognition for his real or alleged past services to the Crown, these distinctions including a knighthood in the Order of Christ, a militia colonelcy, and the *Alcaidaria-mór* of Maragogipe. He was back at Bahia (assuming he had left it) by mid-June, 1730, and was evidently then in the good graces of the viceroy. His death is variously stated to have occurred in 1735 (Calmon) and in 1738 (Golgher), but not even the approximate date of his birth has been ascertained. He left a family of seven children, all of them illegitimate, and is said to have become exceedingly obese in his last years. A long-standing tradition at Bahia alleges that he threw disobedient slaves and other persons who offended him into a lake at his *fazenda,* where they were torn to pieces by *piranhas,* the meat-eating fish which is one of the major hazards of many Brazilian streams.

The evidence about Manuel Nunes Viana is so conflicting that further extensive research is required before a satisfactory assessment can be made of his life and influence, though it is obvious that he was one of the major figures in Bahia and Minas Gerais during his lifetime. His signature in 1717 is that of a barely literate man, but even the Count of Assumar admitted that he had pretensions to culture. He was the proud possessor of Soror Maria Agreda's *Mystica Ciudad de Dios* (1685), Ginés Pérez de Hita's *Las Guerras Civiles de Granada* (1595–1619), the Count of Ericeira's *Portugal Restaurado* (1710), and other books which one would not expect to find in the remote Brazilian Backlands. In addition to sponsoring the publication of the *Compendio Narrativo do Peregrino da America* in 1728, Nunes Viana also subsidized the third volume of the partial edition of Diogo do Couto's *Decadas* which was printed at Lisbon in 1736, judging from the publisher's dedication to this Luso-Brazilian Maecenas.

João da Maia da Gama. Born at Aveiro in 1673, he studied philosophy at the University of Coimbra, but left without completing the course to enlist in the India-bound flagship of the young Viceroy, Count of Villa-Verde, which left the Tagus in March, 1692. The voyage was a disastrous one, sickness, storms, and an enforced stay at the unhealthy island of Moçambique so decimating the passengers and crew, that when the *Nossa Senhora da Conceição* finally reached Goa under jury-rig on May 26, 1693, only 84 out of her original complement of 580 souls were still alive. João da Maia da Gama had rendered yeoman service throughout the voyage, though suffering like everyone else from scurvy and fever, particularly in a hurricane in the Indian Ocean on the night of May 14–15, 1693, which dismasted the ship. Prostrated by illness for months on end after his arrival at Goa, he first saw action in a fight with an English ship during a cruise along the Kanara coast in August, 1694. In January of the following year, he embarked in the squadron which the viceroy led northwards, and he took a prominent part in the destruction of three Arab (Omani) frigates off Rajapur, receiving two bullet wounds in this action. For most of the next two years he served in the Persian Gulf, distinguishing himself in the defeat of another Omani squadron off Cape Ras-al-Hadd (May 13, 1697), and in the defense of the Portuguese factory at Bandar Kung, which was attacked by the Khan of Lara in July of the same year. He was severely wounded on this last occasion by a blunderbuss bullet which passed through his left side, damaging the kidneys, and inflicting injuries which were never properly healed during the rest of his life. While still slowly and painfully recovering he volunteered to sail in an expedition for the relief of Mombasa, which was then besieged by the Arabs of Oman, who eventually took the place on December 13, 1698; but the viceroy rejected his application on medical grounds, and insisted that he should embark with him for Portugal in the great ship *São Pedro Gonçalves*. The Count of Villa-Verde was evidently something of a Jonah, for his return voyage was almost as difficult as his outward one had been six years previously. The *São Pedro* left Goa on December 20, 1698, with 208 people on board, and after a stormy passage round the Cape, reached Bahia on April 23, 1699, with just over half of them left alive. The last lap of the voyage was uneventful, and the Indiaman dropped anchor in the Tagus on October 24 of the same year with only one more fatal casualty.

Early in 1700 he sailed for Mombasa as captain of the frigate *Nossa Senhora do Bom Successo,* but she was accidentally burnt at Bahia en route. Nothing daunted, he fitted out another frigate, the *Santa Escolastica,* with the help of the governor-general of Brazil, but she foundered with great loss of life on November 27, 1700, before she had cleared the Bay of All Saints. João da Maia, who was a strong swimmer, was one of about seventy-five survivors. Despite the crippling nature of his Persian wound, which gave him recurrent trouble and periods of pain, Maia da Gama fought in the early years of the War of the Spanish Succession. His most spectacular feat was in the capture of the little Spanish town of Ferrera, when he vaulted from his horse over the defenders' bulwarks and was the first of the attackers to enter the place under a heavy fire. He also served in the Portuguese squadron which fought under Sir John Leake when the latter destroyed the French Fleet blockading Gibraltar in the Bay of Algeciras in March, 1705. He was governor of Paraíba, 1708–1717, and of the Maranhão-Grão Pará, 1722–1728, as related in the text. After his return to Lisbon, he continued to support the Jesuits of that province against the intrigues of their enemies at court; but his suppurating bullet wound remained troublesome and was the prime cause of his sudden death on November 11, 1731. He was married to a lady from Azurara near Villa do Conde, by whom he had one son and four daughters. He is described as being tall and well-made, with a swarthy complexion, narrow face, black eyes, and a big nose, with a smallpox scar in the middle of his forehead. A Lisbon diarist who seldom mentioned the appointment of a fidalgo to high office without adding some derogatory remark, observed when João da Maia da Gama's appointment as governor of Paraíba was announced, that he was a "very honorable and very worthy man." This was the simple truth as his whole life showed.

ANTÓNIO RODRIGUES DA COSTA. Born at Setubal on December 29, 1656, he studied at the Jesuit College of Santo Antão in Lisbon, where he excelled particularly in Latin, subsequently acting as tutor in this language to several noblemen at Court. He was also proficient in classical Greek, Italian, French, and Spanish, this linguistic skill earning him various official appointments, including the secretaryship of two separate diplomatic missions to Germany (1686) and Austria (1707). Appointed Overseas Councillor in 1709, although he never had first-hand experience of one or another of the Portuguese colonies, as had most of his colleagues, he soon became and remained one of the most trusted and percipient advisers of the Crown in the field of colonial policy. He was a founder member of the Royal Academy of History in 1720, and was created a privy councillor in 1728. Throughout his long life he displayed as much devotion to learning as assiduity in the dispatch of official business; but the demands of this last prevented him from publishing more than a few works (mostly of an historical nature) in Latin and Portuguese. He was a pious but not a bigoted Catholic, and can in some ways be numbered among the *estrangeirados*. In his private correspondence with Manuel de Sousa, the Director of the Mint at Rio de Janeiro, he more than once criticized the "incredible slowness" with which the Crown operated, and the tendency of Dom João V to squander the gold he received from South America on *"empregos inuteis"* instead of on constructive projects such as subsidizing the emigration of married families to Brazil. "The sole objective here is to get as much gold as possible from Brazil for His Majesty," he wrote on February 3, 1720, adding despondently, "and it will all be little enough to squander." He realized that the exactions of the Crown, or of corrupt colonial governors acting in the Crown's name, were bound to arouse lasting resentment among the colonists, whether they were European or American born. He was sadly conscious of the maladministration and inefficiency in high places which marred or frustrated so many sound schemes and promising developments. "I can only say," he wrote in the above-quoted letter, "that we are reaping the fruit of the seeds which we have sown, and that we have no right to blame anyone but ourselves for our mishaps." He foresaw that Brazilian independence was inevitable in the long run, and he seems to have taken an even greater interest in Portuguese India than he did in Portuguese America. The news of the recapture of Mombasa from the Arabs of Oman in 1728, roused him to almost hysterical transports of joy; and his death on February 20, 1732 was hastened by intense chagrin at the tidings that this stronghold had fallen to its Muslim besiegers after a six-month blockade.

DOM LOURENÇO DE ALMEIDA. Son of the Count of Avintes, and brother of D. Tomaz de Almeida, Bishop of Porto and the first Patriarch of Lisbon. He was originally intended for an ecclesiastical career, and studied canon law at the University of Coimbra for several years, but changed his mind after graduating and embarked as a soldier for India in 1697. As stated in the notes (p. 406), the Count of Sabugosa alleged that Dom Lourenço had spent seventeen years in Portuguese India, where he had married and made a fortune by trading in diamonds. This, however, was not entirely correct, for Dom Lourenço's letters-patent as governor of Pernambuco expressly stated that he had served in Portuguese India "for the space of six years, nine months, and sixteen days" in 1697–1704. The Marquis of Angeja, who, as Count of Villa-Verde had been Viceroy at Goa in 1693–1698, wrote of him in 1715: "he was my comrade in India, and I know by personal experience of his great good sense." He served as *fiscal* or rear-admiral of the unsuccessful expedition for the relief of Mombasa in 1698–1699, and in various other campaigns in the Indian Seas, before returning to Europe in 1704. His governorships of Pernambuco in 1715–1718, and of Minas Gerais in 1721–1732, were for long remembered in both those captaincies on account of his tolerant administration and easy-going ways. He was not forgetful of the colonists' interests after his return to Portugal, being a severe critic of Alexandre de Gusmão's capitation- and income-tax scheme, which he denounced as being unjustifiably oppressive. His genuine concern for the welfare of those he governed did not, however, prevent him from feathering his own nest, though it is hard to say whether this was more at their expense or at that of the Crown. It was on his initiative that the chief seat of government in Minas Gerais was moved from Villa do Carmo to Villa Rica, which had for some time surpassed the former in wealth and importance. The fourth Count of Ericeira noted in his diary that when Dom Lourenço de Almeida finally returned to Lisbon in April, 1733, "he did not declare more than 80,000 *cruzados* to the customs, though one of his servants brought a diamond of 82½ carats." The Count stated that Dom Lourenço, when asked by his friends if he had returned from Brazil with a really large fortune, replied in the affirmative but added with engaging cynicism that he had "a lot to buy, a little to give, and nothing to lend." He died at Lisbon on October 17, 1750, a little more than seventy years old.

ANTONIL. Giovanni Antonío Andreoni, to give him his real name, was born of Italian parents in the Tuscan town of Lucca on February 8, 1649. After studying civil law at the University of Perugia for three years, he was received into the Society of Jesus at Rome in May, 1667, and later held teaching posts at the Jesuit Seminary. Padre António Vieira, S.J. took a great fancy to Andreoni and in 1681 persuaded him to accompany him to Brazil, where he stayed for the rest of his life.

Apart from paying brief visits to Pernambuco and Rio de Janeiro, he remained at Bahia for more than forty years, being twice rector of the local college, and Provincial of the Brazilian Province of the Society in 1705-1709. He was an accomplished Latin scholar, and his *Cultura e Opulencia do Brasil por suas drogas e minas,* written in excellent and terse Portuguese, is generally acknowledged to be the best book on the economic and social conditions of Brazil during the first half of the eighteenth century.

Although closely associated with Vieira until the latter's death, and entrusted with the cataloguing and conservation of his unpublished manuscripts, Andreoni held divergent views from his mentor on a number of contemporary problems. As Padre Serafim Leite, S.J. points out, Vieira opposed the enslavement of the Amerindians by the settlers with all the great energy at his command, whereas Andreoni adopted a less intransigent attitude. Vieira did not attack the Jews and actively championed the cause of the New Christians against the Inquisition; Andreoni translated an Italian anti-Semitic work entitled "The Synagogue Undeceived." The chief difference, however, was in their respective attitudes to the foreign members of the Society. Vieira, though he termed his countrymen "the Kaffirs of Europe" in moments of exasperation, was above all things a patriotic Portuguese, and favored their appointment to high office in the Society whenever practicable. Andreoni was, understandably, more conscious of the international aspect of the Order, and was inclined to favor the claims of Italian, German, and even (on a few occasions) of Brazilian-born Portuguese against those from the mother country. The difference continued after Vieira's death, and at the turn of the century the Jesuit General, Tirso González (a Spaniard) reprimanded Andreoni for unduly favoring his Italian colleagues. In 1711, the year of the publication—and suppression—of his *Cultura e Opulencia* at Lisbon, Andreoni complained that if Italian Jesuits were to be considered by the Portuguese as foreigners and hence prohibited from visiting Minas Gerais, he would rather leave Brazil and return to Europe. He remained, however, at Bahia where he died on March 13, 1716.

GLOSSARY

ALDEIA, a village; more particularly an Amerindian mission settlement, supervised by a Jesuit or other missionary.

ALVARÁ, a royal decree.

ARRAIAL, encampment. Applied both to a mining encampment and to a military encampment.

AUTO, affidavit.

BANDEIRA, exploring, slave-raiding, or prospecting party in the bush or jungle.

BANDEIRANTE, member of a *bandeira*.

BANDO, edict; official notification.

BATEIA, bowl or vessel used in washing for alluvial gold.

BICHA, yellow fever.

BICHO, anal gangrene.

CAATINGA, scrub vegetation

CABOCLO, used variously for (a) crossbreed of White and Amerindian stock (b) domesticated Amerindian (c) any low-class person.

CACHAÇA, rum; sugar-cane brandy.

CALHAMBOLA, runaway Negro slave.

CAMARA (SENADO DA CAMARA) municipal or town council.

CAMINHO NOVO, new highway.

CAMINHO VELHO, old highway.

CAPITÃO DO MATO, "Bush-whacking captain," leader of a detachment for hunting down runaway slaves.

CARIJÓ, (a) generic term for Amerindian (b) offspring of a Negro father and Amerindian mother.

CASCALHO, gravel; pebbly subsoil.

CATA, pit, trench, digging.

COMARCA, county; judicial district.

CONSULTA, minute(s) of a council meeting; conclusion reached after discussion in council.

CURRAL, cattle ranch.

DATA, mining claim or allotment.

DONATÁRIO, lord-proprietor.

DONATIVO, contribution, gift; (DONATIVO REAL), contribution to the Crown. Nominally raised by voluntary subscription but in practice often by official pressure.

EMBOABA, derisory term applied by the Paulistas to the Portuguese.

ENGENHO, sugar mill; by extension, sugar plantation.

FAISCADOR, FAISQUEIRO, prospector for alluvial gold or diamonds.

FAZENDA, (a) ranch (b) farm (c) property of any kind (d) the treasury or exchequer.

FIDALGO, nobleman, gentleman.

FILHO(S) DA FOLHA, "Son(s) of the ledger"; Crown pensioners.

GARIMPEIRO, illicit diamond prospector.

GAÚCHO, cowboy or stockman of the Pampa region and southern Brazil.

JUIZ-DE-FORA, Crown judge or magistrate, appointed from a region other than that in which he administered justice.

JUIZ ORDINARIO, a locally elected member of the municipal or town council with judicial powers in minor cases.

LAVOURA, cultivated land(s) or field(s).

LAVRADOR, sharecropper; man working on another's land; also a generic term for a peasant.

LINGUA GERAL, a form of the Tupí-Guaraní Amerindian language spoken by many tribes in Brazil and the Maranhão.

MÁ LINGUA, spiteful gossip; slander.

MAMELUCO, crossbreed between Amerindian mother and white father.

MASCATE, itinerant or ambulant peddler.

MESTIÇO, (a) offspring of a black and white sexual union (b) offspring of Amerindian and white sexual union (c) synonym for Carijó, *q.v.*

MINEIRO, (a) a miner (b) an inhabitant of Minas Gerais, not necessarily a miner.

MINHOTO, a man born in the Portuguese province of Entre Minho e Douro.

MORADOR, a settler; head of a colonial household.

MORRO, a high hill.

OUVIDOR, Crown or Royal judge; senior judicial authority in a *Comarca*.

PANTANAL, low-lying ground, subject to periodical innundation.

PARDO, colored; often synonymous with mulatto.

PARECER, opinion.

PAU A PIQUE, "poles on end"; wattle-and-daub type structure.

PAULISTA, white or halfbreed inhabitant of the region of São Paulo de Piratininga, or of one of its offshoots. The word was also used as a synonym for "Jesuit" in Portuguese Asia, but not so in Brazil.

Glossary

PEÇA, PEÇA DE INDIAS, standard classification for selling Negro slaves as described on p. 5.

PELOURINHO, stone pillar with royal arms, serving as municipal insignia and whipping post.

PODEROSOS DO SERTÃO, powerful landowners who often abused their position in the Backlands.

POMBEIROS, PUMBEIROS, itinerant slave traders in Angola and Benguela, usually mulattoes or mixed bloods.

PROVISÃO, general term for a Crown edict or decree.

QUILOMBO, village community of runaway slaves in the bush or forest.

QUINTO, quint, the Royal fifths.

RECONCAVO, sugar-growing region around Salvador (Bahia).

REGIMENTO, standing-orders; set of instructions; rules.

REGISTRO, toll-point; turnpike.

ROÇA, agricultural allotment; small farm.

SECA, drought.

SENZALA, slave quarters.

SERTÃO (SERTÕES), Backland(s); the bush; the hinterland.

SESMARIA, a grant of land.

SITIO, site; place.

TERÇO, an infantry regiment.

TERMO, a legal or official written declaration.

VAQUEIRO, cowboy; stockman.

VÁRZEA, sugar-growing region round Olinda and Recife.

VEREADOR, alderman; municipal or town councillor.

NOTES

ABBREVIATIONS

AAPB	*Anais do Arquivo Público da Bahia*
ABNRJ	*Anais da Biblioteca Nacional do Rio de Janeiro*
AHU	Arquivo Histórico Ultramarino, Lisboa
ANRJ	Arquivo Nacional, Rio de Janeiro
APEB	Arquivo Público do Estado da Bahia
APM	Arquivo Público Mineiro
APCHB	*Anais do primeiro congresso de história da Bahia*
BA	Biblioteca da Ajuda, Lisboa
BNL	Biblioteca Nacional, Lisboa
BNRJ	Biblioteca Nacional, Rio de Janeiro
Cadaval MSS	*Os Manuscritos do Arquivo da Casa de Cadaval respeitantes ao Brasil*
CR	*Carta Régia*
DH	*Documentos Históricos*
HAHR	*Hispanic American Historical Review*
IHGB	Instituto Histórico e Geográfico Brasileiro
PANRJ	*Publicações do Arquivo Nacional, Rio de Janeiro*
PRO London SP /	Public Record Office London, State Papers/Portugal
RAPM	*Revista do Arquivo Público Mineiro*
RIAGP	*Revista do Instituto Arqueológico e Geográfico Pernambucano*
RIHGB	*Revista do Instituto Histórico e Geográfico Brasileiro*
SPHAN	Serviço do Patrimonio Histórico e Artistico Nacional, Brasil

NOTES TO CHAPTER I

"Empire of the South Atlantic"

(Pages 1–29)

[1] The expression was employed by Dom Francisco Manuel de Mello, writing *ca.* 1660, and by the Jesuit, João Antonio Andreoni, writing under the pseudonym of Antonil in 1710. Cf. E. Prestage, *D. Francisco Manuel de Mello, Esboço biographico* (Coimbra, 1914), pp. 291, 601; André João Antonil, *Cultura e opulencia do Brasil por suas drogas e minas* (Lisboa, 1711), Livro I, cap. 9.

[2] João de Moura *apud* M. C. Kieman, O.F.M., *The Indian Policy of Portugal in the Amazon Region, 1614–1693* (Washington, D.C., 1954), p. 121. Kiemen is, however, mistaken in dating Moura's *parecer* at about 1660.

[3] Fr. António da Conceição, O.E.S.A., "Tratado dos Rios de Cuama, 1696," *apud* J. H. Cunha Rivara, *O Chronista de Tissuary,* II (Nova Goa, 1867), p. 86. D. Sebastião Monteiro da Vide to the Crown, *apud* Accioli-Amaral, *Memorias Historicas da Bahia,* V, 277–278.

[4] "The daily bread of the most considerable part of our British are owing primarily to the labour of Negroes. . . . . The Negro trade therefore, and the natural consequences resulting from it may justly be esteemed an inexhaustable fund of wealth and naval power to the nation:" pamphleteer of 1749, *apud* N. Derr, *History of Sugar,* II (London, 1950), p. 289.

[5] For further details of the African origins of slaves exported to Brazil, see F. Mauro, *Le Portugal et l'Atlantique au XVIIe Siècle, 1570–1670. Étude économique* (Paris, 1960), pp. 147–181.

[6] Domingos de Abreu e Brito, *apud* A. Albuquerque Felner, *Um inquérito à vida administrativa e economica de Angola e do Brasil em fins do século XVI* (Coimbra, 1931), p. 35.

[7] Manuel Fernandes, S.J. (the royal confessor), "Voto sobre as vexaçoins que se fazem aos negros de Angola," MS of *ca.* 1670 in BA, Cod. 50-V-39, Tomo V, doc. 24, fols. 40–41; *Consulta* of the Overseas Council, 9 September 1673, in AHU, "Consultas Mixtas," Cod. 17, fols. 122–124.

[8] *DH,* XXXIII (1936), pp. 366–367; Governor-General of Bahia to the Crown, 7 July 1691, in *Anais do Primeiro Congresso de Historia da Bahia* (Salvador, 1950), II, 296; APEB, "Livro de Ordens Régias, 1700–1701," CR of 7 March 1701; *ibid.,* "Livro de Ordens Régias, 1704," letter of Dom Rodrigo da Costa, Bahia, 30 April 1704.

[9] *Sermoens,* XIV (ed. 1710), p. 253. In H. Cidade's edition (1953), Vol. VII, 39, the expression "felices almas" is misprinted "infelices almas." Cf. also Luiz Vianna Filho, *O Negro na Bahia* (Rio de Janeiro, 1946), pp. 48–60.

[10] Cf. the sources quoted in C. R. Boxer, *Salvador de Sá and the Struggle for Brazil and Angola, 1602–1682* (London, 1952), pp. 224–240, to which should be added A. Brásio, *Monumenta Missionaria Africana. Africa Occidental* (9 vols., Lisboa, 1952–1959), VII, 124–130, 498.

[11] Sir William Godolphin to Mr. Secretary Coventry, 15 May 1678, *apud* R. Southey, *History of Brazil* (3 vols., London, 1810–1819), III, 889.

[12] Law of 28 March 1684 in *Arquivos de Angola,* II, 313–321, and in *DH,* LXXIX (1948), pp. 379–388. CR of 5 March 1697 in APEB, "Livro de Ordens Régias 1696–97," p. 100. CR of 20 January 1719 in ANRJ, "Registro velho de

ordens régias, 1712–1719." For the abortive legislation of 1664, cf. R. Delgado, *História de Angola* (4 vols., Lobito, 1948–1955), III, 284.

13 "No ay diferença entre los Negros y Generos" (D. Gerardo Moro, "natural de la ciudad de Dingle em Irlanda," *Informe en Derecho sobre que la Compañia del Real Assiento de la Gran Bretanha establecida para la introducción de esclavos negros en estas Indias* [Mexico, 1724].)

14 What follows is based mainly on J. A. Gonsalves de Mello [ed.], "Um regimento de feitor-mor de engenho de 1663," in *Boletim do Instituto Joaquim Nabuco de pesquisas sociais,* II (Recife, 1953), pp. 80–87; J. Benci, S.J., *Economia Cristã dos Senhores no governo de escravos. Livro Brasileiro de 1700,* ed. by S. Leite, S.J. (Porto, 1954); Antonil, *Cultura e opulencia do Brasil,* Livro I, caps. 5 and 9; A. Sérgio and H. Cidade [eds.], *Padre António Vieira. Obras Escolhidas* (12 vols., Lisboa, 1951–1954), XI, 1–95; Nuno Marques Pereira, *Compendio Narrativo do peregrino da America* (Lisboa, 1760), pp. 148–166.

15 Benci, S.J., *Economia Cristã,* p. 139.

16 "Um regimento de feitor-mor de engenho," p. 83.

17 CR of 7 February 1698, in APEB, "Livro de Ordens Régias, 1698," Nr. 30; CR of 17 January 1714 in *ibid.,* "Livro de Ordens Régias, 1702–1714," Nr. 48; *provizão* of 5 November 1712, in ANRJ, "Registro velho de ordens régias, 1712–1719," doc. 21. For the Archbishop of Bahia's injunctions that slaves should be adequately fed and clothed, allowed to marry, and attend church, see Sebastião Monteiro da Vide, *Primeiras Constituições do Arcebispado da Bahia* (Coimbra, 1720), pp. 132–133, 160–161.

18 Gaspar Dias Ferreira to the Crown, Amsterdam, 20 July 1645, in *RIAGP,* XXXII (April, 1887), p. 78.

19 João Peixoto Viegas to Salvador Correia de Sá e Benavides, Bahia, 15 July 1680, in *ABNRJ,* XX (1898–1899), p. 221; "Informação do Estado do Brasil e de suas necessidades," anonymous memorial of *ca.* 1690 presented to the Overseas Council, in *Revista do Instituto Histórico e Geográfico Brasileiro,* XXV (Rio de Janeiro, 1862), p. 466. .

20 "Of health and longevity," *apud* Southey, *op. cit.,* III, 898.

21 For the high proportion of Azoreans among the citizens and garrison of Rio de Janeiro, see Dr. Lourenço de Mendonça's printed memorials to the Council of the Indies at Madrid in 1637–1639 (British Museum Pressmark 1324. 1. 9. nrs. 11, 14, 15). For the efforts of João Fernandes Vieira to secure Azorean colonists for northeast Brazil in 1674–1678, cf. J. A. Gonsalves de Mello, *João Fernandes Vieira* (2 vols., Recife, 1956), II, 224–233. For the predominance of Minho men in Bahia, see C. B. Ott, *Formação e Evolução étnica da Cidade do Salvador* (2 vols., Salvador, 1955–1957), I, 43–53, and in Minas Gerais, see my Chapter vii.

22 J. A. Gonsalves de Mello, *António Fernandes de Matos, 1671–1701* (Recife, 1957).

23 Nuno Marques Pereira, *Compendio Narrativo do Peregrino da America* (2 vols., Rio de Janeiro, 1939), I, 385.

24 Simão de Vasconcellos, S.J., *Noticias curiosas e necessarias das cousas do Brasil* (Lisboa, 1668). For an earlier example of what may be termed this "promotion literature," see Simão Estacio da Silveira, *Relação Sumaria das cousas do Maranhão dirigida aos pobres deste Reyno de Portugal* (Lisboa, 1624).

[25] João Peixoto Viegas to the Marquis of Minas, Bahia, 20 December 1687, in *ABNRJ*, XX, 214.

[26] Cf. Caio Prado Júnior, *Formação do Brasil Contemporâneo. Colónia* (4th ed.; São Paulo, 1953), pp. 33–34. "Tendo nôs somente pouoado no Brasil muita parte da marinha, e quasi nenhũa do Çertao," as the Overseas Council reminded the Crown on 8 January 1693 (document printed in E. de Castro e Almeida, *Inventario dos documentos relativos ao Brasil*, VI, 187). Cf. also *RIHGB*, XXV (1862), p. 466.

[27] Antonil, *op. cit.*, Livro I, cap. 9.

[28] Minutes of the Salvador Municipal Council, 3 July 1641, in *Documentos Históricos do Arquivo Municipal. Atas da Camara, 1641–1649* (Salvador, 1949), p. 32; "Indice Abreviado dos documentos do século XVII," in *APCHB*, II (1950), pp. 321, 331, 411.

[29] T. Gage, *The English American. A New Survey of the West Indies, 1648*, ed. by A. P. Newton (1928), pp. 89–92.

[30] Manuel Calado, *O valeroso Lucideno e triumpho da liberdade* (Lisboa, 1648), pp. 30–40.

[31] "... ha muita producção que cauza a Infantaria e outra gente particular, em falta das damas brancas, nas negras damas ..." (António de Oliveira de Cadornega, *História Geral das Guerras Angolanas, 1681* (3 vols., Lisboa, 1940–1942), III, 30.

[32] For the law of 1726 prohibiting any mulatto "até a quarta geração," or any white man married with a "mulher parda," from filling any municipal post, cf. Sérgio Barque de Holanda, *Raizes do Brasil* (Rio de Janeiro, 1936), pp. 28–29. Cf. also Gilberto Freyre, *Nordeste* (1937), p. 146. The observations of Fr. Girolamo Merolla, O.F.M., Cap., on the position of mulattoes in Angola in 1691 are taken from the English translation of his *Viaggio* in Churchill, *Collection of Voyages*, I, 739.

[33] Simão de Vasconcellos, S.J., *Noticias* (1668), pp. 139–140.

[34] C. R. Boxer, *The Christian Century in Japan, 1549–1650* (London, 1951), pp. 83–84, 214, 222; João Ribeiro, *The Historic Tragedy of the Island of Ceilão, 1685*, ed. by P. E. Pieris (Colombo, 1948), p. 62; Alonso de Sandoval, S.J., *Naturaleza, policia, sagrada i profana, costumbres e ritos, disciplina i catechismo evangelico de todos Etiopes* (Sevilla, 1627), pp. 134–137; Fr. Domingo Fernandez Navarrete, O.P., *Tratados historicos, politicos, ethicos, y religiosos de la monarchia de China* (Madrid, 1676), p. 294.

[35] A. Arinos de Mello Franco, *O indio brasileiro e a revolução francesa; as origens brasileiras da teoria da bondade natural* (Rio de Janeiro, 1937).

[36] This is well brought out by Gilberto Freyre, *The Masters and the Slaves* (New York, 1946), pp. 106–113, 158–180.

[37] Officially called the "Estado do Maranhão e Grão-Pará," the state formed a separate governorship from that of Brazil, and at the end of the seventeenth century included the present-day States of Maranhão, Pará, and Amazonas. Ceará, which had formed part of the old State of Maranhão on its formation in 1621, was transferred to the jurisdiction of Pernambuco for practical purposes in 1656.

[38] J. L. Azevedo [ed.], *Cartas do Padre António Vieira* (3 vols., Coimbra, 1925–1928), I, 374–375.

39 Alexander Hamilton, *A New Account of the East Indies, 1688–1723* (1930), I, 17.

40 For a more detailed and documented discussion of this subject, cf. René Ribeiro, *Religião e relações raciais* (Rio de Janeiro, 1956), pp. 38–193; *ibid.*, "Relations of the Negro with Christianity in Portuguese America," in A. S. Tibesar, O.F.M. [ed.], "History of Religion in the New World" (reprinted from *The Americas*, XIV (1958), pp. 118–148.

41 The foregoing pages merely indicate the position during the last quarter of the seventeenth century. Readers desirous of further details concerning the color question and miscegenation at earlier and later periods, cannot do better than consult the excellent work of Freyre, *The Masters and the Slaves,* and Caio Prado Júnior, *Formação do Brasil Contemporâneo. Colónia* (1953).

42 B. Lubbock [ed.], *Barlow's Journal of His Life at Sea in the King's Ships, East and West Indiamen and Other Merchantmen from 1659 to 1703* (2 vols., London, 1934), I, 76–91; A. Shillington and V. Chapman, *The Commercial Relations of England and Portugal* (London, n.d.), p. 217; W. Dampier, *A Voyage to New Holland in 1699* (Argonaut Press, 1939), pp. 37–38.

43 PRO London, SP 89/15, fols. 11–12; C. R. Boxer, "English Shipping in the Brazil Trade, 1640–65," in *The Mariner's Mirror*, XXXVII (1951), pp. 197–230.

44 PRO London, SP 89/11 (1670–1671), fols. 63–64.

45 Cadornega, *História Geral das Guerras Angolanas*, III, 31–33; Ralph Delgado, *História de Angola, 1482–1737* (4 vols., Benguela and Lobito, 1948–1955), III, 118–137, 445–446; IV, 75–78, 85–86, 115, 301–305, 386, 438.

46 João Peixoto Viegas' letters of 1680 and 1687, in *ABNRJ*, XX (1898), pp. 213–223. For the functioning of the convoy system in general, cf. Gustavo de Freitas, *A Companhia Geral do comércio do Brasil, 1649–1720* (São Paulo, 1951), and for the timing of the departure of the Brazil Fleets in 1690, cf. *DH*, XXXIII (1936), pp. 368–370, and CR d. 15 October 1690 in APEB, "Livros de Ordens Régias, 1648–1690."

47 Virginia Rau, *O "Livro de Rezão" de António Coelho Guerreiro* (Lisboa, 1956), gives an excellent picture of this trade based on the ledger of a man who actively participated in it, 1683–1696. Cf. also Gonsalves de Mello, *António Fernandes de Matos, 1671–1701*, pp. 67–70.

48 *ABNRJ*, XX (1898), pp. 220–221.

49 Delgado, *História de Angola*, IV, 303, 322.

50 "... brevemente tornaremos ao primitivo estado dos indios, e os portugueses seremos brasis" (letter dated Bahia, 10 July 1689, in Azevedo, *Cartas de António Vieira*, III, 581). For the smallpox epidemic of 1685 in Angola, cf. Delgado, *História*, IV, 111. For the ravages of the *bicha* or yellow fever in Bahia and Pernambuco, see Azevedo, *Cartas de António Vieira*, III, 525–528, 532–538, 576–580, 617, 634, 638, 642, 654; G. Osorio de Miranda and E. Duarte, *Morão, Rosa & Pimenta* (Recife, 1956), pp. 143–218. For Brazil's financial crisis in 1690–1691, see the Governor-General's dispatch, Bahia, 4 July 1692, in *DH*, XXXIII (1936), pp. 430–440, and the anonymous "Informação do Estado do Brasil e de suas necessidades," in *RIHGB*, XXV (1862), pp. 564–578.

51 V. Magalhães Godinho, "Le Portugal, les flottes du sucre et les flottes de l'or, 1670–1770," in *Annales. Économies-Sociétés-Civilisations* (January–March, 1951), pp. 184–197, or the Portuguese version in *Revista de História*, Nº 15 (July–September, 1953), pp. 69–88; C. R. Boxer, "Vicissitudes of the Anglo-

Portuguese Alliance, 1660–1700," in *Boletim da Faculdade de Letras de Lisboa,* III Serie, Nr. 2 (1958), pp. 5–36; Luis Ferrand de Almeida, *A diplomacia portuguesa e os limites meridionais do Brasil, 1493–1700* (Coimbra, 1957).

[52] Severino Sombra, *História Monetária do Brasil Colonial. Repertorio cronológico* (Rio de Janeiro, 1938), pp. 98–110, gives the best documented survey of Brazil's financial difficulties in the last decade of the seventeenth century.

NOTES TO CHAPTER II
"The Gold Rush in Minas Gerais"
(Pages 30–60)

[1] Maynard to Arlington, Lisbon, 25 November 1670, *apud* Boxer, *Salvador de Sá,* p. 381.

[2] Jaime Cortesão, *Rapóso Tavares e a formação territorial do Brasil* (Rio de Janeiro, 1958).

[3] The original militia *regimento* (Lisboa, 1570), stipulated that a *bandeira* should consist of 250 men, but this number was not adhered to in Brazil. For the introduction of *bandeiras* into the military system of Portuguese India in 1585, see J. H. Cunha Rivara [ed.], *Archivo Portuguez Oriental,* III (Nova Goa, 1861), pp. 103, 118, 154, 200.

[4] The literature on the *Bandeirantes* (a modern term, coined by Taunay) is vast, the fundamental work being Taunay's own lavishly documented *História Geral das Bandeiras Paulistas* (10 vols., São Paulo, 1927–1949).

[5] Delgado, *História de Angola, IV,* 81.

[6] "... porque os portugueses bem sabe Vossa Merce que são homens de pouco trabalho, principalmente fora de seu natural" (Town Council of São Paulo to the Count of Monsanto, January, 1606, *apud* A. Ellis, *O Ouro e a Paulistânia* [São Paulo, 1948, p. 37 n.]).

[7] "El doctor Lourenço de Mendonça sacerdote Comissario del Santo Officio de Potossi en servicio de Vossa Magestade sobre las minas de oro de San Pablo e Brasil, a 21 de junio de 1630" (autograph memorial in BPRJ, Codice 1-2-35, fols. 81–82). Cf. also Boxer, *Salvador de Sá,* pp. 299–302.

[8] Francisco Barreto to the Crown, Bahia, 20 January 1662 in *DH,* XXXIII, 311; António Luís Gonsalves da Camara Coutinho to the Crown, Bahia, 6 July 1692, *ibid.,* p. 444; D. João de Lencastre to the Crown, Bahia, 1 January 1700, *apud* Ellis, *O ouro e a Paulistânia,* pp. 111–112; F. Froger, *A Relation of a Voyage Made in the Years 1695–1697* (London, 1698), pp. 62–63; W. Dampier, *A Voyage to New Holland, 1699* (ed. 1939), p. 57. Cf. also, Taunay, *História Geral,* IX, 3–17, 49–66.

[9] Crown to the Governor of Rio de Janeiro, 16 January 1693, *apud* António Paes de Sande e Castro, *António Paes de Sande, "o grande governador"* (Lisboa, 1951), pp. 199–200. Cf. also *RIHGB,* XXV, 473; Taunay, *op. cit.,* IX, 21–34.

[10] M. S. Cardozo, "The Last Adventure of Fernão Dias Paes, 1674–1681," in *HAHR,* XXVII (Nov., 1946), pp. 467–479; *ibid.,* "D. Rodrigo de Castel-Blanco and the Brazilian El Dorado, 1673–1682," in *The Americas,* I (Oct., 1944), pp. 131–159; Taunay, *op. cit.,* VIII.

[11] Biblioteca Municipal de São Paulo (MS D/ 1/ a/ 43), "Colasam das Noticias dos primeiros descobridores das Minas na America, que fes o Dr. Caetano da Costa Matoso, sendo Ouvidor Geral de Ouro Preto, de que tomou posse em Fevreiro de 1749," fols. 44, 47. Hereafter cited as Codice Costa Matoso. This codex was compiled in 1749–1752, but some of those whose reminiscences are preserved therein had arrived in Minas Gerais before the end of the seventeenth century and others early in the eighteenth. A few of these accounts were published by Taunay, *Relatos Sertanistas* (São Paulo, 1954), but unfortunately with numerous misprints, mistakes, and omissions. He made much better use of this invaluable codex in Vols. IX and X of his monumental *História Geral das Bandeiras Paulistas*, but even there he does not always give adequate references. The thesis of Bahian priority in the occupation of Minas Gerais, originally championed by Orville Derby, has recently been restated by Zoroastro Viana dos Passos, *Em torno da história de Sabará* (2 vols., Rio de Janeiro and Belo Horizonte, 1940–1942), II, and by Salomão de Vasconcelos, "Como nasceu Sabará," *SPHAN,* IX (Rio de Janeiro, 1945), pp. 291 ff., but the weight of contrary evidence adduced by Taunay in Vols. IX and X of his *História Geral* is much more convincing.

[12] Codice Costa Matoso, fol. 67. Cf. also J. P. Calogeras, *As minas do Brasil e a sua legislação* (3 vols., Rio de Janeiro, 1904), I, 74, 336–337. The evidence there adduced seems to me to weaken the arguments in a contrary sense advanced by Sylvio de Vasconcellos, *Vila Rica. Formação e desenvolvimento. Residencias* (Rio de Janeiro, 1956), pp. 161–169.

[13] The classic description of early mining methods is by Antonil, *Cultura e opulencia,* Livro III, cap. 14. Contrary to what is often asserted, Antonil was never in Minas Gerais himself, but he reproduces textually the description sent him by someone who accompanied the governor of Rio, Artur de Sá, thither in 1701–1702. I would hazard a guess that this informant was the governor's secretary, Joseph Rebello Perdigão, who did not return to Rio but settled in the mining region. For handy modern summaries, cf. Calogeras, *Minas do Brasil,* I, 111–132; A. de Lima Junior, *A capitania das Minas Gerais* (ed. 1943), pp. 101–121; Taunay, *História Geral,* IX, 255–275.

[14] Cf. the anonymous memorial presented to the Overseas Council *ca.* 1705, in *ABNRJ,* LVII, 172–184, Antonil, *Cultura e opulencia,* Livro III, caps. 10–12; report of Domingos Certão, Bahia, 15 January 1702, in V. Rau, *MSS Cadaval,* II, 34–36, and that of João de Góis e Aráujo, Bahia, 6 March 1701, *ibid.,* pp. 19–21.

[15] Artur de Sá to the Crown, Rio de Janeiro, 12 June 1697, *apud* M. S. Cardozo, "The Brazilian Gold Rush" (*The Americas,* III, October, 1946, pp. 137–160), p. 137; Dom João de Lencastre to the Crown, Bahia, 12 January 1701, *apud* Rau, *MSS Cadaval,* II, 14–17.

[16] Antonil, *Cultura e opulencia,* Livro III, cap. 5.

[17] Dom João de Lencastre to the Crown, Bahia, 12 January 1701. Cf. penultimate note.

[18] Antonil, *Cultura e opulencia,* Livro III, cap. 17. *Consultas* of the Overseas Council 1708–1709, *apud* Cardozo, "The Brazilian Gold Rush," p. 149.

[19] Dom João de Lencastre to the Crown, 12 January 1701, in Rau, *MSS Cadaval,* II, 14–17; Governor of Rio de Janeiro to Captain-Major of Espirito Santo, 25 September 1702, in ANRJ, "Correspondencia dos governadores do Rio, 1702–1706," Col. 78, Livro 9, fols. 107–108.

[20] CR of 7 February 1701, in APEB, "Livro de Ordens Régias, 1700–1701," fol. 114; *DH*, LXXXIV, 170–171.

[21] D. João de Lencastre to the Crown, 12 January 1701, in Rau, *MSS Cadaval*, II, 14–17; official correspondence of 1703–1704 cited in Cardozo, "The Brazilian Gold Rush," p. 153.

[22] "Informação," of *ca.* 1705 in *ABNRJ*, LVII, 172–186; official correspondence of 1703–1706, cited in Cardozo, *op. cit.*, p. 151; Taunay, *História Geral*, X, 222–225.

[23] *Alvará* and CR of 20 January 1701, in APEB, "Livro de Ordens Régias, 1700–1701," fol. 83; Governor of Rio to the Crown, 2 August 1701, in ANRJ, "Correspondencia dos governadores do Rio, 1702–1706," 13/ 13A, fols. 190–193; CR of 27 February 1711 in APEB, "Livro de Ordens Régias, 1702–1714," Nr. 66A; CR of 28 September 1703 and official correspondence of 1700–1706 cited in Cardozo, *op. cit.*, pp. 150–151; CR of 24 March 1715, in Delgado, *História de Angola*, IV, 301–303; Taunay, *História Geral*, IX, 295–301.

[24] APEB, "Livro de Cartas Régias, 1702–1711," fol. 51.

[25] CR of 2 December 1698, in APEB, "Livro de Ordens Régias, 1698–1699," fol. 80; CR of 7 March 1701 in APEB, "Livro de Ordens Régias, 1700–1701," fol. 126; *ibid.*, 1702–1711, fols. 2–3, 46. Cf. also other relevant official correspondence cited in Mafalda P. Zemella, *O Abastecimento da capitania das Minas Gerais no século XVIII* (São Paulo, 1951), pp. 109, 200–204.

[26] CR of 27 February 1711 and the governor-general's observations of 28 July 1714, in APEB, "Livro de Ordens Régias, 1702–1714," nrs. 64 and 66A.

[27] Codice Costa Matoso, fol. 8. This fecklessness recalls that of the Portuguese adventurers who embarked so eagerly for India in the sixteenth century: "It is an astounding thing to see the facility and frequency with which the Portuguese embark for India. . . . Each year four or five carracks leave Lisbon full of them; and many embark as if they were going no further than a league from Lisbon, taking with them only a shirt and two loaves in the hand, and carrying a cheese and a jar of marmalade, without any other kind of provision" (Alexander Valignano, S.J., apropos of the India Voyage in 1574, *apud* C. R. Boxer, *Tragic History of the Sea, 1598–1622*, London, 1959, p. 15).

[28] Codice Costa Matoso, fol. 30; Antonil, *Cultura e opulencia*, Livro III, cap. 7.

[29] Governor of Rio to the Crown, 20 May 1698 apud Zemella, *Abastecimento das Minas Gerais*, pp. 219–220; Governor of Rio to the Crown, 30 November 1700, *apud* Rau, *MSS Cadaval*, II, 12.

[30] Codice Costa Matoso, fols. 30–35, 44. Cf. Taunay, *Relatos Sertanistas*, pp. 62, 76, and *idem, História Géral*, IX, 115, 121, 136, 237–240, 289.

[31] Antonil, *Cultura e opulencia*, Livro III, cap. 10. This may be compared with the proverb that Portuguese immigrants to India left their consciences behind them on rounding the Cape of Good Hope. Antonil's complaint was echoed by the Conde de Assumar in 1719. Cf. Zemella, *Abastecimento*, pp. 148–149.

[32] Simão Ferreira Machado, *Triunfo Eucharistico* (Lisboa, 1734), p. 18, " ... viose em breve tempo transplantado meyo Portugal a este Emporio"; Ellis, *O ouro e a Paulistânia*, pp. 213–216; A. de Lima Junior, *A Capitania das Minas Gerais* (ed. 1943), pp. 75–83; Sylvio de Vasconcellos, *Vila Rica*, p. 23.

[33] Codice Costa Matoso, fols. 49, 68; Sylvio de Vasconcellos, *op. cit.*, pp. 181–192.

34 J. Mawe, *Travels in the Interior of Brazil* (London, 1812), pp. 72–73. What is essentially the same system still prevails in parts of Brazil today. Cf. T. Lynn Smith, *Brazil. People and Institutions* (Baton Rouge, 1954), pp. 27, 58, 410–411.

35 Sylvio de Vasconcellos, *op. cit.*, pp. 99–125.

36 Antonil, *Cultura e opulencia*, Livro III, cap. 6. The mining code of 19 April 1702 has been printed several times, *inter alia* in F. I. Ferreira, *Repertorio Juridico do Mineiro* (Rio de Janeiro, 1884), pp. 200–208, a fact of which its latest editor, Damião Peres, *Estudos de História Luso-Brasileira* (Lisboa, 1956), pp. 53–63, is apparently unaware. For a comparison of the codes of 1700 and 1702, see Taunay, *História Geral*, IX, 244–248.

37 *Braça*, a fathom (six feet).

38 Codice Costa Matoso, fol. 49; Antonil, *Cultura e opulencia*, Livro III, cap. 6.

39 Codice Costa Matoso, fol. 47. Cf. also Taunay, *História Geral*, IX, 167–170, 445–448.

40 Antonil, *Cultura e opulencia*, Livro III, cap. 17.

41 Codice Costa Matoso, fol. 142; Diogo de Vasconcellos, *História antiga das Minas Gerais* (Bello Horizonte, 1904), pp. 300–304; Taunay, *História Geral*, IX, 396–404; *ibid.*, X, 45–47; Cardozo, "Brazilian Gold Rush," pp. 142, 154–155. *Idem*, "The Collection of the Fifth in Brazil, 1695–1705" (*HAHR*, XX), pp. 377–378.

42 Antonil, *Cultura e opulencia*, Livro III, cap. 17; Cardozo, "Brazilian Gold Rush," pp. 145–146; Taunay, *História Geral*, IX, 310–311.

43 Crown to D. João de Lencastre, 16 March 1701, and other correspondence in APEB, "Livros de Ordens Régias, 1698–1701," *passim*.

44 This and what follows is mainly based on the carefully documented article of Cardozo, "The Collection of the Fifth in Brazil," pp. 359–379. Cf. also Taunay, *História Geral*, X, 19–27.

45 Arquivo Publico Mineiro (APM), Delegacia Fiscal (DF), Codices 5 and 76.

46 Taunay, *História Geral*, IX, 363–366.

47 Carlos de Azevedo, *Um artista Italiano em Goa. Placido Francesco Ramponi* (Lisboa, 1956), p. 38. Ramponi visited Bahia from April 23 to July 14, 1699, during his homeward voyage. The other quotation is from Cardozo, "Collection of the Fifth," p. 376.

48 V. Magalhães Godinho, "Le Portugal, les flottes du sucre et les flottes de l'or, 1670–1770," in *Annales* (Feb.–March, 1951), pp. 192–193.

49 Report of Felix Madureira e Gusmão, 28 July 1705 (?), *apud* Cardozo, "Collection of the Fifth," p. 374.

50 Minute of the Overseas Council, 4 November 1695, *apud* Cardozo, "Collection of the Fifth," p. 372.

NOTES TO CHAPTER III
"Paulistas and Emboabas"
(Pages 61–83)

1 Town Council of São Paulo to the Crown, 7 April 1700, in Taunay, *História Geral*, IX, 473–474.

[2] Taunay, *op. cit.*, IX, 475–478, discusses the various meanings ascribed by different writers to the word *emboaba* (also written *ambuaba, imboaba,* etc.) without coming to any conclusion. My own preference is for the eighteenth-century sources which define *emboaba* as meaning a bird with feathered legs, whence the term was applied in derision to the newcomers from Europe and the coast who wore protective coverings for their legs and feet, in contrast to the Paulistas who normally went barefooted and barelegged in the bush. Cf. Codice Costa Matosa, fol. 37 " ... os Reynões chamados pelos Paulistas ambuabas por desprezo, que na sua lingoa quer dizer galinhas calsadas, que o imitavão pelos calçoens que uzavão de rolos."

[3] Cf. Taunay, *Relatos Sertanistas*, pp. 33, 34; idem, *História Geral,* IX, 478–479.

[4] Cf. *Guerra Civil entre Vascongados e otras naciones en Potosí. Documentos del Archivo Nacional de Bolivia, 1622–1640* (Cuadernos de la Colección de la Cultura Boliviana, Potosí, 1954); Alberto Crespo, *La Guerra entre Vicuñas y Vascongados, Potosí, 1622–1625* (Lima, 1956).

[5] Joseph Alvares de Oliveira, "Historia do distrito do Rio das Mortes ... casos nele acontecidos entre Paulistas e Emboabas" (Codice Costa Matoso, fols. 86–99), an eyewitness account which is my chief authority for the above and for what follows. Cf. also Taunay, *Relatos Sertanistas,* pp. 87–119, and *História Geral,* IX, 487–504. The custom of going about armed to the teeth was not merely inspired by the dangers of life in Minas Gerais, but was also a reflection of the prevailing fashion in Portugal. Every man in the mother country, from nobleman to beggar, went about with a sword "generally five, and sometimes six foot long, which, as they walk, especially on the declivity, trail on the ground after them; on their right side they wear daggers, as long as our swords, and under their clothes, a weapon called *faca da ponta,* or pointed knife, made like a bayonet, with a sharp point and edge, but the back of it notched like a saw; and often besides these arms, in their pockets, a brace of pistols." (Charles Brockwell, *The Natural and Political History of Portugal,* Lisbon, 1726, pp. 20–21.)

[6] Cf. the testimony of André Gomes Ferreira, an Emboaba who reached the Rio das Velhas in 1706, and remained there for the rest of his long life (he was still alive in 1751) " ... o Superintendente Borba ... como juiz supremo deferia a todos com muito agrado e desejava favorecer os confiscados. Tinha meirinho e escrivão e muita gente para as diligencias dos confiscos, muitos livraram e muitos confiscaram." (Codice Costa Matoso, fols., 40–43.)

[7] Codice Costa Matoso, fol. 101. Anonymous paper beginning: "A noticia que tenho de Manuel Nunes Viana ... "

[8] " ... occoreu então pitoresco episódio, o de um desafio em duelo, cousa sobremodo rara entre gente lusa" (Taunay, *História Geral,* IX, 507). This was certainly true of Portugal, Brazil, and West Africa, but dueling was fairly common at certain times in parts of Portuguese Asia. Cf. João Ribeiro, *Fatalidade Historica da Ilha de Ceilão, 1685,* Livro I, cap. 13, and Fernão de Queiroz, S. J., *Conquista Temporal e Espiritual de Ceylão, 1688,* Livro VI, cap. 17.

[9] Sebastião da Rocha Pitta, *História da America Portugueza, 1500–1724* (Lisboa, 1730), Livro IX, para. 22.

[10] The basic documents for the events of 1708 on which my account is primarily based, are: Borba Gato's edict, Caeté, 12 October 1708; Manuel Nunes Viana to Borba Gato, Caeté, 13 October 1708; Borba Gato's reply and second edict, Caeté. October, 1708; Borba Gato to the Governor of Rio de Janeiro, Rio

das Velhas, 29 November 1708; Bento do Amaral Coutinho to the Governor of Rio de Janeiro, Ouro Preto, 16 January 1709. These are all printed in full (from the originals in the AHU Lisbon) by Golgher, *Guerra dos Emboabas,* pp. 74–130. Unfortunately, Senhor Golgher has misread or misunderstood this documentation in many places, thus drawing unwarranted inferences from it. A much better account, based on wider and more critical reading of the AHU documents is the excellent article of Cardozo, "The Guerra dos Emboabas. Civil War in the Minas Gerais, 1708–1709," *HAHR,* XXII (August, 1942), pp. 470–492. Taunay, *História Geral,* IX, 504–518, has made use of the various accounts in the Codice Costa Matosa which were unknown to Golgher and Cardozo, but he has confused his narrative with needless digressions and tedious genealogical asides. J. Soares de Melo, *Emboabas. Chronica de uma revolução nativista. Documentos inéditos,* is unaccountably ignored by Golgher, although Soares de Mello had printed (pp. 229–288) nearly all the documents which Golgher absurdly claims to have "discovered," and which were also utilized by Cardozo and Taunay. There are many other secondary accounts, but they are all more or less misleading, since they rely too heavily (as does Golgher for that matter) on the imaginative fabrications of Diogo Vasconcellos, *História Antiga das Minas Gerais,* an utterly untrustworthy work.

[11] "... fez sua repugnancia sempre e acceitou o posto," as André Gomes Ferreira, then living at Sabará, recalled some forty years later (Codice Costa Matoso, fol. 40).

[12] Cf. p. 53. For Amaral's murder of Pedro de Sousa Pereira, "Procurador da Fazenda da Coroa" at Rio de Janeiro, see the account by the victim's uncle, Martim Correia Vasques, in Frazão de Vasconcellos, *Archivo Nobiliarchico Portuguez,* Serie I, nr. 6 (Lisboa, 1918), pp. 15–16.

[13] For the distinction between Amaral Gurgel and Amaral Coutinho, who are confused by the majority of writers, see Pedro Calmon, *História do Brasil* (3 vols., ed. 1943), III, 28–30, 42–43.

[14] The Sodré Pereira family. One of them was governor of São Tomé in 1695–1696, and another of Pernambuco in 1727–1737.

[15] The best and fullest treatment of the *capão da traição* atrocity is in Taunay, *História Geral,* IX, 548–553. Golgher (*Guerra dos Emboabas,* pp. 120 ff.), tries to make out that the incident never happened, but he ignores the documentary proof given by Soares de Melo, Taunay, and the Codice Costa Matoso. The most important version is that of Joseph Alvares de Oliveira, "História do distrito do Rio das Mortes," in the Codice Costa Matoso, for he was either an eyewitness or was in the immediate vicinity when it happened. Cf. Taunay, *Relatos Sertanistas,* pp. 100–101.

[16] Domingos Duarte de Carvalho to Manuel Mendes Pereira, Rio de Janeiro, 23 January 1709. Cf. Cardozo, "Civil War in Minas Gerais," p. 483; Golgher, *Guerra dos Emboabas,* p. 143; Soares de Melo, *Emboabas,* pp. 256–258.

[17] Luís de Almeida Correia de Albuquerque to Diogo de Mendonça Corte Real, Rio de Janeiro, 6 February 1709. Cf. Cardozo, "Civil War in Minas Gerais," p. 484; Soares de Melo, *op. cit.,* 258–260; Golgher, *op. cit.,* pp. 144–145.

[18] "... e elles na verdade não sabem senão matar gente de tras dos páos."

[19] "Capitollo de hũa carta que veyo do Rio de Janeiro pellas Ilhas remetida a esta corte de peçoa de bom Porte," Rio de Janeiro, 10 February, 1709. Cf.

Cardozo, "Civil War in Minas Gerais," pp. 484–485; Golgher, *op. cit.,* pp. 146–148; Soares de Melo, *op. cit.,* pp. 260–261.

[20] The relevant *termo,* dated Rio de Janeiro, 16 January 1709, is printed in Soares de Melo, *op. cit.,* pp. 246–248, and (with the wrong date) in Golgher, *op. cit.,* pp. 99–101. The commander of the Rio garrison was not invited to this meeting, and the governor was later censured by the Crown for this omission.

[21] D. Fernando Martins Mascarenhas to the Crown, Rio de Janeiro, 14 February 1709, textually transcribed in Soares de Melo, *op. cit.,* pp. 248–254, and (with wrong date) in Golgher, *op. cit.,* pp. 107–114.

[22] D. Fernando Martins Mascarenhas to the Crown, Rio de Janeiro, 16 February 1709, textually transcribed in Soares de Melo, *op. cit.,* pp. 254–256, and Golgher, *op. cit.,* pp. 137–140. Cf. also Cardozo, "Civil War in Minas Gerais," pp. 485–486.

[23] Joseph Alvares de Oliveira, "História do distrito do Rio das Mortes" (Codice Costa Matoso, fols. 86–99), *apud* Taunay, *Relatos Sertanistas,* pp. 89–119. Alvares de Oliveira was an eyewitness of the events which he describes, and one of the Emboaba representatives at the (abortive) agreement made with the Paulistas in the Arraial Novo do Rio das Mortes in April, 1709.

[24] They are exhaustively discussed in Taunay, *História Geral,* IX, 555–562.

[25] Resolutions of the São Paulo Town Council, dated 15 February, and 23 April 1709. Reproduced in extenso by Taunay, *História da Villa de São Paulo no século XVIII, 1701–1711* (n.p., n.d.), pp. 134–137. Cf. also *idem, História Geral,* IX, 575–580.

[26] Golgher, *op. cit.,* pp. 167–175, is in error when he assumes that the Conselho do Estado received the news in June, three months before the Conselho Ultramarino, and that there was bitter rivalry between these two councils. The *consulta* of 7 June 1709, on which he bases this opinion, deals with the complaints made by José Vaz Pinto of his expulsion from the Mines by the Paulistas some four or five years earlier. It has nothing to do with the War of the Emboabas.

[27] "... emquanto não nos dão mayor cuidado os Franceses (ou Ingleses) como se teme e ainda mais destes, por serem nossos amigos" (José Soares da Silva, *Gazeta em forma de Carta,* under date of 15 August 1709, p. 210 of the 1933 edition).

[28] *Consultas* of the Conselho Ultramarino, August, 1709, *apud* Cardozo, "Civil War in Minas Gerais," pp. 488–489; Taunay, *História Geral,* IX, 535–538; cf. also *parecer* of the Marquis of Marialva, 18 October 1709, in Rau, *MSS Cadaval,* II, 62–64.

[29] Frazão de Vasconcellos, "António de Albuquerque Coelho. Notas genealogico-biograficas," in *Arqueologia e História,* Vol. I (Lisboa, 1922), pp. 95–118. The standard biographical sketch by Aureliano Leite, *António de Albuquerque Coelho de Carvalho* (Lisboa, 1944), highly praised and closely followed by Taunay (*História Geral,* IX, 562 ff.), contains many mistakes and is useful only for the documents which it reprints in extenso and without acknowledgments from previously published works.

[30] "Relação da Jornada que eu Frei Manoel da Esperança sendo Vigario Geral fiz ao certam a visitar a Missam do Rio Negro em Companhia do Governador Cappitam Geral do Estado Antonio de Albuquerque Coelho de Carvalho" (BA, Cod. 51-viii-40, nr. 14, fols. 120–126).

[31] Bernardo Pereira de Berredo, *Annaes Históricos do Estado do Maranhão, 1499–1718* (Lisboa, 1749), paras. 1303–1304, 1310, 1333, 1363–1364, 1369, 1372, 1376–1389, 1418–1422; José Soares da Silva, *Gazeta em forma da carta, 1701–1716*, pp. 90, 139, 142, 161, 224.

[32] " ... com barba creçida e em talção e vestia" (Codice Costa Matoso, fol. 37ᵛ.), which, however, gives Sabará as the place of Albuquerque's unheralded and travel-stained arrival.

[33] For this account of Albuquerque's pacification of Minas Gerais, I have depended chiefly on the version of André Gomes Ferreira (Codice Costa Matoso, fols. 40–43), since he was then in the Sabará region. Cf. also Codice Costa Matoso, fols. 37, 49, 73–74, 82–84; Taunay, *História Geral*, IX, 565–570; Cardozo, "Civil War in the Minas Gerais," pp. 489–491.

[34] " ... sendo nossa a conquista," in the words of the São Paulo Town Council's resolution of 15 February 1709.

[35] " ... e que naquellas Minas existia o senhor Governador e capitam general desta repartição a cuja obediencia estivesse com toda a sua gente e cumprisse, e guardasse suas ordens e mandasse cumprir e guardar muito inteiramente como a nosso General," in the words of the São Paulo Town Council's *requerimento* of 24 August 1709.

[36] "Constava este corpo de pouco mais de dois mil homens pretos, Indios da terra, Mamelucos, e muitos poucos brancos" (Albuquerque to the Crown, n.d., n.p., but probably Rio de Janeiro, November, 1709), *apud* Golgher, *Guerra dos Emboabas*, pp. 205–209.

[37] Albuquerque's undated report to the Crown cited in the last note. This report, which is admittedly incomplete, makes no mention of the story found in several other accounts that the Paulista leaders, speaking Tupí among themselves, discussed the advisability of killing Albuquerque there and then, being unaware that he understood what they were saying, since he had learned the *lingua geral* in the Maranhão. Cf. Codice Costa Matoso, fol. 34; Taunay, *História Geral*, IX, 582–583.

[38] The best account of the Rio das Mortes campaign is that by a prominent participant, Joseph Alvares de Oliveira, Codice Costa Matoso, fols. 86–99. Cf. also Taunay, *Relatos Sertanistas*, pp. 104–112; *idem, História Geral*, IX, 581–595.

[39] " ... emboabas e paulistas, que tudo andava arruinando uns contra outros que seriam umas guerras civis se Deus não acudira com sua piedade" (André Gomes Ferreira in Codice Costa Matoso, fol. 40). Cf. also Taunay, *Relatos Sertanistas*, p. 72.

[40] " ... até São Paulo cujas vilas são faceis da conquistar por estarem atiçadas o que me parece deve V.M. ordenar ... " (Albuquerque's undated dispatch to the Crown, *apud* Golgher, *op. cit.*, pp. 207–208); "Se me offereceu dizer a V.M. que na concideração de entender que estes taes vassallos merecião hum exemplar castigo, por desobedientes e absolutos, determinava o darlhos por meio de todo o rigor ... " (Albuquerque to the Crown, Rio de Janeiro, 3 April 1710, *apud* A. Leite, *António de Albuquerque*, p. 50).

[41] Crown to Albuquerque, 22 August 1709, *apud* A. Leite, *op. cit.*, pp. 42–45; Albuquerque's letters-patent as governor of São Paulo e Minas do Oro, Lisbon, 23 November 1709, *apud* A. Leite, *op. cit.*, pp. 56–58; Albuquerque to the São Paulo Town Council (d. Rio, 26 February 1710) and to the Crown (d. Rio, 3 April 1710), *apud* A. Leite, *op. cit.*, pp. 46–53; *Consulta* of the Overseas Council

on the representations of Fr. Francisco de Menezes, Lisbon, 23 November 1709, *apud* Golgher, *op. cit.,* pp. 192–193.

[42] Cf. Taunay, *História Geral,* IX, 597–626, for details.

[43] F. A. Varnhagen, *História Geral* (3d. ed.; São Paulo, n.d.), III, 407–408, for a discussion of Fr. Francisco de São Jeronimo's allegedly anti-Semitic tendencies.

[44] Arquivo Publico Mineiro, Secretaria Geral, hereafter cited as APM(SG), Codice 6, "Primeiro Livro dos Termos deste governo que principiou a servir em 7 de julho de 1710," fols. 3–5 for the original *termo* of 7 July 1710, with the autograph signatures of Albuquerque and thirty-six leading Paulistas and others. Cf. also Taunay, *História Geral,* IX, 607–609.

[45] "E hé sem duvida que as tres partes dos quintos se descaminharão por mais cuidado que se poem nelles" (Albuquerque to the Crown, Rio de Janeiro, 3 April 1710). The original *termos* of 10 November and 1 December 1710, with the autograph signatures of Albuquerque, Borba Gato, and prominent Paulistas and Emboabas are in APM(SG), Codice 6, fols. 10–12.

[46] APM(SG), Codice 6, fols. 14–25, for the original *autos* of 1711 with the autograph signatures of Albuquerque and the founding fathers of the respective townships.

[47] Albuquerque to the Crown, Minas Gerais, 7 August 1711, and *consulta* of the Overseas Council on Albuquerque's previous proposals, Lisbon, 12 July 1711, in A. Leite, *op. cit.,* pp. 77–88. Cf. Taunay, *História Geral,* IX, 613–630; Soares de Melo, *Emboabas,* pp. 264–268.

[48] " ... os que entrão da Bahia e Pernambuco são os mais prejudiciais e absolutos, perturbadores, e de máo exemplo," Albuquerque had written to the Crown (3 April 1710) before leaving on his second expedition to the Mines.

[49] Estimated as covering an area of three million square kilometers by Taunay, *História Geral,* IX, 612.

NOTES TO CHAPTER IV
"The French in Rio de Janeiro"
(Pages 84–105)

[1] Damião Peres, *A diplomacia portuguesa e a Successão de Espanha, 1700–1704* (Barcellos, 1931); R. Lodge, "The Treaties of 1703," in E. Prestage [ed.], *Chapters in Anglo-Portuguese Relations* (Watford, 1935), pp. 152–169, give the best accounts of 1701–1704, from the Portuguese and English viewpoints, respectively.

[2] José Soares da Silva, *Gazeta em forma de carta,* p. 13.

[3] André Ribeiro Coutinho, *O Capitão de Infantaria Portuguez* (2 vols., Lisboa, 1751), II, 157–184, for the difficulties of recruiting in eighteenth-century Portugal.

[4] *Memoirs of the Sieur d'Ablancourt* (ed. London, 1703), p. 21. Cf. also C. Ayres, *Um capitulo da guerra da Restauração, 1660–1668. O Conde de Schönberg em Portugal* (Lisboa, 1897), p. 129.

[5] For the excesses of the allied soldiery, cf. *Gazeta em forma de carta,* pp. 29, 34, "A Milicia estrangeira tem exercitado as operações de suas qualidades, que são heregia e borracheira, em toda a parte por onde passão, e aonde se hospedão." For the excesses of the Portuguese soldiery, cf. Rau, *MSS Cadaval,* II, 69. It

would be easy to multiply such references to the misbehavior of Portuguese, Dutch, and English alike.

[6] C. De La Roncière, *Histoire de la marine française* (Paris, 1932), VI, 527–530, for a succinct account of Du Clerc's expedition from the French side.

[7] Page 104 of the English edition of 1698. The original French edition was published earlier in the same year, and was followed by several editions and translations between 1699 and 1715.

[8] Du Clerc's attack on Rio is extensively documented from the Portuguese side. I have relied chiefly on Fr. Francisco de Menezes' eyewitness account printed in *RIHGB*, LXIX, Parte I, pp. 53–75, the anonymous *Relaçam da Vitoria*, published at Lisbon on February 20, 1711, and on the anonymous eyewitness account printed by E. Brazão, *As expedições de Duclerc e de Duguay-Trouin ao Rio de Janeiro, 1710–1711* (Lisboa, 1940), pp. 15–36. I have also consulted all the sources listed in Varnhagen, *História Geral*, III, 359–363, 382–384. The French sources are listed in De La Roncière, *op. cit.*, VI, 528 n.

[9] Order of battle of the Portuguese forces in Brazão, *op. cit.*, pp. 27–29. Of the 15,300 men who were mustered for the occasion, 4,500 were regular troops. Francisco de Castro Morais had been governor of Pernambuco in 1703–1707 and had commanded the Rio garrison in 1700.

[10] Leite, S.J., *História*, VI, 46–49, for the part played by the Jesuits and their students.

[11] Thomas Pinto Brandão, *Pinto Renascido, empennado, e desempennado* (Lisboa, 1732), pp. 135–139, verses commemorating "A primeira invasão, que os Francezes fizerão no Rio de Janeiro, onde bastarão os Estudantes, e os pretos a destruillos; porque o terço da Infantaria que là se achava, estava no campo a pé quedo, no tempo em que o inimigo entrava pela Cidade: nesta função obrarão os Padres da Companhia como sempre; e as mais Religiões fugirão com o Bispo."

[12] *Apud* Brazão, *op. cit.*, p. 27.

[13] *Ibid.*, pp. 28–29 for a contemporary list of the defenders' casualties.

[14] *Officio* of Castro Morais, 25 June 1711; *consulta* of the Overseas Council, Lisboa, 12 February 1712; summary of Madame Du Clerc's petition; all published in *RIHGB, Tomo Especial do 1º Congresso da História Nacional*, I, 509–517; Varnhagen, *História Geral*, III, 382–384.

[15] *Apud* Brazão, *op. cit.*, pp. 31–32, and Fr. Francisco de Menezes' letter of 6 November 1710, in *RIHGB*, LXIX, Parte I, p. 69.

[16] *Memoires de M. Du Guay-Trouin* ([Paris], 1740), p. 158. Since Du Clerc was murdered on March 18, 1711, news of this could hardly have reached France until after Duguay-Trouin's departure early in June. From the wording of his ultimatum to the governor of Rio on September 19 following (*ibid.*, pp. 181–183), he only heard of the murder after his arrival in Rio.

[17] For the different editions of Duguay-Trouin's *Memoires* and other works on this famous privateer, see De La Roncière, *op. cit.*, VI, 177–178. Modern writers write his name as Du Guay-Trouin, but he always signed his name as Duguay-Trouin, and I have followed his own orthography.

[18] Duguay-Trouin, *op. cit.* (1740), pp. 98–109, for the French version. A Portuguese account in J. Soares da Silva, *Gazeta em forma de carta*, pp. 64–65.

[19] The Rio de Janeiro campaign of 1711 is very fully documented. The French accounts in De La Roncière, *op. cit.*, VI, 530–532, to which should be added the contemporary pamphlets in R. Borba de Moraes, *Bibliographia Brasiliana* (2 vols.,

Amsterdam, 1959), I, 231–232. Portuguese sources in Varnhagen, *História Geral,* III, 363–377; Calmon, *História do Brasil,* III, 47–53; *PAPNRJ,* VII (Rio de Janeiro, 1907), pp. 12–18; to which should be added the accounts of Castro Morais and Gaspar da Costa Ataide in Rau, *op. cit.,* II, 79–80, 104–108. Cf. also an English eyewitness account in H. H. Dodwell [ed.], *The Private Letter-books of Joseph Collett* (London, 1933), pp. 1–6.

[20] He had greatly distinugished himself by saving several lives in the disastrous hurricane which struck shipping in the River Mandoví (Goa) on the night of December 9–10, 1701. For a Portuguese version of the destruction of De Pointis' squadron off Algeciras, see Soares da Silva, *op. cit.,* pp. 34–35. For an indication that Gaspar da Costa was already losing his grip in 1708, see *ibid.,* p. 149.

[21] "Le *Magnanime* manoeuvra avec une fierté qui fit l'admiration de toute l'escadre et fit croire aux Portugais qu'il y avoit des pilotes du pays dans le vaisseau" (contemporary account *apud* De La Roncière, *op. cit.,* VI, 532).

[22] *Private Letter-books of Joseph Collett,* p. 1.

[23] The most reliable contemporary accounts estimate the total number of armed defenders at between 8,000 and 10,000 men, but these figures do not seem to include the armed slaves. Cf. Pizarro e Araujo, *Memorias Históricas do Rio de Janeiro* (ed. Borba de Moraes, 10 vols., Rio, 1945), I, 85, 115. The lower estimate given in Varnhagen, *op. cit.,* III, 365 n., also takes no account of the armed Negroes, who were certainly more numerous than the whites.

[24] Bocage was then *capitão-de-mar-e-guerra* of the scuttled *São Boaventura.* He was married to a Portuguese lady, and was the maternal grandfather of the famous satirical poet, Manuel Bocage.

[25] " ... em todo este tempo se andou oferesendo Bento do Amaral com muita gente que o queria acompanhar para alcansar a ilha das Cobras e a São Diogo aonde heles estavão acampados sem nunca lho consederem" (*apud* Brazão, *op. cit.,* p. 39).

[26] Cf. Rau, *op. cit.,* II, 80; Nuno Marques Pereira, *Compendio Narrativo do Peregrino da America,* chap. xv.

[27] Texts of Duguay-Trouin's ultimatum and of Castro Morais' reply in Duguay-Trouin, *op. cit.* (1740), pp. 181–185. Several contemporary Portuguese sources give the date of the ultimatum as September 8.

[28] " ... com effeito pelas onze horas da noite de domingo, 21 de setembro, se largou miseravelmente a Cidade e se fez a mais porca fugida, que se pode considerar" (Letter of Manuel de Vasconcellos Velho to a friend at Lisbon, dated Rio de Janeiro, 7 December 1711, *apud* Pizarro, *Memorias Históricas,* I, 84–101).

[29] " ... environ 500 hommes," according to Duguay-Trouin, *op. cit.,* p. 139. De La Roncière, *op. cit.,* VI, 537, gives the total as 360. In any event, about 50 officers and men had previously been sent to Bahia. Apart from these French prisoners, there were also about 100 crypto-Jews imprisoned in the city, and a few wounded in the hospitals.

[30] "Leur commandant, nommé Amara [sic], homme en reputation parmi eux, demeura sur la place; M. de Brugnon me présenta ses armes, et son cheval, l'un des plus beaux que j'aye vue" (*Mémoires,* p. 192). This is not surprising when we recall that Bento de Amaral Coutinho was a wealthy sugar planter, and a mineowner in Minas Gerais.

[31] The list of contributors and the Crown's subsequent concessions concerning

repayment are in Pizarro, *op. cit.*, I, 154–155, and Varnhagen, *op. cit.*, III, 385–386. Duguay-Trouin's receipts for the indemnity are in *PAPNRJ*, VII, 16–17.

[32] Albuquerque to the Crown, Rio de Janeiro, 26 November 1711, in *RIHGB*, LV, 215–218, and A. Leite, *op. cit.*, pp. 92–96. The original *portarias* and grants of commissions to the senior officers of the newly raised line regiments and the militia levies are in APM(SG), Codice 8.

[33] Duguay-Trouin was misled by his spies or by his memory when he wrote (*op. cit.*, pp. 195–196), that Albuquerque arrived on October 11, 1711, the day after the capitulation had been signed. This error has been repeated by nearly all subsequent writers, but the sources quoted in the previous note show clearly that on October 11 Albuquerque was still in Minas Gerais. Duguay-Trouin may, however, be correct when he states that Albuquerque on the final stage of his march, "pour s'y rendre plus promptement, il avoit fait mettre l'infanterie en croupe."

[34] José Gomes da Silva and his sons. Duguay-Trouin also released about 100 other crypto-Jews on this occasion (Pizarro, *op. cit.*, I, 101).

[35] *Letter-books of Joseph Collett*, pp. 1–6. The little *Jane* of 180 tons appears in Duguay-Trouin's *Memoires* as a warship of 56 guns.

[36] De La Roncière, *op. cit.*, VI, 538, for Louis XIV's circular letter to the Barbary States on the capture of "la plus florissante colonie des Portugais au Brésil."

[37] Documents in Rau, *op. cit.*, II, 87–88, 104–108.

[38] Manuel Velho's letter of 7 December 1711, in Pizarro, *op. cit.*, I, 98.

[39] Pizarro, *op. cit.*, pp. 153–154; Varnhagen, *op. cit.*, III, 376; Rau, *op. cit.*, II, 87–88, 104–108.

[40] Albuquerque's correspondence on the rehabilitation of Rio in ANRJ, "Registo Velho das Ordens Régias, 1712–1719," Vol. 21 (Col. 78, Livro 19).

NOTES TO CHAPTER V
"Planters and Peddlers"
(Pages 106–125)

[1] Salvador de Sá e Benavides wrote in 1647: "a gente de Pernambuco não he da mais escolhida deste Reyno" (*apud* Boxer, *The Dutch in Brazil*, p. 72n). A visiting Portuguese judge in 1714 was still more outspoken when he said that "os homens nobres de Pernambuco eram caboclos e filhos de degredados" (*apud* Fernandes Gama, *Memorias Históricas*, IV, 270).

[2] Duarte Gomes de Solis wrote from personal and bitter experience of "el grande odio que en Portugal se tiene contra los hombres de negocio" in his *Alegación en favor de la Compañia de la India Oriental* (1628), fol. 70.

[3] F. Froger, *A Relation of a Voyage* (London, 1698), p. 54. Gaspar de Freitas de Abreu wrote to the Prince Regent Dom Pedro, 7 April 1674: "Só nós os Portugueses ficamos com o nome de Judeus ou marranos entre todas as nações, que é grande desgraça, como bem experimentou o Marques de Gouveia em Madrid" (*Boletim Academia das Sciencias*, II Classe, Tomo X, 1915–1916, p. 335). Lord Tyrawley, British envoy to Portugal in 1728–1741, quoted approvingly the

disparaging observation of a French colleague at Lisbon: "What can be expected of a nation, one half of which is looking out for the Messiah, and the other half for Dom Sebastian who has been dead for [nearly] two centuries?"

[4] As Frei Francisco de Menezes wrote from Rio de Janeiro to the Duke of Cadaval, 6 November 1710: "Sua Magestade deu liberdade aos governadores para negociarem. ... até agora sempre governarão, e negociavão, mas era com receio, sempre tinhão mão em si, agora vão pondo isto em taes termos que jà não ha negocio senão o seu ... " (*RIHGB*, LXIX, Pt. I, pp. 73–74).

[5] A popular Oriental saying, of which there were numerous variants, ran: "Were the world a ring, Hormuz would be the jewel in it." Thomas Herbert in *Some Yeares Travaile* (1634), calls it "this universall proverbe," which he rendered into doggerel verse: "If all the world were but a ring, Ormuz the diamond should bring." Cf. A. Wilson, *The Persian Gulf* (Oxford, 1928), p. 101.

[6] H. Koster, *Travels in Brazil* (London, 1816).

[7] Cf. Padre António Gonçalves Leitão's denunciation of the "turbilhão de aventureiros auricedentos, que, todos os annos, nus e miseraveis, aportavam no hospitaleiro Pernambuco. D'esta gente, pois, a mais abjecta de Portugal, ignorante, e sobremaneira mal educada, abundava esta Provincia ... e assim, arvorados em Mascates em breve tempo aquelles estúpidos que em Portugal nem por criados serviam, tornavam-se capitalistas, e, esquecendo-se de seus principios, julgam-se superiores à nobreza do Pais, que tão benignamente os acolhera" (*apud* J. B. Fernandes Gama, *Memorias Historicas da Provincia de Pernambuco* [4 vols., Recife, 1844–1848], IV, 56–57).

[8] *Apud* Pereira da Costa, *Anais Pernambucanos*, V, 21. Cf. Calmon, *História Social do Brasil*, pp. 38–42.

[9] CR of 18 May 1709, in *ABNRJ*, XXVIII, 376; Leite, S.J., *História*, V, 450–452, 471; Mário Melo, *A Guerra dos Mascates como afirmação nacionalista*, pp. 18–19.

[10] In contrast with the "Guerra dos Emboabas," the "Guerra dos Mascates" is extensively documented from both sides, the basic documentation being found in the following works: Fernandes Gama, *op. cit.*, IV, 54–330, being almost entirely based on Padre Gonsalves Leitão's pro-Pernambucan contemporary account; Dr. Manuel dos Santos, "Narração historica das calamidades de Pernambuco, sucedidas desde o anno de 1707 até o de 1715," written in its final form in 1749 by a Mascate supporter, and printed in *RIHGB*, LIII, Pt. I (1890), pp. 1–307; "Relação do levante de Pernambuco em 1710," in *Brasilia*, VI (Coimbra, 1951), pp. 283–329; F. A. Pereira da Costa, *Anais Pernambucanos* (7 vols., Recife, 1951–1958), V, 85–278, *passim;* Varnhagen, *História Geral*, III, 393–407; Pedro Calmon, *História do Brasil*, III, 62–74; Leite, S.J., *op. cit.*, V, 450–459; Rau, *MSS Cadaval*, II, 349–354; Melo, *op. cit.;* Rocha Pitta, *Historia da America Portuguesa*, Livro IX, paras. 51–58. The only detailed account in English, R. Southey, *History of Brazil*, III, 85–107, is heavily biased in favor of the Mascates.

[11] A stone column surmounted by a cross, shield, or the royal arms, which served as the insignia of the municipality and also as a pillory and whipping post for offenders, particularly slaves.

[12] It was alleged that more people had been murdered in Pernambuco in a few years than had been killed in the whole war with the Dutch, 1630–1654. Cf. the list of persons murdered at Olinda and Recife in 1671, in *Anais do IV Congresso da História Nacional*, XI (1951), pp. 123–129. For the general "killing

no murder" attitude prevalent in colonial Brazil, see Calmon, *História Social,* pp. 135–150.

[13] Leite, S.J., *op, cit.,* V, 453; Melo, *op. cit.,* pp. 28–29.

[14] "ad instar dos Venezianos." Bernardo Vieira de Mello was a Pernambucan planter who commanded a Paulista regiment raised to hunt down fugitive Negro slaves. Mascate writers accuse him of conniving at the murder of his daughter-in-law by his wife and son, André Vieira de Mello, under particularly revolting circumstances (*RIHGB,* LIII, 68–74).

[15] For slightly differing versions of the Pernambucan planters' demands, cf. Pereira da Costa, *op. cit.,* V, 190–194; *RIHGB,* LIII, 56–57, 60–62; *Brasília,* VI, 304–308; Rau, *op. cit.,* II, 352–354.

[16] Fernandes Gama, *op. cit.,* IV, 69.

[17] Melo, *op. cit.,* pp. 69–78; prints the Bishop's own account in his letter to the Crown, Olinda, 7 November 1711. The Mascate version is given in Captain João da Mota's letter, Recife, 30 November 1711, *op. cit.,* pp. 81–90.

[18] " ... pois se valião de pedaços de tijollo e barro, e até com genipapos verdes se atiravão" (Manuel dos Santos in *RIHGB,* LVIII, 110).

[19] For the original Camarão and Henrique Dias, see the definitive biographies by J. A. Gonsalves de Mello, *D. Antonio Felipe Camarão Capitão-Mor dos Indios da Costa do Nordeste do Brasil,* and *Henrique Dias Governador dos pretos, crioulos e mulatos do Estado do Brasil,* both published at Recife in 1954. The two leaders concerned in the War of the Mascates were Dom Sebastião Pinheiro Camarão and Domingos Rodrigues Carneiro.

[20] This correspondence is printed in Fernandes Gama, *op. cit.,* IV, 77–86, 101–114, and in *RIHGB,* LIII, 120–140.

[21] Fernandes Gama, *op. cit.,* IV, 130–131.

[22] Fernandes Gama, *op. cit.,* IV, 121–135; Manuel dos Santos in *RIHGB,* LIII, 198–199. The Mascate author claims that Christovão de Mendonça Arrais was allowed to disembark after nightfall, to avoid participating in this humiliating procession. He also states that when the prisoners reached the jail, they were soon helped with clothes and money by charitable citizens, "uns por caridade, e outros por conhecimento."

[23] Manuel dos Santos in *RIHGB,* LIII, p. 141.

[24] *Ibid.,* pp. 190–192.

[25] Arquivo Publico do Estado de Pernambuco, Recife; "Livro de Registo de Portarias, 1711–1716," fols. 9–10; "Bando que se lançou para que se evitassem vocabulos mal soantes e palavras offensivas entre todos estes povos," d. 4 November 1711.

[26] The sufferings of the persecuted planters are related at great length with many supporting documents in Fernandes Gama, *op. cit.,* IV, 186–281. The leading matrons of the captaincy wrote to the viceroy at Bahia (28 May 1714) stating that they were enduring a tyranny which surpassed the worst excesses of the Dutch when they were masters of Pernambuco (*ibid.,* p. 272).

[27] Gama, *op. cit.,* IV, 259–271.

[28] *Ibid.,* IV, 310–312, for typical allegations.

[29] Gama, *op. cit.,* IV, 246–248. The new viceroy of Brazil, Dom Pedro de Noronha, Marquis of Angeja, also wrote to the Crown in favor of the perse-cuted Pernambucans in 1714, but his dispatches arrived after the king had de-

cided on a policy of clemency as a result of Albuquerque's representations. Cf. Angeja's letters in *DH*, XXXIX, 360–369.

[30] D. Manuel Alvares da Cunha was recalled to Portugal in 1715, and transferred to the See of Angra in the Azores five years later. For the Crown amnesty, d. 7 April 1714, see Gama, *op. cit.,* IV, 281–285, and for its implementation by the governor, "Bando que se lançou sobre o perdam que SM foy servido confirmar aos naturais de Olinda," Recife, 4 June 1714 (APEP, "Livro do Registo de Portarias, 1711–1716," fol. 285).

[31] Pereira da Costa, *op. cit.,* V, 210. For the use of *marinheiro* as a derogatory term for unsuccessful Portuguese immigrants at Recife in 1941, see Melo, *op. cit.,* pp. 19–20 n.

NOTES TO CHAPTER VI
"Bay of All Saints"
(Pages 126–161)

[1] Gilberto Freyre, *Baía de Todos os Santos e de quase todos os pecados* (Recife, 1926), reprinted in the collected edition of his works.

[2] "... podendose com muita razão dizer que o Brasil tem o corpo na America e a alma na Africa," as Padre António Vieira, S.J., wrote in the unpublished *Vida* of his English-born colleague, João de Almeida (*apud* J. L. d'Azevedo, *História de António Vieira,* I, 408).

[3] Ramponi, *apud* C. Azevedo, "Um artista italiano em Goa," p. 35. An archipiscopal estimate of 1706 gave the population of the six parishes of Salvador as 4,296 hearths (*fogos*) with 21,601 communicants, which had risen to 6,719 hearths and 37,543 communicants fifty years later (Accioli-Amaral, *Memorias Historicas da Provincia da Bahia,* V, 503). C. B. Ott, *Formação e Evolução do Salvador,* I, 63, accepts the accuracy of Caldas' calculation in 1759 that the total population of the city and the *Reconcavo* amounted to 103,096 souls.

[4] Leite, S.J., *História,* VII, 191–208, for a documented account of the Bahia citizens' vain attempt to get the Jesuit College recognized as a university.

[5] Dampier, *A Voyage to New Holland in the Year 1699* (ed. J. A. Williamson, London, 1939), pp. 33–43.

[6] An observation confirmed by the remarks of many other foreign travelers who visited Portugal's overseas possessions. Cf. my *Salvador de Sá,* pp. 52–53.

[7] *Letters from the Island of Teneriffe, Brazil, the Cape of Good Hope and the East Indies. By Mrs. Kindersley* (London, 1777), pp. 15, 34–35. Mrs. Kindersley visited Bahia in 1764 but most of her observations are equally applicable to the first half of the eighteenth century.

[8] *Voyage de Marseille a Lima* (Paris, 1720), II, 130–131, *apud* M. S. Cardozo, "Lay Brotherhoods of Colonial Bahia," pp. 13–14.

[9] "Viagem que fes o Arcebispo de Goa Primaz da India Oriental na náo *São Francisco de Borja* o anno de 1691" (British Museum, Add. MSS 20953, fol. 251).

[10] Germain Bazin's excellent *L'Architecture religieuse baroque au Brésil* (2

vols., Paris, 1956), is lavishly illustrated and provided with a full bibliography of relevant books and articles. My succinct description is based chiefly on R. C. Smith, "The Arts in Brazil. Baroque Architecture," in *Portugal and Brazil*, pp. 349-384; *idem*, "Nossa Senhora da Conceição da Praia and the Joanine style in Brazil," in *Journal of the Society of Art Historians* XV (October, 1956), pp. 16-23; *idem*, *As Artes na Bahia. Arquitectura Colonial* (Salvador, 1955); John Bury, "Jesuit Architecture in Brazil," in *The Month*, n.s., IV (1950), pp. 385-408; *idem*, "The Borrominesque Churches of Colonial Brazil," in *The Art Bulletin*, XXXVII (March, 1955), pp. 27-53.

11 *Relation succinte et sincère de la Mission du père Martin de Nantes, Prédicateur Capucin, Missionaire Apostolique dans le Brezil parmy les Indiens appelés Cariris* (Quimper, *ca.* 1707), pp. 93-95. Fr. Martin was in the captaincy of Bahia, 1671-1688.

12 Leite, S.J., *op. cit.*, VII, 233-247, for a discussion of the lack of religious vocations in seventeenth- eighteenth-century Brazil, and the steps taken by the Jesuits to cope with the problem.

13 "A India e a Religião costumão dar boa acolhida a este genero de gente. Siso será destinarlhe" (D. Francisco Manuel de Mello, *Carta de Guia de Casados*, Lisboa, 1651, p. 125).

14 "... porque está hoje o mundo (e principalmente este Estado do Brasil) em taes termos, que mais parecem alguns sacerdotes mercadores negociantes, que Ministros de Deos, a curas de almas," wrote Nuno Marques Pereira when discussing the laxity of the colonial clergy in chapter 23 of his *Compendio Narrativo do Peregrino da America*. These and other clerical misdemeanors were also denounced by Archbishop Sebastião Monteiro da Vide, *Primeiras Constituições do Arcebispo da Bahia* (Coimbra, 1720), pp. 183-199. How ineffective the archiepiscopal admonitions were can be seen from numerous complaints in the official correspondence between Bahia and Lisbon, such as those in APEB, "Ordens Régias," Vol. XIV, doc. 226; *ibid.*, Vol. XVII, doc. 4A; *ibid.*, Vol. XXVII, no. 7A; Accioli-Amaral, *op. cit.*, V, 489-495. Le Gentil de la Barbinais is particularly scathing in his denunciation of the Bahia clergy in 1717 (*Nouveau Voyage autour du monde*, 3 vols., Paris, 1728), III, 202-203, 206-209, 216-219.

15 Extracts from the cuckolded planter's pathetic petition are given by Augusto de Lima Junior, *Notícias Históricas. De Norte a Sul* (Rio, 1953), pp. 61-70. This clerical Casanova was also accused of habitually soliciting married women, "como a fez à mulher de João Correia, boticário, e de Valentim de Goiás, cravador de diamantes, e outras mais de que se tem seguido perniciosas consequencias, sem ele haver tido o menor castigo."

16 "... Ia vos disse que o peyor Religioso, he melhor que o melhor secular ... " (Martim Affonso da Miranda, *Tempo de Agora*, 2 vols., Lisbon, 1622-1624, I, 123 of the 1785 reprint). Cf. Thomé Pinheiro da Veiga, *Fastigimia* (ed. 1911), p. 347. The transcendent dignity of the sacerdotal calling was often expressed in Portuguese devotional literature by terming the priests *Creadores do seu Creador*, "Creators of their Creator."

17 Nuno Marques Pereira, *Compendio Narrativo* (ed. 1760), pp. 234-235.

18 *Relation Succinte* (*ca.* 1707), p. 146.

19 As a true-blue Protestant she could not forbear to add: "were the Roman Catholic priests to take as much care of the morals of their flock, as they do to attach them to the church, they would be the most virtuous common people

in the world" (*Letters,* pp. 50–51). The good lady was evidently quite unaware of the extent to which many of these worshipers retained a strong infusion of their ancestral religions, which have survived to the present day in the Afro-Brazilian cults of *Xângo* and *Candomblé*.

[20] "... exercice violent qui ne convenoit gueres à son age, ni à son caractère: mais c'eut été une impieté digne du feu, au sentiment de ce peuple, s'il avoit refusé de rendre cet hommage au Saint dont on celebroit la Fête," observed Le Gentil de la Barbinais disapprovingly (*Nouveau Voyage,* III, 218).

[21] Cardozo, "The Lay Brotherhoods of Colonial Bahia," in *Catholic Historical Review,* XXXIII (April, 1947), pp. 12–30, and Bazin, *op. cit.,* I, 10–19, for documented discussion of the brotherhoods and their roles.

[22] "Encore aujourd'hui celui qui visite à Rio le siège de l'établissement dit 'de la Pénitence,' impressionné par les portraits solonnels des anciens Ministres, par la profusion d'or de l'église, par le luxe du consistoire, croit pénétrer dans une sorte de Jockey-Club religieux" (Bazin, *op. cit.,* I, 13).

[23] Viceroy to Crown, Bahia, 6 August 1729 (APEB, "Ordens Régias, Vol. XXV, doc. 55.) Sabugosa estimated the annual total of Masses involved at 24,311, "que reduzido todo este numero de missas a dinheiro, emporta 4 contos, 432,960." For the vicissitudes of the Luanda Misericordia, see Padre Brásio's article in *Studia,* IV (July, 1959), pp. 106–149. For the establishment of the Villa Rica Misericordia, see *RAPM,* XVI, 399.

[24] E. Prestage, *O Dr. António de Sousa de Macedo, Residente de Portugal em Londres, 1642-46* (Lisboa, 1916), p. 9. Thomé Pinheiro da Veiga's *Fastigimia* was first published at Oporto in 1911, though written three centuries earlier.

[25] Archbishop of Bahia's pastoral of 20 July 1751, quoted in *Anais do IV Congresso da História Nacional,* Tomo XI (Rio, 1951), p. 85.

[26] CR of 1 March 1700, in Accioli-Amaral, *op. cit.,* II, 149. Cf. also Nuno Marques Pereira, *Compendio Narrativo,* chap. xiii, and Le Gentil de la Barbinais, *op. cit.,* III, 202–204, for the prostitution of female slaves by their lady owners.

[27] *Provizão* of 5 November 1711, in ANRJ, "Registo Velho de Ordens Régias," Vol. XXI, fol. 9; CR of 11 January 1690, in APEB, "Ordens Régias," Vol. II, doc. 56.

[28] CR of 31 March 1722 and attached papers in APEB, "Ordens Régias," Vol. XVII, doc. 23.

[29] CR of 27 February 1698 in APEB, "Ordens Régias," Vol. VI, doc. 43; Viceroy to Crown, 30 September 1728, in *ibid.,* Vol. XXIV, doc. 122; CR of 12 May 1732, in *ibid.,* Vol. XXIX, fols. 89 ff. Cf. Delgado, *História de Angola,* IV, 434. The archives of the Camara Municipal at Luanda contain a worm-eaten codex (which I examined in 1955) entitled "Registro dos degredados condenados por varios crimes vindos do Brasil, 1663-1757." There is another codex covering the years 1757-1793, and a third relating to the year 1768. They give the origin of each individual and particulars of his (or her) crime and sentence, and are of great sociological interest.

[30] Carlos de Azevedo, *Um Artista Italiano em Goa,* p. 39. Cf. Pedro Calmon, *História social do Brasil,* pp. 135–150.

[31] *A Voyage to New Holland in 1699* (ed. 1939), p. 36.

[32] Count of Sabugosa's correspondence with the Crown, 1724-1725, in APEB, "Ordens Régias," Vol. XX, docs. 114–115A, and that of his successor, the Count

of Galveas, in 1735–1736, in *ibid.,* Vol. XXXIII, fols. 46–47. Cf. *DH,* XC (1950), p. 93. For the difficulties of recruiting in Portugal itself, cf. Chap. iv, p. 85 above.

[33] CR of 29 April 1730 and viceregal reply of 3 August 1730, in APEB, "Ordens Régias," Vol. XXVII, fols. 84–85; Viceroy to Crown, 29 November 1731, in *ibid.,* Vol. XXVIII, fol. 296. Cf. also Nuno Marques Pereira, *Compendio Narrativo* (ed. Academia Brasileira), I, 371, 386. *PANRJ,* X, 146–149, for applications for discharge on compassionate grounds by the soldiers of the garrison of Rio de Janeiro.

[34] CR of 13 January 1731 and viceregal reply of 10 June 1731, in APEB, "Ordens Régias," Vol. XXVIII, docs. 17–17A. Cf. the CR of 27 January 1728 addressed to the Governor of Minas Gerais, ordering that whites and colored should be mixed in the militia, so that the latter should "ficarem mais sujeitos e obedientes." This was reiterated on 13 January 1731 (*RAPM,* XVI [1911], pp. 342–343).

[35] CR of 24 February 1731 and viceregal reply of 13 July 1731, in APEB, "Ordens Régias," Vol. XXVIII, docs. 32–32A; *Alvará* of 9 October 1716, for the conditions of military service in Angola (copy APEB, Vol. XI, doc. 67).

[36] Correspondence between the Crown and the governor-general at Bahia, in APEB, "Ordens Régias," Vol. XI, docs. 13–14.

[37] For documented accounts of the mutinies of 1688 and 1728, see Accioli-Amaral, *op. cit.,* II, 161–167, 376; Luiz Monteiro da Costa, *Na Bahia Colonial* (Salvador, 1958), pp. 111–136.

[38] See his orders for the extermination of a tribe of hostile Amerindians, which gave the Crown occasion to remind him that women and children and those who surrendered should be spared (Accioli-Amaral, *op. cit.,* II, 168, 343, 363–364).

[39] Sabugosa to the Crown, 30 April 1731, and Crown's reply of 26 October 1732 (author's collection); *DH,* XC, 246–247. For the powers conferred on the governors-general and viceroys of Brazil during this period, see the documents printed in Accioli-Amaral, *op. cit.,* II, 317–319, and summarized in E. M. Lobo, *Administração colonial Luso-Espanhola nas Américas* (Rio de Janeiro, 1952), pp. 289–291.

[40] For Sabugosa's viceroyalty, I have relied principally on his original correspondence with the Crown preserved in APEB, "Ordens Régias," Vols. XV–XXXI, part of which (down to Vol. XXII) is calendared in *AAPB,* Vol. XXXII (Salvador, 1952). Relevant documents are also scattered throughout Accioli-Amaral, *op. cit.,* particularly Vols. II, V, and VI, but unfortunately this work has no index. The same applies to the *Documentos Historicos.*

[41] For some typical instances of the feud between the Count of Sabugosa and the *Ouvidor Geral* at Bahia, cf. Accioli-Amaral, *op. cit.,* II, 349–351, and for the former's dislike of Dom Lourenço de Almeida (*ibid.,* VI, 77–81).

[42] Lord Tyrawly to Lord Newcastle, Lisbon, 2 January 1740 (PRO, London, SP 89/40).

[43] A printed copy of the *alvará em forma de lei* of 24 July 1713, in APEB, "Ordens Régias," Vol. IX, doc. 34. For some typical instances of red tape and bureaucratic delays, cf. J. L. d'Azevedo, *O Marquez de Pombal e a sua epoca* (Lisboa, 1909), pp. 43–46; Bazin, *op. cit.,* I, 9–11. This procrastination was not confined to Lisbon, as one might think from the strictures of Lord Tyrawly and others. Stamford Raffles, after returning to London from his governorship of Java in 1816, found many of his dispatches unopened in the India Office

(*Narrative of the Early Life and Services of Captain D. Macdonald I.N.* 3d ed.; Weymouth, n.d., p. 239.

[44] Cf. the dispatches of the Conde das Galveas in APEB, "Ordens Régias," Vol. XXXIII, fols. 129, 376–377; *ibid.*, Vol. XXXIV, fol. 104. For the overworked secretariat at Government House in Ouro Preto, Minas Gerais, in 1724, see D. Lourenço de Almeida's dispatch in *RAPM*, XVI, 375.

[45] "Se a pessoa a quem Vossa Magestade encarrega o governo deste Brasil não hé capaz de erigir hũa villa, dar-lhe o termo, e ouvir as Camaras a que dantes estava repartido, e se a dita villa pode com o gasto do conselho ou não, não he tambem capaz de se lhe encarregar o governo da Bahia e deste Estado" (Marquis of Angeja to the Crown, 13 July 1718, *apud* Accioli-Amaral, *op. cit.*, II, 332–333). Cf. also Angeja's dispatch, 30 May 1715 (*DH*, XL, 25–28).

[46] Sabugosa added that the population of Maragogipe had increased from some 40 households in 1700 to 426 in 1724, "entre os quais ha mais de 2,500 almas de confissão." Sabugosa to the Crown, 1 April 1724, and supporting documents (author's collection). Cf. also *DH*, XC, 136–137, 155; Accioli-Amaral, *op. cit.*, II, 160, 325, 364.

[47] Correspondence between the Viceroy and the Crown, 1728–1730, in APEB, "Ordens Régias," Vol. XXVI, fol. 49; Vol. XXVII, docs. 36–38; Accioli-Amaral, *op. cit.*, II, 84–91, 359–360.

[48] The minutes of the Salvador Municipal Council Meetings from 1625 to 1700 have been published in six volumes (Salvador, 1945–1951), and for an historical survey of the Council's activities, see Affonso Ruy, *História da Camara Municipal do Salvador* (Salvador, 1953). Accioli-Amaral prints many documents in the *Memorias Historicas*, 6 vols., *passim*. Cf. also the correspondence of the viceroys and governors-general with the Bahia Municipal Council, 1697–1726, in *DH*, LXXXVII, 1–224.

[49] Sabugosa's correspondence with the Crown, 1729–1732, and supporting documents (author's collection). Cf. also *DH*, LXXXVII, 24–25, 41; *DH*, XC, 244–246; Rau, *MSS Cadaval*, II, 338; Wanderley de Araujo Pinho, *História de um engenho do Reconcavo* (Rio de Janeiro, 1946); *PANRJ*, X, 157–159.

[50] Edicts of 31 August 1636 and 1663 in Accioli-Amaral, *op. cit.*, II, 94, 384; Viceroy to Crown, 22 January 1725 and 22 August 1726, in APEB, "Ordens Régias," Vols. XX and XXI; Antonil, *Cultura*, Livro III, cap. 10.

[51] " ... se a mandioca é o pão, a aguardente é o vinho com que os homens tem algum alento ... e até os meninos morriam de frialdade" (Document of 1663 calendared in *Anais do I Congresso de Historia da Bahia*, II, p. 169). For the ravages of Demon Rum in Angola cf. Delgado, *História*, IV, 125–126.

[52] Xavier Lopes Villela to the Crown, Bahia, 10 March 1726, in APEB. "Ordens Régias," Vol. XXIII, No. 85E; correspondence of Sabugosa with the Crown, 29 May 1729–28 August 1729, ni APEB, "Ordens Régias," Vols. XXV–XXVI. Antonil, *Cultura e Opulencia*, Livro III, gives an excellent account of the tobacco trade at the opening of the eighteenth century.

[53] Accioli-Amaral, *op. cit.*, VI, 16–126, 200–216, print many documents relating to the development of the Bahian gold mines in the eighteenth century. For the services of Pedro Leolino Mariz, cf. Varnhagen, *História Geral*, IV, 155–159.

[54] Between 30 August 1728 and 29 July 1729 the Mint at Bahia received gold from the Minas Novas amounting to 113 *arrobas* 11 pounds and 59 *oitavas,* and between 29 July 1729 and 15 April 1730, gold amounting to 107 *arrobas* 8

pounds, 31 *oitavas* and 24 grains (Detailed list showing how much gold was received from each individual miner in APEB, "Ordens Régias," Vol. XXVIII, docs. 16B and 16C). In a dispatch of 16 February 1738, the Count of Galveas informed the Crown that the gold received by the Bahia Mint from the mines in the hinterland between 1 September 1735 and 31 August 1736 and reduced to coin amounted to 55 *contos*, 620,345 *reis*, ready for dispatch to Portugal. Another 2, 641½ *oitavas* and 29½ grains of gold were received from the Jacobina mines for the six months ending 31 December 1737 (APEB, "Ordens Régias," Vol. XXXV, fols. 42–47, including a list of individual remittances). Cf. also the statistics of gold production from these mines in Accioli-Amaral, *op. cit.*, VI, 99–100, 209–212, 252–254.

[55] *Letters*, pp. 42–43.

[56] APEB, "Ordens Régias," Vol. XXXIII, fols. 270–271.

[57] Cf. the numerous documents relating to the trade with Whydah, and difficulties with the Dutch of Elmina (Mina) which are indexed under the word *Ajudá* in the *Anais do Arquivo Público da Bahia*, Vols. XXXI (1949), and XXXII (1952). The difficulties persisted down to the end of the century (Accioli-Amaral, *op. cit.*, V, 350–351). For the actual founding of the fort at Whydah in 1721, see the contemporary "Memoria" printed in *Arquivo das Colonias*, I (Lisboa, 1917), pp. 162–165.

[58] Sabugosa to the Secretary of State, Bahia, 3 March 1731, with supporting documents, in APEB, "Ordens Régias," Vol. XXVII, fols. 174–185.

[59] Count of Galveas to the Secretary of State, incomplete and undated but *ca.* February, 1738, in APEB, "Ordens Régias," Vol. XXXV, fols. 54–56. Printed in Viana Filho, *O Negro na Bahia*, pp. 155–160. The Viceroy Count of Atouguia, writing to the Crown on 6 September 1753, stated that the records of the Customs House showed that 90,809 Negro slaves were imported into Bahia during the twenty years from 1728 to 1748 (Accioli-Amaral, *op. cit.*, II, 397, 429. The majority of these slaves were from Dahomey.

[60] Secretary of State to D. João de Lencastre, Lisbon, 20 January 1701, in Accioli-Amaral, *op. cit.*, II, 302–304. The itemized list of seizures of contraband tobacco shows that among the culprits were a discalced Carmelite friar and some Bernardine nuns.

[61] *Provizão em forma de lei*, printed 8 February 1711 and reissued in October, 1715 (copy in APEB, "Ordens Régias," vol. X, doc. 32).

[62] Anon., *Description de la ville de Lisbonne ou l'on traite de la cour, de Portugal, des colonies Portugaises, & du commerce de cette capitale* (Paris, 1730), p. 248.

[63] Crown to Viceroy, 22 March 1718, in Accioli-Amaral, *op. cit.*, II, 338–339; Viceroy to Crown, 3 October 1733, in APEB, "Ordens Régias," Vol. XXX, doc. 161; Le Gentil de la Barbinais, *Nouveau Voyage*, III, 168. The same thing happened at Rio de Janeiro (ANRJ, "Correspondencia dos Governadores do Rio, 1702–1706," 13/13A, fols. 470–471).

[64] Mahé de la Bourdonnais to De Clos Rivière, Pondicherry, October, 1730, and attached documents, Lisbon, December, 1730 (author's collection). For other seamen from Saint Malo who were trading with India and Brazil in 1728, see *RIHGB* (ed.), *Catalogo de documentos sobre a história de São Paulo, existentes no Arquivo Histórico Ultramarino de Lisboa* (Rio de Janeiro, 1956), II, 58 ff. For La Bourdonnais' connections with the Portuguese at Goa, cf. *Studia*, IV, 35–39 (where he is wrongly split into two persons).

[65] *Description de la ville de Lisbonne* (1730), pp. 229-230, 245-247.

[66] Tyrawly to Newcastle, Lisbon, 22 August 1738 (PRO, London, SP 89/40); the estimates of gold exports for the year 1733 as given independently by Assumar and Pombal *apud* J. Cortesão, *Alexandre de Gusmão*, I (1), 54-57; where, however, the date is misprinted as 1713.

[67] CR of 10 February 1696, in APEB, "Ordens Régias," Vol. V, doc. 15.

[68] Tyrawly to Newcastle, Lisbon, 2 January 1739 (PRO, London, SP 89/40).

[69] Cf. Le Gentil de la Barbinais, *op. cit.*, III, 163-164, 198-199, 244. For the Portuguese Crown's refusal to recognize the appointment of an English or any other consul in Brazilian ports in 1719, see *PANRJ*, X, 63.

[70] Leite, S.J., *História*, V, 92-95. Padre Leite estimates that at the time of the seizure of the Jesuits' property by Pombal in 1760, their College library at Bahia contained at least 15,000 volumes.

[71] Waldemar Mattos [ed.], *Documentos historicos do Arquivo Municipal. Registro das marcas dos ensaidores de ouro e prata, 1725-1845* (Salvador, 1952), and S. Leite, S.J., *Artes e Oficios dos Jesuitas no Brasil* (Rio de Janeiro, 1953), give much information about the goldsmiths and silversmiths of Bahia, and about the Jesuits who exercised a wide variety of arts and crafts, respectively.

[72] The complete works of Gregorio de Matos have been edited by the Academia Brasileira in six volumes (*Obras Completas*, 1923-1933).

[73] The edition of the unpublished works of the Academia dos Esquecidos, promised by the Academia Brasileira in 1944 has not yet appeared at the time of writing.

[74] *AAPB*, XXXII (1952), pp. 305-310.

[75] *Apud* R. Gallop, *Portugal. A Book of Folk-ways* (London, 1936), p. 253. Le Gentil de la Barbinais had a much lower opinion of the *modinha* at Bahia in 1717-1718: "Les Portugais en longues robbes de chambre, le rosaire en Echarpe, l'Epée nue sous la Robbe, & la guitarre à la main se promenoient sous les balcons de leurs Dames, et là d'une voix ridiculement tendre, ils chantoient des aires qui me faisoient regretter la musique chinoise, ou nos gigues de basse Bretagne" (*Nouveau Voyage*, III, 205).

NOTES TO CHAPTER VII
"Rich Town of Black Gold"
(Pages 162-203)

[1] Simão Ferreira Machado, *Triunfo Eucharistico. Exemplar de Christandade Lusitana em Villa Rica, Corte da Capitania das Minas, aos 24 de Mayo de 1733* (Lisboa, 1734), pp. 24-25.

[2] Francisco Tavares de Brito, *Itinerario Geografico do Rio de Janeiro até as Minas do Ouro* (Sevilla, 1732), p. 19 " ... Esta Serra he hum Potosí de Ouro."

[3] Dom Lourenço de Almeida's dispatch of April, 1722 in F. A. Lopes, *Os Palacios de Vila Rica. Ouro Preto no ciclo do ouro* (Belo Horizonte, 1955), pp. 153-154; Martinho de Mendonça's dispatch of 1734 in A. Lima Junior, *Vila Rica do Ouro Preto* (Belo Horizonte, 1937), p. 73, where, however, it is wrongly dated; *RAPM*, XXIV, Pt. I (1933), pp. 347-348, 350-351, for fuller ex-

tracts. Assumar's opinion in "Discurso Historico e Politico," ed. Xavier da Veiga, *A Revolta de 1720 em Vila Rica* (Ouro Preto, 1898), p. 149.

[4] D. Lourenço de Almeida's dispatch of June, 1731, in F. A. Lopes, *Vila Rica,* p. 154; *provizam* of 1 March and CR of 14 March 1732, in APEB, "Ordens Régias," Vol. XXVIII, fols. 58–61. Cf. also Ott, *Formação,* II, 77; the Crown had been asked to take a similar step as early as 1695, but had then refused. Cf. Accioli-Amaral, *Memorias Historicas,* II, 283. There is a thoughtful discussion of the problem in Caio Prado Júnior, *Formação, Brasil Colónia,* pp. 351 ff.

[5] W. L. Schurz, *This New World* (London, 1956), p. 62.

[6] Le Gentil de la Barbinais, *Nouveau Voyage,* III, 204.

[7] Luís Vahia Monteiro to the Crown, 5 July 1726, *apud* M. P. Zemella, *O abastecimento das Minas Gerais no século XVIII* (São Paulo, 1951), pp. 202–203. For slave prostitution in Minas Gerais, see Manuel de Affonseca's dispatch of February, 1732, in F. A. Lopes, *Vila Rica,* pp. 155–157.

[8] Overseas Council's minute of 25 September 1725 and Gomes Freire de Andrada's observation in A. Lima Junior, *Capitania das Minas Gerais* (ed. 1943), pp. 149–153. Cf. also Xavier da Veiga, *Ephemerides Mineiras,* I, 94–95.

[9] CR of 30 May 1753 and Gomes Freire de Andrada's reply of 23 September 1753, in APM, Cod. 100 (SG), fol. 24. I owe this reference to the kindness of Dr. Curt Lange.

[10] Anonymous account by an old-timer who had reached Villa Rica in 1712, in Codice Costa Matoso, fol. 37ᵛ. For the order of 1715, cf. Xavier da Veiga, *op. cit.,* III, 145.

[11] APM, Cod. 19(DF) for the years 1718–1719, for example, shows "Minas" as the most numerous group, with "Angolas" and "Benguelas" next, and "Carijós" third.

[12] " ... a gente mesquinha de que abundão para sua ruina todas as nossas praças": Francisco de Sousa, S.J., *Oriente Conquistado a Jesu Christo pelos Padres da Companhia de Jesus da Provincia de Goa* (2 vols., Lisboa, 1710), II, 53–54.

[13] Luís Vahia Monteiro to the Crown, 5 July 1726, *apud* Zemella, *Abastecimento,* p. 202; José Freire de Monterroyo Mascarenhas, *Epanaphora Indica* (Lisboa, 1746), p. 21.

[14] Manuel dos Santos, "Calamidades de Pernambuco," in *RIHGB,* LIII, p. 7; Fr. José de Jesus Maria, O.F.M., *Azia Sinica e Japonica, 1745* (ed. C. R. Boxer, 2 vols., Macao, 1941–1950), II, 229–240.

[15] G. N. Clark, "The Other Face of Mercantilism," in *Trans. Royal Hist. Soc.,* IX (1959), pp. 87–89.

[16] Caio Prado Júnior, *Formação. Brasil Colónia,* p. 93.

[17] CR of March 1721 in Lopes, *op. cit.,* pp. 152–153.

[18] CR of 11 May 1753, and Gomes Freire de Andrada's reply of 3 March 1754 in APM cod. 100 (SG), fols. 46–47. I owe this reference to the kindness of Dr. Curt Lange.

[19] "Regimento para os Capitães do mato," d. Ribeirão do Carmo, 6 and 7 March 1716, in Cod. Costa Matoso, fols. 46–47. Another dated 17 December 1722 is printed in *RAPM,* II (1897), pp. 389–391, and summarized in Lopes, *op. cit.,* pp. 129–130.

[20] Commonplace-book of D. Rodrigo de Menezes, São Paulo, 1721, in IHGB, MS L89, 1509, fol. 18; Xavier da Veiga, *Ephemerides Mineiras,* I, 94–95; II, 402;

III, 132; CR of 27 January 1726 in *RAPM*, XVI (1911), p. 375. For Spanish America, cf. C. H. Haring, *The Spanish Empire in America* (New York, 1947), pp. 218, 231, 271. W. L. Schurz, *This New World*, pp. 182–184, claims that the situation improved after 1750.

[21] Report of 14 November 1759, in Lopes, *op. cit.*, p. 133.

[22] Anonymous and undated proposal of *ca.* 1750 in Codice Costa Matoso, fols. 259–264.

[23] Petition of the Senate of Mariana, May, 1755, and the Count of Arcos' comments, Bahia, 10 August 1756, in Accioli-Amaral, *Memorias Historicas*, II, 427–429.

[24] Luís Gomes Ferreira, *Erario Mineral dividido em doze Tratados* (Lisboa, 1735), pp. 2, 31–32, 50–55, 72–73, 393, 422, 426, for this and what follows. For other eyewitness accounts of the mistreatment of slaves in colonial Brazil, see the sources quoted in Chapter i note 14, to which should be added Luís dos Santos Vilhena, *Recopilação de Noticias Soteropolitanas e Brasilicas* (ed. Braz do Amaral, 2 vols., Salvador, 1927).

[25] Fr. Jerome de Merolla, O.F.M. (Cap.), *apud* Churchill, *Voyages* (1704 ed.), I, 659.

[26] Martinho de Mendonça de Pina de Proença, "Reflexões sobre a sistema da capitação," *ca.* March, 1734, in J. Cortesão, *Alexandre de Gusmão. Obras Várias*, pp. 418–419.

[27] Codice Costa Matoso, fols. 181–187. Cf. Appendix III above. For other estimates of the 1730's, see Cortesão, *op. cit.*, II (1), pp. 59, 418–419.

[28] *Erario Mineral*, p. 55; APM (SG), Codices 6, 12, 19, 23, 25–28, 30–31, 38–39, 46, 54–56, 58, 60, 62, 68.

[29] Clado Ribeiro Lessa [ed.], *Viagem de Africa em o reino de Dahomé* (São Paulo, 1957); Ott, *Formação*, I, 70–75; II, 16–17; Report of the Count of Arcos on the trade with Dahomey, d. Lisbon, 19 October 1760 (author's collection).

[30] Extracts from Assumar's correspondence with the Crown in 1718–1719, in Lopes, *op. cit.*, pp. 126–130. For the abortive slave revolts of 1724, 1735, and 1756, cf. Xavier da Veiga, *Ephemerides*, II, 77–86, 407; IV, 431.

[31] Bazin, *L'Architecture religieuse*, II, 60–116, and other sources there quoted.

[32] Report of the Vicar of Catas Altas, d. 3 November 1750, in Cod. Costa Matoso, fol. 80. Cf. Bazin, *op. cit.*, II, 63–68.

[33] Dom Braz da Silveira to the Crown, 2 June 1716, in APM, Cod. 4 (SG), fols. 447–449; complaints of the Town Councils of Minas, 22 July 1716, in APM, Cod. 6 (SG), fols. 67–68; Xavier da Veiga, *Ephemerides*, I, 188–189.

[34] "Rendimento da mitra do Bispado da Mariana," in Cod. Costa Matoso, fols. 418–420.

[35] Xavier da Veiga, *op. cit.*, I, 67, 197, 203, 252, 320–321, 333; II, 212, 278, 340; III, 85–86, 385–386; IV, 103, 157, 174–175, 267, 325.

[36] Curt Lange (ed.), *Arquivo de Música Religiosa da Capitania Geral das Minas Gerais. Siglo XVIII* (Mendoza, 1951); *idem, Monumenta Musicae Brasiliae* (in press); *idem, Historia da Musica na Capitania Geral das Minas Gerais* (in preparation).

[37] J. Mawe, *Travels in the Interior of Brazil* (ed. 1812), pp. 78–79. For the complicated code regulating disputes between miners over the sub-soil, irrigation and other rights, see Codice Costa Matoso, fols. 422–423.

[38] Decree of 19 February 1752 and CR of 29 February 1752, in Cod. Costa

Matoso, fol. 364. Cf. also Xavier da Veiga, *op. cit.*, I, 204–206, 265–266; IV, 222.

[39] *Erario Mineral* (1735), pp. 52–55, 67, 387. The Portuguese mania for phlebotomy is thus described in the anonymous *Description de la Ville de Lisbonne* (1730), pp. 117–120: "Dans les malades ordinaires, ils commencent par ordonner *huma meia duzia de sangrias,* c'est à dire, demi douzaine de saignées; & quand le mal se rend opiniâtre, ils poussent l'ordonnance jusqu'à quinze et vingt ... "

[40] *Erario Mineral* (1735), passim; Andrade & Duarte (eds.), Morão, *Rosa e Pimenta,* especially pp. 393–340. Cf. also Sergio Buarque de Holanda, *Caminhos e Fronteiras* (1957), pp. 85–104, for the "Botica da Natureza" of the Paulistas.

[41] "Vereações da Camara de Ouro Preto," in *ABNRJ,* XLIX (1927); *Lei* of 29 August 1720, in Lopes, *op. cit.,* pp. 183–186; Accioli-Amaral, *Memorias Historicas,* II, 257–258, where the date is wrongly given as 1726; "Reflexos" of Martinho de Mendonça in Cortesão, *op. cit.,* II (1), p. 420. Cf. also Xavier da Veiga, *op. cit.,* IV, 227.

[42] M. Cardozo, "Tithes in Colonial Minas Gerais," pp. 175–182. For a more detailed study of Brazil in general, see Oscar de Oliveira, *Os dizimos eclesiasticos do Brasil nos periodos da Colonia e do Imperio* (Juiz de Fora, 1940). The *propinas* levied in mid-eighteenth-century Minas Gerais are listed in Codice Costa Matoso, fols. 328–352.

[43] M. F. Zemella, *O Abastecimento das Minas Gerais no século XVIII* (1958); Myriam Ellis, "Contribuição ao estudo do abastecimento das zonas mineradoras do Brasil on século XVIII" (1958); the extract concerning Manuel Nunes Viana is from APM (DF), Cod. 17, fol. 47ᵛ. This "Rio Grande" is not the actual one of that name but a section of the river Jequitinhonha, where early eighteenth-century maps show a "passagem da Bahia." The Jequitinhonha was formerly termed Rio Grande for the greater part of its course. Cf. Mawe, *Travels* (1812), p. 240. Some relevant figures for the contracts of 1710–1750 from the Codice Matoso are printed in Appendix V above.

[44] Newcastle to Tyrawly, Whitehall, 20 November 1739 (PRO, SP 89/40).

[45] The instructions of 1719 specified that the gold bars should be stamped at one end with the royal arms and at the other end with an armillary sphere. The weight and carats of the bar, as also the year of its founding, were stamped on both sides, in the middle. A pattern bar of 1730 in the Mint at Rio de Janeiro measures 450 mm long and 35 mm wide, and is stamped with the weight of 3 marcs, 7 ounces, 1 dram, 39 grains. Cf. K. Prober, "A Casa de Fundição de Sabará," pp. 5–35. For surveys of the legislation on quints and gold in 1706–1750, cf. Sombra, *História Monetaria,* pp. 139–196; A. de Salles Oliveira, *Moedas e Barras de Ouro* (São Paulo, 1944), pp. 196–207; M. Cardozo, *Alguns Subsídios para a história da cobrança do quinto na Capitania de Minas Gerais até 1735* (Lisboa, 1937).

[46] Anonymous account in Codice Costa Matoso, fol. 39.

[47] He had entertained Assumar in great style on the Count's arrival in 1717, and the governor then recommended him to the Crown as being one of nine persons who "mais se têm distinguido, e mais zelosas se têm mostrado no serviço de Sua Magestade neste governo das Minas" (Rau, *Cadaval MSS,* II, 194).

[48] The revolt of 1720 and its aftermath is very fully documented, at any rate from Assumar's side. Cf. the original *termos* in APM, Codice 6 (SG), fols. 91–104; Assumar's correspondence in *RAPM,* VI, 202–217; and the *Discurso Histórico Politico* inspired by him (ed. Xavier da Veiga, Ouro Preto, 1898).

[49] "Desde o governo do Conde de Assumar acabou o tempo de terem os Mineiros negros valentões para instrumento das suas desordens, e jà naquelle tempo se fez conhecer aos Mineiros que hé mais suave o jugo da sogeição civil que da liberdade licencioza," wrote Martinho de Mendonça in his "Reflexões" of 1734. Sixteen years later Alexandre de Gusmão wrote of Assumar in his "Reparos:" "Elle, com a sua sagacidade, e com os rigores necessarios, que então praticou, reduziu o povo das Minas a uma sugeição que tem felismente continuado até o presente" (Cortesão, *Gusmão*, II (1), pp. 249, 421).

[50] A. de Lima Junior, *Vila Rica de Ouro Preto* (Belo Horizonte, 1957), p. 73.

[51] Count of Galveas to the Crown, 1 April 1734, in M. Cardozo, "Subsídios," pp. 30–31.

[52] " ... sendo a maior parte da gente de que se compõe, negros, mulatos, foragidos com pouca consciencia e com a nimia liberdade, e pouco temor de castigo, que lhes facilitam os vastos sertões da América" (Cortesão, *op. cit.,* I (2), p. 366.

[53] Some authorities, such as Kurt Prober, maintain that Villa Rica was the only place where a smelting-house functioned before 1751, but the production figures for those established at Sabará and São João d'El Rei in 1734 are given in Codice Costa Matoso, fol. 180.

[54] Gusmão's original plan and the modification which it subsequently underwent are fully discussed in Cortesão, *op. cit.,* I (1), pp. 349–404, and the documents printed in *idem, Obras Várias,* and *Documentos biográficos.* Cf. also *RAPM,* XII, 605–676.

[55] Anonymous eyewitness account in Codice Costa Matoso, fol. 50. *Se non è vero ...* , but the story does show that there were a number of elementary schools in Minas Gerais.

[56] Protests of the Town Councils of Minas Gerais against the capitation tax in 1741–1751, in Codice Costa Matoso, fols. 243–258, and *RAPM,* II, 287–309.

[57] Cardozo, "Alguns subsídios," pp. 25–27; and A. de Lima Junior, *Noticias Historicas* (1953), pp. 169–177, give some typical examples, drawn chiefly from the printed correspondence of Luís Vahia Monteiro in *ABNRJ.* It would be easy to extend the list.

[58] The best summary of this famous scandal, based on the original papers in the AHU, Lisboa, is by A. de Lima Junior, *op. cit.,* pp. 179–218.

[59] This prince, who was also the protector of Manuel Nunes Viana, was fond of taking pot shots with a fowling piece at fishermen on the Tagus, a diversion which he described as "duck shooting."

[60] Sabugosa to the Crown, Bahia, 8 January 1733 (APEB, "Ordens Régias," Vol. XXX, doc. 25). This codex also contains some documents relating to Inacio de Sousa Ferreira and his gang. For his connections with associates in London, see *RAPM,* VI, 654–655. For the activities of coiners and forgers in São Paulo during these years, see *RIHGB, Catalogo dos documentos sobre a história de São Paulo existentes no AHU de Lisboa* (14 vols., Rio de Janeiro, 1956–1959), II, 222–223, 251–252, 327; III, 65.

NOTES TO CHAPTER VIII
"Diamond District"
(Pages 204–225)

[1] The Overseas Councillor, António Rodrigues da Costa, appealed in 1732 "... à primeira e principal maxima dos Senhores Reis de Portugal, a qual foy sempre tratarem os seus vassallos como Pais e não Senhores" (*apud* J. Cortesão, *Alexandre de Gusmão*, I (1), pp. 344–345). The peculiar nature of the paternalism of the Crown of Portugal was well brought out by A. Gavy de Mendonça, *Historia do Cerco de Mazagão* (Lisboa, 1607), cap. ix.

[2] Cortesão, *op. cit.*, I (1), pp. 76–78.

[3] The Count of Sabugosa, who lost no opportunity of traducing Dom Lourenço de Almeida (cf. p. 145 above), wrote to Martinho de Mendonça some years later: "O padre António Xavier de Sousa teve comigo várias conferências e também Felipe de Santiago que ambos eles e algumas outras pessoas convieram em que Dom Lourenço de Almeida conheceu logo as pedras por preciosas; eu com muita razão me persuadi ao mesmo, porque em cinco anos que estive em Goa, fiquei tão prático, que facilmente as distinguiria das outras; veja V. M. agora se com dezassete que o dito D. Lourenço residiu na India e trazendo o seu dote e cabedal que adquiriu com a sua boa economia empregado nelas, se poderia enganar" (*apud* A. de Lima Junior, *História dos diamantes nas Minas Gerais. Século XVIII*, Rio de Janeiro, 1945, p. 21). For further details and differing accounts of the discovery of Brazilian diamonds, cf. *ibid.*, pp. 15–31; *RAPM*, II, 271–282; Joaquim Felício dos Santos, *Memórias do distrito Diamantino* (3d. ed., Rio de Janeiro, 1956), pp. 60–66.

[4] The classic account of the diamond mines of Golconda is by the famous Huguenot traveler and jeweler, J. B. Tavernier (V. Ball & W. Crooke [eds.], *Travels in India by Jean-Baptiste Tavernier*, 2 vols., Oxford, 1925, II, 41–62, 352–354).

[5] Dom Lourenço de Almeida's correspondence concerning diamonds with the Crown in 1729–1730, in A. de Lima, *op. cit.*, pp. 27–30; "Regimento dos Diamantes," d. Villa Rica, 26 June 1730, in APM (SG), Cod. I, fols. 89–92; cf. also *RAPM*, XVI (1), pp. 439–441; Felício dos Santos, *Memórias*, pp. 61–71; A. de Lima, *op. cit.*, pp. 32–39. Mawe states that in his day the District measured "about sixteen leagues from north to south, and about eight from east to west," Tijuco being roughly in the center of it (*Travels*, p. 247, and map at p. 137).

[6] Tyrawly to Newcastle, Lisbon, 14 February 1738, in PRO London, SP 89/40. Cf. the criticism of colonial justice at Bahia in 1718 by Le Gentil de la Barbinais, *Nouveau Voyage*, III. For Pires Pardinho, see Cortesão, *op. cit.*, II (2), 152 n., and Vol. I, index; correspondence of Martinho de Mendonça in *RAPM*, XVI (2), 239–460; Felício dos Santos, *op. cit.*, p. 94.

[7] Cf. the correspondence printed by A. de Lima, *op. cit.*, pp. 59–81; Southey, *History*, III, 276–280.

[8] Cf. Felício dos Santos, *op. cit.*, pp. 72–78.

[9] "Condições para a extracção de diamantes em 20. vi. 1739," in APM (SG),

I, 141–147; Sabugosa to the Crown, Bahia, 16 January 1732, in Accioli-Amaral, *Memórias Históricas,* VI, 85–86; correspondence of Galveas and Martinho de Mendonça in *RAPM,* XVI (2), 277–278, 305–310, 405, 416–418, 421, 431. Cf. also Felício dos Santos, *op. cit.,* pp. 85–92.

[10] Assumar to the Crown, Ribeirão do Carmo, 1 January 1720, in APM (SG), IV, fols. 770–775. Joseph Rodrigues de Oliveira was also something of an engineer, architect, and cartographer. He designed the first barracks for the dragoons and drew several maps of Minas Gerais, some of which are in the AHU, Lisboa. He was later governor of Santos from 1738 until August, 1744, when he became insane, dying shortly afterwards.

[11] For the *motins do sertão,* in which a woman landowner, Maria da Cruz, played a leading part, see Martinho de Mendonça's correspondence in *RAPM,* I, 649–672; *ibid.,* XI, 373–397.

[12] The rates of pay for the dragoons of Minas Gerais are in Codice Costa Matoso, fol. 436. Details of barracks construction and other administrative matters in Lopes, *op. cit.,* pp. 165–178. Cf. also *RAPM,* XVI (1), 372–386, for successive legislative enactments concerning the dragoons.

[13] For the *garimpeiros* and *calhambolas,* see F. dos Santos, *op. cit.* (1956), pp. 95–102.

[14] For contemporary descriptions of diamond mining (or, rather, washing) in 1735 and 1778, see A. de Lima, *op. cit.,* pp. 41–58, and for early nineteenth-century methods see Mawe, *Travels* (1812), pp. 219–317.

[15] *Bandos* of 9 January 1735 and 1 March 1743, for example.

[16] Mawe states that in his day the Negroes worked generally "in a waistcoat and a pair of drawers, and not naked, as some travellers have stated" (*op. cit.,* p. 225). In the eighteenth century, however, they were more scantily clad: "Todos os Negros andão nûs durante o serviço das lavagens, aonde só se lhes permitte o estarem cobertos com a sua tanga, que he hum pedaço de baeta involto á roda da cintura" (BNRJ, Codice I – 18 – 1 – 14, "Do Descobrimento dos diamantes e differentes methodos que se tem practicado na sua extracção," fol. 43. For the original capitation figures for slaves working in the Serro do Frio in 1736–1749, see Codice Costa Matoso, fols. 181–187.

[17] BNRJ, Cod. I – 18 – 1 – 14, fols. 41–43. Cf. A. de Lima, *op. cit.,* pp. 56–58, for an apparently identical version in AHU, Lisboa.

[18] Mawe, *op. cit.* (1812), pp. 223–225.

[19] For further details, cf. F. dos Santos, *op. cit.* (ed. 1956), pp. 68–69, 104–107, 160–171; Xavier de Veiga, *op. cit.,* IV, 186–190, 289–290.

[20] Cf. A. de Lima, *op. cit.,* pp. 83–92, where, however, the two João Fernandes de Oliveira are telescoped into one.

[21] BNRJ, Cod. I – 18 – 14 – 1, fol. 32.

[22] The romantic story of the vicissitudes of the Caldeira Brants as narrated by Felício dos Santos, *op. cit.* (1956), pp. 102–125, is corrected in some respects by the more prosaic documents published by A. de Lima, *op. cit.,* pp. 187–207. Where the details differ, I have followed the latter and better documented version.

[23] *Alvará de ley* dated 11 August and published at Lisbon 30 August 1753.

[24] Reproduced in full by A. de Lima, *op. cit.,* pp. 137–167.

[25] British Museum Add MS 13981, fol. 44 (118); J. L. d'Azevedo, *O Marquez de Pombal e a sua epoca* (Lisboa, 1909), p. 134.

²⁶ John Gore's correspondence of 1733, printed in A. de Lima, *op. cit.*, pp. 62–72. Contract figures from BNRJ, Cod. I – 18 – 1 – 14, fol. 32. *Extracção Real* figures from F. dos Santos, *op. cit.*, p. 183. The last-named author states (*ibid.*, pp. 96, 112) that the five original codices of diamond-entry books, *Livros das Entradas dos Diamantes para o Cofre,* were transferred from Tijuco to the archives at Ouro Preto in 1847. The archives were subsequently removed to Belo Horizonte, but these codices could not be traced when I asked for them there in March, 1959.

²⁷ Gilberto Freyre, *O Mundo que o Portugues creou* (Rio de Janeiro, 1940). A Brazilian friend, who prefers to remain anonymous, remarked to me that another book, equally relevant, could be written under the title of *O Mundo que o Portugues não conseguiu impedir.*

NOTES TO CHAPTER IX
"Cattle Country"
(Pages 226–245)

¹ Virginia Rau (*Sesmarias medievais portuguesas,* Lisboa, 1946) has an excellent discussion of the *Lei de sesmarias* in its historical setting.

² APEB, "Livro de Ordens Régias," Vol. VI, no. 113.

³ Lynn Smith (*Brazil,* ed. 1954, p. 137) points out that the evils of modern Brazilian latifundianism derive from the extensive grants of land given to people who cannot cultivate a hundredth part of it, but who will not sell or rent it, in the hope that one day it will become much more valuable.

⁴ APEB, "Livro de Ordens Régias," Vol. VI, no. 111.

⁵ Pedro Calmon, *História da Casa da Torre. Una dinastia de pioneiros* (Rio de Janeiro, 1939 and 1958).

⁶ *Cultura e Opulencia,* Livro IV, chaps. 1–4.

⁷ Cf. the Crown's order of 7 February 1726 that these landholders, and others who are mentioned by name, should produce their title deeds within one year for examination at Lisbon. They were also to explain how they came by such vast estates, and what they were doing to develop them. The Crown urged that similar investigations should be made of the extensive landholdings of the Benedictines (APEB, "Livro de Ordens Régias," Vol. XXI, nos. 29–29A).

⁸ Capistrano de Abreu, *Capitulos de História Colonial* (ed. 1954), pp. 217–219.

⁹ Dampier, *A Voyage to New Holland in 1699* (ed. 1939), p. 41. Similar remarks on the leanness of Brazilian cattle were made by most foreign visitors.

¹⁰ See Fr. Martin de Nantes, O.F.M., *Relation Succinte, passim,* and S. Leite, S.J., *História,* V, 293–315, for the difficulties between the missionaries and the House of Torre. Cf. also the documents calendared in *Anais do primeiro Congresso de História da Bahia,* II, 4083–4100, 4239–4241, and on pp. 355–387.

¹¹ Fr. Martin de Nantes, *op. cit.,* pp. 35–36. For the payment of Amerindian cattle drovers from the *sertão,* see D. João de Lencastre's dispatch of 26 July 1702, in Rau, *MSS Cadaval,* II, 48–53.

¹² Originally and variously spelled as Piagohy, Piaguhuy, and Piagui. There

are three well-documented works on the penetration and settlement of this region: F. A. Pereira da Costa, *Chronologia Historica do Estado do Piauhy* (Recife, 1909); Barbosa Lima Sobrinho, *Pernambuco e o São Francisco* (Recife, 1929); *idem, O Devassamanto do Piauí* (Rio de Janeiro, 1946). Save where otherwise stated, I have relied chiefly on the documents printed in these works, although I have not always drawn the same deductions from them as have those authors. Cf. also Carlos Eugênio Porto, *Roteiro do Piauí* (Rio de Janeiro, 1955).

[13] For Domingos Affonso Sertão (Mafrense) and the Jesuit estates in Piauí, see S. Leite, S.J., *op. cit.,* V, 550–565, especially p. 552 for the statistics of 1739. Domingos Affonso's will was first printed in *RIHGB,* XX, 144 ff.

[14] Padre Miguel de Carvalho's report to the Bishop of Pernambuco, dated Piauí, 2 March 1697, and the documents relating to the foundation of the parish church of Nossa Senhora da Vitoria da Mocha de Piauí are in E. Ennes, *Os Palmares. Subsídios para a sua história* (Lisboa, 1937), pp. 148–171.

[15] The information given on the events of 1711–1712 in the works cited above, note 12, is here supplemented from the documents calendared in Rau, *op. cit.,* II, 235–254, 379–400.

[16] Rau, *ibid.* The difficulty of reaching a reliable conclusion on the causes of the Amerindian revolt is illustrated by a comparison of the evidence given in the indigenes' favor by two Jesuit Padres, António de Sousa Leal, and João Guedes (Rau, *op. cit.,* pp. 385, 396). Padre Sousa Leal relates how António da Cunha and some whites wished to justify the projected murder of certain captive Amerindians by drawing up a (false) affidavit of their alleged misdeeds. "But João da Costa, now a clergyman at Bahia, saying that it was not necessary to sign papers in order to kill Tapuyas, seized a musket and fired at the chief. In the ensuing confusion, the other whites only succeeded in killing twelve Indians, António da Cunha leaving João da Costa for dead on the ground," having shot him accidentally. Padre Guedes, in his version of the same incident, alleges that António da Cunha and his brother deliberately shot João da Costa because the latter strongly objected to the proposed massacre.

[17] F. A. Oliveira Martins, *Um herói esquecido. João da Maia da Gama* (2 vols., Lisboa, 1944), prints in full the report of Maia da Gama, dated Lisbon, 28 April 1730. The description of Piauí is in Vol. II, 14–38.

[18] As Southey aptly observed: "The name of Rio Grande, or the Great River, often and inconveniently as the Portuguese and Spaniards have bestowed it, has never been more injudiciously applied than to the channel, a few miles only in length, by which the waters of the Lagoa dos Patos discharge themselves into the sea" (*History,* III, 564). The name was soon extended by the Portuguese to include the region west of Lakes Mirim and Patos, as far as the Spanish Jesuit missions. For the plethora of Brazilian rivers called "Rio Grande," some of them quite insignificant streams, see Taunay, *História Géral,* X, Pt. 3, p. 31. Eighteenth-century documents refer to this region indifferently as São Pedro do Rio Grande do Sul and Rio Grande de São Pedro, whereas the modern usage is Rio Grande do Sul.

[19] The colonial history of Rio Grande do Sul and the vicissitudes of the Colonia do Sacramento are very well documented in numerous books and articles. The most important are listed in the bibliography to a suggestive essay by J. H. Rodrigues, *O Continente do Rio Grande* (Rio de Janeiro, 1954), to which should be added Cortesão, *Alexandre de Gusmão,* I (2) (1956).

[20] Governor of Rio de Janeiro to the Crown, 8 January 1718, in *PANRJ*, X (1910), pp. 29–32.

[21] André Ribeiro Coutinho's report *apud* J. H. Rodrigues, *Continente do Rio Grande*, p. 32. André Ribeiro Coutinho, after receiving an excellent education at the Jesuit College of Santo Antão (Lisbon), served with distinction in the War of the Spanish Succession, and in the expedition against the Turks at Corfu in 1716. During the next two years he fought in Austria-Hungary under Prince Eugene, participating in the siege and capture of Belgrade. From 1723 to 1734 he served on the west coast of India, where he was chiefly occupied in the fortification of Bassein and its district. Returning to Portugal in October, 1735, he was sent to Brazil in the following March. He took part in the relief of Sacramento and the abortive attack on Montevideo, and was the governor of São Pedro do Rio Grande from April, 1737 to December, 1740. For his activities in later years when a garrison commander at Rio de Janeiro, see pp. 315–316.

[22] Cf. the documents of 1740–1742 calendared in *PANRJ*, VIII, 165, 168, 171–174.

[23] *Bola (Bolas)*, a form of lasso or lariat with two or more balls or stones instead of a noose. These are swung round the head and discharged so as to wind round and entangle cattle.

[24] Report of Domingos Ferreira Chaves, Ceará, 23 November 1719, in Rau, *op. cit.*, pp. 248–254.

[25] *Parecer* of the Duke of Cadaval, Lisbon, 30 July 1713, in Rau, *ibid.*, II, 119–220.

NOTES TO CHAPTER X
"Moving Frontiers and Monsoons"
(Pages 246–270)

[1] The struggle for Sacramento, which lasted on and off for almost exactly a century, can be studied in the following richly documented works, on which I have relied here: J. Costa Rêgo Monteiro, *A Colónia do Sacramento, 1680–1777* (2 vols., Porto Alegre, 1937); J. Cortesão, *Alexandre de Gusmão*, II (1), III (2); J. Cortesão (ed.), *MSS. da Colecção de Angelis. Colónia do Sacramento, 1669–1749* (Rio de Janeiro, 1954). Cf. also Simão Pereira de Sá, *História Topographica e Belica da Nova Colónia do Sacramento* (ed. Capistrano de Abreu, Rio de Janeiro, 1900); Mario Rodrigues, "Dom Pedro of Braganza and Colônia do Sacramento, 1680–1705" (*HAHR*, XXXVIII, 179–208).

[2] For the prosperity of Sacramento in 1735, see Southey, *History*, III, 287–289, 294–295; Rêgo Monteiro, *Sacramento*, I, pp. 202 ff. For the backward state of agriculture in eighteenth-century Portugal see J. F. Bourgoing [ed.], *Voyage du ci-devant Duc du Chatelet en Portugal* (2 vols., Paris, 1798).

[3] Southey, *op. cit.*, III, 294; Cortesão, *Gusmão*, I (2), pp. 39, 71, 275–276, 296–298, 388.

[4] "A Nova Colonia do Sacramento por mercê de Deus se conserva; por metterem nella um presidio fechado sem mulherio, que é o que conserva os homens, por que se não tem visto em parte alguma do mundo fazerem-se novas povoações sem casaes" (*RIHGB*, XXV, 473).

[5] For the frequency of desertions from Sacramento and complaints of condi-

tions there in the first half of the eighteenth century, see the documents calendared in *PANRJ*, VIII, 64, 65, 67, 171, 202; *PANRJ*, X, 99, 134–135, 150, 162, 214–215, 221, 264.

6 Southey, *op. cit.*, II, 219–223; *PANRJ*, X, 214–230. It is interesting to note that colonists from the Canary Islands were being sent to this part of South America just when the Portuguese were sending some from the Azores and Madeira.

7 "... que a Praça da Colonia era de tanta importancia para a sua Coroa, que não a trocaria pelo mais vantajoso equivalente que lhe offerecessem os Castelhanos" (Costa Rêgo Monteiro, *Sacramento*, I, 179, and II, 140. Cf. also Southey, *op. cit.*, III, 218).'

8 The siege of Sacramento in 1735–1737, is fully documented in the works of Pereira de Sá and Costa Rêgo Monteiro quoted in note 1 above. For the diplomatic rupture with Spain and the tortuous negotiations that culminated in the Armistice of Paris (March, 1737), see Cortesão, *Gusmão*, I (2), pp. 59–132, although this author does not do justice to the Spanish viewpoint.

9 R. Walter, *A Voyage Round the World in the Years 1740–1744 by George Anson Esqre* (London, 1748), pp. 46–47. Rodolfo Garcia in his lengthy note to the third edition of Varnhagen's *História Geral*, IV, 97, completely misunderstands Anson's remarks about Brigadier Silva Pais. Far from being complimentary, they are definitely denigrating and imply that Silva Pais was embezzling Crown funds for the fortifications.

10 *PANRJ*, X, 9–10, 29–31, for the governor's reports of March 1, 6, 1718.

11 Cortesão, *Gusmão*, I (2), pp. 245–259, and III (2), pp. 438–480, for a fully documented account of the colonization plans.

12 *Condiçoens com que se arremata o assento do transporte dos Cazaes desta Corte, e das Ilhas para o Brazil a Feliciano Velho de Oldemberg* (Lisboa, 1747). Cf. Cortesão, *Gusmão*, III (2), pp. 459–467.

13 "Regimento" of 5 August 1747, in J. Cortesão, *Gusmão*, III (2), pp. 448–451; Alan Villiers, *Sons of Sindbad* (London, 1940).

14 Caio Prado Júnior, *Formação*, pp. 109–110.

15 Rodrigo Cezar de Menezes to the Crown, São Paulo, 25 December 1721, and *termo* dated Cuiabá, 6 November 1721, in the MS letter book (*Livro-copiador*) of this governor of São Paulo in the library of the Instituto Histórico e Geográfico Brasileiro, Rio de Janeiro (L. 89. 1509, fols. 144, 161–162). Taunay prints another copy of this *termo* (*História Geral*, X (3), 15–16), but dates it 1720.

16 *RIHGB, Catalogo de documentos sobre a história de São Paulo existentes no Arquivo Histórico Ultramarino de Lisboa* (14 vols., Rio de Janeiro, 1956–1959), Vol. I, 339.

17 José Barbosa de Sá, "Relação das povoaçoens do Cuyabá e Mato Grosso de seos principios thé os prezentes tempos," dated 15 August 1775, and printed in *ABNRJ*, XXIII (Rio de Janeiro, 1901–1904), pp. 5–58. This is the basic source from which all subsequent writers have derived their accounts. Cf. also Taunay, *op. cit.*, X (3), and *idem, História das Bandeiras Paulistas*, II.

18 José Barbosa de Sá, apud *ABNRJ*, XXIII, 5–16.

19 José Barbosa de Sá apud *ibid.*, XXIII, 23–24.

20 Sérgio Buarque de Holanda, *Monções* (Rio de Janeiro, 1945), p. 91; *RIHGB, Documentos do AHU sobre São Paulo*, II, 25.

21 Discussed at length by Taunay in his *História Geral*, X (3), pp. 217–246, who

considers that Sebastião Fernandes do Rego, *Provedor* of the royal fifths and of the smelting-house at São Paulo, was the real culprit.

[22] For Rodrigo Cezar de Menezes' activities in Cuiabá and São Paulo, cf. Washington Luís, *Contribuição para a história da Capitania de São Paulo. Governo de Rodrigo Cézar de Meneses* (São Paulo, 1918); Taunay, *História Geral*, X (3), *passim*, and *idem*, *História das Bandeiras Paulistas*, II, *passim*.

[23] For detailed technical descriptions of the types of canoes used in the São Paulo "monsoons" of the eighteenth century, cf. Buarque de Holanda, *Monções*, pp. 19–65, and Taunay, *História das Bandeiras*, II, 151–158.

[24] There were a number of other rivers which were less used for all or part of the eighteenth century. They are enumerated in the anonymous "Demonstração dos diversos caminhos de que os moradores de São Paulo se servem para os Rios Cuiabá e Provincia de Cochiponé," printed in Taunay, *Relatos Sertanistas*, pp. 201–207. Cf. also Buarque de Holanda, *Monções*, pp. 124–184.

[25] "Não se sabia que gentio era, adonde habitava, e que nome tinha, por não ser o nome de Payaguá thé então conhecido" (José Barbosa de Sá, apud *ABNRJ*, XXIII, p. 15). The Portuguese had obviously forgotten that they had encountered the Paiaguá a century earlier in Paraguay. Cf. Boxer, *Salvador de Sá*, pp. 90–93, for a summary of early Luso-Spanish contacts with both Paiaguá and Guiacurú.

[26] José Barbosa de Sá, apud *ABNRJ*, XXIII, 26–28. Documents from the Evora Library published by Taunay reduce the number of the losers' casualties to 107, and the amount of gold lost to about 12 *arrobas* (*História das Bandeiras*, II, 78).

[27] "... o negro nú intujucado escoregavalhes pelas maons como hum porco, não havião forças que o sojugasem; a hum arrancou a lingoa pellos goellas a outro troseo o pescoso que lhe pos a cara para as costas, dava-lhes murros nos narizes com a mao feixada que os deixava atordoadas thé que o sojeitarão e levarão vivo com tudo o mais que vinha na monção, escapando somenté dous brancos e dous pretos em huma canoa ligeira que trouçerão a noticia do que virão e prezenciarão que tudo depozerão fielmente" (*ABNRJ*, XXIII, 32–33).

[28] "... Manuel Rodrigues do Prado, mulato fusco, natural da villa de Pindamonhangaba da Capitania de Sam Paulo, a quem chamavão por alcunha Manduasú. Vinha este piloteando huma canoa com sua mulher tambem mulata junto a si sercou o gentio introu aos tiros com elles carregandolhe as armas e elle a fazer pontarias sertas que não errava huma; com tanto exforso, valor e presteza e sem largar o remo das maons, dando rizadas e asenando aos infieis que chegasem que os atemorizou e fes retirar e postos elles em fuga ainda mandou remar a canoa sobre elles, matando alguns" (*ABNRJ*, XXIII, 33).

[29] Buarque de Holanda, *Monções*, p. 167.

[30] Cf. the quotations from eighteenth-century records in Taunay, *História das Bandeiras*, II, 93, 94, 101.

[31] One detachment under the command of the Portuguese Ensign, José Peixoto da Silva Braga, descended the river Tocantins to Belem do Pará. Cf. his original account as printed in Taunay, *Relatos Sertanistas*, pp. 121–137.

[32] Taunay, *História das Bandeiras Paulistas*, Vol. II, for a detailed account of the pioneer days in Goiás and Mato Grosso, 1720–1750.

[33] "... e sómente na villa ficarão sete homens brancos entre seculares e clerigos, e alguns carijós que gente preza só algum page que servia a seo senhor de porta a dentro" (*ABNRJ*, XXIII, 37).

[34] Padre José Manuel de Sequeira *apud* Buarque de Holanda, *Monções*, pp. 86–87.

[35] The adventurous journey of Manuel Felix de Lima is recounted at great length in Southey, *op. cit.*, III, 311–344, from the original autograph account that was then in the poet's possession.

NOTES TO CHAPTER XI
"Missionaries and Settlers in Amazonia"
(Pages 271–292)

[1] Lynn Smith, *Brazil* (ed. 1954), p. 91.

[2] "... agora se está já fazendo de nossa lavra aguardente de açucar que é o vinho da terra (e de que gostam generalmente todos mais que do de Europa), para se dar ordinaria dele ... " (Padre António Vieira, S.J., to the Jesuit General, Rio das Almazonas, 24 March 1661). Cf. S. Leite, S.J., *História*, IV, 153–154.

[3] Vieira to the Padre Provincial do Brasil, 1654 (*Cartas*, I, 373–374).

[4] Vieira to the Jesuit General, 21 March 1661 (S. Leite, *Novas Cartas Jesuíticas*, pp. 290–291); F. A. Oliveira Martins, *João da Maia da Gama*, II, 5–114.

[5] Cf. the sarcastic marginal annotations of Dom António de Ataide in a copy of the *Relação Sumaria* apud C. R. Boxer, "The Naval and Colonial Papers of D. António de Ataide, 1567–1647" (*Harvard Library Bulletin*, V, 34–35).

[6] For the natural products which circulated as money in Maranhão-Pará, cf. J. F. Lisboa, *Obras Completas* (2 vols., Lisboa, 1901), II, 182–183, 186, 189–193; S. Sombra, *História Monetaria* (ed. 1938), pp. 150–151, 185; *Livro Grosso do Maranhão*, II, 27, 86–87, 102; *Revista de História* (São Paulo), X, 231–235.

[7] António Vieira, S.J., "Resposta aos Capitulos" (1662), apud *Obras Escolhidas*, V, 269, 292.

[8] *Obras Escolhidas*, V, 317; *ibid.*, XI, 113–114. Fr. M. C. Kiemen, O.F.M., *The Indian Policy of Portugal in the Amazon Region, 1614–1693*, says what can fairly be said on behalf of the friars in seventeenth-century Maranhão-Pará, but I feel that Vieira's indictment still stands on the whole.

[9] Letter of Padre Bettendorff, S.J., 20 July 1673, *apud* S. Leite, S.J., *História*, VII, 295.

[10] Vieira, *Cartas*, I, 468. A more moderate but pretty damning indictment of Portuguese mistreatment of the Amerindians of Amazonia is in his "Resposta aos Capitulos" of 1662 (*Obras Escolhidas*, V, 174–315). Cf. also Azevedo, *Jesuitas no Grão-Pará*, pp. 155–157, 171, 196, 380. Recent research estimates the total number of Amerindians in Brazil at the time of the Portuguese discovery as something under a million at the most.

[11] *Livro Grosso do Maranhão*, I, 263, 273–274, 284; *ibid.*, II, 78–79, 172, 263, for some typical examples.

[12] "O Maranhão e o Pará é uma Rochela de Portugal, e uma conquista para conquistar, e uma terra onde Vossa Magestade é nomeado mas não obedecido" (Vieira, *Cartas*, I, 422).

[13] The *Regimento* of December, 1686 and the supplementary *alvará* of April, 1688, are printed in full by S. Leite, S.J., *História*, IV, 369–380, and summarized

by M. Kiemen, O.F.M., in *Indian Policy*, pp. 158–162. For subsequent additions and amendments, see Jacinto de Carvalho, S.J., [ed.], *Regimento & Leys sobre as Missões do Maranhão & Pará, e sobre a liberdade dos Indios* (Lisboa, 1724).

[14] CR of 9 March 1718 in *Livro Grosso do Maranhão*, II, 152–154; Lisboa, *Obras Completas*, II, 178–179.

[15] Vieira's *Regulamento* is printed in full from the only existing copy in Leite, S.J., *História*, IV, 106–124. It is interesting to compare this with the regulations for the Spanish Jesuit Reductions of Paraguay.

[16] The Jesuit Visitor of Maranhão-Pará to the Crown, 13 June 1718, in Leite, S.J., *História*, IV, 387–394.

[17] The regional *juntas das missões* which functioned at various places in Portuguese Asia and America should not be confused with the central *junta das missões* established at Lisbon in 1655 as an advisory council to the Crown.

[18] " ... logrando-se com isso terem esses moradores, não só quem os sirva, mas quem vá aos certões a buscar as drogas que nelles se produzem, e ajudem a defender as nossas mesmas terras do acometimento dos Indios do Corço nossos inimigos" (CR of 12 April 1709, in *Livro Grosso*, II, 28).

[19] For the use and abuse of Amerindian village labor, cf. *Livro Grosso*, I, 249, 263, 273–274, 284; *ibid.*, II, 115–116, 139, 152–154, 169, 221; S. Leite, S.J., *História*, IV, 125–132. The complaints of the misuse of Amerindian wet nurses recall those made of similar practices in Spanish America, as can be seen from R. Konetzke, *Colección de documentos para la historia de la formación social de Hispano America, 1493–1810* (2 vols., Madrid, 1958), II, 45, 552.

[20] *Livro Grosso do Maranhão*, I, 131, 184, 194, 205, 225, 266, 272; *ibid.*, II, 20, 37, 88, 158–160, 232, 245, 250, for some typical complaints. Cf. also Azevedo, *op. cit.*, pp. 169, 172–175, 196, 203, 215, 220, 235–236, 240, 251–253, 310, 323, 351.

[21] "O homem está doido nesta materia" (*apud* Azevedo, *op. cit.*, p. 255). For a survey of D. João V's relations with the Jesuits, see Rodrigues, S.J., *História*, VI (1), pp. 425–454.

[22] Oliveira Martins, *João da Maia da Gama*, I, 114–115.

[23] For Silva Nunes' accusations and the Jesuits' defense, cf. Azevedo, *op. cit.*, pp. 187–226; Maia da Gama's "Resposta" of 26 May 1730, *apud* Oliveira Martins, *op. cit.*, I, 106–113; Jacinto de Carvalho's memorials listed in Leite, S.J., *História*, VIII, 150–153, to which should be added three letters signed by Carvalho and dated Lisbon, 13 and 18 January and 18 March 1730, respectively, in the writer's collection.

[24] "A segurança dos Sertões e das mesmas povoaçoens do Maranhão e de toda a America consiste na amisade dos Indios" (*Livro Grosso do Maranhão*, I, 71. Cf. also *ibid.*, pp. 134, 229).

[25] C. M. de La Condamine, *Relation abrégée d'un voyage fait dans l'interieur de l'Amerique Meridionale ... en descendant la Rivière des Amazons* (Paris, 1745; reprinted, Maestricht, 1778).

[26] G. Edmundson [ed.], *Journal of the Travels and Labours of Father Samuel Fritz, S.J., in the River of the Amazons between 1686 and 1723* (ed. Hakluyt Society, London, 1922); CR of 13 May 1721 ordering that the *resgates* should be undertaken annually—a reversal of previous policy—in *Livro Grosso do Maranhão*, II, 181–183.

[27] "Nous crûmes en arrivant au Para, à la sortie des bois de l'Amazone, nous voir transportés en Europe. Nous trouvâmes une grande ville, des rues bien

alignées, des maisons riantes, la plupart rebâties depuis trente ans en pierre et en moilon, des Eglises magnifiques" (La Condamine, *Voyage*, ed 1778, pp. 173-174).

[28] For the missionary jurisdictional division of 1693-1695, cf. Leite, S.J., *História*, VI, 133-138, and Kiemen, O.F.M., *op. cit.*, pp. 170-180.

[29] Azevedo, *op. cit.*, pp. 228-230; Leite, S.J., *História*, IV, 138-140.

[30]Leite, S.J., *op. cit.*, IV, 155-164; La Condamine, *op. cit.* (ed. 1778), pp. 180-181.

NOTES TO CHAPTER XII
"Portuguese America in Mid-Century"
(Pages 293-325)

[1] Cf. the representations of the municipal councils of the principal towns in Minas Gerais dated 1750-1751 in Codice Costa Matoso, fols. 243-257.

[2] J. Cortesão, *Alexandre de Gusmão*, I (2), pp. 231-264.

[3] " ... está no conhecimento de se defender a Colonia mais por reputação que por interesse."

[4] Tyrawly to Newcastle, Lisbon 2 January 1740 (PRO London SP 89/40). The mutual dislike of D. João V and Isabel Farnese emerges very clearly in the well-documented works of Jaime Cortesão, Eduardo Brazão, and Caetano Beirão, which are cited in the bibliography.

[5] Cf. the map in Cortesão, *op. cit.*, I, pp. 276-277.

[6] For the work of the *Padres Mathematicos* in Brazil, cf. J. Cortesão, *op. cit.*, I (2), pp. 7-26, reproduced virtually *ipsissima verba* in *Studia*, I, 123-150; S. Leite, S.J., *História*, VIII, 130-132; *ibid.*, IX, 130-137.

[7] "Le corps des ingénieurs est peut-être en ce moment le moins mauvais des corps militaires du Portugal, quoi'qu'il renferme encore beaucoup d'ignorans et de sujets très-peu propres au métier que le hasard, plutôt que le goût, leur a fait embrasser" (J. F. Bourgoing, *Voyage du ci-devant Duc de Chatelet*, II, 8-9).

[8] J. Cortesão, *op. cit.*, I (1), p. 320. For eighteenth-century engineers in Pernambuco, cf. Pereira da Costa, *Anais Pernambucanos*, V, 11-17.

[9] C. Ferreira Reis, *A Amazonia que os Portugueses revelaram*, p. 48.

[10] "Diario do IV Conde da Ericeira," *Biblos*, XVIII (1942), pp. 486, 488.

[11] Cf. the correspondence of the Secretary of State with the Viceroy of India on this project in Accioli-Amaral, *Memórias Históricas*, II, 179-181.

[12] *Livro Grosso do Maranhão*, II, 172; Rau, *MSS Cadaval*, II, 280, 388-393; *ABNRJ*, XXVIII, 344-345; Pereira da Costa, *op. cit.*, V, 66-67, 298-303, for some typical instances.

[13] "Informação Geral da Capitania de Pernambuco," dated 1749, in *ABNRJ*, XXVIII, 120-496, especially pp. 133-135, 344-345, 402-404; Soterio da Silva Ribeiro [pseudonym of Fr. Manuel de Madre de Deus, O.F.M.], *Suma Triunfal da nova e grande celebridade do glorioso e invicto martir Gonçalo Garcia com uma colecção de varios folguedos e danças &c* (Lisboa, 1753), summarized in Pereira da Costa, *op. cit.*, VI, 53-61.

[14] Cf. Pereira da Costa, *op. cit.*, V, 116; *ABNRJ*, XXVIII, 477-478. Although Pereira da Costa does not give his source, it was evidently another copy of the

"Informação," which he dates 1746, and from which he quotes extensively elsewhere in his work. The difference between the two figures is mainly due to Pereira da Costa making no distinction between the *engenhos moentes* and the *fogos mortos.*

[15] CR of 18 February 1730 in *ABNRJ,* XXVIII, 248–249.

[16] *ABNRJ,* XXVIII, 482–483, for further details of Pernambuco's trade in 1749. For the export of specie from Pernambuco to Portugal, cf. Pereira da Costa, *op. cit.,* VI, 71–72.

[17] Prices ranged from 400 to 1,400 *reis* the *arroba,* according to grade and quality for the Bahian sugars, those from the other regions being 100 *reis* less in each category. CR of 27 January 1751, and Pereira da Costa, *op. cit.,* V, 117–118. It is interesting to compare these prices with those obtaining half a century earlier, as given by Antonil, *Cultura e opulencia,* Livro III, chap. 11.

[18] Galveas' correspondence with the Crown in APEB, "Livros das Ordens Régias," 1735–1749. Cf. also Accioli-Amaral, *op. cit.,* II, 168–178, 387–404.

[19] Cf. the statistics published by Ott, *Formação e Evolução,* II, 91.

[20] Cf. the documents calendared in *PANRJ,* VIII, 56–61.

[21] Caio Prado, *Formação,* pp. 296–339, has an excellent discussion of Portuguese colonial legislation in Brazil at the end of the eighteenth century, and most of what he says there is equally applicable here.

[22] " ... não obstante se terem degulado e enforcado muitos, depois que governo este Estado, he tal o genio dos homens que vivem no sertão mays remoto que a sua liberdade e tirannia as faz esquecer estes exemplos" (Count of Sabugosa to the Crown, Bahia, 16 September 1732 in Accioli-Amaral, *op. cit.,* II, 342). For Angeja's equally drastic attitude, cf. Le Gentil de la Barbinais, *Voyage,* III, 162–163. Cf. also APEB, "Livros das Ordens Régias," 1698–1701; *ABNRJ,* XXVIII, 188–193, 343–344; Accioli-Amaral, *op. cit.,* II, 373–381.

[23] " ... porque a vaidade os obriga mais que toda a conveniencia, porque neste clima e em tães homens he o vicio que mais se conserva," as the Governor of São Paulo observed in a dispatch to the Crown dated 25 December 1721, apropos of the Paulista discoverers of the mines of Cuiabá. Cf. also the remarks of the Count of Assumar in Rau, *MSS Cadaval,* II, 194; Southey, *History,* III, 155.

[24] "Eu não peço a Sua Magestade que me faça fidalgo nem que me de habito de Christo porque o mundo está tam cheio delles que inda ejde ser conhecido por homem que não tem abito como antigamente hera conhecido António Fernandez polo do abito" (Diogo do Couto to the Count of Vidigueira, Goa, December, 1607).

[25] " ... se vos não devia permittir a tal faculdade, asy por não haver nesse Estado as continuas guerras que ha no da India por mar e em terra, não só com os Reys de Azia, mas e muitas vezes com as naçoens da Europa, nas quaes os meus vassallos se fazem merecedores das taes honras" (Crown to Viceroy of Brazil, Lisbon, 6 January 1715, in reply to a viceregal request for permission to confer twelve *foros* of *fidalgo* and twelve habits of the three Military Orders yearly.)

[26] " ... os filhos da India, que dizem à boca cheya, que Fidalguia sò a da India; e que a do Reino he sombra à vista della" (Fr. Inacio de Santa Teresa, "Estado do presente Estado da India," MS of 1725 in the writer's collection).

[27] Thousands of the *cartas de sesmaria* issued by Gomes Freire de Andrada in Minas Gerais during the years 1739–1753, are published in the *RAPM,* of which

those printed in Vol. XVI (1), pp. 160–233 may be taken as typical. For forestry conservation, cf. *Ephemerides Mineiras*, III, 86–87.

[28] Documents calendared in Rau, *op. cit.*, II, 134, 180; *RAPM*, XVI (2), 382; *PANRJ*, X, 202–203.

[29] For the Minas Gerais contracts in 1750, cf. Codice Costa Matoso, fols. 325–327; *RAPM*, XVI (2), pp. 427, 443; Myriam Ellis, "Contribuição ao estudo do abastecimento das zonas mineradoras do Brasil no século XVIII," in *Revista de História*, XXXVI (São Paulo, 1958), pp. 429–467. The same author is also responsible for the standard work on the salt gabelle in colonial Brazil, *O monopólio do sal no Estado do Brasil, 1631–1801* (São Paulo, 1955). For royal decrees concerning Brazilian contracts in general and those of Pernambuco in particular, cf. *ABNRJ*, XXVIII, 132–133, 283–336.

[30] Memorial of the Town Council of Villa Rica, 3 April 1751, in Codice Costa Matoso, fols. 248–249. Cf. p. 188 above, for the increase of farming at the expense of mining.

[31] "Relache de *l'Arc-en-ciel* à Rio de Janeiro, 1748," published with a commentary by M. S. Cardozo in *HAHR*, XXI (1941), pp. 425–435. The anonymous author's portrait sketch of Gomes Freire begins: "Quoique Don Fernand Freire [*sic*] commence à se ressentir des approches de la vieillesse et qu'il dejà essuye plusieurs attaques de goutes, il etoit encore d'une assez belle representation."

[32] A good idea of Gomes Freire's manifold preoccupations and the energy with which he tackled them can be obtained from the selection from his correspondence for the years 1736–1737 printed in *RAPM*, XVI (2), pp. 239–460.

[33] André Ribeiro Coutinho, *O Capitão de infantaria portuguez, com a theoria e pratica das suas funções, exercitados assim nas Armadas Terrestres, a navaes, como nas Praças e Corte* (2 vols., Lisboa, 1751). The work was dedicated to Gomes Freire, and the study of the battle of Fontenoy is in Vol. II, 304–309.

[34] J. F. Pinto Alpoim, *Exame de artilheiros que comprehende Arithmetica, Geometria, e artilharia, com quatro appendices* (Lisboa, 1744); *Exame de Bombeiros que comprehende dez tratados; geometria, trigonometria, longmetria, altimetria, Morteiros, pedreiros, batteria dos morteiros &c.* (Madrid, 1747). Both these works were likewise dedicated to Gomes Freire.

[35] "As tropas que levou Gomes Freire para a sua guarda foram sòmente quatro companhias de granadeiros, tais e tão faustosos e bem disciplinados que assombraram os castelhanos," the future Marquis of Pombal wrote to his brother, Francisco Xavier de Mendonça Furtado, on 13 May 1753 (*apud* d'Azevedo, *Jesuitas no Grão-Pará*, p. 329 n.).

[36] "On voit aussi à Lisbonne plusieurs maisons qu'ont été de même construites en Amérique; elles sont en bois; les morceaux arrivent équarris et numérotés: trois ou quatre jours après le débarquement de la charpente, la maison est achevée et habitable. Pendant que j'étois à Lisbonne, le ministre de Naples en ocupoit une de cette espèce, qui étoit très commode et très bien distribuée" (J. F. Bourgoing, *Voyage du Chatelet*, II, 97).

[37] " ... só o dispenseiro da fragata tomara nesse Corte 10,000 cruzados a risco, que empregara em varios generos ... e eu faço hoje muy pouca differença dos capitaens das Naus de El Rey aos dos navios mercantes, porque tanto huns como outros querem voltar para o Reino, não quando El Rey manda mas no tempo que lhe pareçe" (Sabugosa to Secretary of State, Bahia 18 September 1732, in APEB, "Ordens Régias," Vol. XXIX, fol. 132). For the frequent changes rung

on the dates fixed for the departure and return of the Brazil fleet after the *alvará* of 1690, cf. Sabugosa to Secretary of State, 5 October 1729, in APEB, "Ordens Régias," Vol. XXVI, fol. 91; Conde das Galveas' representation cf. *ca.* February, 1738 in APEB, *ibid.,* XXXV, fol. 55; documents in *ABNRJ,* XXVIII, 144–145.

[38] Laws of 24 December 1734 and 28 February 1736 in Sombra, *História Monetaria do Brasil,* p. 175; paras. 19–23 of the *regimento* given to the *capitão-de-mar-e-guerra* José Soares de Andrade, commander of the Rio de Janeiro convoy in 1734 (University of Sao Paulo, Lamego MS 73). Cf. also the documents of 1720–1736 in *ABNRJ,* XXVIII, 140–144.

[39] For the various laws enacted against goldsmiths in the years 1688 to 1766, cf. *RAPM,* XVI (1), pp. 453–456; Xavier da Veiga, *Ephemerides,* I, lxvii, pp. 152–153, 203, 391, 409; *ibid.,* Vol. II, 407; *ibid.,* III, 170–175; Sombra, *op. cit.,* pp. 110, 179, 182.

[40] Petition of the town council of São Jorge de Ilheus, 30 May 1748, in APEB, "Ordens Régias," Livro 1748–1750; Accioli-Amaral, *op. cit.,* II, 388. For the embezzlements in the Bahia *Donativo Real,* see the Count of Atouguia's dispatch of September 6, 1753 in Accioli-Amaral, *op. cit.,* II, 396–398. For Pernambuco's contribution, see Pereira da Costa, *Anais Pernambucanos,* V, 379–382. The original *termo* of the representatives of the town councils of Minas Gerais concerning the collection of their quota of the *Donativo Real* is in APM, Cod., 6 (S.G.), fols. 152–156.

[41] " ... em hum paiz de grande rellaxação e ignorancia, aonde os Ecleziasticos são os mais cubiçozos e desordenados" (*Parecer* of Manuel Galvão de Lacerda in a discussion of the Overseas Council on the difficulties of collecting the royal fifths in Brazil, Lisbon, 28 December 1730. MS in private hands).

[42] "Problema que em duas palavras resolvo dizendo, que o dito principe para poder conservar Portugal necessita totalmente das riquezas do Brazil e de nenhuma maneira das de Portugal, que não tem para sustentar o Brazil, de que se segue, que he mais commodo e mais seguro estar onde se tem o que sobeja, que onde se espera o de que se carece." *Instrucções inéditas de D. Luís de Cunha a Marco António de Azevedo Coutinho* (ed. Azevedo e Baião, Coimbra 1929), pp. 211–218.

[43] " ... e bem se deixa ver que, posto em uma balança o Brasil, e na outra o reino, ha de pesar com grande excesso mais aquella que esta; e assim a maior parte e a mais rica não soffrerá ser dominada pelo menor, mais pobre; nem a este inconveniente se lhe poderá achar facil remedio" (this *parecer* of 1732 has been printed several times in the *RIHGB,* VII, in 1845, 1866, and 1911, but the text here followed is that in Cortesão, *op. cit.,* III (2), pp. 23–30).

BIBLIOGRAPHY

NOTE.—This is not a bibliography of Portugal and Brazil in the reigns of Dom Pedro II and Dom João V, but a list of the full titles of the printed books and manuscripts cited in the footnotes, together with brief critical or explanatory remarks where these may be helpful.

ACCIOLI-AMARAL, *Memorias Historicas e politicas da Provincia da Bahia. Do Coronel Ignacio Accioli de Cerqueira e Silva. Annotador Dr. Braz do Amaral* (6 vols., Salvador, Bahia, 1919–1940).
A most useful and richly documented work, but somewhat unsystematically arranged and lacking an index.

Anais do Arquivo Público da Bahia (32 vols., Salvador, Bahia, 1917–1952).
Title varies somewhat, the first volumes having been entitled *Annaes do Arquivo Publico e do Museu do Estado da Bahia.*
Vols. 31 and 32 of this series are particularly useful.

Anais da Biblioteca Nacional do Rio de Janeiro (Rio de Janeiro, 1876 to date).
A particularly useful and richly documented series.

Anais do Primeiro Congresso de Historia da Bahia (5 vols., Salvador, 1950–1951).
Vol. II of this series is particularly useful.

Anais do IV Congresso de História Nacional, 21-28 Abril de 1949 (10 vols., Rio de Janeiro, 1950–1951).
Edited by the Instituto Histórico e Geográfico Brasileiro.

ANDRADE AND DUARTE [eds.], *Morão, Rosa e Pimenta. Notícia dos três primeiros livros em vernáculo sobre a medicina no Brasil. Estudo crítico de Gilberto Osório de Andrade. Introducções históricas, interpretações e notas de Eustáquio Duarte. Prefácio de Gilberto Freyre* (Recife, 1956).

ANTONIL, ANDRÉ JOÃO [pseudonym of Giovanni Antonio Andreoni, S.J.], *Cultura e opulencia do Brasil por suas drogas, e minas, com varias noticias curiosas do modo de fazer o assucar; plantar, & beneficar o Tabaco; tirar ouro das minas; & descubrir as da Prata; E dos grandes emolumentos, que esta conquista da America Meridional dá ao Reyno de Portugal com estes, & outros generos, & Contractos Reaes* (Lisboa, 1711).
None of the later editions (1837, 1898, 1923, 1950, etc.) are satisfactory, which is doubly unfortunate in view of the exceeding rarity of the original. I have used the British Museum copy which should be added to the six listed by Borba de Moraes, *Bibliographia Brasiliana*, Vol. I, p. 34.

Arquivo Nacional do Rio de Janeiro. "Correspondencia dos Governadores do Rio, 1702–1706" (Col. 78/9/ Armario 4) and "Registo velho de Ordens Régias, 1712–1719," Vol. 21 (Col. 78/19) were the only codices

Bibliography

I had time to examine personally, reliance being placed otherwise on the documents catalogued or published in the *Publicações do Arquivo Público Nacional*, q.v.

Arquivo Público do Estado da Bahia.

The principal collection used was the "Livros de Ordens Régias" for the period 1695–1750. These codices contain the correspondence between the Crown at Lisbon and the viceroy (or the governor-general) at Bahia. Those for the years 1695–1727, inclusive, are catalogued in Vols. XXXI and XXXII of the *Anais do Arquivo Público da Bahia* (Salvador, Bahia, 1949–1952) which afford a good idea of the scope of this series.

Arquivo Público do Estado de Pernambuco, Recife. "Livro de Registo das Portarias, 1711–1716."

Codex of 317 leaves in folio, interesting for the aftermath of the *guerra dos Mascates*.

While at Recife, I was able to examine, through the kindness of Professor José António Gonsalves de Mello, his transcripts from the letter-book (*copiador*) of Luís Cardoso, 1687–1711, the original of which is in the archives of the local branch of the Third Order of Saint Francis.

Arquivo Publico Mineiro.

The principal sections consulted were: "Secretaria do Governo" (S.G.) and "Delegacia Fiscal" (D.F.) for the years 1710–1750.

Arquivos de Angola (Luanda, 1933 to date).

AZEVEDO, CARLOS DE, *Um Artista Italiano em Goa. Placidio Francisco Ramponi* (Lisboa, 1956).

A Portuguese translation of the hitherto unpublished Italian MS. Ramponi visited Bahia on his homeward voyage in 1699.

AZEVEDO, JOÃO LUCIO d', *Os Jesuitas no Grão-Pará. Suas missões e a colonização* (2d. rev. ed., Coimbra, 1930).

Still the best survey of the subject within the compass of one volume. See also under Vieira, S.J., António.

BARBINAIS, LE GENTIL DE LA, *Nouveau Voyage autour du monde, par L. G. de la Barbinais; enrichi de plusieurs plans, vues et perspectives des principales villes et ports du Perou, Chily, Brésil et de la Chine &c.* (3 vols., Paris, 1728).

The first edition, which I have not seen, is dated 1725.

BAZIN, GERMAIN, *L'Architecture religieuse baroque au Brésil* (2 vols., Paris, 1956).

The definitive work on this subject.

BENCI, S.J., JORGE, *Economia Christã dos Senhores no governo dos escravos. Livro Brasileiro de 1700. 2a. edição, preparada, prefaciada e anotada por Serafim Leite, S.J.* (Porto, 1954).

Bibliography

I have used this second edition in default of the exceedingly rare original (Rome, 1705) which I have never seen.

BERREDO, BERNARDO PEREIRA DE, *Annaes Historicos do Estado do Maranhão, em que se dà noticia do seu descobrimento, e tudo o mais que nelle tem succedido desde o anno em que foy descoberto até o de 1718* (Lisboa, 1749).
Biblioteca Munícipal de São Paulo, Codice Costa Matoso, MS D/1/a/43. *See* Costa Matoso below.

Biblioteca Nacional, Rio de Janeiro, "Do Descobrimento dos Diamantes, e differentes methodos que se tem praticado na sua extracção" (Cod. I-18-14-1).
Anonymous MS of 287 folio pages, covering the period 1729–1790.

Biblos. Revista da Faculdade de Letras da Universidade de Coimbra (Coimbra, 1925 to date).

BORBA DE MORAES. *See* MORAES

BOURGOING, JEAN FRANÇOIS, *Voyage du ci-devant Duc du Chatelet, en Portugal, où se trouvent des détails intéressans sur les colonies, sur le tremblement de terre de Lisbonne, sur M. de Pombal et la cour; Revu, corrigé sur le manuscrit, et augmenté de notes sur la situation actuelle de ce royaume et de ses colonies par J. Fr. B.* (2 vols., Paris, 1798–1808).
There is an English translation, published by J. Stockdale, 2 vols., London, 1809. The first French edition was published in 1797.

BOXER, C. R., *Salvador de Sá and the Struggle for Brazil and Angola, 1602–1686* (London, 1952).

Brasilia. Revista de assuntos brasileiros. Published by the University of Coimbra, 1942 to date.

BRAZÃO, EDUARDO, *As expedições de Duclerc e Duguay-Trouin ao Rio de Janeiro, 1710–1711* (Lisboa, 1940).
Prints two hitherto unpublished documents from the Ajuda Library, of which that on the Duclerc expedition is the most important.

——, *Dom João V. Subsídios para a história do seu reinado* (Porto, 1946).

——, "Diário de Francisco Xavier de Menezes 4º Conde da Ericeira, 1731–33." Published serially in *Biblos*, Vols. XVI–XVIII.

——, *Relações Externas de Portugal. Reinado de D. João V* (2 vols., Oporto, 1938).

BURY, JOHN, "Jesuit Architecture in Brazil," *The Month*, New Series, Vol. IV (1950), pp. 385–408.

——, "The Borrominesque Churches of Colonial Brazil," *The Art Bulletin*, Vol. XXXVII (March, 1955), pp. 27–53.

CADORNEGA, ANTONIO DE OLIVEIRA DE, *História Geral das Guerras Angolanas* (3 vols., Lisboa, 1940–1942).

Bibliography

Written at Luanda in 1680–1681, this valuable work was edited by José Matias Delgado and Manuel Alves da Cunha.

CAIO PRADO JÚNIOR, *Formação do Brasil contemporâneo. Colônia* (4th ed.; São Paulo, 1953).

A most admirable work vitiated only by the lack of an index. Already a classic, it deals primarily with Brazil on the eve of independence, but much of what the author writes is applicable to an earlier period.

CALMON, PEDRO, *Historia do Brasil, 1500–1800* (3 vols., São Paulo and Rio de Janeiro, 1939–1943).

Since my own work first went to press, this edition has been superseded by the seven-volume edition of 1961, of which volumes 3–4 cover the period 1695–1750.

——, *Historia Social do Brasil, I, Espirito de Sociedade colonial* (3d. ed.; São Paulo and Rio de Janeiro, 1941).

——, *História da civilização Brasileira* (5th ed.; São Paulo and Rio de Janeiro, 1945).

All these three works of Pedro Calmon are excellent examples of effective synthesis.

——, *História da Casa da Torre. Uma dinastia de pioneiros* (Rio de Janeiro, 1939).

CALOGERAS, JOÃO PANDÍA, *As minas do Brasil e a sua legislação* (3 vols., Rio de Janeiro, 1904).

CARDOZO, MANUEL DA SILVEIRA SOARES, "Alguns subsídios para a história da cobrança do quinto na capitania de Minas Gerais até 1735" (Lisboa, 1938).

A reprint of 45 pages from *I Congresso da História da expansão Portuguesa no Mundo*, III Seccão (Lisboa, 1937).

——, "The Collection of the Fifth in Brazil, 1695–1709," *HAHR*, Vol. XX, No. 3 (August, 1940), pp. 359–379.

——, "The *Guerra dos Emboabas*, Civil War in Minas Gerais, 1708–1709," *HAHR*, Vol. XXII, No. 3 (August, 1942), pp. 470–492.

——, "The Brazilian Gold Rush," *The Americas*, Vol. III (October, 1946), pp. 137–160.

——, "The Lay Brotherhoods of Colonial Bahia," *The Catholic Historical Review*, Vol. XXXIII, No. 1 (April, 1947), pp. 12–30.

——, "Tithes in Colonial Minas Gerais," *Catholic Historical Review*, Vol. XXXVIII, No. 2 (July, 1952), pp. 175–182.

——, "A French Document on Rio de Janeiro, 1748," *HAHR*, Vol. XXI, No. 3 (August, 1941).

These richly documented articles form the best treatment of their re-

Bibliography

spective topics in English. The author varies his name between the full
form and Manuel (or Manoel) Cardozo.

CARNAXIDE, VISCONDE DE, *O Brasil na administracão Pombalina. Economia
e Política Externa* (São Paulo and Rio de Janeiro, 1940).
Though principally concerned with the reign of Dom José I, this book
contains valuable information about the production of gold in Minas
Gerais in the first half of the eighteenth century.

CASTRO E ALMEIDA, EDUARDO DE, *Inventario dos documentos relativos ao
Brasil existentes no archivo da marinha e ultramar de Lisboa* (6 vols.,
Rio de Janeiro, 1913–1921). Reprinted from the *ABNRJ*.
Extremely useful guide to documents which have since been trans-
ferred to the AHU, Lisbon.

*Catalogo de documentos sobre a história de São Paulo, existentes no Ar-
quivo Histórico Ultramarino de Lisboa* (14 vols., Rio de Janeiro, 1956–
1959).
Published as a special series ("Tomo Especial") in the *RIHGB*. Since
the documents are concerned with the São Paulo captaincy at its widest
extent, this series also includes much material concerning the Minas
Gerais, Goiás, Mato Grosso, Rio de Janeiro, etc.

CHATELET, DUC DU, *See* BOURGOING, J. FR.

CODICE COSTA MATOSO. *See* COSTA MATOSO.

CODICE MANUEL DE SOUSA. *See* SOUSA, MANUEL DE.

COLLETT, JOSEPH, *The Private Letter-Books of Joseph Collett* (London,
1933). Edited by H. H. Dodwell.

CORTESÃO, JAIME, *Raposo Tavares e a formação territorial do Brasil* (Rio
de Janeiro, 1958).

———, *Alexandre de Gusmão e o tratado de Madrid* (8 vols., Rio de
Janeiro, 1950–1959).
An excellent and lavishly documented work, marred only by the confusing way in which the volumes are numbered, resulting in Parte I,
tomo I appearing two years after Parte II, tomo I. Subdivided into sections entitled *Obras varias; Documentos biograficos; Antecedentes do
Tratado; Negociações.*

———, *Manuscritos da colecção de Angelis. Colonia do Sacramento, 1669–
1749* (Rio de Janeiro, 1954).

———, *Manuscritos da colecção de Angelis. Antecedentes do Tratado de
Madrid. Jesuítas e Bandeirantes no Paraguai, 1703–1751* (Rio de Janeiro,
1955).

COSTA MATOSO, CAETANO, "Colasam das Noticias dos primeiros descobridores
das Minas na America, que fes o Dr. Caetano da Costa Matoso, sendo

Bibliography

Ouvidor Geral do Ouro Preto, de que tomou posse em Fevreiro de 1749," Biblioteca Munícipal de São Paulo, MS D/1/a/43.

Priceless repository of original MSS on the history of Minas Gerais (and on some other regions of Brazil and the Maranhão-Pará as well) collected by a crown judge at Ouro Preto between 1749 and 1752.

COUTINHO, ANDRÉ RIBEIRO, *O Capitão de Infantaria Portuguez, com a theorica, e pratica das suas funções, exercitadas assim nas Armadas terrestres e navaes, como nas Praças, e Corte* (2 vols., Lisboa, 1751).

DAMPIER, WILLIAM, *A Voyage to New Holland* [in 1699]. Edited with introduction, notes and illustrative documents by J. A. Williamson (London, 1939).

Originally published in two parts, 1703 and 1709, being reprinted with continuous pagination in 1729.

DELGADO, RALPH, *História de Angola* (4 vols., Benguela and Lobito, 1948–1955). In progress. These 4 vols. cover the period 1575–1737.

Description de la ville de Lisbonne, ou l'on traite de la Cour, de Portugal, de la langue Portugaise, & des Moeurs des Habitans; du gouvernement, des revenues du Roi, & de ses forces par Mer et par Terre; des colonies Portugaises, et du commerce de cette capital (Paris, 1733).

This anonymous account gives one of the best brief descriptions of Portugal in the reign of Dom João V.

Documentos Historicos da Bibliotheca Nacional do Rio de Janeiro (Rio de Janeiro, 1928 to date).

This monumental series is particularly rich in eighteenth-century documents, but unfortunately the majority of the 120-odd volumes published to date are not indexed.

DUGUAY-TROUIN, RENÉ, *Memoires de Monsieur Du Guay-Trouin, Lieutenant General des armées navales de France, et commandant de l'Ordre Royal Militaire de Saint Louis* (1 vol., with atlas of plates [Paris], 1740).

First authentic and best edition of a work which had many less satisfactory ones in the eighteenth century.

EDMUNDSON, GEORGE [trans. and ed.]. *Journal of the Travels and Labours of Father Samuel Fritz S.J., in the River of the Amazons between 1686 and 1723* (London, 1922).

ELLIS, MYRIAM, *O monopólio do sal no Estado do Brasil, 1631–1801* (São Paulo, 1955).

———, "Contribuição ao estudo do abastecimento das zonas mineradoras do Brasil no século XVIII," *Revista de História*, Vol. XXXVI (São Paulo, 1958), pp. 429–467.

———, *Aspectos da pesca da baleia no Brasil colonial* (São Paulo, 1959).

Bibliography

ELLIS JUNIOR, ALFREDO, *O Ouro e a Paulistânia* (São Paulo, 1948).

FERNANDES GAMA, JOSÉ BERNARDO, *Memorias Historicas da Provincia de Pernambuco, precedidas de um ensaio Topographico-Historico* (4 vols., Pernambuco, 1844–1848).
Professor J. A. Gonsalves de Mello kindly lent me his copy of this exceedingly rare work, which is based largely on original manuscripts for the period 1695–1750.

FERREIRA, FRANCISCO IGNACIO, *Repertorio Juridico do Mineiro. Consoldição alphabetica e chronologica de todas as disposições sobre Minas, comprehendendo a legislação antiga e moderna de Portugal e do Brasil* (Rio de Janeiro, 1884).

FERREIRA REIS, ARTHUR CEZAR, *Limites e Demarcações na Amazônia Brasileira, I: A Fronteira colonial com a Guiana Francesca* (Rio de Janeiro, 1947).
Of the numerous works by this author on the colonial history of the Amazon region, this is the fullest and best documented for the period with which we are concerned.

———, *Estadistas Portugueses na Amazônia* (Rio de Janeiro, 1948).

FREITAS, GUSTAVO DE, *A Companhia Geral do comércio do Brasil, 1649–1720. Subsídios para a história económica de Portugal e do Brasil* (São Paulo, 1951).

FREYRE, GILBERTO, *Casa-Grande e Senzala. Formação da familia brasileira sob o regime de economia patriarcal* (4a edição, definitiva, 2 vols., Rio de Janeiro, 1943).

———, *The Masters and the Slaves. A Study in the Development of Brazilian Civilization* (New York, 1946).
Translation of the fourth edition of *Casa-Grande e Senzala* by Samuel Putnam.

GODINHO, VITORINO MAGALHÃES, "Le Portugal, les flottes du sucre et les flottes de l'or, 1670–1770," *Annales—Économies—Sociétés—Civilisations* —(Jan./Mar. 1951), pp. 184–197.
A Portuguese version of this short but highly suggestive essay was later published in the Brazilian *Revista de Historia*, No. 15 (July–September, 1953), pp. 69–88.

GOLGHER, ISIAS, *Guerra dos Emboabas. A primeira guerra civil nas Americas. Estudo baseado em documentação inédita* (Belo Horizonte, 1956).
Despite the pretentious way in which this book is written, it adds virtually nothing to the documents already published and used more judiciously by J. Soares de Mello, Taunay, and Manuel Cardozo (*q.v.* respectively).

GOMES FERREIRA, LUÍS, *Erario Mineral dividido em doze Tratados ... Autor*

425

Bibliography

L.G.F. cirurgião approvado, natural da Villa de S. Pedro de Rates, e assistente nas Minas do ouro por discurso de vinte annos (Lisboa, 1735).

An invaluable work for the social history of Minas Gerais, containing much information which cannot be found elsewhere.

GONSALVES DE MELLO, JOSÉ ANTONIO, *Antônio Fernandes de Matos, 1671–1701* (Recife, 1957).

A model monograph.

Hispanic-American Historical Review (Baltimore and Durham, North Carolina, Duke University Press, 1918 to date).

HOLANDA, SERGIO BUARQUE DE, *Monções* (Rio de Janeiro, 1945).

A classic of its kind. Some of the material is embodied in the same author's later work, *Caminhos e Fronteiras. Edição ilustrada* (Rio de Janeiro, 1957).

Instituto Histórico e Geográfico Brasileiro.

The only codex which I had time to examine in any detail was the letter-book of D. Rodrigo Cezar de Menezes, governor of São Paulo in 1721–1726: "Heste livro tem tudo o que fes o ex^mo Senhor General no tempo em que gouvernou a cidade de São Paulo e toda sua capitania, tomando posse do governo em 3 de setembro 1721" (L. 89, 1509).

KIEMEN, O.F.M., MATHIAS C., "The Indian Policy of Portugal in America, with Special Reference to the Old State of Maranhão, 1500–1755," reprinted from *The Americas*, Vol. V, No. 4 (April, 1949), pp. 131–171, 439–460.

———, *The Indian Policy of Portugal in the Amazon Region, 1614–1693* (Washington, D.C., 1954).

KINDERSLEY, MRS., *Letters from the Island of Teneriffe, Brazil, the Cape of Good Hope, and the East Indies* (London, 1777).

LA CONDAMINE, CHARLES MARIE DE, *Relation abrégé d'un voyage fait dans l'interieur de l'Amerique Meridionale depuis la côte de la Mer du Sud, jusqu'aux côtes du Brésil & de la Guyane, en descendant la rivière des Amazones lue a l'Assemblée publique de l'Académie des Sciences le 28 Avril 1745* (Paris, 1745).

I have used the Maestricht edition of 1778. For the numerous editions and variants of this work, see Borba de Moraes, *Bibliographia Brasiliana*, Vol. I, 378–381.

LE GENTIL. *See* BARBINAIS.

LEITE, AURELIANO, *Antonio de Albuquerque Coelho de Carvalho, Capitão-General de São Paulo e Minas do Ouro no Brasil* (Lisboa, 1944).

Contains some useful documents but usually without indication of their source.

Bibliography

LEITE, S.J., SERAFIM, *História da Companhia de Jesus no Brasil* (10 vols., Lisboa and Rio de Janeiro, 1938–1950).

——, *Artes e ofícios dos Jesuitas no Brasil, 1549–1760* (Lisboa, 1953). Taken together the works of this author form the definitive history of the Jesuits in Brazil, based as they are òn a wealth of manuscript and printed sources.

LIMA JUNIOR, AUGUSTO DA. *A Capitania das Minas Gerais* (Rio de Janeiro, 1943). Second edition of a book first published in 1940.

——, *História dos diamantes nas Minas Gerais* (Lisboa, and Rio de Janeiro, 1945). In many ways more reliable than Santos' work, *q.v.*

——, *Vila Rica do Ouro Preto. Sintese histórica e descritiva* (Belo Horizonte, 1957).

——, *Notícias Históricas. De Norte a Sul* (Rio de Janeiro, 1954). Although the author of these works does not always give the source for his quotations from historical documents, I see no reason to doubt their essential accuracy, as some of his Brazilian colleagues do.

LISBOA, JOÃO FRANCISCO, *Obras de João Francisco Lisboa, natural do Maranhão, precedidas de uma noticia biographica pelo Dr. Antonio Henriques Leal e seguidas de uma apreciação critica do illustre escritor Theophilo Braga. Editores e revisores, Luiz Carlos Pereira de Castro e o Dr. A. Henriques Leal* (2 vols., Lisboa, 1901).

Livro Grosso do Maranhão, 1647–1745 (2 vols., Rio de Janeiro, 1948). Forms Vols. 66 and 67 of the *ABNRJ*.

LOPES, FRANCISCO ANTONIO, *Os Palácios de Vila Rica. Ouro Preto no ciclo do ouro* (Belo Horizonte, 1955). Particularly valuable for its copious documentation from the Arquivo Publico Mineiro.

MACHADO, SIMÃO FERREIRA, *Triunfo Eucharistico exemplar da Christandade Lusitana na solemne trasladação do Divinissimo Sacramanto de Igreja da Senhora do Pilar em Villa Rica, corte da capitania das Minas aos 24 de Mayo de 1733. Dedicado à soberana senhora do Rosario pelos Irmãos Pretos da sua irmandade, e a instancia dos mesmos exposto á publica noticia por Simam Ferreira Machado natural de Lisboa, e morador nas Minas* (Lisboa, 1734). Several times reprinted, but always with errors and omissions, so I have used this rare first edition.

MARQUES PEREIRA, NUNO, *Compendio Narrativo do Peregrino da America, em que se tratam de varios discursos espirituaes, e moraes, com muitas advertencias, e documentos contra os abusos que se achão introduzidos pela malicia diabolica no Estado do Brasil* (Lisboa, 1760).

This is the fourth edition. The three previous ones are dated 1728, 1731, and 1732. I have also used the sixth (two-volume) edition published by the Academia Brasileira de Letras in 1939, which contains the second part for the first time.

MARTIN DE NANTES, O.F.M., Cap., *Relation Succinte et sincere de la Mission du Père Martin de Nantes, Prédicateur Capucin, Missionaire Apostolique dans le Brézil parmy les Indiens appellés Cariris* (Quimper, ca. 1707).

My quotations are from the facsimile edition edited with an introduction and notes by F. G. Edelweiss (Salvador, Bahia, 1952).

MAWE, JOHN, *Travels in the Interior of Brazil, Particularly in the Gold and Diamond Districts of that Country* (London, 1812).

Although Mawe visited Minas Gerais in the first decade of the nineteenth century, much of what he says about mining methods is equally applicable to a century earlier.

MELLO, J. SOARES DE, *Emboabas. Chronica de uma revolução nativista. Documentos inéditos* (São Paulo, 1929).

Still the best work on the subject in Portuguese.

MELO, MÁRIO, *A Guerra dos Mascates como afirmação nacionalista* (Pernambuco, 1941).

Prints many of the relevant documents in the Arquivo Historico Ultramarino, Lisboa, in full.

MONTEIRO, J. COSTA RÊGO, *A Colônia do Sacramento, 1680–1777* (2 vols., Porto Alegre, 1937).

MONTEIRO DA COSTA, LUIZ, *Na Bahia Colonial. Apontamentos para história militar da cidade do Salvador* (Salvador, Bahia, 1958).

MORAES, RUBENS BORBA DE, *Bibliographia Brasiliana. A Bibliographical Essay on Rare Books about Brazil Published from 1504 to 1900 and Works of Brazilian Authors Published Abroad before the Independence of Brazil in 1822* (2 vols., Amsterdam and Rio de Janeiro, 1959).

Cf. the reviews of this work in *Studia. Revista Semestral*, Vol. IV (Lisboa, 1959), pp. 335–359, and in *HAHR*, Vol. XXXIX (August, 1959), pp. 474–478.

OLIVEIRA MARTINS, F. A., *Um heroí esquecido. João da Maia da Gama* (2 vols., Lisboa, 1944).

OTT, CARLOS B., *Formação e evolução étnica da Cidade do Salvador. O Folklore Bahiano* (2 vols., Salvador, 1955–1957).

PEREIRA DA COSTA, FRANCISCO AUGUSTO, *Anais Pernambucanos* (7 vols., Recife, 1951–1958).

Originally compiled in the late nineteenth and early twentieth centuries

428

Bibliography

this work leans heavily on Fernandes Gama (*q.v.*) but also contains much material from other printed and manuscript sources, unfortunately not always with adequate references.

———, *Chronologia Historica do Estado do Piauhy, desde as seus primitivos tempos até a proclamação da Republica em 1889* (Recife, 1909).

PITTA, SEBASTIÃO DA ROCHA, *Historia da America Portugueza, desde o anno 1500 do seu descobrimento até o de 1724* (Lisboa, 1730).

Since there are several later and more accessible editions, my quotations from this work are given in "Book" and "paragraph" form.

PIZARRO E. ARAUJO, JOSÉ DE SOUSA DE AZEVEDO, *Memorias Historicas da provincia do Rio de Janeiro* (9 vols., Rio de Janeiro, 1820–1822).

All citations in the text are taken from the second edition by Borba de Moraes (10 vols., Rio de Janeiro, 1945).

PORTO SEGURO. *See* VARNHAGEN.

Public Record Office London, State Papers Portugal.

SP 89/40 covering the years 1738–1741 is the codex from which most of my quotations are taken.

Publicações do Arquivo Nacional, Rio de Janeiro (Rio de Janeiro, 1886– to date).

Vols. V, VII–XI, XV and XXI are particularly rich in revelant material.

RAU, VIRGINIA, *O "Livro de Rezão" de António Coelho Guerreiro* (Lisboa, 1956).

———, and MARIA FERNANDES GOMES DA SILVA [eds.], *Os Manuscritos do Arquivo da Casa de Cadaval respeitantes ao Brasil* (2 vols., Coimbra, 1955–1958).

The second volume of this invaluable series contains the eighteenth-century documents.

Relaçam da vitoria que os Portuguezes alcançàrão no Rio de Janeiro contra os Francezes, em 19 de Setembro de 1710. Publicada em 20 de Fevereyro (Lisboa, 1711).

This pamphlet, a reprint of which appeared next day (21. ii. 1711) is ascribed by some bibliographers to the pen of the Count of Ericeira.

Revista do Arquivo Publico Mineiro (25 vols., Belo Horizonte, 1896–1938).

Particularly valuable for the documents which it reproduces from the regional archive, one of the richest in Brazil.

Revista de História (41 nrs., São Paulo, 1950–1960. In progress).

Not to be confused with the earlier Portuguese publication of the same title (16 vols., Lisboa, 1912–1928).

Revista do Instituto Arqueologico Histórico e Geografico Pernambucano Recife, 1863 to date).

429

Bibliography

Revista do Instituto Histórico e Geografico Brasileiro (Rio de Janeiro, 1838 to date).

Contains much useful material but often very carelessly edited. Misprints, errors, and omissions, consequently abound.

RIBEIRO ROCHA, MANUEL, *Ethiope Resgatado, empenhado, sustentado, corregido, instruido, e libertado. Discurso theologico-juridico, em que se propoem o modo de comerciar, haver, e possuir validamente, quanto a hum, e outro foro, os Pretos cativos Africanos, e as principaes obrigações, que correm a quem delles se servir* (Lisboa, 1758).

An exceedingly rare work by a Portuguese priest domiciled at Bahia, which is basic for the study of Negro slavery in Brazil in the eighteenth century.

RIBEIRO DE LESSA, CLADO, *Crónica de uma Embaixada Luso-Brasileira à Costa d'Africa em fins do século XVIII, incluindo o texto da viagem de Africa em o Reino de Dahomé escrita pelo Padre Vicente Ferreira Pires no ano de 1800 e até o presente inédita* (São Paulo, 1957).

RODRIGUES, JOSÉ HONORIO, *O Continente do Rio Grande* (Rio de Janeiro, 1954).

A short but suggestive and well-documented historical essay.

RONCIÈRE, CHARLES DE LA, *Histoire de la Marine Francaise, VI: Le Crépuscule du grande règne, l'apogée de la guerre de course* (Paris, 1932).

RUY, AFFONSO, *Historia da Camara Municipal do Salvador* (Salvador, Bahia, 1953).

Based primarily on material in the local archives.

RYDER, A. F. C., "The Re-establishment of Portuguese Factories on the Costa da Mina to the Mid-Eighteenth Century," *Journal of the Historical Society of Nigeria*, Vol. I, No. 3 (December, 1958), pp. 157–183.

This important and well-documented article only came to my notice after the present work had gone to press.

SALLES OLIVEIRA, ALVARO DE, *Moedas do Brasil*, I, *Moedas e Barras de Ouro. Elementos para o seu estudo* (São Paulo, 1944).

No more was published of this valuable work, owing to the premature death of the author.

SANTOS, JOAQUIM FELICIO DOS, *Memórias do distrito Diamantino* (Rio de Janeiro, 1956).

Third edition of a work first published in 1868 and justly regarded as a classic, this book is in some ways superseded by the more recent and better documented *História* of A. de Lima Junior, *q.v.*

SHILLINGTON, V. M. and CHAPMAN, A. B. W., *The Commercial Relations of England and Portugal* (London, n.d., but apparently 1907).

SILVA, ANTONIO DA, *Directorio Practico da Prata e Ouro, em que se mo-*

Bibliography

stram as condiçoens, com que se devem lavrar estes dous nobilissimos metaes; para que se evitem nas obras os enganos, e nos artifices os erros (Lisboa, 1720).

The author, who died in 1723, was assayer of the mint at Lisbon.

SILVA, JOSÉ SOARES DE, *Gazeta em forma de Carta*, I; *Anos de 1701–1716* (Lisboa, 1933).

All published to date, this first volume coming down only to the year 1709.

SMITH, ROBERT C., *As Artes na Bahia, I: Arquitectura Colonial* (Salvador, Bahia, 1955).

——, "The Arts in Brazil. Baroque Architecture," *in* H. V. Livermore, ed., *Portugal and Brazil. An Introduction* (Oxford, 1953), pp. 349–384.

SMITH, T. LYNN, *Brazil. People and Institutions* (Baton Rouge, 1954).

An excellent compendium.

SOMBRA, SEVERINO, *Historia Monetaria do Brasil Colonial. Repertorio cronológico com introdução, notas e carta monetária. Edição revista e aumentada* (Rio de Janeiro, 1938).

A most useful work, but it is in some respects being supplemented by the articles of Alvaro da Veiga Coimbra, "Noções de Numismática Brasileira," appearing serially in the São Paulo *Revista de História* at the time of writing (1959).

SOUSA, MANUEL DE, "Cartas originaes de El Rey e de varios Ministros escriptos a meo tio o senhor Manuel de Souza, Provedor que foy da Caza da Moeda do Rio de Janeiro."

Codex in folio, containing 150 original dispatches and private letters from the Crown, the Overseas Council, and various viceroys and governors in Brazil, addressed to Manuel de Sousa, 1695–1721 (author's collection). Manuel de Sousa was superintendent of the mint at Rio de Janeiro from 1702 until his death in March, 1722.

SOUTHEY, ROBERT, *History of Brazil* (3 vols., London, 1810–1819).

Studia. Revista Semestral (Lisboa, 1958 to date).

Edited by the Centro de Estudos Históricos Ultramarinos, Lisbon.

TAUNAY, AFFONSO DE ESCRAGNOLLE, *História Geral das Bandeiras Paulistas escripta á vista de avultada documentação inedita dos archivos Brasileiros, Hespanhoes e Portuguezes* (10 vols., São Paulo, 1924–1949).

Diffuse and rambling, but the basic work on the subject owing to the copious citations from original documents.

——, *História das Bandeiras Paulistas* (2 vols., São Paulo, 1951).

An abridged version of the *História Geral*.

——, *Sob El Rey Nosso Senhor. Aspectos da vida setecentista Brasileira sobretudo em São Paulo* (São Paulo, 1923).

Bibliography

One of Taunay's best books. Reprinted from the *Anais do Museu Paulista*, Vol. I.

——, *Collectanea de mappas da cartographia Paulista antiga, abrangendo nove cartas, de 1612 a 1837, reproduzidas da collecção do Museu Paulista* (São Paulo, 1922).

——, *Relatos Sertanistas. Colectanea, introdução e notas de A. de E.T.* (São Paulo, 1953).

Although no indication whatever of this fact is given, the documents printed herein were nearly all taken from the Codice Costa Matoso (*q.v.*) at São Paulo, and from a miscellany in the Evora Public Library (Codex CXVI/2–15). Unfortunately, the editing was very carelessly done and the work abounds in errors and misprints. Where possible, I have checked the printed versions with the MS originals.

Taunay had originally printed these *Relatos* in the *Revista do Instituto Histórico e Geográfico de São Paulo*, Vol. XLIV (São Paulo, 1948), where they appear with the same misprints, errors, and omissions as in the 1953 version which I have used.

——, *Subsidios para a historia do trafico africano no Brasil* (São Paulo, 1941).

The best survey of the Negro slave trade during the colonial period in Brazil. Includes some material from the Codice Costa Matoso.

Universidade de São Paulo. Biblioteca Geral da Faculdade de Filosofia. MSS da Colecção Lamego.

Though primarily of seventeenth-century interest, this collection contains some valuable original-papers of the period 1695–1750.

VARNHAGEN, FRANCISCO ADOLFO DE (also styled BARÃO DE PORTO SEGURO) *História Geral do Brasil antes da sua separação e independência de Portugal* (5 vols., São Paulo, n.d.)

The publishers of the third and fourth editions of this standard work have, for reasons known only to themselves, taken every precaution to conceal in what years their respective volumes were published. My own copy apparently comprises Vols. I and II of the fourth edition (1948) and Vols. III, IV, and V of the third edition (1928–1936?).

VASCONCELLOS, DIOGO DE, *Historia Antiga de Minas Gerais* (Belo Horizonte, 1904).

——, *História Média de Minas Gerais* (Belo Horizonte, 1918).

Though frequently quoted as a standard work, and reprinted as such in 1948, this work should be used with caution, as the author was strongly influenced by the belated romanticism of the period in which he wrote. On the other hand, he did draw largely on the unpublished documents in the archives of Minas Gerais.

432

Bibliography

VASCONCELLOS, SYLVIO DE, *Vila Rica. Formação e desenvolvimento. Residencias* (Rio de Janeiro, 1956).
Chiefly concerned with architecture and housing.

VEIGA, JOSÉ PEDRO XAVIER DA, *Ephemerides Mineiras, 1664-1897* (4 vols., Ouro Preto, 1897).

————, *A Revolta de 1720 em Vila Rica. Discurso Historico-Politico* (Ouro Preto, 1898).
Integral publication of the Count of Assumar's version of the revolt at Villa Rica in 1720.

VERGER, PIERRE, *Notes sur le culte des Orisa et Vodun à Bahia, la Baie de tous les Saints, au Brésil et à l'ancienne côte des Esclaves en Afrique* (Dakar, 1957).
The most authoritative study of this subject by a writer familiar with it on both sides of the Atlantic.

VERNEY, LUÍS ANTÓNIO, *Verdadeiro Methodo de Estudar para ser until à Republica, e à Igreja; proporcionado ao estudo, e necessidade de Portugal* (2 vols., Valencia, 1746).
There is a good annotated edition of this work in five volumes (Lisboa, 1949-1952) by António Salgado Junior, which is essential for the study of the mentality of the educated Portuguese in the reign of Dom João V.

VIANA PASSOS, ZOROASTRO, *Em tôrno da História do Sabará* (2 vols., Belo Horizonte, 1940-1942).
The documents published in the second volumes are particularly useful.

VIANNA FILHO, LUIZ, *O Negro na Bahia* (Rio de Janeiro, 1946).

VIDE, SEBASTIÃO MONTEIRO DA, *Constituiçoens Primeyras do Arcebispado da Bahia* (Coimbra, 1720).
There is an earlier Lisbon edition of 1719, and a later one of 1765; all three are rare. The constitutions were drawn up at the diocesan synod of 1707.

VIEIRA, S.J., ANTÓNIO, *Sermoens do Padre António Vieira* (14 vols., Lisboa, 1679-1710).
This collection, now rare, is still the most satisfactory edition of the sermons.

————, [J. L. de Azevedo, ed.], *Cartas do Padre António Vieira* (3 vols., Coimbra, 1925-1928).

————, [António Sérgio and Hernâni Cidade, eds.], *Padre António Vieira. Obras Escolhidas* (12 vols., Lisboa, 1951-1954).

VILHENA, LUIS DOS SANTOS, *Recopilacão de Noticias Soteropoliterras e Brasilicas contidas em XX cartas* (2 vols., Salvador, Bahia, 1927).
Edited by Braz do Amaral, these letters by the Portuguese professor

of Greek at Salvador in 1787–1798 give a wealth of information which is equally applicable to the first half of the eighteenth century.

WANDERLEY DE ARAUJO PINHO, JOSÉ, *História de um engenho do* Reconcavo, *1552–1944* (Rio de Janeiro, 1946).

A richly illustrated and documented work by a descendant of the old planter-aristocracy.

ZEMELLA, MAFALDA P., *O Abastecimento da Capitania das Minas Gerais no século XVIII* (São Paulo, 1951).

Should be consulted in conjunction with Myriam Ellis' essay on the same topic, *q.v.*

INDEX

Academy of History, 159, 362, 367.
Academy of the Forgotten, 159–160.
Acting and actors, 181–182.
Affonso Mafrense (or Sertão), Domingo, 230, 234–236, 243.
Agriculture, difficulties of, 13, 257–258, 303–304; in Minas Gerais, 50, 187–188, 310; in the *Reconcavo* of Bahia, 150–152, 304; around Sacramento, 247–248, 250; in Cuiabá, 257–258; in Piauí, 235–236; in Várzea of Pernambuco, 302–303; and mining, 321. *See also,* Maize, Manioc, Sugar, etc.
Aguiar, Bernardo Carvalho de. *See* Carvalho de Aguiar.
Aguilar, Sebastião Pereira de, 76, 77.
Ajudá. *See* Whydah.
Albuquerque, António Coelho de Carvalho de, biographical sketch, 75–76; governor of Rio de Janeiro, 75, 76, 104–105; governor of São Paulo and Minas Gerais, 80–82; dismisses Manuel Nunes Viana, 77; difficulties with Paulistas, 78–81; reconciled with Paulistas, 81–83; pacification of Minas Gerais by, 77, 308; founds new townships, 82–83; and the relief of Rio de Janeiro, 83, 91–92, 98, 100–102; and the Pernambucan planters, 123; accused of private trade, 83; return to Portugal, 105, 123; and the collection of the fifths, 82.
Aldeias (mission villages), establishment of, 20–21; rules and regulations for, 281–286; numbers of, 290–291; and episcopal visitation, 287; white men imprisoned in, 288; how financed, 282, 289; daily life in, 282–283.
Almeida, Captain João de, 214.
Almeida, Dom Lourenço de, biographical sketch, 368–369; governor of Pernambuco, 124, 196; of Minas Gerais, 163, 206; feud with the Count of

Sabugosa, 145, 406; implicated in diamond smuggling, 187, 206, 406; accused of private trade, 187; inaugurates smelting-houses, 196–197; his regulations for the diamond diggings, 207–208; his opinion of the Mineiros, 163–166; consulted on capitation tax, 197, 369.
Alpoim, José Fernandes Pinto, 298, 315.
Amaral Coutinho, Bento do, 68–70, 72, 75–76, 88–89, 97, 100.
Amaral Gurgel, Francisco do, 53, 68–69.
Amazon, description of the river, 271–273.
Amazonia, as defined in this book, 274.
Amerindians, Portuguese opinion of the, 18–20, 288; enslavement of the, 21–22, 31–33, 167, 277–290 *passim;* Jesuits and liberty of the, 20–21, 277–290; Portuguese miscegenation with, 19–20, 31, 32, 167, 286; as hunters and trappers, 2; as cattle drovers, 233; as rowers, 22, 272–273, 277, 285; liability to disease, 278; healthy appearance of, 18–19; mission villages *(aldeias)* of, 281–286; in Minas Gerais, 36, 167. *See also* Carijó, Tapuyá, Tapes, etc.
Andreoni. *See* Antonil.
Angeja (Dom Pedro de Novonha) Count of Villa-Verde and Marquis of, 147, 308, 364, 366, 369.
Angola, slave trade with, 4–7, 153–154, 303, 304, 306, 313; military drafts for, 140, 143; pattern of trade with Brazil and Portugal, 25–28; deportation of convicts to, 140, 170, 301; social position of mulattoes in, 17. *See also* Luanda, Bantu, etc.
Anhangüera, 267–268.
Ant, "King of Brazil," 13.
Antonil, 369.
Arcos, Count of, 172–173.
Ardra, 153, 154, 155, 176.

435

Index

Index

Index

Spices, South American, 278–279, 285, 291, 299–300.
Sugar and the sugar trade, 11, 24–27; at Bahia, 24, 149–152, 304; in Pernambuco, 302–304. *See also* Planters.
Sutil, Miguel, 256.

Tapes, 240, 249.
Tapuyá(s), 62, 172, 234, 235, 409; rebellion of the Northern, 236–237.
Tijuco, Arraial do, 207, 210, 218–220.
Tithes, 180, 189–190, 286.
Tobacco, tobacco planting, and tobacco trade, 11, 25–27, 151–152, 155, 230, 277, 286, 299, 303; planters claim exemption from distraint for debt, 151–152.
Tolls and taxes, 188–190, 347–350.
Torture, use of judicial, 139–140.
Trails to the Mines, 39–41, 43–44, 250–261.
Treaty of Madrid, 293–295.
Treaty of Tordesillas, 292.
Treaty of Utrecht, 104.
Tupí-Guaraní language (*lingua geral*), 31, 286, 388.
Tyrawly, Lord, on character of D. João V, 145–146; on gold exports from Portugal to England, 157; on English participation in the Brazil trade, 157–158; on bribery and corruption, 209; on Jewish strain in the Portuguese, 392–393.

Vagrancy, 167–169, 263, 269, 301, 322.
Vaqueiros, 23, 44, 231–245, 322.
Vasconcellos, Dom António Pedro de, 250.

Vasconcellos, Simão de, S.J., quoted, 18–19.
Velho, Domingos Jorge, 233–234.
Venereal disease, 185.
Viana, Manuel Nunes, biographical sketch, 65, 364–365; in War of Emboabas, 66–77; repels D. Fernando Martins Mascarenhas, 73–74; accepts orders of António de Albuquerque, 78; personal appearance of, 190; his Rio São Francisco estates, 230.
Viegas, João Peixoto, 13, 27, 230.
Vieira, António, S.J., quoted, 5, 272–273, 274, 277, 370; mentioned, 11, 12, 17, 22, 28.
Villa Rica de Ouro Preto, foundation of, 82, 162; growth of, 51, 162–163; apogee in eighteenth century, 162–203 *passim;* revolt at, 193–196; capital of Minas transferred to, 369; Mint and smelting-house at, 163, 192–196, 197; religious processions at, 177–178, 181, 182; Misericordia of, 136; Municipal Council of, 187, 196; compared with Potosí, 163.

Whydah, slave trade with, 46, 153–155, 165, 175–176, 303, 305–306, 400.
Women, shortage of white, 164–165, 248, 301, 322; white prohibited from leaving Brazil, 165; prostitution of slave, 16, 131, 138, 140, 165, 174; alleged Luso-Brazilian preference for colored, 16, 55, 165; seclusion of Luso-Brazilian, 137–138, 253–254; fecundity of Minho, 11.

Yellow Fever, 29.

443

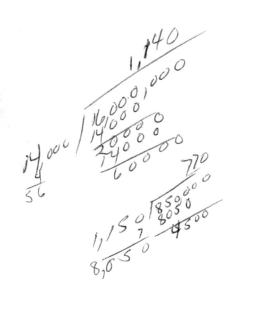

70

760